The Evangelical Crackup?

In the series *Religious Engagement in Democratic Politics*, edited by Paul A. Djupe

Edited by PAUL A. DJUPE AND
RYAN L. CLAASSEN

The Evangelical Crackup?

The Future of the Evangelical-Republican Coalition

TEMPLE UNIVERSITY PRESS
Philadelphia • *Rome* • *Tokyo*

TEMPLE UNIVERSITY PRESS
Philadelphia, Pennsylvania 19122
www.temple.edu/tempress

Library of Congress Cataloging-in-Publication Data

Names: Djupe, Paul A., editor. | Claassen, Ryan L., 1972– editor.
Title: The evangelical crackup? : the future of the Evangelical-Republican coalition /
   edited by Paul A. Djupe and Ryan L. Claassen.
Description: Philadelphia : Temple University Press, 2018. | Series: Religious engagement
   in democratic politics | Includes index.
Identifiers: LCCN 2018010262 (print) | LCCN 2018025533 (ebook) |
   ISBN 9781439915233 (E-book) | ISBN 9781439915219 (cloth) |
   ISBN 9781439915226 (pbk.)
Subjects: LCSH: Evangelicalism—United States. | Christianity and politics—
   United States. | Christians—Political activity—United States. |
   Republican Party (U.S. : 1854–)
Classification: LCC BR1642.U6 (ebook) | LCC BR1642.U6 E93 2018 (print) |
   DDC 261.70973/09051—dc23
LC record available at https://lccn.loc.gov/2018010262

Contents

PART III   LEGAL, CONSTITUTIONAL BATTLES AND MORALITY POLITICS

PART IV   THE LASTING POLITICAL CONTRIBUTIONS OF EVANGELICALISM

Acknowledgments

We first recognize the decades of rigorous religion and politics research that preceded our work, renewing scholarly interest in the role of religion in American politics and identifying evangelicals as an increasingly important group in regard to understanding political divisions. Second, we are grateful for the unique set of circumstances we were able to observe in the 2016 presidential election. While we are not especially thankful for the turbulent politics the election produced, the hotly contested Republican primary and divisions among evangelical elites that persisted through the general election created a perfect storm in which to assess the political proclivities of evangelicals. Dissension in the ranks of elites and the possibility of dissension among evangelical voters inspired us to investigate the possibility of an "evangelical crackup." The voting loyalties of white evangelicals proved unshakable in 2016, but the unique circumstances of the election cast their loyalties in a new and revealing light.

At the elite level, the rifts that began with dissension about endorsing the Republican nominee continue to reverberate, and herein lies a real paradox. How does a candidate with less unified support from evangelical elites redouble the voting loyalty of the laity? Some elites seem so vexed by this paradox that they are attempting to redefine evangelicalism to exclude their partisan opponents. True, one might be able to re-create a bygone era of evangelical political unity by redefining who is in and who is out, but doing so will fail to reveal anything of substance about the role of religion in the political lives of evangelicals. Those insights will reveal themselves only when evangelical political behavior now and in the past is carefully examined. All of which is to say we believe this book wrestles with profoundly important issues—issues that will help inform views about evangelicals' current political loyalties and that will highlight the forces behind ongoing shifts within evangelicalism.

We owe many intellectuals debts, collectively and individually—too many to list exhaustively but some who need to be mentioned specifically. Most important, we are grateful to the contributors for their outstanding chapters that engage these issues empirically and intellectually. This collection of chapters is proof that the study of religion and politics is robust, creative, and engaging.

We thank Ted Jelen and Elizabeth Oldmixon for their careful attention to this project during the review stage and for the many insights they provided. Ted never learned how to say no to a request for a review, and a great number of scholars in the field have benefited from his suggestions. He passed just as this book was entering production, and he will be missed. We also thank several anonymous reviewers for their help and ideas. We thank the great team at Temple University Press for investing in this project. At the risk of sounding awkward, we also thank each other, since it was much more interesting and fun working on this together. Finally, we thank our families for their support for our work.

The Evangelical Crackup?

Introduction

PAUL A. DJUPE
RYAN L. CLAASSEN

What is a crackup? Dictionaries offer a range of meanings. *Oxford Living Dictionaries* reports "crack up" as a phrasal verb meaning to "suffer an emotional breakdown under pressure" or to "burst into laughter."[1] *Merriam-Webster* adds "to damage."[2] It is safe to say that the state of the relationship between the Republican Party and white evangelicals is no laughing matter and that our meaning tracks best with "strain."[3] As 2016 ticked along, we wondered whether the Republican Party was on a path that would strain, damage, or destroy the coalition with evangelicals. The election results, however, saw evangelicals double-down on Republican loyalty. When we began to write this book, we were confronted with a rather unexpected fact pattern. The unusual events of 2016 shined new light on the political priorities of evangelicals and what they expect from the Republican Party. Whether there was a crackup or not, 2016 was a gift to those who study religion and politics.

The unprecedented candidates and events of the presidential election let us see seams that had not been exposed for decades. Put differently, when evangelicals do things that are consistent with Republican priorities and Republicans do things that are consistent with evangelical priorities, it is almost impossible to study what causes what. The 2016 election was different. It presented evangelical elites advocating against Republicans, Republican infighting, a Republican nominee far from evangelical orthodoxy, and candidates other than the eventual winner with far better conservative Christian bona fides.

If we were quickly disabused of the idea that evangelicals might break with the Republican Party, we were equally quickly enlightened with a new set of possibilities about what makes that connection endure. This book does not focus solely on 2016 but takes in varying sweeps of recent history to make sense of where evangelicals and the Republican Party are now and will likely head.

It is important to remember that not long ago, George W. Bush's electoral success appeared to be evidence that the Christian Right movement that began in the 1960s had come of age. Of course, this had been said before about the movement, when then-candidate Ronald Reagan told the Religious Roundtable, "I know you can't endorse me. But I want you to know that I endorse you and what you're doing" (quoted in Lamb 2015). George H. W. Bush rebranded himself a chimerical born-again Episcopalian in honor of the Christian Right's influence. And groups like the Christian Coalition had galvanized a large, mostly evangelical voting bloc to help sweep the Republican Party into Congress in 1994. But not long after President George W. Bush began his terms, the Christian Coalition was on the brink of financial ruin, Ralph Reed (its former leader) had been exiled under a cloud of scandal, and David D. Kirkpatrick (2007) was writing the article "The Evangelical Crackup." Ten years later, this article inspires our book's title.

Evidence of the crackup came in the form of disagreement among evangelical leaders over which candidate to anoint and party nominations that seemed to repudiate evangelical influence. For example, on November 7, 2007, televangelist Pat Robertson endorsed former New York mayor Rudy Giuliani for the Republican nomination for president. While Giuliani promised to make judicial nominations Robertson's followers would find congenial, the two men shared few policy views in common, especially on such stalwarts as abortion (Kirkpatrick and Cooper 2007). Just a month earlier, a prominent group of evangelicals did the very opposite—threatening to leave the party if Giuliani became the nominee (Djupe and Calfano 2013).

In the end, the GOP nominee in 2008 was John McCain, a candidate some saw as symbolizing a Republican Party rejection of evangelical influence. After all, it was John McCain in 2000 who labeled the Reverend Jerry Falwell (founder of Liberty University) one of the "agents of intolerance" and decried the influence of the Christian Right in the Republican Party. And in 2012, the Republican nominee, Mitt Romney, was no hard-core social conservative either—he was once a supporter of abortion rights as Massachusetts governor. Furthermore, Romney belonged to a religious group with whom evangelicals had long been at odds—Mormons (Campbell, Green, and Monson 2014). Paradoxically, despite apparent discord at the elite level, ordinary evangelicals in the electorate maintained a consistent voting record, with solid majorities supporting the Republican throughout this period. Therefore, continued evangelical support begs the question of the basis for the connection to the Republican Party and just what, if anything, and who, if anyone, is directing the ship.

Perhaps the most perplexing connection of evangelicals to the Republican Party was their support for Donald Trump's candidacy in 2016. Witness the now-famous photo at a Trump rally where a sign read, "Thank you Lord Jesus for President Trump." To be sure, evangelical preferences were spread across a range of candidates in the primaries, but a high proportion of Trump supporters were "Trumpvangelicals." Maggie Haberman and Thomas Kaplin (2016) wrote, "Brash, thrice-married, cosseted in a gilded tower high above Fifth Avenue and fond of swearing from the stage at his rallies, Mr. Trump, who has spent his career in pursuit, and praise, of wealth, would seem an odd fit for voters who place greater value on faith, hope and charity."

High levels of evangelical support for Trump were all the more baffling in a field with several very religious contenders, such as Ted Cruz. The first words of Ted Cruz's first campaign ad proclaimed, "Were it not for the transformative love of Jesus Christ, I would have been raised by a single mom without my father in the house." Nevertheless, Trump attracted mass support in the absence of much elite evangelical support and with nontrivial elite-level antipathy. According to Russell Moore, head of the Southern Baptist Convention's Ethics and Religious Liberty Commission, "He's someone who has spoken in vulgar and harsh terms about women, as well as in ugly and hateful ways about immigrants and other minorities. I don't think this is someone who represents the values that evangelicals in this country aspire to" (Taylor 2015). Trump would go on to claim 81 percent of white evangelicals' votes in the 2016 presidential election.

This, then, is the puzzle that we engage in this book. If we are honest, almost none of us expected to conduct research under a Trump administration. There are very few who thought he would win. Accordingly, at least the tone of the following chapters has changed, but the content has not. Our intent is to pull apart the strands that mark the relationship between evangelicals and the Republican Party. Much conventional wisdom received a hostile reception in 2016.

We lay out the various arguments that have been posed for why evangelicals attached and remain attached to the Republican Party. Naturally, this serves as an overview of and introduction to the book. We distinguish between macrohistorical forces, organizational intermediaries, and microsocial and psychological forces that operate on religious communities. Of course, these three interrelate and demonstrate a great deal of continuity over time, which makes assessing causal relationships particularly difficult.

Macrohistorical Roots of Scholarly Interest in Evangelicals

Mid-twentieth-century Republicans visiting twenty-first-century America would be surprised to learn that evangelical groups now dominate the Republican Party and that a crackup may be in the works. At that time, *mainline*

Protestantism and Republican identity were nearly synonymous. Barry Goldwater, Republican nominee for president in 1964, quipped, "Mark my word, if and when these preachers get control of the party, and they're sure trying to do so, it's going to be a terrible damn problem" (quoted in Rymel 2016). The decline of mainline influence and the rise of evangelical groups in the Republican coalition surely rank among the most notable political transformations of the past half century (Claassen 2015; Green 2007; Green et al. 1996; Jelen 1991; Kohut et al. 2000; Layman 2001, 2010; Putnam and Campbell 2010; Smidt et al. 2010).

In the early 1960s, 64 percent of Republican activists were from mainline traditions, but in 2008 that number had fallen to just 21 percent (Claassen 2015, 20–21). Political scientists often devote substantial attention to single-digit shifts in the political coalitions, so the more than 40 percent decline in the presence of mainline activists in the Republican Party is notable, to say the least. Much of the void left by their decline was filled by evangelical activists. In the early 1960s, only about 20 percent of Republican activists were from evangelical traditions, but by 2008 that number had risen to 47 percent—a strong plurality (Claassen 2015, 20–21). These percentages reflect the religious affiliations of partisan activists, using the survey responses of ordinary Americans captured in the American National Election Studies, but the shifts are similarly evident in studies of national convention delegates (Layman 2001, 2010); analogous shifts are also evident in the party's voting coalitions (Brooks and Manza 2004; Claassen 2015; Layman 2001, 2010; Green 2007; Smidt et al. 2010). In Chapter 2 of this book, Geoffrey Layman and Mark Brockway provide updated figures through 2016 along with analyses of the different ways in which evangelical activists shape Republican policy positions and norms about intraparty and interparty compromise. For those who have been following evangelical ascendency in the Republican Party, this chapter is the new state of the art. Similarly, Kimberly Conger provides updated figures for Christian Right organizational strength and activity at the state level in Chapter 6, along with an assessment of the ways organizational strength structured the Trump vote. In Chapter 13 Tobin Grant and Joshua Mitchell detail how the movement, in its search for political opportunities, helps diffuse policy initiatives throughout American counties.

Many attribute the decline of mainline dominance and the rise of evangelical Protestants within the Republican Party to fundamental changes in religious divisions within the United States (Wuthnow 1988, 1989) that gave rise to a culture war (Hunter 1991). Geoffrey Layman put it this way, "The culture war theorists argue that, just as past cultural clashes affected party politics in important ways, the current conflict should reshape contemporary party politics making the Republican Party into a coalition of religious and cultural traditionalists" (2001, 12). For much of American history, evangelicalism dominated religious thought and practice—even in religious traditions now designated as mainline (Marsden 1990). However, as American society experienced the benefits and problems associated with the Industrial Revolution, a rift emerged among religious people in their orientations toward modernity (Green 2007; Putnam and Campbell 2010; Wald and Calhoun-Brown 2014; Wuthnow 1988, 1989). Many within the denominations we now think of as mainline (e.g., Presbyterian, Episcopalian, Methodist) gravitated toward a more progressive theology that was less at odds with scientific discoveries and modern life, and many others abandoned organized religion altogether. Modern-day evangelicals come from denominations that resisted challenges to religious orthodoxy (e.g., Southern Baptists, Pentecostals, Seventh-Day Adventists).

The culture wars pit religious and secular progressives against the defenders of religious traditionalism. Over time the Democratic Party adopted political positions that were more congenial to religious and secular progressives, and the Republican Party adopted political positions that were more congenial to traditionalists. Accordingly, the religious orientations that distinguished modern-day evangelicals from other religious people became politically salient. And the rising political salience of evangelical identity coincided with a demographic boom in their numbers. Robert D. Putnam and David E. Campbell note, "The rise of evangelicals at the most conservative end of the religious spectrum, followed after 1990 by the rise of the nones at the most liberal end of the spectrum, has in effect polarized the spectrum as a whole" (2010, 105–106).

If evangelicals were once propelled out of politics by embarrassing defeats in their efforts to oppose Darwin's theory of evolution and their efforts to defend racially segregated schools (e.g., Rev. Jerry Falwell's Lynchburg Christian Academy), the set of Christian Right organizations generally credited with bringing evangelicals into the Republican fold coalesced in the late 1970s around abortion and sexual politics more generally. These issues were framed as legal and constitutional battles in which evangelicals' Christian moral duties were aligned with their civic duties. Political wins in the Congress and White House were highlighted as essential in the legal fight, insofar as political opponents were accused of having staffed the federal courts with activist judges. Christian Right organizations mobilized so-called values voters by identifying stalwart opponents of abortion as candidates for elected office and calling on evangelicals to support these candidates as a matter of Christian duty. While the organizations appear weakened and the recent Supreme Court decision regarding gay marriage seems like another embarrassing defeat, abortion rights are much more limited now than in the immediate aftermath of *Roe v. Wade* (Phillips 2016), and some worry the Democratic Party has permanently lost its congressional majority.

While this account of events represents the conventional wisdom about the forces behind the rise of evangelicals within the Republican Party, significant questions remain about whether moral issues represent a Trojan horse for long-standing divisions in American politics over issues of racial equality. Is the conventional wisdom correct in attributing evangelical migration from the Democratic Party to the Republican Party to their conservative positions on the issue of abortion? Or, alternatively, is opposition to federal efforts to reduce racial inequality an important part of understanding increasing evangelical support for the Republican Party? In Chapter 3, Ryan Claassen brings a wealth of survey data to bear on these questions and finds that conventional wisdom underplays the importance of racial attitudes in regard to understanding evangelical political behavior but also finds evidence that abortion and other moral issues matter.

Organizational Intermediaries

The connection between evangelicals and the Republican Party could once upon a time be characterized by a go-to set of active organizations with prominent leaders and media profiles. The rise of secularism in the 1960s inspired increasing political involvement of organizations, such as the Moral Majority, the Religious Roundtable, and the Christian Voice, beginning in the late 1970s and early 1980s. Founded in the wake of conservative televangelist Pat Robertson's failed 1988 presidential bid, the Christian Coalition is "dedicated to defending America's Godly heritage by getting Christians involved in their government again," according to Roberta Combs (quoted in Sala 2005, 103). Consistent with its mission, the organization devoted enormous resources in the 1990s to mobilizing its membership (see, e.g., Rozell and Wilcox 1995).

By the end of the first decade of the twenty-first century, that was no longer true. While some Christian Right political organizations are still in operation, many have ceased to exist and the set of notables has become more diffuse. For instance, the Christian Coalition in the 2000s was a skeleton of its former glory under Ralph Reed in the early 1990s. The Family Research Council continues to operate but has had a much reduced and more controversial profile since Rev. James Dobson cut ties with the organization in 2003. Meanwhile, liberal-leaning evangelical organizations, such as Sojourners, continue to chug along, and the Obama campaigns were exceptional, by all accounts, in their deliberate courtship of liberal-leaning evangelicals (Smidt et al. 2010).

As early as the late 1990s after the Clinton impeachment trial, evangelicalism appeared to show signs of changing political course. For example, conservative Christian Rod Dreher (2013) wrote about the "Benedict Option," which is modeled on Saint Benedict, the founder of modern monasticism. The Benedict Option encourages conservative Christians to withdraw from politics. Additionally, some megachurch clergy are now pushing a different set of issues that could appeal more broadly than the traditional culture-wars and sexual-politics issues. These "new evangelicals," such as Rick Warren of Saddleback Church in California, are not stepping into the shoes of the late Reverend Jerry Falwell, who launched the Moral Majority in the late 1970s. Instead, they are creating new movements within evangelicalism, including the emergent church movement (see Chapter 10), partly in reaction to the divisive politics of the Christian Right.

Also notable, the demographic trends that paved the way for greater evangelical influence—mainline decline and evangelical growth—in the late twentieth century are no longer uniformly positive for evangelical denominations. In the early 2000s evangelicalism appears to have succumbed to the more general malaise that emptied pews in other religious traditions in the United States several decades earlier. For the first time, some denominations at the heart of evangelicalism are not growing. The Southern Baptist Convention is on the decline after more than two hundred years of growth, only propped up by growth in its Hispanic membership (see Chapter 9). Other evangelical religious bodies, including nondenominational churches, continue to buck the trend (Stetzer 2015), but the new members are increasingly nonwhite and less likely to support the Republican Party. A May 7, 2014, report from the Pew Research Center on Religion and Public Life indicated that growth in the percentage of Hispanic evangelicals is partly fueled by a decline in the percentage of Hispanics who are Catholic, from 67 percent in 2010 to 55 percent in 2013.

Demographic changes among evangelicals are clearly linked to changes in the orientation of evangelicals toward issues that once fell outside a narrow set of sexual-politics issues, such as the radical shift in the stances of evangelical organizations on immigration beginning in 2009, when the National Association of Evangelicals passed a resolution calling for comprehensive immigration reform. Is there a growing generational divide among young and old evangelicals? In Chapter 8, Jeremy Castle explores the politics of young evangelical liberals and the extent to which they differ from other liberals. From a different perspective, in Chapter 12 Juhem Navarro-Rivera, Daniel A. Cox, Robert P. Jones, and Paul A. Djupe explore the social networks of young and older evangelicals and how their pattern of contacts helps connect them with, and divides them from, the rest of the evangelical community.

In Chapter 4, Kevin den Dulk examines the rhetoric of Republican and evangelical elites to investigate related questions about what the Republican Party did to attract evangelicals and what evangelicals brought to the Republican Party. Here Republicans continue to build on prior successes by redoubling their support for religious traditionalism in the culture wars—the rhetoric lining up more closely with the conventional wisdom. Likewise, in Chapter 5, Andrew R. Lewis examines the dramatic shift among evangelicals to adopt a politics of rights as a way to bolster claims amid shrinking levels of support.

Microsocial and Psychological Connections

Documenting the macromovements of religious groups among the parties hinges on accurate measurements that document where people can be exposed to identity, values, and policy cues that would help link their religion with political choices. We continue to debate just what an evangelical is (see Chapter 7), in part, because religion and religious connections continue to evolve with society. Terms like "born again" or even "evangelical" come in and out of fashion, leaving scholars grappling with ways of connecting with individual voters.

Group membership merely scratches the surface of how religion is present in people's lives. Indeed, scholars have different definitions for "religious group," which then points toward the individual-level attribute that matters in connecting to political groups. In general, the more aggregated the religious group, the more psychological the measurement. Those who are concerned with the evangelical religious tradition are more concerned with religious identities and religious belief markers that place them in that movement. Ronald J. McGauvran and Elizabeth Oldmixon present a good example in Chapter 15.

This is not to say that we can assume religious traditions are unified in their theologies, politics, social status, or anything else. Consider the emergent church—a protest movement rejecting the authoritarian religion and politics of modern evangelicalism, which Ryan P. Burge documents in Chapter 10. Given the attention to the role of authority in post–World War II social science, it is important to consider the religious roots of this orientation, which Burge does with a new measure that disentangles authority from orthodoxy.

However, religion is also experienced in congregations, a fact that points toward a decidedly more social experience that may be quite varied across congregations. That is, the degree of vertical integration of religion is a function of social ties and political information flow through them. One of the purported strengths of evangelicalism flows from the social insularity of evangelicals, which Jacob R. Neiheisel, Paul A. Djupe, and Anand E. Sokhey discuss in Chapter 11. Just how insularity promotes integration into the evangelical or Christian Right movements is not obvious, however, and depends on generational relations (see Chapter 12). For example, in Chapter 1, Paul A. Djupe and Brian R. Calfano explain that evangelical support for Trump continued apace despite vocal opposition by several evangelical elites because few evangelicals knew about opposition to Trump by evangelical leaders, and even when exposed to such opposition, they ignored it when embedded in pro-Trump religious communities.

Political Opportunity Structure

As our introduction intimates, the set of political opportunities factors heavily into the viability of Christian Right politics. Earlier in the twentieth century, the legacy of slavery and the one-party South undercut the potential for a mass conservative Christian movement. The nationalization of politics from the New Deal, but especially in the regulatory revolution of the 1960s and 1970s, created the raw materials for the Christian Right but also meant that the movement would be subject to its vagaries. That is, winners suffer from having little to mobilize against, and the Christian Right has been declared dead at regular intervals since "the preachers gave it to Reagan" in 1980 (Martin 1996, 220).

One way to keep that critical tension is to create it through lawsuits. The legal wing of the Christian Right has only gotten stronger through time, its place cemented by the opening of Christian law schools. Daniel Bennett highlights the close ties of legal advocacy and the movement in Chapter 14.

Conclusion

All of this underscores the political importance of evangelicals in contemporary America. Investigating changes within American religion and the ways in which those changes affect politics has long been of interest to scholars of religion and politics. But interest in religion became mainstream within political science because of the sense of urgency associated with a simmering culture war fueled by conflict between evangelicals devoted to political protection of traditionalism and religious progressives and unaffiliated Americans with very different political goals. Indeed, this conflict lies at the heart of much of the research into political polarization, and the literature on polarization is burgeoning (witness the 1,610 citations Google Scholar currently credits to *Culture War?* by Fiorina, Abrams, and Pope 1991). Evangelicals achieved a place of prominence within religion and politics research, and political science research more generally, because they are viewed as a key group of culture-war combatants.

Accordingly, even the slightest whiff of a crackup in the alliance between white evangelicals and the Republican Party merits significant attention. At the elite level, the Christian Right organizations widely credited with cementing the alliance recently appear in disarray and disrepair. Republican nomination politics have seen the candidates most congenial to evangelical concerns go down in defeat. Yet there is little indication that elite-level discord is affecting rank-and-file voting. Against the benchmark of the George W. Bush elections—a candidate whom evangelicals embraced as one of their own (he spoke the language of a born-again Christian even if he hailed from a mainline denomination)—white evangelical support for the Republican nominee continued apace in the elections of 2008 (Smidt et al. 2010) and 2012 (Guth and Bradberry 2013). If anything, Trump appears to have fared slightly better in 2016 than George W. Bush did in his elections (Smith and Martinez 2016). This seeming paradox raises a host of fascinating questions about the forces behind evangelical voting behavior and what the future holds.

To provide some critical perspective about what the future holds, we invited two luminaries in the field of religion and politics to reflect on evangelicalism in the 2016 election and what the election means for evangelical politics going forward. Robert Wuthnow and John Green, who wrap things up in Chapters 16 and 17, provide insightful perspectives and serve as our oracles concerning future possibilities. Finally, in Chapter 18, we review the themes of this book through the lens of the counterfactual. As mentioned earlier, 2016 created opportunities to observe evangelical voting behavior in new circumstances—thus providing answers to several interesting "what-if" questions. For example, what if evangelical elites offered vocal opposition to the Republican nominee? We both review the lessons of 2016 and reflect on important counterfactuals that have not yet come to pass, as we offer our concluding thoughts about the present state of evangelical politics in the United States.

NOTES

1. *Oxford Living Dictionaries*, s.v. "crack up," available at https://en.oxforddictionaries.com/definition/crack_up (accessed May 23, 2018).

2. *Merriam-Webster Learner's Dictionary*, s.v. "crack," available at http://www.learnersdictionary.com/definition/crack[1] (accessed May 23, 2018).

3. This book focuses almost exclusively on white evangelicals; for ease of communication, we generally use "evangelicals" and "white evangelicals" interchangeably.

REFERENCES

Brooks, Clem, and Jeff Manza. 2004. "A Great Divide? Religion and Political Change in U.S. National Elections, 1972–2000." *Sociological Quarterly* 45 (3): 421–450.

Campbell, David E., John C. Green, and J. Quin Monson. 2014. *Seeking the Promised Land: Mormons and American Politics*. New York: Cambridge University Press.

Claassen, Ryan. 2015. *Godless Democrats and Pious Republicans? Party Activists, Party Capture, and the "God Gap."* New York: Cambridge University Press.

Djupe, Paul A., and Brian R. Calfano. 2013. *God Talk: Experimenting with the Religious Causes of Public Opinion*. Philadelphia: Temple University Press.

Dreher, Rod. 2013. "Benedict Option." *American Conservative*, December 12. Available at http://www.theamericanconservative.com/articles/benedict-option/.

Fiorina, Morris P., S. J. Abrams, and J. C. Pope. 1991. *Culture War? The Myth of a Polarized America*. New York: Pearson Longman.

Green, John C. 2007. *The Faith Factor: How Religion Influences American Elections*. New York: Praeger.

Green, John C., James L. Guth, Corwin E. Smidt, and Lyman A. Kellstedt. 1996. *Religion and the Culture Wars: Dispatches from the Front*. Lanham, MD: Rowman and Littlefield.

Guth, James L., and Leigh A. Bradberry. 2013. "Religion in the 2012 Election." In *The American Elections of 2012*, edited by Steven E. Schier and Janet Box Steffenmeier, 190–214. New York: Routledge.

Haberman, Maggie, and Thomas Kaplin. 2016. "Evangelicals See Donald Trump as Man of Conviction, If Not Faith." *New York Times*, January 18. Available at https://www.nytimes.com/2016/01/19/us/politics/evangelicals-see-donald-trump-as-man-of-conviction-if-not-faith.html.

Hunter, James Davison. 1991. *Culture Wars: The Struggle to Define America*. New York: Basic Books.

Jelen, Ted G. 1991. *The Political Mobilization of Religious Beliefs*. New York: Praeger.

Kirkpatrick, David D. 2007. "The Evangelical Crackup." *New York Times*, October 28, p. A38.

Kirkpatrick, David D., and Michael Cooper. 2007. "In a Surprise, Pat Robertson Backs Giuliani." *New York Times*, November 8. Available at http://www.nytimes.com/2007/11/08/us/politics/08repubs.html.

Kohut, Andrew, John C. Green, Scott Keeter, and Robert C. Toth. 2000. *The Diminishing Divide: Religion's Changing Role in American Politics*. Washington, DC: Brookings Institution.

Lamb, W. Scott. 2015. "35th Anniversary of Reagan's 'I Know You Can't Endorse Me. But I Endorse You'—to Evangelicals." *Washington Times*, August 21. Available at https://www.washingtontimes.com/news/2015/aug/21/w-scott-lamb-this-day-in-us-history-reagans-endors/.

Layman, Geoffrey C. 2001. *The Great Divide: Religious and Cultural Conflict in American Party Politics*. New York: Columbia University Press.

———. 2010. "Religion and Party Activists: A 'Perfect Storm' of Polarization or a Recipe for Pragmatism?" In *Religion and Democracy in the United States*, edited by Alan Wolfe and Ira Katznelson, 221–254. Princeton, NJ: Princeton University Press.

Marsden, George M. 1990. *Understanding Fundamentalism and Evangelicalism*. Grand Rapids, MI: Eerdmans.

Martin, William. 1996. *With God on Our Side*. New York: Broadway Books.

Phillips, Amber. 2016. "14 States Have Passed Laws This Year Making It Harder to Get an Abortion." *Washington Post*, June 1. Available at https://www.washingtonpost.com/news/the-fix/wp/2016/06/01/14-states-have-passed-laws-making-it-harder-to-get-an-abortion-already-this-year.

Putnam, Robert D., and David E. Campbell. 2010. *American Grace: How Religion Divides and Unites Us*. New York: Simon and Schuster.

Rozell, Mark, and Clyde Wilcox, eds. 1995. *God at the Grass Roots: The Christian Right in the 1994 Elections*. Lanham, MD: Rowman and Littlefield.

Rymel, Tim. 2016. "Donald Trump Is a Christian! Can You Believe It? Really. Can You?" *Huffington Post*, June 27. Available at https://www.huffingtonpost.com/tim-rymel/donald-trump-is-a-christi_b_10689674.html.

Sala, James. 2005. *How to Talk to Christians*. 2nd ed. Austin, TX: TDP.

Smidt, Corwin E., Kevin R. den Dulk, Bryan T. Froehle, James M. Penning, Stephen V. Monsma, and Douglas L. Koopman. 2010. *The Disappearing God Gap? Religion in the 2008 Presidential Election*. Oxford: Oxford University Press.

Smith, Gregory A., and Jessica Martinez. 2016. "How the Faithful Voted: A Preliminary Analysis." Pew Research Center, November 9. Available at http://www.pewresearch.org/fact-tank/2016/11/09/how-the-faithful-voted-a-preliminary-2016-analysis/.

Stetzer, Ed. 2015. "The Rapid Rise of Nondenominational Christianity: My Most Recent Piece at CNN." *Christianity Today*, June 12. Available at http://www.christianitytoday.com/edstetzer/2015/june/rapid-rise-of-non-denominational-christianity-my-most-recen.html.

Taylor, Jessica. 2015. "True Believer? Why Donald Trump Is the Choice of the Religious Right." *NPR*, September 13. Available at http://www.npr.org/sections/itsallpolitics/2015/09/13/439833719/true-believer-why-donald-trump-is-the-choice-of-the-religious-right.

Wald, Kenneth D., and Allison Calhoun-Brown. 2014. *Religion and Politics in the United States*. 7th ed. Lanham, MD: Rowman and Littlefield.

Wuthnow, Robert. 1988. *The Restructuring of American Religion*. Princeton, NJ: Princeton University Press.

———. 1989. *The Struggle for America's Soul: Evangelicals, Liberals, and Secularism*. Grand Rapids, MI: Eerdmans.

PART I

Activists, Candidates, and the Partisanship of Evangelicals

1

Evangelicals Were on Their Own
in the 2016 Elections

PAUL A. DJUPE
BRIAN R. CALFANO

Donald Trump is perhaps the most unlikely Republican presidential candidate to garner the highest concentration of white evangelical support in any election in the era of surveys. Twice divorced, crude, and uncivil, Trump inspired the #NeverTrump hashtag used by a number of evangelical elites and publications, despite his offerings of a judicial pick and pro-life stance. For instance, in an op-ed in the *Christian Post*, Napp Nazworth (2016) argued, "Don't fall for the temptation to vote for Donald Trump. . . . The fact that Trump uses Satan-like tactics should concern Evangelicals." Max Lucado (2016), San Antonio pastor and best-selling author, took to his website (and then the *Washington Post*) to argue, "[Trump's] insensitivities wouldn't be acceptable even for a middle school student body election. But for the Oval Office? And to do so while brandishing a Bible and boasting of his Christian faith?" And the executive editor of *Christianity Today*, Andy Crouch (2016), in a piece published less than a month before the election, charged, "Evangelicals, of all people, should not be silent about Donald Trump's blatant immorality."

Did anyone hear them? Would it make a difference if they did? These questions take us to the core of religious influence in politics, covering the two principal functions of religion and public opinion. For a suite of potential reasons, religion can *expose* people to information that may shape their political outlooks, and religion can drive how people respond to, or "adopt," that information. Most research on religion and public opinion makes assumptions about these exposure and adoption processes (for an extended discussion of exposure and adoption, see Djupe and Calfano 2013), assuming that elites are present and powerful, that people talk to each other and provide persuasive information, and that people acquire meaningful identities to help sort through the noise. But those assumptions are problematic, especially in the context of the 2016 election, where competing signals have been recorded.

Answering these questions satisfactorily is essential business for understanding the place of religion in public life. To remain an effective force, religion must remain independent, retaining the ability to overcome reflexivity (e.g., knee-jerk partisanship). Instead, religion must be able to deliberate over its political choices and select the ones that best accord with its values. Ideally, participants would be exposed to a range of considered views that enable critical thinking, which here might include the #NeverTrump elites (the Nazworth piece was paired with a thoughtful counterpiece by Richard Land [2016]) but should be expanded to anyone willing to present his or her views publicly.

Put differently, the "evangelical crackup" may be referring to the link between evangelical adherents and organized religion, represented by clergy and other affiliated elites. If adherents are not exposed to elite messages, and, even more troubling, if they are unwilling to consider them, then we might tentatively conclude that evangelicalism has a waning influence on American politics. At least, this is the conclusion we are looking to assess.

We draw on a national survey of white Christians conducted in the week before the election through Qualtrics Panels. Our analysis of these data from white evangelicals, mainline Protestants, and Roman Catholics shows widespread ignorance about evangelical elites and a considerable amount of projection of their own beliefs about support for Trump onto clergy and national elites. We also embedded an experiment in this survey to overcome the variability of exposure, and what we find suggests little willingness to consider credible counterviews.

The Role of Elites in Public-Opinion Formation

Much of the reason scholars focus on political elites writ large is the public's general ignorance (Delli Carpini and Keeter 1996) and the tendency of people, including those well informed, to follow leader dictates (Milgram 1974; Zaller 1992). In American politics, party labels often function as part of the elite influence mechanism (see Rahn 1993; Cohen 2003), with party identity serving as a social identity cue that makes elite pronouncements acceptable (Mackie, Gastardo-Conaco, and Skelly 1992; Popkin 1994). Part and parcel of elite influence is the public's use of shortcuts in taking elite cues on political matters without much in the way of critical thought (McGuire 1969; Iyengar and Valentino 2000; see also Nie, Verba, and Petrocik 1976). Cues function as shortcuts, which explains why most scholars suggest that people utilize peripheral processing of political information (Petty and Cacioppo 1996).

Yet the tidy picture of elite-to-mass influence painted by the Michigan School and related social-psychological studies of party identity's effects tell only part of the story of elite-based influence. In reality, the scope of political elites in American politics extends far beyond elected and party officials who can rely on a well-established brand name in garnering public support. In the case of religious elites, for example, there are no automatic party cues to rely on in making arguments about what "ought" to be in the world (see Wald, Owen, and Hill 1988; Djupe and Gilbert 2009). Religious leaders (e.g., pastors, bishops) have to make the case for parishioners to adopt the elite's preferred view of things through a combination of appeals to spiritual authority, reason, group identity, shared experiences, and related items (Hadden 1969; Stark et al. 1971). There is far less evidence to support the direct influence of these religious leaders over parishioners than scholars have found for party elites (Djupe and Gilbert 2009), though there is some (e.g., Djupe and Calfano 2013; Djupe and Gwiasda 2010; Margolis forthcoming; Wald 1992). Anemic influence may be especially true for religious elites who communicate political instead of religious messages (Kohut et al. 2000) and for elites who lead religious communities that are less exclusive in membership and outlook (Finke and Stark 2005).

There is also the issue of the larger context in which religious elites carry out their work. Two types of context are relevant to this project. The first is institutional in nature and regards the presence of hierarchical structures within religious denominations. Generally, institutional higher-ups have some sway over local elites, influence that may even be considered welcome and sought after (Ammerman 1981; Calfano 2009; Calfano, Michelson, and Oldmixon 2017). The Roman Catholic Church is the classic hierarchical structure, but we could include the Episcopal Church, the Evangelical Lutheran Church in America, and the Presbyterian denominations. However, evangelical denominations tend to be more congregational, with less of a top-down chain of command or, for a growing number (Stetzer 2015), no denominational structure at all. This means that local elites leading evangelical communities may be perceived as independent brokers of political influence in the eyes of their local congregants. And there are fewer hard-coded links from elites to members in the pews.

The second type of context regards the cue information a religious elite offers. Stephen P. Nicholson's (2011) work on political-source cues finds that people are responsive to both the cue giver and the intended beneficiary of what the cue aims to accomplish. In fact, the endorsement of an unpopular group or entity was found to overwhelm the source cue's influence. That is, disagreement can overwhelm even credible sources. We return to both of these context-based points later.

Of all the things we know about elites, there remain several areas ripe for investigation about how the public views and responds to these leaders. For example, we do not have much of a sense of how the public treats elites who change their known views on controversial and salient topics. In today's polarized political environment, a position change, real or perceived, can run the risk of alienating substantial segments of followers (and their resources, including monetary contributions). At this point, there is a movement in the Southern Baptist Convention for stripping the position of prominent Never Trumper Russell Moore (Gjelten 2016). Thus, some political leaders may find toeing the community line (e.g., supporting Republicans) as the safest strategy. But position change by elites happens more than one might think, particularly for elected officials who often campaign using one type of rhetoric while governing in a different, usually less strident, way.

If we know a considerable amount about the extent to which interest-group leaders cooperate to achieve goals (see, e.g., Berry and Wilcox 2015; Cigler and Loomis 2011), we do not have much in the way of evidence about coordination between elites across institutional and political domains. In the case of religious elites (like clergy) and political candidates, coordination is generally forbidden by existing federal tax regulations. Even if these elites could solve their coordination problem, however, scholars have not been able to gain much leverage on questions having to do with how the public perceives coordination and/or collaboration between elites from different domains (e.g., the political, corporate, religious, celebrity, sports, and related worlds). Since much of the appeal elites have over their groups is steeped in the in-group cues based in social identity, there is at least some reason to expect that elite "crossover" is not viewed favorably, particularly among groups with more exclusive boundaries. By the same token, however, it could just as easily be that some publics find collaboration between elites across domains to be a positive development, especially when certain values or group norms are considered threatened.

Finally, and most important for our purposes, we do not know whether the public views elites as part of a hierarchy in which some leaders are considered more influential than others when they are involved in the same political or religious institution or movement. A classic example from the religion and politics literature is whether Catholics are more persuaded by messages from their bishops or local priests (e.g., Djupe 2001). Scholars have provided context for the institutional dynamics in play for both sets of religious leaders (e.g., Cavendish 2001; Wald 1992), but they have not directly assessed this elite-hierarchy question from the standpoint of mass influence.

Interestingly, the Catholic question has an evangelical Protestant analog. Pastors of mainline and evangelical congregations may function as cue givers who encourage people to use what they hear in the local church setting to look for supporting cues from or simply project supportive cues onto religious elites working in national capacities as ministry leaders and media personalities. There is also the possibility that the public does not find complementary links between their local clergy and national religious elites because of some social identity motive; however, evidence from Robert P. Jones (2016) about the feelings of anxiety about social status among sizable portions of religious publics leading up to the 2016 election suggests that evangelicals may have created their own form of national institution to rival the Catholic Church (minus the ecclesiastical hierarchies, of course).

Projection is more likely in the absence of information, and there are good reasons to think that credible cues from local elites were not plentiful. First, although Trump made overt efforts to court religious voters in 2016, he has had a personal and professional life full of behavior that many social conservatives should have been hard pressed to condone. Supporting Trump would have been taking the risk of deviating from the predominant expectations congregants have of these elites. In terms of elite coordination, there were certainly those religious elites with national reputations who supported Trump (including Jerry Falwell Jr. and Pat Robertson), but this does not necessarily mean that all or even a majority of local pastors followed their lead. This is the point at which context comes back into play. Trump appeared to be a divisive candidate and also appeared to inspire a great deal of loyalty from backers. This presents perhaps the worst of situations for clergy to step into if there was any disagreement in the congregation. Thus, likely personal ambivalence as well as organizational hazards should undermine the clergy's degree of engagement with the candidates.

There is some evidence to address this situation. Writing in the *Washington Post's Monkey Cage* blog, Paul A. Djupe and colleagues found, using data from September 2016, that just 9 percent of white evangelicals reported hearing about Trump from their clergy; 6 percent heard about Clinton (Djupe et al. 2016). They also used an experiment to assess the effect of exposure to anti-Trump messages (using a version of Nazworth's op-ed) and found that evangelicals expressed less support for Trump after such exposure. The upshot is that evangelicals would listen at this stage of the campaign but were simply not hearing such messages. In the end, resolving the major unknown pieces of the religious elite puzzle requires multiple research designs and hypotheses. What we focus on here pertains to the question of how publics are connected and respond to religious elites. As stated, whether or not local and national elites coordinate their efforts at political influence, the public may connect these dots for them by combining complementary cues about political candidates and topics into a seamless set of directions. In this way, we suspect the public is active in creating its own coherent elite hierarchy, which is an interesting twist on the notion of an uninformed and disinterested electorate. In the case of religious elites at least, the religious public may be motivated enough to match cues from disparately located elites in supporting their decision to support Trump. This may simply be an attempt to align one's party identity with cues from elites outside the partisan domain proper. But even if it is, the act of combining elite cues in determining vote preference shows a level of engagement with elite-provided information that scholars have heretofore overlooked.

Research Design

A week before the election, we contracted with Qualtrics Panels to survey 1,091 white evangelicals, mainline Protestants, and Catholics. We imposed no quotas on the sample but did survey only adults. As is appropriate to surveying a graying set, the survey is older (average age = fifty-six) and more female (59 percent), and 34 percent have completed a four-year college degree. The sample leans heavily toward the Republican Party, with which 47 percent identify (including leaners); 31 percent are Democrats.

We undertook two strategies to address the exposure and adoption questions that are so central to religious influence. We asked respondents the level of support they perceive for Trump from their clergy, congregations, and communities, as well as whether their clergy addressed a number of political issues, including the presidential candidates. We also asked their perceptions of support for Trump by a set of evangelical elites who have either a media or a social media presence (see Figure 1.1). About half of them opposed Trump, and half offered him their support. We believed that it would be unlikely that most respondents would know these figures (a belief that was ratified in the data), so we offered an explicit "Don't know" response along with "Supports Trump" and "Opposes Trump."

The expected vagaries in exposure to these elites and anti-Trump sentiment would make any observational study of adoption difficult. Therefore, we controlled exposure in an experimental context by presenting respondents with an op-ed styled on the one offered by *Christianity Today*'s executive editor (Crouch 2016). The 2×3 set of conditions varied the gender of the author—either John or Jane Warren—and then varied whether there was positive reaction from evangelicals, negative reaction from evangelicals, or no specified reaction.[1] It read (condition choices in brackets separated by "//"):

November 1, 2016 AP—Colorado Springs, CO
Leaders of the evangelical publication *Christianity Today* have decided to wade into presidential politics. Though they try to stay neutral in presidential politics, the publication's publisher, [John // Jane] Warren, wrote a long article called "Speak Truth to Trump." In it, Warren argued, "We are not indifferent when the gospel is at stake. The gospel is of infinitely greater importance than any campaign. There is hardly any public person in America today other than

Trump who has more exemplified the 'earthly nature' that Paul urges the Colossians to shed: 'sexual immorality, impurity, lust, evil desires, and greed, which is idolatry' (3:5). Enthusiasm for a candidate like Trump gives our neighbors ample reason to doubt that we believe Jesus is Lord. They see that some of us are so self-interested, and so self-protective, that we will ally ourselves with someone who violates all that is sacred to us." [no statement // But some evangelicals interviewed in North Carolina for this story shot back that *Christianity Today* is being a traitor to the Republican Party. As one voter said, "We ARE the party. We chose Trump, and we are telling our representatives to back a specific candidate, not what some elitist magazine we have never read tells us!" // Some evangelicals interviewed in North Carolina for this story agreed with *Christianity Today* and see the magazine as supporting the Republican Party, if not its current presidential candidate. As one voter said, "We ARE the party, and Trump's candidacy too shall pass. *Christianity Today* understands exactly where we're coming from."] Trump continues to trail Democrat Hillary Clinton in most national polls.

The experiment was presented at the beginning of the survey; the questions about elite stances and congregation and clergy support were presented near the end—more than five minutes of questions apart in the survey. We begin discussion with the observational items and close with a brief presentation of the results of the experiment.

Results: Support from Evangelical Elites

We compiled a list of evangelical elites who took divergent stands on Trump's candidacy and who have a media platform and/or robust social media presence. Shown in Figure 1.1, that group included stalwarts of the Christian Right—Pat Robertson (700 Club), Mike Huckabee (former presidential candidate), Jerry Falwell Jr. (Liberty University), and Tony Perkins (Family Research Council)—who expressed support for Trump. But the list also included new evangelical leaders who leaned against or were staunchly opposed to his candidacy: Rick Warren (Saddleback Church), Beth Moore (head of Living Proof ministries and has a huge Twitter following—see Beaty 2016; Burge 2017), Michael Gerson (*Washington Post* columnist and former George W. Bush speechwriter), Russell Moore (head of Southern Baptist Ethics and Religious Liberty Commission [ERLC]), and Jen Hatmaker (American Christian author, speaker, blogger, and television presenter). We also listed *Christianity Today* to see if respondents were paying attention to the experimental treatment detailed in the previous section, which mentioned the magazine.

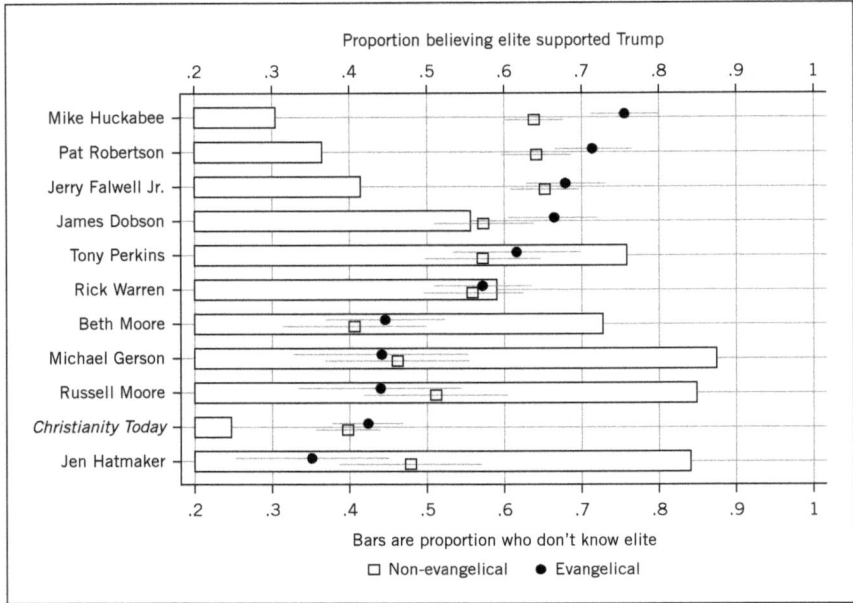

Figure 1.1 Perceived Trump support among evangelical elites
Note: Lines are 90 percent confidence intervals.

Figure 1.1 shows widespread ignorance about most of these leaders—the bars show the proportion of the sample that did not know how the elite stood on Trump. Most of those leaders are well above 50 percent. The least well known are also the ones most opposed to Trump—such as Russell Moore and Michael Gerson (87 percent do not know their stance). Most do not have population-level or really even group-level reach. They do not need to have that level of reach to be influential, but it is worth pointing out.

Of those respondents willing to venture an opinion, they by and large have correct perceptions. Huckabee, Falwell, and Robertson did support Trump's candidacy. They were in the news quite a bit and are widely known as Christian Right Republicans. Tony Perkins was a supporter, too, but received less media coverage, so about 40 percent did not think he was a Trump supporter (he was, at least after the nomination contest, when he supported Ted Cruz). Rick Warren appeared to take no position on Trump, so it is not surprising that the results are nearly split. The elites at the bottom of the list did at least make statements critical of Trump. Yet the results still suggest that more than 40 percent of evangelicals thought Beth and Russell Moore (no relation), Gerson, and *Christianity Today* were in support of Trump. There is more error among non-evangelicals, which is to be expected, but it is often not significantly different from what evangelicals guess.

Results: Congregational Links to National Figures

There are numerous ways that individuals can become aware of elite position taking, especially now that we are engulfed in social media. Nevertheless, organizations and other entities (such as social networks) are important to help individuals connect with elites. Congregations and clergy are just such actors that we think help knit together movements. They can relay information from elites, build support for the movement's goals, and make individuals aware of opportunities for getting involved. The actual evidence to assess this notion regarding particular movements is rather sparse, however, beyond the civil rights movement (e.g., Morris 1984).

Here, we can assess whether more political evangelical congregations help individuals connect with evangelical elites. There is a relatively lively debate about what constitutes a political church (see Djupe and Gilbert 2009), but we use the number of political topics that individuals perceive their clergyperson to have addressed in the past year (Donald Trump, Hillary Clinton, immigration in America, abortion, importance of voting/participating in the election, Islam in America, religious freedom, poverty, and same-sex marriage/gay rights). The average number of topics perceived was 2.4 among evangelicals, 2.0 among Catholics, and 1.8 among mainline Protestants.

Figure 1.2 shows the link between being in a political church and perceptions of evangelical elites.[2] The top panel reports the rate of selecting the "don't know" option for the listed elites (the measure tallies up the "don't know" responses and divides by the eleven elites listed). Being in a political church does nothing to connect Catholics and mainliners to evangelical elites, as expected, but it does for evangelicals. Their rate of claiming ignorance drops by 10 percent of the scale from the least to the most political churches. It is not clear if this measure captures comfort with politics (see, e.g., Mondak and Anderson 2004) or reflects the actual transmission of knowledge. For that, the bottom panel of Figure 1.2 is instructive. Evangelicals in highly political churches know the correct position of 0.5 more elites. Political churches make no difference for the other traditions. To an extent, we find that political evangelical congregations help make informational ties to evangelical elites.

Results: Clergy Trump Support and Its Links

Clergy are not neutral conduits for political information, of course, so it is worth investigating the extent to which they were perceived to engage the campaign. Figure 1.3 shows the percentage of respondents who reported hearing their clergy talk about Trump as well as their perceived support level for Trump. Perceived clergy support for Trump was tepid among respondents,

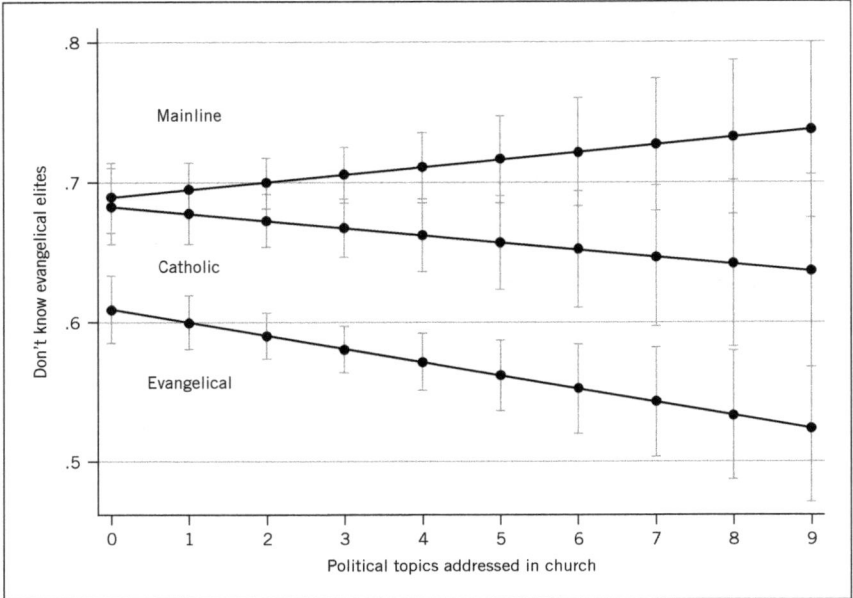

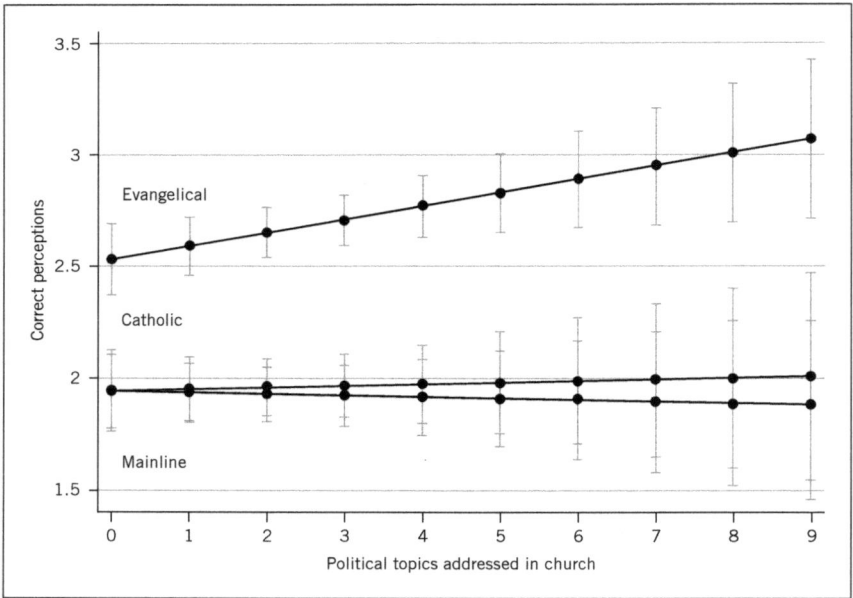

Figure 1.2 Rates of choosing "don't know" evangelical elites' support for Trump (*top*) and correct perceptions of evangelical elites' support for Trump (*bottom*)

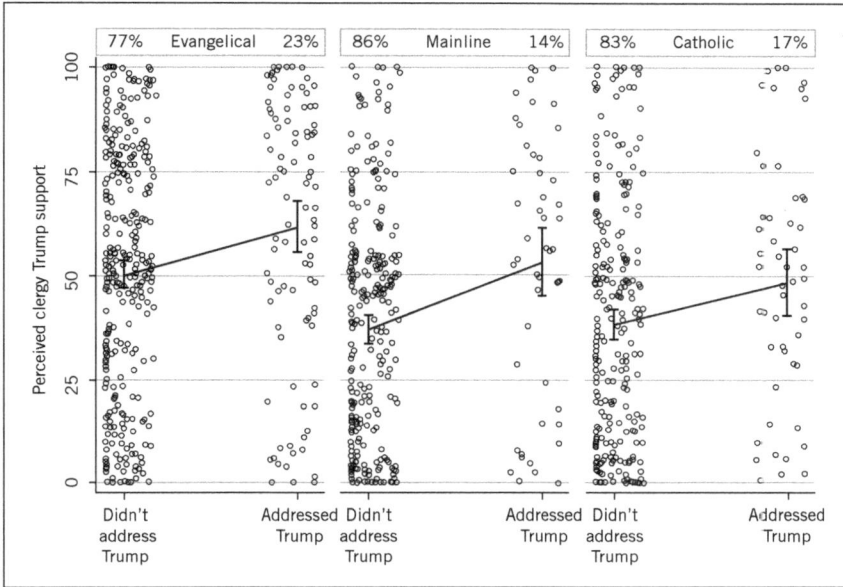

Figure 1.3 Perceived Trump support by clergy who addressed Trump

but it was uniformly higher when the clergy talked about Trump. In each case, those addressing Trump were seen as ten points more supportive. However, only 23 percent of evangelicals reported their clergy addressing Trump. This is a low figure but slightly higher than the 17 percent of Catholic priests and the 14 percent of mainline pastors and up quite a bit from late September, when only 9 percent reported hearing their evangelical clergyperson address Trump (Djupe et al. 2016).

It is clear, though, that there was nothing monolithic about the evangelical religious community's support for Trump. In fact, most could be said to be left to their own devices in evaluating the candidates. That interpretation gains steam in Figure 1.4, which shows the rather tight link between community support for Trump and perceived clergy support. There are very few clergy who are "off-diagonal"—standing resolute for Trump in anti-Trump country. While there are more evangelicals living in pro-Trump communities, there is wide variation that corresponds to wide variation in perceived clergy support for Trump. Among evangelicals, 38 percent of their clergy and 32 percent of their communities are perceived to have less than 50 percent support for Trump.

Those perceptions of their clergy and community are linked to how evangelicals view national evangelical elites. As Figure 1.5 shows, the greater support they perceive for Trump from their clergy, the greater the support they perceive from the listed evangelical elites. The effect is huge, increasing

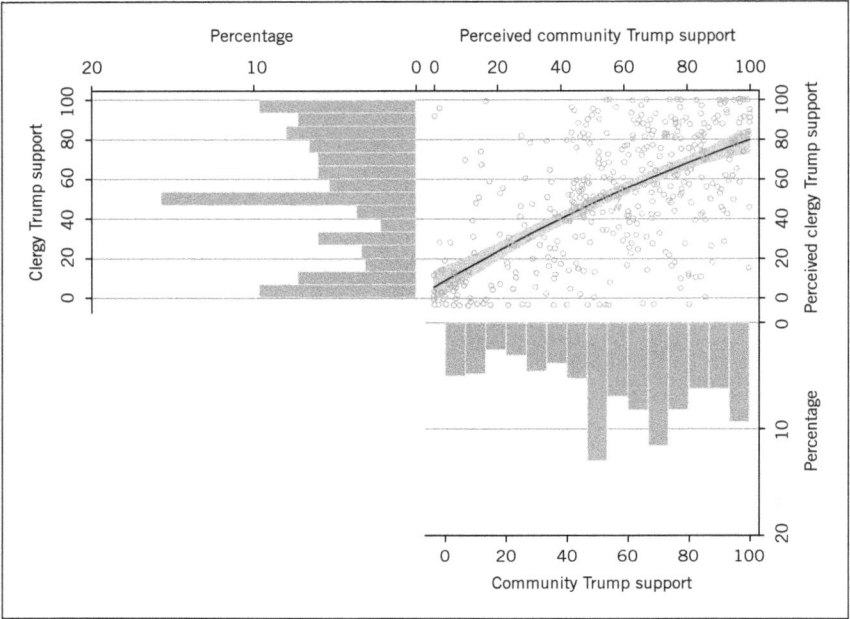

Figure 1.4 Link between community and clergy Trump support

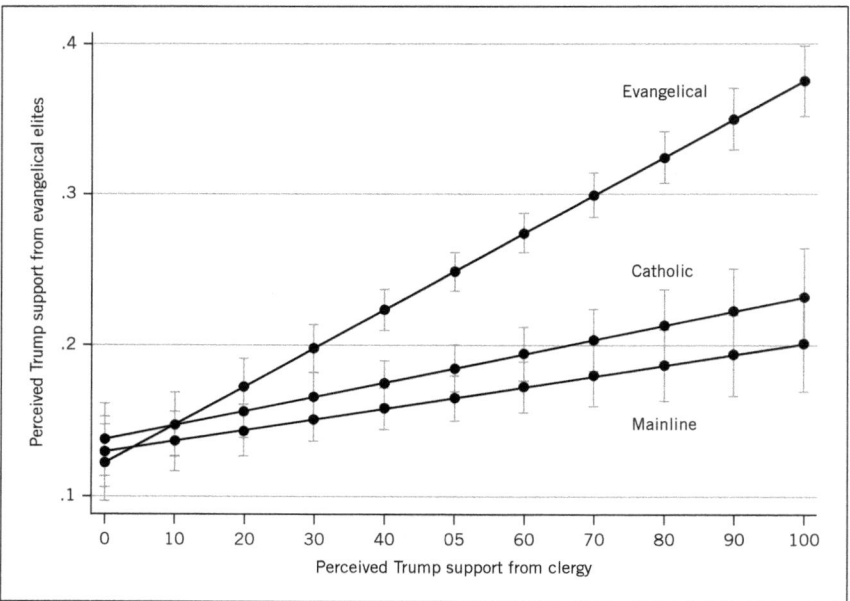

Figure 1.5 Link between evangelicals' view of elites and perceptions of views of clergy and community

from 12 percent support to 37 percent support (for the rest, most just simply do not know). For the other traditions, there is a modest (90 percent significance level) increase among mainliners and Catholics of about 10 percent or less. There is also a modest increase in perceived elite support for Trump when evangelicals live in pro-Trump communities (not shown). The same shift from 0 to 100 percent support in the community nets a ten-point shift in perception of evangelical elite support for Trump.

Experimental Results

In our experiment, we were not looking to study the effects of exposure but the conditions associated with adoption of what we suspect was novel information for most—statements by credible evangelical elites critical of Trump. It is impossible not to notice the gender divide in the list of elites used in our survey. While there were women who endorsed Trump, many more walked away from historic commitments in the face of "The Tape," among other crude behavior (Beaty 2016). We also sought to capture the community component involved in reaction to elites. That is, evangelical perception of others' support for Trump appears to be conditioned by how supportive their community is. Thus, we varied the inclusion of a statement expressing support for or opposition to the anti-Trump comments (one-third of the sample was not exposed to such a statement).

Figure 1.6 shows those results for evangelicals. The first panel (upper left) shows how the six statements were received as indexed by a feeling thermometer for Trump. Effectively, there was no reaction whatsoever, as mean thermometer ratings in all six conditions varied insignificantly. However, it is noteworthy that feelings toward Trump were *higher* when the anti-Trump statement was attributed to a woman (Jane Moore).

The remaining panels focus attention on how men and women evangelicals may have responded differently to the statement for each of the mass-support conditions. This was a fruitful endeavor. Men tend to shift their feelings toward Trump more than women do, and they do so in reaction to the gender of the elite. In the condition (upper right) where there was no statement of mass support, men react negatively to the woman elite—they report distinguishably more positive feelings toward Trump. In the case where the mass is said to agree with the elite, men react more negatively to the male elite. And in the case where the mass is said to disagree with the elite, there is little movement at all.

This suggests that evangelical men are more likely to react in negative ways to novel information than to emphasize agreement, once again ratifying Christian Smith's (1998) sense of evangelicals as "embattled." In this way, our results highlight the importance that community distributions play in evangelicals' reception of information. This should not be surprising in a

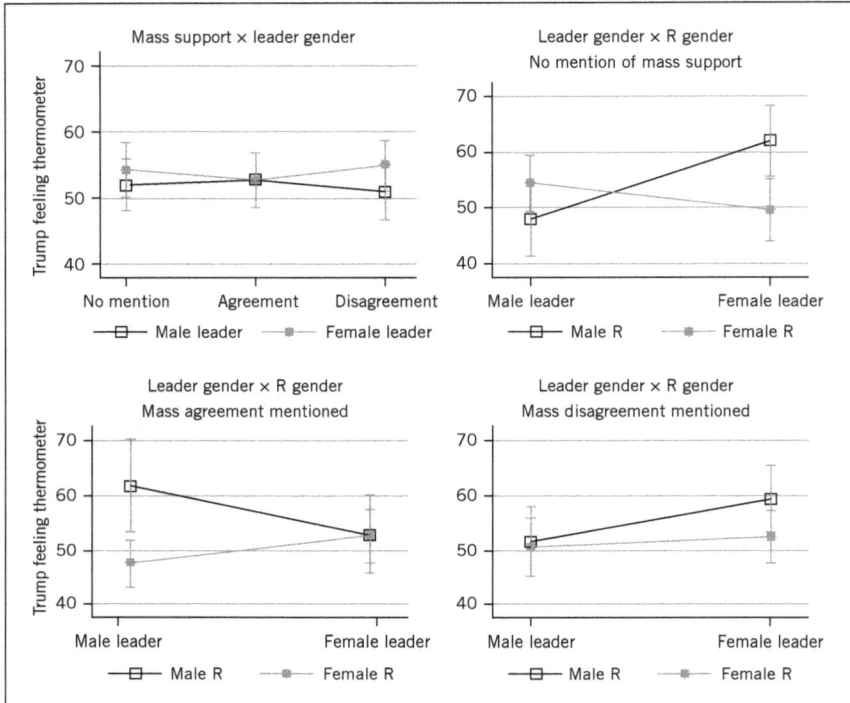

Figure 1.6 Effect of gender on evangelical men and women's reactions to anti-Trump comments

faith tradition that places heavy importance on personal responsibility enforced by community norms and surveillance. But it differs from the emphasis scholars have traditionally placed on the privately held beliefs of individual evangelicals. Put differently, these suggest that evangelicals cling less to in-group cues, which strikes us as eminently credible here coming from *Christianity Today*, and react more strongly to out-group cues that help reinforce their attitudes.

Conclusion

In this chapter, we seek to envision the evangelical crackup a bit differently, looking to check the linkages evangelicalism had within, from the top to the bottom. It would be too strong to suggest there is a hollow core, but it would not be too strong to indicate that those linkages are as fragmented as the religious tradition itself. There are few ties to evangelical elites, and evangelicals at the grassroots appear to supply cues from their read of their own congregation and community.

In some ways this is the strength of the movement—it was designed to be a grassroots religious group, taking its leadership from among the local faithful (at least, in the case of the Baptists). This practice relieved pressure to supply the pastorate, but it also invited local experimentation even as it insulated congregations from some measure of disagreement. Of course, this is also the weakness, since evangelical views do not then travel out into the community at the same rate as they do in the mainline tradition (e.g., Granovetter 1973), and it is difficult to reorient the views of evangelicals toward a new goal. Put differently, evangelical elites do not have the infrastructure to attempt to shape affiliates' views or act as a counterweight to Republican officials who do have that organizational and media infrastructure. And evangelicals appear to reject new information from nontraditional sources that stand against community momentum.

When pushed to their logical conclusion, the results suggest the inability of evangelical elites to point the faithful in new directions. This would be a crackup of sorts if such elites had had this power in the past. Unfortunately, at least for academic scoring, there are very few test cases like Trump in the past that would expose fault lines and weakness. Nevertheless, the evidence at hand reveals evangelicals in the mass public have weak connections to evangelical elites. Their clergy are generally unwilling to discuss and criticize candidates for office. And evangelicals react negatively when evangelical leaders are critical of Republican candidates. All told, the lack of elite evangelical engagement may have paved the way for evangelical support for Trump, but criticism might have fallen on deaf ears, especially late in the campaign.

NOTES

1. Randomization was successful, and there is no significant variation in demographics across the six treatment cells: age ($p = .88$), female ($p = .38$), education ($p = .39$), or evangelical ($p = .42$).

2. We use a simple model that controls for age, education, gender, clergy's Trump support, and political interest.

REFERENCES

Ammerman, Nancy. 1981. "The Civil Rights Movement and the Clergy in a Southern Community." *Sociological Analysis* 41:339–350.

Beaty, Katelyn. 2016. "'No More': Evangelical Women Are Done with Donald Trump and His Misogyny." *Washington Post*, October 13. Available at https://www.washingtonpost .com/news/acts-of-faith/wp/2016/10/13/no-more-evangelical-women-are-done-with -donald-trump-and-his-misogyny.

Berry, Jeffrey M., and Clyde Wilcox. 2015. *The Interest Group Society.* 5th ed. New York: Routledge.

Burge, Ryan P. 2017. "Trump and the Prosperity Gospel." *Religion in Public*, January 26. Available at https://religioninpublic.blog/2017/01/26/trump-and-the-prosperity-gospel/.

Calfano, Brian Robert. 2009. "Choosing Constituent Cues: Reference Group Influence on Clergy Political Speech." *Social Science Quarterly* 90:88–102.

Calfano, Brian Robert, Melissa R. Michelson, and Elizabeth A. Oldmixon. 2017. *A Matter of Discretion: The Politics of Roman Catholic Priests in the US and Ireland.* Lanham, MD: Rowman and Littlefield.

Cavendish, James C. 2001. "To March or Not to March: Clergy Mobilization Strategies and Grassroots Antidrug Activism." In *Christian Clergy in American Politics,* edited by Sue E. S. Crawford and Laura R. Olson, 203–224. Baltimore: Johns Hopkins University Press.

Cigler, Allen J., and Burdett A. Loomis. 2011. *Interest Group Politics.* 8th ed. Washington, DC: CQ Press.

Cohen, Geoffrey L. 2003. "Party over Policy: The Dominating Impact of Group Influence on Political Beliefs." *Journal of Personality and Social Psychology* 85:808–822.

Crouch, Andy. 2016. "Speak Truth to Trump." *Christianity Today,* October 10. Available at http://www.christianitytoday.com/ct/2016/october-web-only/speak-truth-to-trump .html.

Delli Carpini, Michael X., and Scott Keeter. 1996. *What Americans Know about Politics and Why It Matters.* New Haven, CT: Yale University Press.

Djupe, Paul A. 2001. "Cardinal O'Connor and His Constituents: Differential Benefits and Public Evaluations." In *Christian Clergy in American Politics,* edited by Sue E. S. Crawford and Laura R. Olson, 188–202. Baltimore: Johns Hopkins University Press.

Djupe, Paul A., and Brian Robert Calfano. 2013. *God Talk: Experimenting with the Religious Causes of Public Opinion.* Philadelphia: Temple University Press.

Djupe, Paul A., and Christopher P. Gilbert. 2009. *The Political Influence of Churches.* New York: Cambridge University Press.

Djupe, Paul A., and Gregory W. Gwiasda. 2010. "Evangelizing the Environment: Decision Process Effects in Political Persuasion." *Journal for the Scientific Study of Religion* 49:73–86.

Djupe, Paul A., Anand E. Sokhey, Amanda Friesen, and Andrew R. Lewis. 2016. "When Evangelical Clergy Oppose Trump, Their Flocks Listen. But They're Not Speaking Up." *Washington Post,* November 4. Available at https://www.washingtonpost.com/news/ monkey-cage/wp/2016/11/04/when-evangelical-clergy-oppose-trump-their-flocks -listen-but-theyre-keeping-quiet.

Finke, Roger, and Rodney Stark. 2005. *The Churching of America, 1776–2005: Winners and Losers in Our Religious Economy.* New Brunswick, NJ: Rutgers University Press.

Gjelten, Tom. 2016. "Evangelical Leader under Attack for Criticizing Trump Supporters." *NPR,* December 20. Available at http://www.npr.org/2016/12/20/506248119/anti-trump -evangelical-faces-backlash.

Granovetter, Mark. 1973. "The Strength of Weak Ties." *American Journal of Sociology* 78:1360–1380.

Hadden, Jeffrey K. 1969. *The Gathering Storm in Churches.* Garden City, NY: Doubleday.

Iyengar, Shanto, and Nicholas Valentino. 2000. "Who Says What? Source Credibility as a Mediator of Campaign Advertising." In *Elements of Reason,* edited by Arthur Lupia, Matthew D. McCubbins, and Samuel L. Popkin, 108–129. New York: Cambridge University Press.

Jones, Robert P. 2016. *The End of White Christian America.* New York: Simon and Schuster.

Kohut, Andrew, John C. Green, Scott Ketter, and Robert C. Toth. 2000. *The Diminishing Divide: Religion's Changing Role in American Politics.* Washington, DC: Brookings Institution Press.

Land, Richard C. 2016. "The Presidential Election: An Excruciating Choice." *Christian Post,* August 23. Available at http://www.christianpost.com/news/the-presidential-election -an-excruciating-choice-168428/.

Lucado, Max. 2016. "Decency for President." *Max Lucado* (blog), February 24. Available at https://maxlucado.com/decency-for-president/.

Mackie, Diane M., M. Cecilia Gastardo-Conaco, and John J. Skelly. 1992. "Knowledge of the Advanced Position and the Processing of In-Group and Out-Group Persuasive Messages." *Personality and Social Psychology Bulletin* 58:145–151.

Margolis, Michele F. Forthcoming. "How Far Does Social Group Influence Reach? Elites, Evangelicals, and Immigration Attitudes." *Journal of Politics*. Available at http://www .michelemargolis.com/uploads/2/0/2/0/20207607/eit_november_2015.pdf.

McGuire, William J. 1969. "The Nature of Attitudes and Attitude Change." In *Handbook of Social Psychology*, 2nd ed., edited by Gardner Lindzey and Elliot Aronson, 136–314. Reading, MA: Addison-Wesley.

Milgram, Stanley. 1974. *Obedience to Authority.* New York: Harper and Row.

Mondak, Jeffery J., and Mary R. Anderson. 2004. "The Knowledge Gap: A Reexamination of Gender-Based Differences in Political Knowledge." *Journal of Politics* 66 (2): 492–512.

Morris, Aldon D. 1984. *The Origins of the Civil Rights Movement: Black Communities Organizing for Change.* New York: Free Press.

Nazworth, Napp. 2016. "Why Evangelicals Shouldn't Vote for Trump." *Christian Post*, August 23. Available at http://www.christianpost.com/news/why-evangelicals-shouldnt-vote-for -donald-trump-168426./

Nicholson, Stephen P. 2011. "Dominating Cues and the Limits of Elite Influence." *Journal of Politics* 73:1165–1177.

Nie, Norman, Sidney Verba, and John R. Petrocik. 1976. *The Changing American Voter.* Cambridge, MA: Harvard University Press.

Petty, Richard E., and John T. Cacioppo. 1996. *Attitudes and Persuasion: Classic and Contemporary Approaches.* Boulder, CO: Westview Press.

Popkin, Samuel L. 1994. *The Reasoning Voter: Communication and Persuasion in Presidential Campaigns.* 2nd ed. Chicago: University of Chicago Press.

Rahn, Wendy. 1993. "The Role of Partisan Stereotypes in Information Processing about Political Candidates." *American Journal of Political Science* 37:472–497.

Smith, Christian. 1998. *American Evangelicalism: Embattled and Thriving.* Chicago: University of Chicago Press.

Stark, Rodney, Bruce D. Foster, Charles Y. Glock, and Harold E. Quinley. 1971. *Wayward Shepherds: Prejudice and the Protestant Clergy.* New York: Harper and Row.

Stetzer, Ed. 2015. "The Rapid Rise of Nondenominational Christianity: My Most Recent Piece at CNN." *Christianity Today*, June 12. Available at http://www.christianitytoday.com/ edstetzer/2015/june/rapid-rise-of-non-denominational-christianity-my-most-recen .html.

Wald, Kenneth D. 1992. "Religious Elites and Public Opinion: The Impact of the Bishops' Peace Pastoral." *Review of Politics* 54 (1): 112–143.

Wald, Kenneth D., Dennis E. Owen, and Samuel S. Hill. 1988. "Churches and Political Communities." *American Political Science Review* 82:531–548.

Zaller, John R. 1992. *The Nature and Origins of Mass Opinion.* New York: Cambridge University Press.

2

Evangelical Activists in the GOP

Still the Life of the Party?

GEOFFREY LAYMAN
MARK BROCKWAY

Party activists are a fundamentally important part of the American two-party system. They exert considerable influence on the candidates the parties nominate, their policy priorities, and their political cultures (Miller and Jennings 1986; Aldrich 1983; Layman 2014). Moreover, because the U.S. parties are relatively decentralized and open to new participants, new groups of activists—championing new candidates or demanding new policies—find it fairly easy to infiltrate and gain influence within party politics (Cohen et al. 2008).

No group of party activists has been more important or influential than evangelical Protestant activists in the contemporary Republican Party. Largely apolitical or Democratic through the 1970s (Oldfield 1996; Green et al. 1996), evangelicals turned to Republican activism in the 1980s and grew increasingly involved in the 1990s and 2000s (Oldfield 1996; Layman and Weaver 2016). The value of evangelical activism to the GOP gave evangelicals considerable influence within the party, pushing it to the right on moral and cultural issues and making cultural conservatism a prerequisite for party nominations (Green and Jackson 2007; McTague and Layman 2009; Carmines and Woods 2002). Evangelical activists also have helped spur the GOP's rightward shift on economic and foreign-policy issues and encouraged a more strident style in Republican politics (Layman 2010). In short, evangelical Republican activists have been important to the GOP's full-scale participation in the "culture wars" and its entrenched position in the unyielding political wars waged by the Republican and Democratic Parties.

However, several trends in American religious and political life suggest that evangelical activists' continued dominance of Republican politics may not be assured. Indeed, the fact that the last three Republican presidential nominees—John McCain, Mitt Romney, and Donald Trump—all lacked prior ties to the evangelical movement may suggest that an evangelical "crackup" is on the horizon.

In this chapter, we examine the presence and influence of evangelical activists in the Republican Party and assess whether they are rising or declining. We first consider the theoretical reasons for evangelical activists' considerable impact on the GOP and then assess the empirical evidence for evangelical activists' party influence. We examine changes over time in the representation of evangelicals in the Republican activist base, compare the policy positions and political orientations of evangelical activists to those of other active Republicans, and evaluate the role that evangelical activists played in Donald Trump's presidential nomination and election in 2016.

Party Activism, Evangelicalism, and the Life of the Republican Party

Because the American parties rely heavily on the physical, intellectual, and financial resources provided by activists (Layman 2014), activists play a prominent role in party politics. In fact, one leading view of the American parties contends that policy-demanding activists represent the very essence of the parties—parties exist primarily to pursue the goals of policy-oriented activists, and these policy goals provide the principal rationale for party organization (Cohen et al. 2008; Karol 2009; Bawn et al. 2012). Another leading view of parties sees office seekers—political candidates and elected officials—as the preeminent party actors and winning elections as the primary party goal. However, because activists or benefit seekers provide essential resources for office seekers, their goals place important constraints on the strategies and activities of party candidates and office holders (Aldrich 1995; Schlesinger 1991; Miller and Schofield 2003).

Specifically, party activists exert influence on party politics in at least three important ways. First, because the American parties nominate their candidates through a participatory process (consisting of primary elections and/or local party caucuses), in which involvement generally is limited to people who are particularly interested and engaged in politics, activists exert a great deal of influence over whom the parties nominate for president, Congress, and other public offices (Aldrich 1995; Carsey and Layman 1999; Polsby et al. 2011). Second, their importance for party nominations and for successful general election campaigns means that activists exert considerable influence over the parties' policy positions. Activists tend to hold policy positions that are more ideologically extreme than those of the average voter (McClosky, Hoffmann, and O'Hara 1960; Layman et al. 2010), and they tend to be ideological "purists," eschewing politically pragmatic compromise in favor of adherence to ideological principles (Wildavsky 1965; Soule and Clarke 1970). Thus, their influence helps create partisan policy differences even if strategic party candidates and leaders would prefer to stake out ground closer to the ideological center (Aldrich 1983; Layman et al. 2010). Third, party activists play an essential role in the process of partisan change (Karol 2009). They are often the catalysts for the emergence of new political issues; they encourage party candidates and office holders to adopt clear positions on these issues; and, through their interaction with less active citizens, they help translate change among political elites into change in the parties' coalitions in the mass electorate (Carmines and Stimson 1989; Layman 2001).

A particularly good example of activist influence on the parties is evangelical activists in the Republican Party. Because committed evangelical Protestants have high levels of religious devotion (Smith 1998), adhere strongly to core religious beliefs (Smidt 2013), and typically belong to strict churches that demand a good deal from their members (Finke and Stark 2005), political issues and causes that are connected to their faith spur them to relatively high levels of political activism (Green, Guth, and Fraser 1991; Green and Jackson 2007; Swartz 2012). Moreover, evangelical churches, religious networks, and faith-based institutions provide impressive organizational resources for mobilizing believers into political activity (Oldfield 1996). This combination of religion-based passion and institutional resources has spurred evangelicals to relatively high levels of participation in Republican nomination politics and made evangelicals a highly important base of Republican support in general elections (Oldfield 1996; Green, Rozell, and Wilcox 2006).

Ryan Claassen (2015) reminds us of other important resources for evangelical Protestants: size and growth. Evangelicals are prominent in Republican activism not just because they have religious zeal and a capacity for political mobilization but also because they represent a large segment—approximately 25 percent (Green 2010; Smidt 2013)—of the American citizenry and a growing segment of American Christianity. As mainline Protestantism has rapidly declined, evangelicalism—which has grown slightly as a percentage of the populace (Green 2010; Smidt 2013)—has become a sharply growing portion of U.S. Christians. This growth in evangelicalism's share of the American religious market is an important reason for its growing presence in the Republican activist base (Claassen 2015).

The prominence of evangelical activists in Republican nominations and general election campaigns has given them considerable influence over the GOP's policy agenda. Evangelical activists and the Christian Right organizations with which they have been associated are greatly concerned with moral and cultural issues such as abortion, homosexuality, and religion in the public square. Thus, their influence has helped make moral and cultural issues a higher priority for the Republican Party and has driven the party to the right on those issues (Green and Guth 1988; Layman 2001, 2010; Swartz 2012; Green and Jackson 2007). Evangelicals' strong presence and influence also have encouraged other Republican activists to adopt more conservative cultural views and have helped push the GOP's mass coalition to the moral and cultural right (Layman 2010; Layman et al. 2010).

Evangelical activists also support the GOP's staunch and growing conservatism on issues outside the moral and cultural realms. Evangelicalism long has been associated with free-market sensibilities and opposition to a large social-welfare role for government (J. M. Wilson 2009), and some scholars attribute this to the individualistic character of evangelical Protestant theology (e.g., Barker and Carman 2000). Evangelical theology also has been linked to opposition to environmental regulation (Guth et al. 1995; Barker and Bearce 2013); staunch support for Israel (Mayer 2004); and support for an aggressive, militaristic, and interventionist U.S. foreign policy (Barker, Hurwitz, and Nelson 2008; Guth 2009). Accordingly, evangelical Republican activists are highly conservative on social-welfare, environmental, and foreign-policy issues (Layman 2010).

Evangelical activists also may have contributed to an increasingly strident tone to Republican politics. Ideologically motivated activists tend to value principle over pragmatism and compromise (J. Q. Wilson 1962; Lupton, Myers, and Thornton 2015). Religiously driven evangelicals may be more likely than other party activists to view politics as a contest between good and evil and to deride compromise on policy principles (Layman 2010). Evangelical activists also may strongly support the Tea Party, a movement that shares their steadfast conservatism and disdain for compromise (Campbell and Putnam 2011; Smidt 2013).

Is the Party Influence of Evangelical Activists Waning?

Although students of religion and politics have touted the influence of evangelical activists on contemporary Republican politics, there are several reasons why that influence may be declining. First, the trends in American religion that helped fuel evangelical dominance in GOP politics may now be working against them. Although maintaining membership and attendance rates far better than those of mainline Protestantism, evangelical Protestantism now is demonstrating declining church attendance, lower rates of adherence among younger people, and sharply declining growth rates (Jones 2016).

Second, the Christian Right organizations that helped mobilize evangelicals into Republican politics in the 1980s and 1990s generally have decentralized and atrophied. There is no longer a central organization like the Moral Majority or the Christian Coalition to activate and focus evangelical political participation (Wilcox and Robinson 2011).

Third, younger evangelicals seem to be less committed than their elders to culturally conservative politics. Although they are even more pro-life on abortion than older evangelicals, younger evangelicals are more supportive of LGBT (lesbian, gay, bisexual, and transgender) rights (Smidt 2013). They also care more than older evangelicals about traditionally liberal issues such as the environment, poverty, and social justice (Smith and Johnson 2010; Wilcox and Robinson 2010). Importantly, younger evangelicals are not noticeably less Republican than their elders (Smith and Johnson 2010; Smidt 2013), and the most devout among them are still very culturally conservative (Castle 2015; Lewis 2016). However, they may be weaker candidates than their elders for culturally motivated party activism.

Finally, the influence that party activism has provided evangelicals within the Republican Party may be sowing the seeds of its own demise. Geoffrey Layman (2010) shows that the longer devout evangelicals are active in the GOP, the more likely they are to adopt pragmatic political norms such as supporting compromise for the sake of electoral victory. That political pragmatism may be reflected in the support that evangelical activists and leaders have lent to recent Republican presidential candidates who had previously been critical of the Christian Right (e.g., John McCain in 2008), who had liberal positions on key cultural issues (e.g., Rudy Giuliani in 2008, Donald Trump in 2016), or whose personal lifestyles did not seem to conform to conservative Christian values (e.g., Trump). And some evangelical and Christian Right leaders have decried such support as evidence that evangelicals have sold out their faith-based values for political power and Republican electoral success (Thomas and Dobson 2000; Gerson 2016).

That evangelical activists have supported electorally viable candidates does not necessarily mean their influence in Republican politics has dwindled. Indeed, all recent Republican presidential nominees—McCain, Romney, and Trump alike—have aggressively courted evangelical support and have emphasized their conservative bona fides on the cultural issues on which they agree with the Christian Right. However, this may mean that evangelical influence has become less distinctive, growing more similar to that of conservative political activists in general.

The Influence of Evangelical Activists in the GOP: Assessing the Evidence

We turn now to the empirical evidence on the influence of evangelical activists in the Republican Party. We first assess temporal change in evangelical strength among Republican activists, turning to the longest-running series of surveys of American party activists: the Convention Delegate Study (CDS) surveys of national party convention delegates from 1972 to 2012.[1]

In Figure 2.1, we trace the presence of evangelical Protestants who attend church frequently and infrequently in Republican national convention delegations from 1972 to 2012. For comparison's sake, we also include frequently and infrequently attending mainline Protestants and Catholics, as well as delegates claiming no religious affiliation.[2] The figure shows that, while there has not been much change in the representation of nonreligious people or of Catholics, there has been a clear shift in the types of Protestants represented in the Republican activist base. In the 1970s and 1980s, GOP activists were predominantly mainline Protestants—mostly frequent attenders, but less devout mainliners also had a strong presence. However, just as their share of the larger population has declined, there has been a sharp recent decrease in the presence of mainline Protestants—both frequent and infrequent attenders—at Republican national conventions.

Meanwhile, devout evangelical Protestants have steadily increased as a percentage of Republican convention delegates since 1980, and their rise has been sharpest since the early 1990s. Less devout evangelicals have remained a very small percentage of Republican activists throughout the last four decades, but committed evangelicals have become far and away the largest

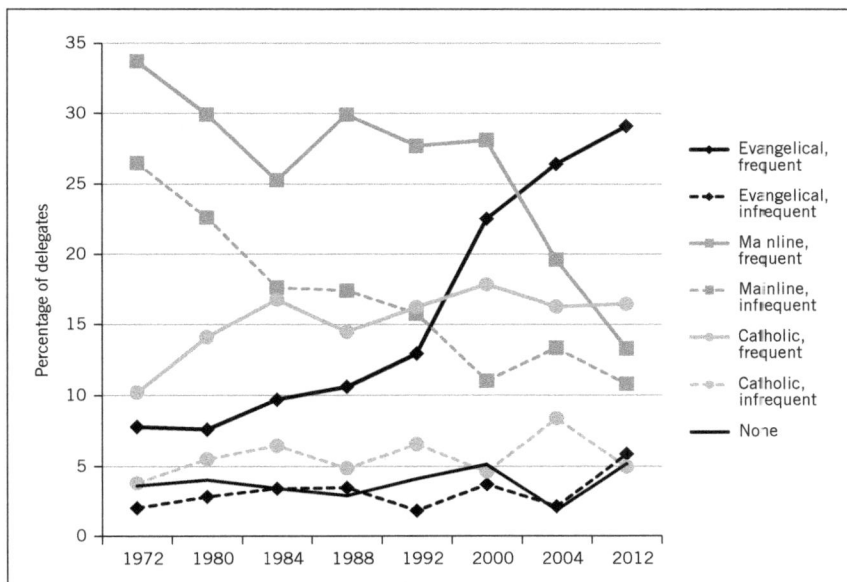

Figure 2.1 Religious tradition and frequency of worship attendance of Republican National Convention delegates, 1972–2012
Source: Convention Delegate Study surveys, 1972–2012.

religious group among delegates to Republican national conventions. To be sure, devout evangelicals are far from a majority in the Republican activist base. However, at the same time that some observers have suggested a decline in evangelical influence in the GOP, the trends in their representation at the highest levels of Republican Party activism suggests just the opposite. The GOP is not a party only of committed and politically active evangelicals, but it has become more so over the last few decades.

If the influence of devoted evangelical activists in Republican politics has increased (at least numerically), then the next question is: Are committed evangelicals different from other Republican activists in regard to policy preferences, views about politically important groups, and political norms?

To answer that question, we use the 2012 CDS survey to compare committed evangelicals to other groups of Republican activists—evangelicals with low levels of religious commitment and non-evangelical activists with both low and high levels of religious commitment—on several dimensions of political attitudes and orientations.[3] These include four types of policy issues: moral and cultural issues, economic issues, racial issues, and illegal immigration.[4] They also include general ideological identification (a seven-point scale ranging from extremely liberal to extremely conservative) and feeling-thermometer ratings (on scales of 0 to 100) of two groups that have been particularly important in recent Republican politics: the Tea Party has been embraced by large segments of the GOP activist base, but Muslims have been criticized intensely by many Republican political leaders.

Finally, our set of political orientations taps into activists' political norms—specifically, their preferences for pragmatic compromise over ideological purity. We include a scale of "party pragmatism" that gauges activists' rating of the importance of intraparty harmony and electoral success relative to ideological conviction.[5] We also include a scale of "support for government compromise" (a seven-point scale ranging from "elected officials should stand up for their principles no matter what" to "elected officials should compromise with their opponents in order to get things done for the country"). In Figure 2.2, we show the mean values for all these indicators (all ranging from zero for the most liberal issue position or least pragmatic political norm to one for the most conservative issue position or most pragmatic political norm) for each group of activists along with the 90 percent confidence intervals around the means.

Not surprisingly, committed evangelicals are more conservative than less devout evangelicals or either group of non-evangelicals on cultural issues, although the difference between the two groups of religious devotees is just shy of statistical significance. Devout evangelicals also are the most conservative of the groups on economic issues, with a mean score that is much more conservative than that of either non-evangelical group. The same pattern holds for feelings about the Tea Party and for ideological identification. However, on economic issues, ideology, and attitudes toward the Tea Party,

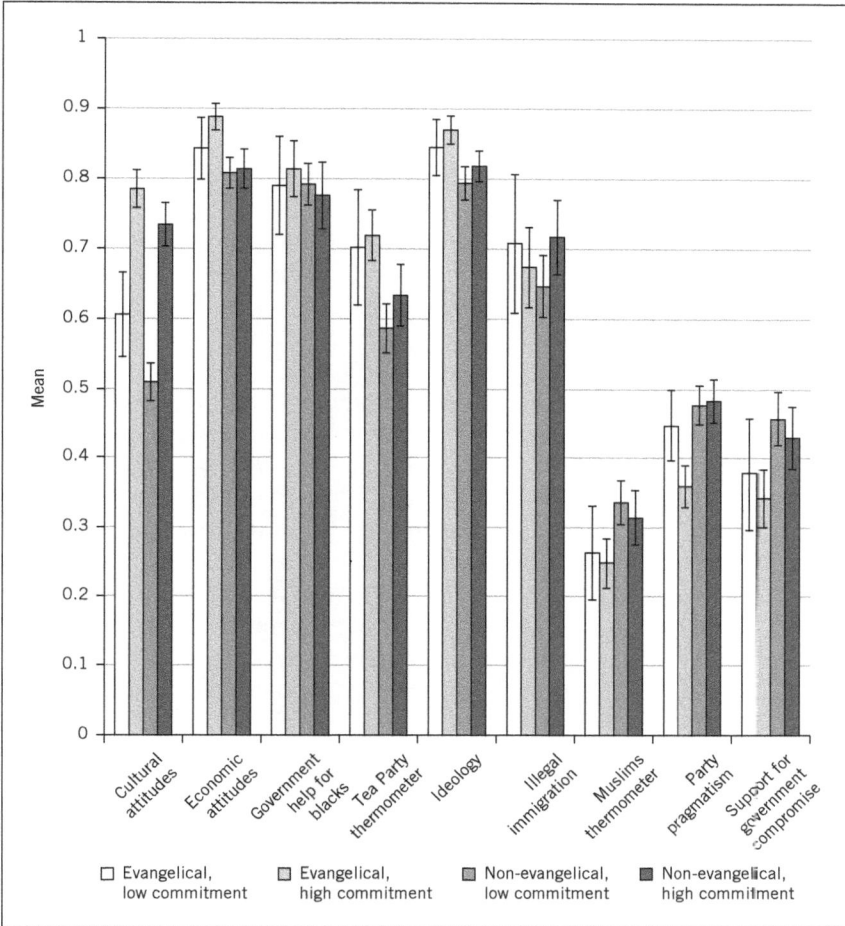

Figure 2.2 Political attitudes and orientations of Republican Party activists by religious tradition and religious commitment

Source: Convention Delegate Study, 2012.

Note: Ideology and cultural, economic, racial, and illegal immigration attitudes all range from most liberal to most conservative. The bars are the mean value for each group. The solid lines represent the 90 percent confidence interval around the mean.

committed evangelicals are not significantly different from evangelicals with low levels of religious commitment.

This suggests that devout evangelical activists' economic conservatism and Tea Party support may stem not from their religious commitment but from the general ideological conservatism of evangelicals. By extension, this may mean that membership in a religious tradition remains consequential for political attitudes. Contrary to the culture-wars thesis, some of the conservatism of committed evangelical activists may stem not from their religious devotion but simply from the fact that they are members of the highly conservative evangelical faith tradition.

However, neither religious tradition nor religious commitment is consequential for Republican activists' racial attitudes. On the issue of government assistance for African Americans, all activist groups are highly, and equally, conservative.

The next two sets of bars may shed light on how sympathetic evangelical activists were to the 2016 presidential candidacy of Donald Trump. Two of Trump's signature themes were taking a harder line on illegal immigration and a tougher stance toward Muslims, including a temporary ban on Muslims entering the United States. We capture attitudes toward these proposals through agreement that illegal immigration is "one of the major threats" to the United States and through feeling-thermometer ratings of Muslims. On illegal immigration, devout evangelical activists were likely no more or less supportive than other groups of Republican activists of Trump's hard-line stance, as their feeling of threat from illegal immigration is not different from that of less committed evangelicals or either group of non-evangelicals. Committed evangelical activists may have been a uniquely strong base of support for Trump's aggressive stance toward Islam, as they rate Muslims significantly lower than either group of non-evangelical activists.

Turning to political norms, it appears that committed evangelical activists remain a particularly strong force for a "purist" approach to conservative Republican politics. In their norms about party politics, committed evangelicals are significantly less supportive than less devout evangelicals or either group of non-evangelical activists of intraparty compromise, unity, and moderation relative to standing firm for ideological principles. In regard to government compromise, devout evangelicals take a dimmer view of compromise to "get things done"—and are more supportive of "standing up for principles"—than either group of non-evangelical activists. With the data at hand, we cannot say whether purist norms have risen or declined among committed evangelical activists. However, we can say that a purist outlook on politics remains alive and well for this group.

In short, evangelical activists still bring a distinct voice to the Republican Party. They are more conservative than non-evangelical activists, and they are less supportive of intraparty and interparty compromise. Devoted evangelical activists still push the GOP toward greater conservatism and greater stridency.

Evangelical Activists and the Nomination of Donald Trump

In 2016, the Republican Party nominated Donald Trump, a presidential candidate who supported same-sex marriage and transgender bathroom choice, who praised Planned Parenthood, who has been divorced twice, and whose personal behavior and language do not seem to match conservative Christian norms. That Trump won the GOP nomination (and eventually the election); that he won over candidates such as Ted Cruz and Ben Carson, who themselves are highly devout evangelical Christians and steadfast supporters of the Christian Right's cultural agenda; and that he won despite strong opposition from many evangelical leaders suggested to some observers that the influence of evangelical activists and the Christian Right movement on the Republican Party was greatly diminished (e.g., Merritt 2016; Posner 2016). However, Trump was endorsed by some prominent evangelical leaders (including Jerry Falwell Jr., president of Liberty University and son of Moral Majority founder Jerry Falwell), emphasized his strong commitment to nominating only pro-life federal judges, ultimately promised to defund Planned Parenthood, and received relatively strong support from evangelicals in the Republican primaries and general election (Layman 2016; Brockway, Campbell, and Layman 2016).

We can assess the degree to which evangelical activists supported Trump and how that compared to Trump support among non-evangelical Republican activists by using exit polls conducted by the National Election Pool of media organizations at Republican primaries and caucuses in twenty-six states. In the top part of Figure 2.3, we compare the percentage of evangelical and non-evangelical votes captured by Donald Trump and by the two leading evangelical candidates, Ted Cruz and Ben Carson, across those twenty-six states.[6]

This comparison indicates that Trump did better with non-evangelicals than with evangelicals. In fact, Trump performed better with non-evangelicals than with evangelicals in twenty-four of these states. However, while the gap between evangelicals and non-evangelicals was substantial in support for Cruz and Carson (nearly seventeen percentage points), it was relatively small in support for Trump (less than four percentage points). In fact, Trump still won a clear plurality of evangelical votes. It is clear that Trump won the GOP nomination with the help of evangelical activists, not in spite of them.

However, that does not necessarily mean that Trump's evangelical support base was the same as that of earlier Republican nominees. Given his own lack of religious commitment and his shaky credentials as a cultural conservative, it is possible that Trump did better with less devout evangelical activists than with evangelical devotees.

To see if evangelical support for Trump varied by religious commitment, we turn to the American National Election Studies (ANES) 2016 Pilot Study, which contains individual-level data on both religious affiliation and church attendance.[7] We define Republican-nomination activists as respondents who (1) identified as either independents or Republicans, (2) indicated a preference

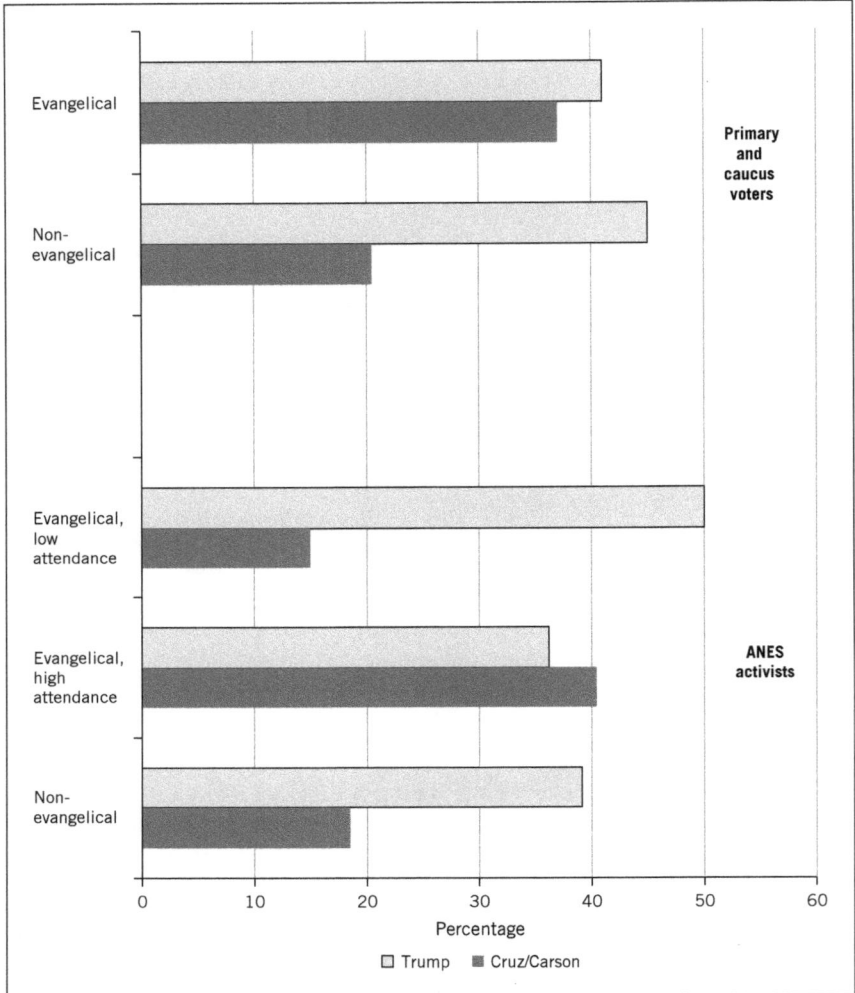

Figure 2.3 Republican primary voting by religion, worship attendance, and political activism, 2016

Source: National Election Pool exit polls, 2016; American National Election Studies 2016 Pilot Study.

for one of the Republican presidential candidates, (3) said that they were more than 70 percent likely to vote in the 2016 election, and (4) participated, or were very likely to participate, in one additional political activity (including donating money to a campaign, participating in a march or protest, signing a petition, sharing political information, or attending a political meeting). In the bottom part of Figure 2.3, we compare levels of support for Trump and for Cruz and Carson (combined) among evangelical activists with low and high levels of church attendance and among non-evangelical Republican-nomination activists.[8]

It turns out that high-attendance evangelicals were the least likely of the three groups to support Trump, and they were far and away the most likely to support either Cruz or Carson. Importantly, Trump still received significant support from committed evangelicals—in fact, he received noticeably more support than any other single candidate. However, less committed evangelical activists were a good bit more likely than their more devout brethren to prefer Donald Trump as the Republican presidential nominee. Layman (2016) finds the same pattern among all ANES Pilot Study respondents—activists and nonactivists—and uncovers several reasons why infrequently attending evangelicals provided such strong support for Trump. These include the fact that less committed evangelicals have, compared to high-attendance evangelicals, lower income and education levels, greater concern for immigration and jobs, and less positive feelings toward racial minority groups.

In short, both committed and less committed evangelical activists provided strong support for Donald Trump. However, Trump's strongest support came not from the committed core of evangelical Republican activism but from evangelicals less devoted to their faith.

Conclusion

In this chapter, we show that, in important ways, evangelical Republican activists are still the "life of the party." The share of Republican activists represented by committed evangelicals has continued to grow and is larger than that of any other religious group. And it is a distinctive influence. Committed evangelicals are more conservative than other Republican activists—not only on the cultural and moral issues that traditionally have driven evangelical activism but also on economic issues and in general ideology. Devout evangelicals also have helped foster the inflexible style of contemporary Republican politics. They are more opposed to compromise and more committed to standing on principle than other groups of Republican activists.

That stronger commitment to ideological principle may help explain why the most devout evangelical activists were somewhat less likely than their less devout brethren as well as non-evangelical activists to support Donald Trump for the Republican presidential nomination in 2016. However, committed Republican activists still provided strong support for Trump and, most likely, helped rather than hurt his nomination and election bids. Whether Trump's presidency represents a decline in evangelical influence in the GOP remains to be seen. However, it seems clear that Trump won the Republican nomination and the White House with the help of evangelical activists, not in spite of them. Evangelical party activists remain a very important part of contemporary Republican politics.

NOTES

1. The CDS surveys were administered by Warren E. Miller, M. Kent Jennings, and various colleagues from 1972 to 1988; by Miller and Richard Herrera in 1992; by Herrera, Thomas Carsey, John Green, and Geoffrey Layman in 2000; by Green, Herrera, Layman, and Rosalyn Cooperman in 2004; and by Cooperman, Green, Herrera, Layman, Kimberly Conger, Kerem Ozan Kalkan, and Gregory Shufeldt in 2012. See Miller and Jennings 1986; Herrera 1992; Layman 2001; Layman et al. 2010; and Layman and Weaver 2016 for more details about the methodology of and response rates to the various CDS surveys. For the survey data, see https://www.icpsr.umich.edu/icpsrweb/ICPSR/series/00116.

2. Respondents were grouped into religious traditions based on religious affiliation, using the classification scheme presented in Kellstedt and Green (1993) and Steensland et al. (2000). For all three Christian traditions in the figure, frequent church attenders are respondents who said they attend church "once or twice a month" or more frequently, and infrequent church attenders are respondents who said they attend "a few times a year" or less frequently.

3. We turn now to a more nuanced measure of religious commitment, based not just on frequency of worship attendance but also on the amount of guidance in one's life received from religion and one's view of the Bible. We rescaled attendance (ranging from "never attend" to "attend more often than once a week"), religious guidance (ranging from "no guidance" to "a great deal of guidance"), and view of the Bible (ranging from "a good book, but not the word of God" to "the actual word of God, to be taken literally word for word") to range from zero to one and took each respondent's mean score on the three scales (or each of the scales on which she or he had nonmissing values). We then classified respondents with scores at or below the median for all Republican delegates as low commitment and all Republican delegates above the median as high commitment. A factor analysis, using principal components extraction, of the three indicators of religious commitment produced only one factor with an eigenvalue greater than one, with that factor explaining 68 percent of the total variance across the indicators. The alpha coefficient for the commitment scale is .77.

4. The cultural-issues scale includes abortion attitude (the standard four-category scale ranging from "By law, a woman should always be able to obtain an abortion as a matter of personal choice" to "By law, abortion should never be permitted"), attitudes on same-sex marriage (ranging from "The law should define marriage as a union between two people regardless of their gender" to "The law should define marriage only as a union between one man and one woman"), and feeling-thermometer ratings of "gay men and lesbians" and "feminists." A factor analysis of the four indicators produced a single factor with an eigenvalue greater than one (explaining 60 percent of overall variance), and the alpha for the scale is .78. The economic-issue scale includes government services and spending (a seven-point scale ranging from "government should provide many more services and increase spending a lot" to "government should provide many fewer services, reducing spending a lot"); government providing health insurance (a seven-point scale ranging from "the government should provide a health insurance plan for all Americans" to "all Americans should be responsible for their own health insurance plans"); and a Likert scale of agreement with the statement "In order for the U.S. to fund government obligations, it is important that Congress periodically raise the federal debt ceiling." A factor analysis of those three items produced one factor with an eigenvalue greater than one (explaining 56 percent of the overall variance), and the alpha for the scale is .62. For both cultural- and economic-issue attitudes, the scales were formed by rescaling all items to range from zero to one and then taking each respondent's mean on all of the items in each scale on which she or he had nonmissing values. Racial attitudes are

measured through respondents' self-placement on a scale ranging from "the government in Washington should make every effort to help improve the social and economic position of blacks" to "government should not make any special effort to help blacks because blacks should help themselves." Illegal-immigration attitudes are measured through a Likert scale of agreement with the statement "One of the major threats to the future of the United States is illegal immigration."

5. The scale consists of Likert scales of agreement with five statements: "One should stand firm for a position even if it means resigning from the party," "The party should play down some issues if it will improve the chances of winning," "It is best to minimize disagreement within the party," "The party should select a nominee who is strongly committed on the issues," and "Choosing a candidate with broad electoral appeal is more important than a consistent ideology." All items were rescaled to range from zero to one, with higher scores representing greater support for intraparty compromise, and each respondent's scale score is her or his mean on all of the items on which she or he had nonmissing values. A factor analysis of the five indicators produced a single factor with an eigenvalue greater than one (explaining 53 percent of the overall variance). Alpha for the scale is .77.

6. We accessed the Republican exit-poll data at http://www.cnn.com/election/primaries/polls. Evangelicals are exit-poll respondents identifying themselves as a "born-again or evangelical Christian."

7. The ANES 2016 Pilot Study is available at http://electionstudies.org/studypages/anes_pilot_2016/anes_pilot_2016.htm. The study includes twelve hundred respondents. Evangelicals are defined as individuals identifying themselves as "born-again Christians" and who are not African Americans.

8. Respondents with "low" levels of church attendance said that they attend "a few times a year" or less often. "High"-attendance respondents attend "once or twice a month" or more often. The number of respondents in our categories of activists is admittedly small: twenty low-attendance evangelical activists, forty-seven high-attendance evangelical activists, and ninety-two non-evangelical activists.

REFERENCES

Aldrich, John H. 1983. "A Downsian Spatial Model with Party Activism." *American Political Science Review* 77 (4): 974–990.

———. 1995. *Why Parties? The Origin and Transformation of Party Politics in America*. Chicago: University of Chicago Press.

Barker, David C., and David H. Bearce. 2013. "End-Times Theology, the Shadow of the Future, and Public Resistance to Addressing Global Climate Change." *Political Research Quarterly* 66 (2): 267–279.

Barker, David C., and Christopher Jan Carman. 2000. "The Spirit of Capitalism? Religious Doctrine, Values, and Economic Attitude Constructs." *Political Behavior* 22 (1): 1–27.

Barker, David C., Jon Hurwitz, and Traci L. Nelson. 2008. "Of Crusades and Culture Wars: 'Messianic' Militarism and Political Conflict in the United States." *Journal of Politics* 70 (2): 307–322.

Bawn, Kathleen, Martin Cohen, David Karol, Seth Masket, Hans Noel, and John Zaller. 2012. "A Theory of Political Parties: Groups, Policy Demands and Nominations in American Politics." *Perspectives on Politics* 10 (3): 571–597.

Brockway, Mark, David E. Campbell, and Geoffrey C. Layman. 2016. "Secular Voters Didn't Turn Out for Clinton the Way White Evangelicals Did for Trump." *Washington Post*, November 18. Available at https://www.washingtonpost.com/news/monkey-cage/wp/2016/11/18/secular-voters-didnt-turn-out-for-clinton-the-way-white-evangelicals-did-for-trump.

Campbell, David E., and Robert D. Putnam. 2011. "Crashing the Tea Party." *New York Times*, August 16. Available at http://www.nytimes.com/2011/08/17/opinion/crashing-the-tea-party.html.

Carmines, Edward G., and James A. Stimson. 1989. *Issue Evolution: Race and the Transformation of American Politics*. Princeton, NJ: Princeton University Press.

Carmines, Edward G., and James Woods. 2002. "The Role of Party Activists in the Evolution of the Abortion Issue." *Political Behavior* 24 (4): 361–377.

Carsey, Thomas M., and Geoffrey C. Layman. 1999. "A Dynamic Model of Political Change among Party Activists." *Political Behavior* 21 (1): 17–41.

Castle, Jeremiah J. 2015. "Rock of Ages: Subcultural Religious Identity and Public Opinion among Evangelical Millennials." Ph.D. diss., University of Notre Dame.

Claassen, Ryan L. 2015. *Godless Democrats and Pious Republicans? Party Activists, Party Capture, and the "God Gap."* New York: Cambridge University Press.

Cohen, Marty, David Karol, Hans Noel, and John Zaller. 2008. *The Party Decides: Presidential Nominations before and after Reform*. Chicago Studies in American Politics. Chicago: University of Chicago Press.

Finke, Roger, and Rodney Stark. 2005. *The Churching of America, 1776–2005: Winners and Losers in Our Religious Economy*. New Brunswick, NJ: Rutgers University Press.

Gerson, Michael. 2016. "Evangelical Christians Are Selling Out Faith for Politics." *Washington Post*, June 23. Available at https://www.washingtonpost.com/opinions/evangelical-christians-are-selling-out-faith-for-politics/2016/06/23/f03368de-3964-11e6-8f7c-d4c723a2becb_story.html.

Green, John C. 2010. "Religious Diversity and American Democracy." In *Religion and Democracy in the United States: Danger or Opportunity?*, edited by Alan Wolfe and Ira Katznelson, 46–88. Princeton, NJ: Princeton University Press.

Green, John C., and James L. Guth. 1988. "The Christian Right in the Republican Party: The Case of Pat Robertson's Supporters." *Journal of Politics* 50 (1): 150–165.

Green, John C., James L. Guth, and Cleveland R. Fraser. 1991. "Apostles and Apostates: Religion and Politics among Party Activists." In *The Bible and the Ballot Box*, edited by James L. Guth and John C. Green, 113–136. Boulder, CO: Westview Press.

Green, John C., James L. Guth, Corwin E. Smidt, and Lyman A. Kellstedt. 1996. *Religion and the Culture Wars: Dispatches from the Front*. Lanham, MD: Rowman and Littlefield.

Green, John C., and John S. Jackson. 2007. "Faithful Divides: Party Elites and Religion." In *A Matter of Faith: Religion in the 2004 Presidential Election*, edited by David E. Campbell, 37–62. Washington, DC: Brookings Institution.

Green, John C., Mark J. Rozell, and Clyde Wilcox, eds. 2006. *The Values Vote? The Christian Right and the 2004 Elections*. Washington, DC: Georgetown University Press.

Guth, James L. 2009. "Religion and American Public Opinion: Foreign Policy Issues." In *The Oxford Handbook of Religion and American Politics*, edited by Corwin E. Smidt, Lyman A. Kellstedt, and James L. Guth, 243–265. New York: Oxford University Press.

Guth, James L., John C. Green, Lyman A. Kellstedt, and Corwin E. Smidt. 1995. "Faith and the Environment: Religious Beliefs and Attitudes on Environmental Policy." *American Journal of Political Science* 39 (2): 364–382.

Herrera, Richard. 1992. "The Understanding of Ideological Labels by Political Elites: A Research Note." *Western Political Quarterly* 45:1021–1035.

Jones, Robert P. 2016. *The End of White Christian America*. New York: Simon and Schuster.

Karol, David. 2009. *Party Position Change in American Politics: Coalition Management*. Cambridge: Cambridge University Press.

Kellstedt, Lyman A., and John C. Green. 1993. "Knowing God's Many People: Denominational Preference and Political Behavior." In *Rediscovering the Religious Factor in American Politics*, edited by David C. Leege and Lyman A. Kellstedt, 53–71. Armonk, NY: M. E. Sharpe.

Layman, Geoffrey. 2001. *The Great Divide: Religious and Cultural Conflict in American Party Politics*. New York: Columbia University Press.

———. 2010. "Religion and Party Activists: A 'Perfect Storm' of Polarization or a Recipe for Pragmatism?" In *Religion and Democracy in the United States: Danger or Opportunity?* edited by Alan Wolfe and Ira Katznelson, 212–254. Princeton, NJ: Princeton University Press.

———. 2014. "Party Activists." In *Guide to U.S. Political Parties*, edited by Marjorie R. Hershey, Barry C. Burden, and Christina Wolbrecht, 209–221. Washington, DC: CQ Press.

———. 2016. "Where Is Trump's Evangelical Base? Not in Church." *Washington Post*, March 29. Available at https://www.washingtonpost.com/news/monkey-cage/wp/2016/03/29/where-is-trumps-evangelical-base-not-in-church.

Layman, Geoffrey C., Thomas M. Carsey, John C. Green, Richard Herrera, and Rosalyn Cooperman. 2010. "Activists and Conflict Extension in American Party Politics." *American Political Science Review* 104 (2): 324–346.

Layman, Geoffrey C., and Christopher L. Weaver. 2016. "Religion and Secularism among American Party Activists." *Politics and Religion* 9 (2): 271–295.

Lewis, Andrew R. 2016. "Learning the Value of Rights: Abortion Politics and the Liberalization of Evangelical Free Speech Advocacy." *Politics and Religion* 9 (2): 309–331.

Lupton, Robert N., William M. Myers, and Judd R. Thornton. 2015. "Political Sophistication and the Dimensionality of Elite and Mass Attitudes, 1980–2004." *Journal of Politics* 77 (2): 368–380.

Mayer, Jeremy D. 2004. "Christian Fundamentalists and Public Opinion toward the Middle East: Israel's New Best Friends?" *Social Science Quarterly* 85 (3): 695–712.

McClosky, Herbert, Paul J. Hoffmann, and Rosemary O'Hara. 1960. "Issue Conflict and Consensus among Party Leaders and Followers." *American Political Science Review* 54 (2): 406–427.

McTague, Michael John, and Geoffrey C. Layman. 2009. "Religion, Parties, and Voting Behavior: A Political Explanation of Religious Influence." In *The Oxford Handbook of Religion and American Politics*, edited by Corwin E. Smidt, Lyman A. Kellstedt, and James L. Guth, 330–370. New York: Oxford University Press.

Merritt, Jonathan. 2016. "Trump Reveals the End of the Religious Right's Preeminence." *The Atlantic*, February 27. Available at http://www.theatlantic.com/politics/archive/2016/02/the-demise-of-conservative-christian-political-prominence/471093/.

Miller, Gary, and Norman Schofield. 2003. "Activists and Partisan Realignment in the United States." *American Political Science Review* 97:245–260.

Miller, Warren E., and M. Kent Jennings. 1986. *Parties in Transition: A Longitudinal Study of Party Elites and Party Supporters*. New York: Sage.

Oldfield, Duane M. 1996. *The Right and the Righteous: The Christian Right Confronts the Republican Party*. Lanham, MD: Rowman and Littlefield.

Polsby, Nelson W., Aaron Wildavsky, Steven E. Schier, and David A. Hopkins. 2011. *Presidential Elections: Strategies and Structures of American Politics*. 13th ed. Lanham, MD: Rowman and Littlefield.

Posner, Sarah. 2016. "Is This the End of the Religious Right?" *New York Times*, May 10. Available at http://www.nytimes.com/2016/05/10/opinion/campaign-stops/is-this-the-end-of-the-religious-right.html.

Schlesinger, Joseph A. 1991. *Political Parties and the Winning of Office*. Ann Arbor: University of Michigan Press.

Smidt, Corwin E. 2013. *American Evangelicals Today*. Lanham, MD: Rowman and Littlefield.

Smith, Buster G., and Byron Johnson. 2010. "The Liberalization of Young Evangelicals: A Research Note." *Journal for the Scientific Study of Religion* 49 (2): 351–360.

Smith, Christian. 1998. *American Evangelicalism: Embattled and Thriving*. Chicago: University of Chicago Press.

Soule, John W., and James W. Clarke. 1970. "Amateurs and Professionals: A Study of Delegates to the 1968 Democratic National Convention." *American Political Science Review* 64:888–898.

Steensland, Brian, Jerry Z. Park, Mark D. Regnerus, Lynn D. Robinson, W. Bradford Wilcox, and Robert D. Woodberry. 2000. "The Measure of American Religion: Toward Improving the State of the Art." *Social Forces* 79 (1): 291–318.

Swartz, David R. 2012. *Moral Minority.* Philadelphia: University of Pennsylvania Press.

Thomas, Cal, and Ed Dobson. 2000. *Blinded by Might: Why the Religious Right Can't Save America.* Grand Rapids, MI: Zondervan.

Wilcox, Clyde, and Carin Robinson. 2011. *Onward Christian Soldiers? The Religious Right in American Politics.* 4th ed. Boulder, CO: Westview Press.

Wildavsky, Aaron. 1965. "The Goldwater Phenomenon: Purists, Politicians, and the Two-Party System." *Review of Politics* 27:393–399.

Wilson, J. Matthew. 2009. "Religion and American Public Opinion: Economic Issues." In *The Oxford Handbook of Religion and American Politics*, edited by Corwin E. Smidt, Lyman A. Kellstedt, and James L. Guth, 191–216. New York: Oxford University Press.

Wilson, James Q. 1962. *The Amateur Democrat.* Chicago: University of Chicago Press.

3

Understanding the Political Motivations of Evangelical Voters

RYAN L. CLAASSEN

W hy do more white evangelicals vote Republican now than in previous decades? The conventional wisdom has Christian Right political organizations materializing in the wake of the *Roe v. Wade* decision in 1973 and forming an alliance with the Republican Party around the creation of an antiabortion plank in the platform in 1980 (e.g., Kohut et al. 2000, 127). Having secured a partisan home for so-called values voters, these organizations are then credited with mobilizing a group that had allegedly withdrawn from politics after the embarrassment of being lampooned for their beliefs in the Scopes Monkey Trial in 1925. Now white evangelicals are widely credited with being one of the largest and most important groups in the Republican coalition.

Granted, exit polls of the views of evangelicals on moral issues reveal a strong correlation with their votes, but evidence that moral issues are correlated need not mean that moral issues explain the voting trends. Empirically, it is impossible to document the role of an attitude in shaping a trend by analyzing only its correlation. In addition to assessing whether an attitude matters, efforts to explain trends must consider both changes in the distribution of the attitude over time and changes in the relationship of the attitude over time with the vote. For example, if abortion attitudes have not changed over time and the link between abortion attitudes and vote choice has not changed over time, then abortion attitudes cannot explain why evangelicals have become more consistently Republican over the years.

Substantively, the focus on moral issues may be too narrow. One of the more pointed challenges to the moral-issues explanation is that the evangelical vote is driven by racial attitudes (Leege et al. 2002). After all, because the Republican Party espouses conservative positions on both moral and racial issues (since at least 1964 and Barry Goldwater's opposition to the Voting and Civil Rights Acts), it is difficult to distinguish values voters from voters who oppose federal efforts to address persistent problems of racial inequality.

If one of the reasons an evangelical crackup appeared imminent was the poor fit between Trump's biography and the assumption that morality politics drive evangelical political behavior, perhaps the crackup was averted for reasons that have very little to do with abortion or gay marriage. This chapter is devoted to developing a deeper understanding of the complicated political motivations of white evangelical voters. Is Trump's support among evangelicals similar to the support George Wallace received (an election when issues of racial inequality were front and center)? Or have the culture wars overtaken the racial politics of the 1960s and created new political alliances? The answers to these and other, related questions reveal significant problems with the values-voters narrative. The narrow view of morality politics that is so popular in contemporary political commentary is too narrow to explain voting trends. Racial attitudes matter as least as much as and perhaps much more than morality politics.

Conventional Wisdom: Scopes Led Evangelicals to Hide

How does the conventional wisdom stack up against the historical record? On its face, quite well. It is certainly true that many evangelicals were deeply humiliated by media portrayals of William Jennings Bryan as a Bible-quoting buffoon during the Scopes Monkey Trial. Bryan was an evangelical (Cumberland Presbyterian tradition), was a leader in the Democratic Party (three times the presidential nominee), and represented the state of Tennessee in prosecuting John Scopes (a substitute teacher) for teaching evolution. A critical point in the trial occurred when defense attorney Clarence Darrow called on Bryan to testify as a biblical expert. Darrow questioned Bryan for two hours regarding the scientific basis of biblical accounts. An exchange regarding an objection from the prosecution's table during Bryan's questioning sums things up pretty well. Describing the defense's purpose for its line of questioning, Bryan said it was "to cast ridicule on everybody who believes in the Bible." In response Darrow quipped, "We have the purpose of preventing bigots and ignoramuses from controlling the education of the United States" (Moran 2012, 22). Bryan was ridiculed in the media and died five days after the trial.

So it is possible that evangelicals shied away from public-policy battles after the Scopes Trial (Cizik 2005), but accounts of withdrawal undersell the short-term legal win and the longer-term political win, let alone ongoing opposition to the theory of evolution that has persisted to the present day. After all, the prosecution (Bryan's side) won—although Scopes's conviction was reversed on appeal—and evolution was effectively banned from biology texts in much of the United States for several decades. In fact, it seems equally plausible that the effects of political *victory* buoyed political efficacy among evangelicals despite efforts to ridicule evangelical opposition to teaching evolution in the national media. Empirically, analyses of voter turn-out and rates of campaign activism among white evangelicals in the 1960s and early 1970s indicate white evangelicals were participating at rates similar to those from other religious traditions (Claassen 2015). Unfortunately, the data I use to examine participation in the 1960s are not available dating all the way back to 1925. The point here is that participation among white evangelicals was not distinctively low in the two decades prior to their alleged political awakening at the end of the 1970s. So the withdrawal thesis does not receive much support from an examination of historical political participation among white evangelicals.

Conventional Wisdom: Christian Right Organizations Mobilized Evangelicals

When did the organizations the conventional wisdom credits with stimulating recent political involvement among white evangelicals begin? It is true that most organizations currently associated with the Christian Right movement postdate the *Roe v. Wade* decision and have been vocal abortion opponents. For example, James Dobson founded Focus on the Family in 1977 and the Family Research Council in 1981. Robert Grant and Richard Zone founded the Christian Voice in 1978. Jerry Falwell founded the Moral Majority in 1979. Pat Robertson created the Christian Coalition in 1989. It is also true that abortion is first mentioned in the Republican platform in 1976, and by 1980 the Republican platform not only mentions abortion but advocates for a constitutional amendment outlawing the practice (Fisher 2012).

These dates have a great deal of meaning if the story of white evangelical withdrawal after Scopes is true. However, it seems that story was much exaggerated. Still, it is possible that Christian Right organizations stimulated exceptional participation once on the scene. There have been modest participation improvements among evangelicals (Claassen and Povtak 2010). However, these increases are also evident in religious traditions not associated with the Christian Right—the participation of religious groups is rising and falling together. More damning still, participation increases among evangelicals are entirely a function of socioeconomic status gains. Evangelicals are wealthier and better educated now than they were in the 1960s, and both of these are strong predictors of participation. True, the Christian

Coalition sent out many voting guides, but when one compares evangelicals before and after the founding of the Christian Right organizations, poor evangelicals participate at lower rates more recently—there are just fewer poor evangelicals now. So, taken together, white evangelical political participation prior to *Roe v. Wade* is not unusually low, the trend in participation among white evangelicals is not distinctive relative to members of other religious traditions, and—to the extent white evangelical participation has increased over time—that trend is a function of socioeconomic status gains (Claassen 2015).

Clearly, white evangelicals were active politically after the Scopes Trial and before Christian Right organizations were on the scene, but to what end? According to Randall Balmer, white evangelicals were not politically active opponents of abortion during this period. Regarding historic evangelical attitudes about abortion, Balmer (2014) writes,

> In 1968, for instance, a symposium sponsored by the Christian Medical Society and *Christianity Today*, the flagship magazine of evangelicalism, refused to characterize abortion as sinful, citing "individual health, family welfare, and social responsibility" as justifications for ending a pregnancy. In 1971, delegates to the Southern Baptist Convention in St. Louis, Missouri, passed a resolution encouraging "Southern Baptists to work for legislation that will allow the possibility of abortion under such conditions as rape, incest, clear evidence of severe fetal deformity, and carefully ascertained evidence of the likelihood of damage to the emotional, mental, and physical health of the mother." The convention, hardly a redoubt of liberal values, reaffirmed that position in 1974, one year after *Roe*, and again in 1976.

Evangelical Motivations: Racial or Abortion Attitudes?

Contrary to the conventional wisdom that has evangelicals mobilizing in the late 1970s to oppose abortion, Balmer's work highlights the political involvement much earlier of white evangelicals resisting federal efforts to desegregate the schools. First, it must be mentioned that white evangelicals are concentrated in the South. More than half of all white evangelicals live in the eleven former Confederate states. Second, it is also worth emphasizing that a state-enforced system of white supremacy and racial segregation was reestablished in the South shortly after the end of the Civil War with the termination of Reconstruction efforts in 1877. Much of that system remained intact nearly a century later, even after *Brown v. Board of Education* in 1954; the Civil Rights Act in 1964; and several legal cases related to implementing school desegregation plans, culminating in *Alexander v. Holmes County*

Board of Education in 1969. Therefore, many white evangelicals reacted in much the same way as other whites in the South to the prospect of integrated schools. However, when it became clear that resisting federal efforts to integrate public schools was futile, white people in the South began creating racially segregated private schools. In this way, one can disentangle evangelicals from the general population by identifying their schools. For example, in 1967 Rev. Jerry Falwell founded the Lynchburg Christian Academy in Lynchburg, Virginia, as a private school for white students and a ministry of the Thomas Road Baptist Church.

By February 1970 in Holmes County, Mississippi, all 904 white students were withdrawn from the public school system ("Segregation Academies" 1973). Black parents sued to prevent new segregated private schools from enjoying federal support in the form of tax-exempt status. Prior to the resolution of this case in *Green v. Kennedy* (1970) and *Green v. Connally* (1971), tax-exempt status had not been considered as public funding. Thereafter, racially discriminatory admissions practices were grounds for revoking or denying tax-exempt status—but whether racial segregation due to religious beliefs was still protected by the Supreme Court remained an open question. And at this point a real political movement among white evangelicals to protect the tax-exempt status of their segregated evangelical schools begins.

The question was not resolved until 1983 when the Supreme Court ruled against Bob Jones University (another prominent segregated evangelical school). Were evangelicals involved in a political fight prior to *Roe v. Wade*? Whole school districts across the South were emptied of white students, and segregated religious schools received much political support from white evangelicals opposed to racial integration (Balmer 2006). An evangelical political movement to oppose school integration was widespread and institutionalized—white evangelicals created and worked politically to defend private, segregated schools. Also there was organizational support in the form of amicus curiae briefs filed in support of Bob Jones University by evangelical groups such as the American Baptist Churches, the United Presbyterian Church, and the National Association of Evangelicals (Devins 2000). Rank-and-file white evangelicals and evangelical institutions were active alongside segregated evangelical schools opposing federal desegregation efforts. The effort was not limited to a fringe element at Bob Jones University.

Balmer (2006) links the political efforts of white evangelicals resisting school integration to the modern-day Christian Right movement by verifying that the same individuals acted as leaders of both. When the Internal Revenue Service (IRS) began sending questionnaires to evangelical schools—including Falwell's—regarding their admissions policies in the wake of *Green v. Connally*, Paul Weyrich (founder of the Heritage Foundation and the man credited with coining the phrase "moral majority") saw evangelical leaders rally in a way he had not seen before. Although defending segregated schools worked as a catalyst for motivating white evangelicals politically, segregation was no longer a palatable political issue in the mass public (Balmer 2006). Evangelical leaders made a calculated decision to build a movement around abortion to elect Republicans who would defend evangelical schools against IRS scrutiny. Accordingly, Balmer credits Ronald Reagan's promise to rein in the IRS and Jimmy Carter's refusal to support a constitutional amendment banning abortion with evangelical support for Reagan in 1980.

> When Reagan addressed a rally of 10,000 evangelicals at Reunion Arena in Dallas in August 1980, he excoriated the "unconstitutional regulatory agenda" directed by the IRS "against independent schools," but he made no mention of abortion. Nevertheless, leaders of the religious right hammered away at the issue, persuading many evangelicals to make support for a constitutional amendment out-lawing abortion a litmus test for their votes. . . . Although abortion had emerged as a rallying cry by 1980, the real roots of the religious right lie not the defense of a fetus but in the defense of racial segrega-tion. (Balmer 2014)

Putting Conventional Wisdom to the Test: Which Issue Moved Evangelicals to the Republican Column?

Having highlighted the historical role of racial conservatism among white evangelicals, I now turn to an empirical study in which the associations be-tween voting behavior and abortion attitudes are compared to the associa-tions between voting behavior and racial attitudes. I am by no means the first to assert that racial attitudes matter a great deal when trying to under-standing the political behavior of white evangelicals. For example, David C. Leege and colleagues (2002) conduct a rigorous analysis and conclude that the literature has been too willing to ascribe the political behavior of white evangelicals to issues such as abortion when racial attitudes are more impor-tant. They write, "In fact, from 1968 to 1988 almost the entire story of the white evangelical shift from Democrats to Republicans is anchored in race and the role of the federal government seeking to assure greater opportunity for minorities" (Leege et al. 2002, 243). My analysis is similar and updates theirs to include recent elections.

My data come from the American National Election Studies (ANES) Time Series Cumulative Data File (1948–2012) and the ANES 2016 Time Series Study.[1] Because I am concerned with the role of attitudes about race and abortion explaining the voting behavior of white evangelicals, I am lim-ited to data beginning in 1972 because of question availability. My work diverges from the work mentioned earlier that asserts abortion attitudes explain the voting behavior of white evangelicals. That work rests on a variety of empirical demonstrations that the abortion views of white evangelicals are strongly related to their voting behavior. I do not attempt to undermine that evidence. However, I do question whether this empirical evidence explains longitudinal variation in the voting behavior of evangelicals. Studies estimating correlations between abortion attitudes and voting cannot—without additional analyses—estimate the portion of longitudinal change due to abortion attitudes. Even evidence of a strengthening correlation over time is not evidence that abortion attitudes moved voting behavior over time. For example, the correlation might strengthen while the distribution of abortion opinion changes in a direction that would lead to fewer Republican votes. A different type of analysis is required to estimate the role of attitudes shifting longitudinal voting behavior.

Results

I use econometric techniques to decompose into component parts the trend in voting from 1972 to 2016 among white evangelicals.[2] Evangelicals are identified using Brian Steensland and colleagues' (2000) method for categorizing church denominations into major religious traditions.[3] Figure 3.1 is a theoretical diagram of the analyses I conduct. It shows that the trend in voting (a) would be different from the analogous trend after controlling for policy attitudes (a'). Estimating precisely which portion of the trend in voting is due to which attitude is the object of this study.

First, the "a" path shown in Figure 3.1 is the total observed linear trend in voting. Essentially a is estimated by regressing whether individuals voted for the Republican or not (nonvoters are omitted; votes for the Democrat or other candidates are coded as zeros) on a variable measuring the year in which the individual was interviewed for the ANES (1972–2016 recoded to range from zero to one).

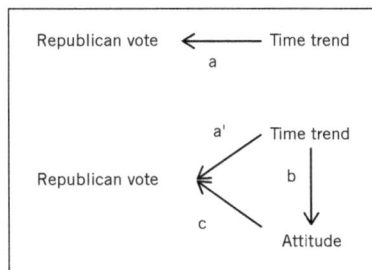

Figure 3.1 Econometric model for decomposing voting trends

The second model shown in Figure 3.1 estimates the same linear trend, now designated a', controlling for racial and abortion attitudes. The portion of the linear trend in voting that is due to attitudes is the difference between trends in the full model and the reduced model $(a - a')$. This difference is the indirect effect of time through attitudes and can also be computed by multiplying b and c, where b captures over-time changes in attitudes and c captures the effect of attitudes on voting, and $a = a' + (b \times c)$. The term $b \times c$ captures the idea that change in voting is the product of the effect of the attitude and changes in its distribution over time. This is the empirical equivalent of the theoretical point made previously. To understand the role of an attitude shaping a longitudinal change in voting, one must examine *both* the effect of the attitude and the changing distribution of that attitude.

For example, if abortion views were dichotomous and pro-lifers were 25 percent $(c = .25)$ more likely to vote Republican than pro-choicers, and over time pro-life evangelicals increased from 50 percent to 70 percent $(b = .20)$, that change in opinion combined with the effect of the attitude would cause a 5 percent increase in Republican voting $(.25 \times .20 = .05)$. In this scenario, a quarter of the 20 percent of new pro-life evangelicals would vote Republican, for a 5 percent gain. Note that absent a congenial distributional change in abortion attitudes, abortion would not affect the longitudinal trend in voting even if abortion were a robust predictor of vote choice.

Figures 3.2–3.4 provide the longitudinal trends for all my measures from 1972 to 2016 in the ANES data described earlier. Figure 3.2 presents the voting

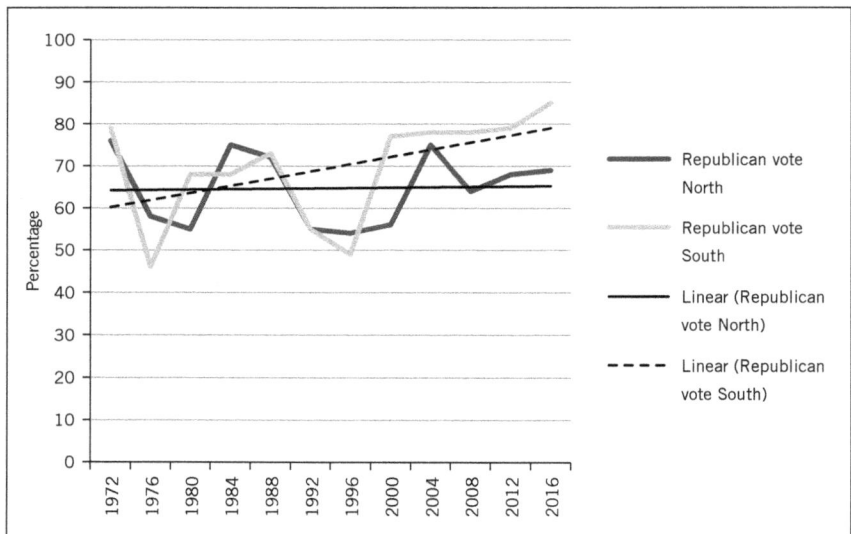

Figure 3.2 Percentage of white evangelicals voting Republican, 1972–2016

trend (percentage voting Republican) among white evangelicals, sorted by whether they reside in the South (the eleven former Confederate states) or not (designated "North"). In addition to the plots, I include the linear trends. Initially it is tempting to see similar voting trends in the plots in Figure 3.2, but there are several places early on where gaps emerge. Since 1996 there has been a more substantial difference, and these differences are more evident in the linear trends. That is, white evangelicals in the South are trending toward the Republican Party, while white evangelicals in the North are trending very weakly (not statistically significantly different from no trend) in the other direction.

To measure views about racial attitudes and abortion attitudes, I use the following items from the ANES:

> **Racial attitudes:** Some people feel that the government in Washington should make every effort to improve the social and economic position of blacks. Others feel that the government should not make any special effort to help blacks because they should help themselves. Where would you place yourself on this scale, or haven't you thought much about it? It ranges from 1 = Government should help minority groups/blacks to 7 = Minority groups/blacks should help themselves.
>
> **Abortion attitudes:** There has been some discussion about abortion during recent years. Which one of the opinions on this page best agrees with your view?[4]
> 1. By law, abortion should never be permitted.
> 2. The law should permit abortion only in case of rape, incest, or when the woman's life is in danger.
> 3. The law should permit abortion for reasons other than rape, incest, or danger to the woman's life, but only after the need for the abortion has been clearly established.
> 4. By law, a woman should always be able to obtain an abortion as a matter of personal choice.

Again for white evangelicals in the South and North, respectively, each item is plotted in Figure 3.3 (racial attitudes) and Figure 3.4 (abortion attitudes). Although white evangelicals in the South are consistently more conservative in their racial attitudes, the conservative trends are similar for both groups. For abortion, evangelicals in the North begin somewhat more liberal and converge on the more conservative attitudes of white evangelicals in the South. Consequently, there is a longitudinal trend in the North, but a very weak (not statistically significant) trend in the South.

With these data in hand, I compute all of the estimates described in Figure 3.1. The model enables me to compare the indirect effect of time through abortion attitudes to the indirect effect of time through racial attitudes (i.e., there are separate b and c coefficients for each attitude measure in

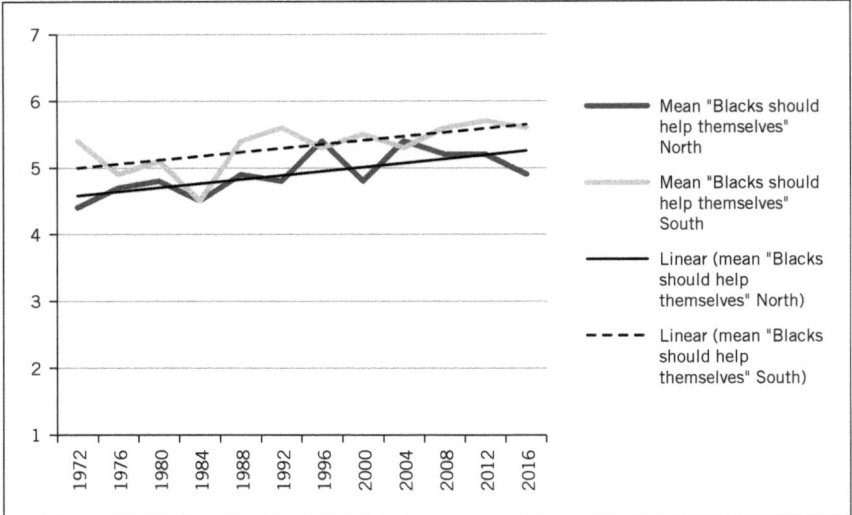

Figure 3.3 Racial attitudes of white evangelicals, 1972–2016

Note: Scale ranges from "Government should help minority groups/blacks" (1) to "Minority groups/blacks should help themselves" (7).

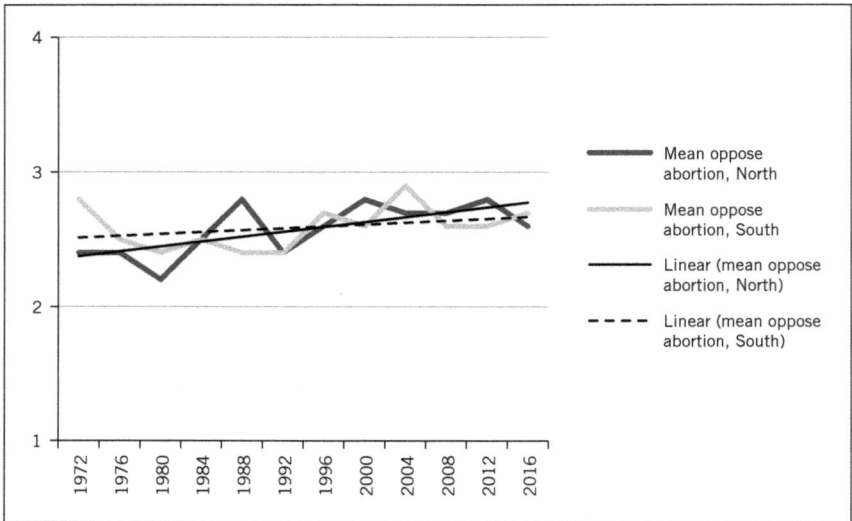

Figure 3.4 White evangelical attitudes on abortion

Note: Scale ranges from the belief that abortion should always be permitted (1) to the belief that it should never be permitted (4).

the model). These indirect effects are graphed in Figure 3.5. As expected, the lighter-colored bars indicate substantial effects of racial attitudes, both in the South and in the North. These indicate that the combined impact of the trend toward more conservative racial attitudes and the correlation between conservative racial attitudes and voting for Republicans have pushed white evangelicals toward the Republican Party over time. In the North, the effect of abortion on Republican voting is very similar, each attitude contributing about 3.5 percent more Republican support over the entire period (1972–2016). However, recall from Figure 3.2 that white evangelicals in the North are actually about 4.3 percent more *Democratic* in their voting in 2016 than in 1972 (linear trend). The proper interpretation, then, is that the weak Democratic trend among white evangelicals in the North would be about 7 percent more Democratic but for the conservative trends in racial and abortion attitudes that restrain that movement. Racial and abortion attitudes are pushing some white evangelicals in the North toward the Republican Party, but other forces are pushing more white evangelicals in the other direction.

In the South, the combined effect of the two attitudes is about 4 percent more Republican support over the entire period. In contrast to that in the North, more of the movement in the South is due to racial attitudes. In the South the indirect effect involving abortion attitudes is only about half the effect of racial attitudes and cannot be distinguished from zero statistically. Each of the other three indirect effects represented by the four bars graphed in Figure 3.5 is statistically significant. Since the voting trend in the South charted in Figure 3.2 shows about 17 percent greater Republican support in 2016 than in 1972 (linear trend), the interpretation is that the strong Republican voting trend would have been weaker had it not been for increasing racial conservatism.

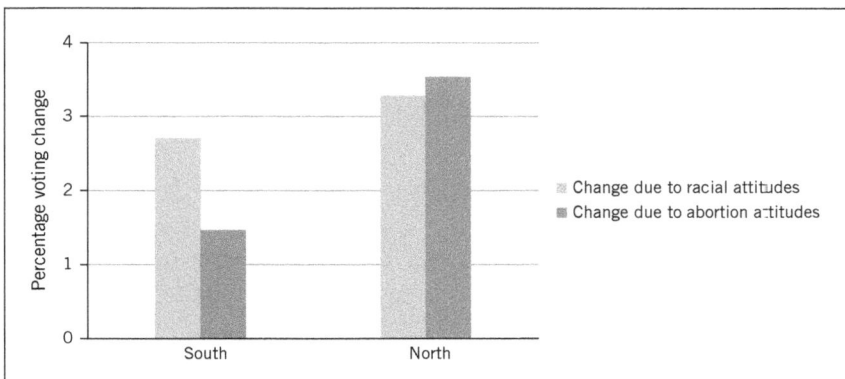

Figure 3.5 Percentage voting change due to abortion and racial attitudes, 1972–2016

Summarizing, there are two key findings in Figure 3.5. First, racial attitudes are robust predictors of Republican voting trends in both the North and the South. The ongoing role of conservative racial attitudes cannot be neglected in developing a deeper understanding of the changing voting behavior of white evangelicals. Though it is tempting to infer that trends in evangelical politics are best explained by the issues most discussed by their political organizations—abortion and gay marriage—the historical record of evangelical political opposition to federal efforts to enforce racial equality remains a potent factor to this day.

Second, in the South abortion attitudes hardly matter at all in regard to explaining trends in the voting behavior of white evangelicals. I hasten to add that this does not mean that abortion is not linked to vote choice. Although I do not report them, I did estimate voting models for individual elections for these groups, and abortion is generally a strong predictor of voting—hence the conventional wisdom. However, there is neither a trend toward greater reliance on abortion attitudes over time (an interaction term between abortion attitudes and time is not statistically significant) nor significant movement in the abortion attitudes of white evangelicals in the South. So religion and politics research asserting that abortion is linked to vote choice is correct. However, the evidence does not support the additional inference that, because abortion is linked to the vote, it is behind the *trend*. For white evangelicals in the South, it is a very minor player.

Conclusion

Against this empirical backdrop, Trump's success among white evangelicals comes into sharper focus. As Balmer (2016) writes in the *Washington Post*:

> [Trump's] racially and ethnically charged rhetoric has included assaults on everyone from Latinos to Muslims . . . condemned and even ridiculed those agitating for racial justice . . . and suggested that a Black Lives Matter protester at one of his own rallies should be "roughed up."

A big part of Trump's appeal among white evangelicals has roots in Wallace's strong showing among white evangelicals in 1968, Reagan's promise to protect the tax-exempt status of segregated evangelical schools in 1980, and more general opposition in the Republican Party to federal efforts to enforce racial equality. Abortion, gay marriage, and other so-called moral issues are consistently linked to vote choice, but the rightward drift of white evangelical voters cannot be explained without recognizing the force of conservative racial attitudes. The reasons the crackup did not occur may well be about the politics of race.

Furthermore, it bears emphasizing that conservative racial attitudes are pushing white evangelicals into the Republican column in *both* the North and the South. It is probably not very surprising that white evangelicals in the South have conservative racial attitudes. The trend toward greater conservatism documented in Figure 3.3 might be mildly surprising in a post–Jim Crow society, but perhaps less so when one considers the recent history of riots and a national protest movement over the racial disparity in civilian deaths at the hands of the police. Great progress has been made in regard to legal racial discrimination, but de facto racial residential segregation and segregation in schools remain extremely high, and trends in racial disparities in unemployment, income, health, and so on remain equally troubling. The problems that stimulated the civil rights movements of the 1950s and 1960s are different but no less pressing. So it might not come as much of a surprise that there is a trend toward more conservative racial views shown in Figure 3.3 among white evangelicals in both the North and the South.

Future research should investigate in greater detail the possibility that racial attitudes lie at the heart of Trump's populist and nationalist appeal—both in the South and in the North. If blaming minority groups for social problems is a key element in populist and nationalist rhetoric, Trump may have harnessed an important and often overlooked public-opinion trend among white evangelicals. It would provide more empirical leverage on whether race or cultural conservatism explains Trump's support in 2016 if Trump had not reversed his pro-choice positions and promised to oppose abortion and appoint like-minded judges. But these analyses suggest that in a race against another fairly pro-choice candidate, a pro-choice position might not have cost much in the way of white evangelical support because of the effect of racial attitudes.

Finally, I emphasize that the statistical tendencies do not speak for all white evangelicals—whether in the North or the South. The statistical tendencies tell about the dominant themes in a group, and white evangelicals are a very diverse group. I conclude by noting there are many progressive voices within evangelicalism and many evangelicals who support candidates who highlight the social problems faced by racial, ethnic, and cultural minority groups and promote policies designed to address them.

NOTES

1. To include 2016 data prior to its incorporation into the cumulative file by the ANES, the necessary variables were coded within the 2016 Time Series Data File and appended to the Cumulative Data File.

2. The "KHB" method is used to estimate the paths in Figure 3.1 and also to decompose the indirect effects of abortion and racial attitudes. See Karlson, Holm, and Breen 2012; Karlson and Holm 2011; and Kohler, Karlson, and Holm 2011.

3. All analyses here are limited to white evangelicals. The Steensland et al. 2000 method distinguishes evangelical Protestants from mainline Protestants, black Protestants, Catholics,

Jews, other religious traditions, and unaffiliated and nonreligious individuals. See appendix A in Claassen 2015 for a full listing of denominations in each tradition.

4. This item is reverse-coded so that conservative is high to match other opinion items. The question also appeared in slightly different form from 1972 to 1980, and the two items VCF0837 and VCF0838 have been merged.

REFERENCES

Balmer, Randall. 2006. *Thy Kingdom Come: How the Religious Right Distorts the Faith and Threatens America; An Evangelical's Lament*. New York: Basic Books.

———. 2014. "The Real Origins of the Religious Right." *Politico Magazine*, May 27. Available at http://www.politico.com/magazine/story/2014/05/religious-right-real-origins-107133.

———. 2016. "Trump's Success with Evangelical Voters Isn't Surprising: It Was Inevitable." *Washington Post*, May 16. Available at https://www.washingtonpost.com/posteverything/wp/2016/05/16/trumps-success-with-evangelical-voters-isnt-surprising-it-was-inevitable.

Cizik, Richard. 2005. "A History of the Public Policy Resolutions of the National Association of Evangelicals." In *Toward an Evangelical Public Policy: Political Strategies for the Health of the Nation*, edited by Ronald J. Sider and Diane Knippers, 15–35. Grand Rapids, MI: Baker Books.

Claassen, Ryan L. 2015. *Godless Democrats and Pious Republicans? Party Activists, Party Capture, and the "God Gap."* New York: Cambridge University Press.

Claassen, Ryan L, and Andrew Povtak. 2010. "The Christian Right Thesis: Explaining Longitudinal Change in Participation among Evangelical Christians." *Journal of Politics* 72:2–15.

Devins, Neal. 2000. "*Bob Jones University v. United States*, 461 U.S. 574 (1983)." In *Religion and American Law: An Encyclopedia*, edited by Paul Finkelman, 50–52. New York: Garland.

Fisher, Marc. 2012. "GOP Platform through the Years Shows Party's Shift from Moderate to Conservative." *Washington Post*, August 28. Available at https://www.washingtonpost.com/politics/gop-platform-through-the-years-shows-partys-shift-from-moderate-to-conservative/2012/08/28/09094512-ed70-11e1-b09d-07d971dee30a_story.html.

Karlson, K. B., and A. Holm. 2011. "Decomposing Primary and Secondary Effects: A New Decomposition Method." *Research in Social Stratification and Mobility* 29:221–237.

Karlson, K. B., A. Holm, and R. Breen. 2012. "Comparing Regression Coefficients between Same-Sample Nested Models Using Logit and Probit: A New Method." *Sociological Methodology* 42:286–313.

Kohler, U., K. B. Karlson, and A. Holm. 2011. "Comparing Coefficients of Nested Nonlinear Probability Models." *Stata Journal* 11:420–438.

Kohut, Andrew, John C. Green, Scott Keeter, and Robert C. Toth. 2000. *The Diminishing Divide: Religion's Changing Role in American Politics*. Washington, DC: Brookings Institution Press.

Leege, David C., Kenneth D. Wald, Brian S. Krueger, and Paul D. Mueller. 2002. *The Politics of Cultural Differences*. Princeton, NJ: Princeton University Press.

Moran, Jeffrey P. 2012. *American Genesis: The Evolution Controversies from Scopes to Creation Science*. Oxford: Oxford University Press.

"Segregation Academies and State Action." 1973. *Yale Law Journal* 82 (7): 1436–1461.

Steensland, Brian, Jerry Z. Park, Mark D. Regenerus, Lynn D. Robinson, W. Bradford Wilcox, and Robert D. Woodberry. 2000. "The Measure of American Religion: Toward Improving the State of the Art." *Social Forces* 79 (1): 291–318.

4

The GOP, Evangelical Elites, and the Challenge of Pluralism

KEVIN R. DEN DULK

The popular narrative about religion in the 2016 presidential election barely needed writing. It jumped out from the top-line result of the exit polls: Eight in ten white evangelical voters reported Republican candidate Donald Trump as their choice. Social scientists later nuanced that number, noting that different measures of evangelical identification produce somewhat lower figures. Nevertheless, no amount of analysis will likely challenge the basic fact that white evangelicals reprised their role in 2016 as a reliable bloc in the Republican coalition. While evangelical voters were uneasy with Trump in the primaries, when they gave their strongest support to candidates with clearer conservative bona fides, the evangelical rank and file eventually found their way back to their familiar rut in the two-track road of American polarization.

But what about more prominent evangelical voices? Did the denominational leaders, parachurch executives, best-selling theologians, megachurch pastors, media celebrities, political activists, or popular pundits reflect the near consensus of their own constituencies? Here the narrative did not write itself. The basic story line is fracture and conflict rather than coalescence, as evangelical elites fell out with one another over their views of the GOP standard-bearer. But explaining these disagreements is not straightforward. Did elites simply disagree about who was the lesser of two evils? Did they have diverging calculations about whether their agenda on abortion, same-sex marriage, or religious liberty stood a better chance with a Republican candidate, even one as morally troubling as Trump? Or is the better explanation found in the deeper waters of competing perspectives on identity, pluralism, and justice?

It is easy to see how these questions apply to the 2016 election, but these elite-level political disagreements among evangelicals are actually part of an older story, an echo of a decades-long history of uneasy alliances between the Republican Party and the evangelical establishment. In some cases those tensions result from evangelical leaders whose experience and commitments contrast with those of their conservative brethren. Those evangelicals—progressives, most African Americans—have found a more comfortable home among the Democrats. But even within the conservative movement of the so-called Christian Right, influential evangelicals are no monolith. Journalists and social scientists often miss these consequential elite-level differences by focusing on the domain of "morality politics," because here most conservative evangelicals generally agree about the hot-button issues of abortion, marriage, and child rearing. If we expand the picture, however, from nitty-gritty policy issues to more fundamental convictions, the image becomes less clearly defined.

This chapter examines disagreements among evangelical elites and the response of the GOP by shifting focus away from policy preferences to the more fundamental domain of culture. The chapter starts with the following question: How has dynamic cultural change—and particularly the challenges of *pluralism*—divided the evangelical establishment? By pluralism, I do not mean diversity of one sort or another: racial, religious, sexual, ideological. Pluralism is not a synonym for diversity but a *response* to it. It is a cluster of ideas and norms wedded to action and focused on how to navigate claims that challenge what one takes to be true. Pluralism is not merely a set of attitudes about policy issues; it is indeed only secondarily about politics. As a result, even agreement about policy *goals* related to diversity can reveal differing underlying *orientations* about pluralism. I argue that the challenges of pluralism have become a centrifugal force for prominent evangelicals; they are increasingly pushed apart by their response to cultural diversity.

Different orientations to pluralism are not simply a result of theological or social distinctions within the evangelical subculture. They are also shaped and activated by outside forces, including partisan efforts to craft an agenda amenable to the faithful. To borrow Clyde Wilcox's (2009) apt metaphor, the GOP and conservative evangelical elites have "coevolved" through a process of mutual adaptation. The Republicans embraced evangelicals in the 1980s as part of a big-tent conservatism, but the party has often struggled to maintain the loyalty of prominent religious voices. Big tents, after all, are hard to keep up. Parties are better at aggregation; they seek to flatten and combine diverse perspectives and channel citizen preferences. What to do, then, with an increasingly fractured evangelical elite? Over the past two decades, the GOP could have advanced an inclusive strategy—that is, expand the tent even further and enfold those emerging evangelical perspectives that are more conciliatory on race, interfaith relations, and other areas of cultural conflict. But the Republican Party took a different path, at least in its messaging to elites. It doubled-down on an exclusivist approach that highlights the threats that new social forces represent to a vision of Judeo-Christian America. Using Republican Party platforms, I trace the coevolution of the GOP and evangelical elites from 1996 to 2016, a two-decade period of roiling change that culminated in a remarkable alliance that helped bring Donald Trump to the White House. I begin with a brief sketch of evangelical-elite perspectives on pluralism and then move to analysis of GOP efforts to adapt its message to these shifting perspectives.

Evangelical Elites and Pluralism: Snapshots

My focus is evangelical elites rather than the rank and file. This requires distinguishing the elite from the mass and evangelicals from other religious groups. But the meanings of both terms—"evangelical" and "elite"—are not uncontroversial. The term "evangelical" has never been more divisive than in the wake of the 2016 presidential election, when even some key leaders in the evangelical subculture wondered if the label had melted in the political heat. I simply stipulate to the conventional scholarly descriptions laid out in the first chapter of this book. Evangelicalism is a range of Protestant faith expressions that is capacious yet nevertheless connected by key ecclesial affiliations (i.e., churches that are part of self-identifying evangelical denominations) and traditionalist beliefs about the authority of the Bible, the person of Jesus Christ, and the way of salvation.

Who, then, are evangelical elites? Clergy in specific churches? Leaders of key denominational agencies? Advocates at evangelical-heavy think tanks and interest groups? Activists who claim the label and happen to be the most vociferous? By "elites" I do not necessarily mean leaders with numerous followers. Because my goal is to understand the coevolution of evangelical elites and the GOP on questions of pluralism, I focus on prominent evangelicals who are connected in identifiable ways to decision making within the Republican Party. For my purposes, in other words, "elite" refers to evangelicals who participate in what political scientists call the "party network," a concept that suggests that the formal party organization is "only one part of an extended network of interest groups, media, other advocacy organizations, and candidates" (Koger, Masket, and Noel 2009, 633). These party-based networks are the creatures of interest groups and activists—"intense policy demanders"—who build coalitions of interests and shape those interests into common agendas (see, e.g., Bawn et al. 2012). These networks have an outsized influence on nominating candidates and generating governing majorities (Cohen et al. 2008).

How do we know an evangelical member of such a party network when we see one? While my approach in this study is selective and not highly formalized, I can identify evangelicals who participate in the Republican network in two basic ways: invitation and office. The GOP and its candidates have often actively recruited evangelicals to participate in the party network; we can readily observe some of those elites in organized workgroups, convention committees, or advisory bodies. But other evangelicals who lack that invitation can still have influence, usually because they occupy a position in an evangelical organization that matters to the party. In fact, I have included in this study public figures who have explicitly critiqued and sometimes even rejected the Republican Party's agenda, but their prominence in certain key organizations qualifies them as intense policy demanders.

James Dobson, for example, has periodically excoriated the Republican Party and threatened to withdraw his support, but his standing as founder of the evangelical-heavy Focus on the Family (and the Family Research Council, its advocacy arm) positions him squarely as an influential player in the party network. More recently, Russell Moore, a vocal critic of the party (and especially its 2016 nominee), still counts as part of the network, in large part because of his key position as president of the Southern Baptist Convention's (SBC) Ethics and Religious Liberty Commission (ERLC). So, too, does Franklin Graham, heir to the legacy and parachurch organization of the famed evangelist Billy Graham. The younger Graham renounced his affiliation with the Republican party in 2015 (over Planned Parenthood funding) but has continued to take an active interest in GOP politics. He strongly supported (though did not explicitly endorse) Trump as the party's nominee in 2016, and he was one of six clergy who prayed at his inauguration.

Many of these evangelical elites were brought into party politics as part of the Christian Right movement. While not all members of the Christian Right are evangelicals, and not all evangelicals are members of the Christian Right, the political movement is certainly rooted heavily in the evangelical tradition, and most of its leaders have an evangelical extraction. The names are familiar: Jerry Falwell Sr., who led one of the initial charges with his formation of the Moral Majority in 1979; Pat Robertson, who enlisted Ralph Reed to strengthen the grassroots of the movement, largely through the Christian Coalition in the 1990s; James Dobson, whose Family Research Council was led through much of the 1990s by Gary Bauer and in the 2000s by Tony Perkins; and countless others.

What brought these leaders into the political fray? The broad social forces that motivated the Christian Right movement are discussed elsewhere in this book, but it is worth highlighting several areas that shape evangelical approaches to pluralism. One school of thought about the Christian Right points to hot-button concerns about marriage, education, abortion, and other matters in the category of family, reproduction, and child rearing. The sexual revolution and other cultural changes of the 1960s were an affront to traditionalist perspectives on family and society. What progressives saw as a liberation, evangelical conservatives imagined as a slide into moral decay, domination of secular thinking, and societal disintegration—and they saw government as both complicit and a mechanism for change. Another school of thought focuses on the prerogatives of race. Race does indeed cut across the evangelical tradition, such that most white evangelicals are conservative, while most of their black coreligionists are not (Emerson and Smith 2000). Randall Balmer (2004) and others have argued that the history of evangelicalism goes hand in hand with the politics of racial division epitomized in the embrace of segregationist policies by many southern evangelicals throughout much of the twentieth century. A third school of thought suggests that mounting religious diversity over the past half century has generated greater social anxiety and cultural retrenchment (Wuthnow 2005). For many evangelicals, politics was a way to reassert religious primacy against those new religious traditions—not to mention *ir*religion—that undermined the norms and values of a "Christian nation."

Whatever the creation story, however, the through-line is the challenge of pluralism, the underlying debate over the appropriate response to diversity in family structure, human sexuality, race and ethnicity, and religion itself. As it emerged in the early 1980s, the Christian Right saw diversity in culture through a polarized lens symbolized in the name of its vanguard organization: Moral Majority. In this view, the culture was divided in two: the majority of citizens, rooted in a vision of Judeo-Christian identity; and a largely secular minority using the mechanisms of elite power to supplant that vision. Falwell and others sought to rally the majority to return the culture to its faith-based moorings. By most accounts, however, the Moral Majority's strategy was ineffective, but the Christian Right experienced a "second coming" in the early 1990s as the Christian Coalition and other groups adopted a larger agenda and began to adapt the language of choice, equality, and rights to conservative goals (Moen 1992; Rozell and Wilcox 1996).

By the end of the 1990s a split emerged among evangelical elites over the basic question of whether cultural engagement was worth the costs. The man who coined the phrase "moral majority," Paul Weyrich of the Free Congress Foundation, published an open letter advising evangelicals to withdraw from the broader "culture of decadence," an "ever-widening sewer" whose roots in Judeo-Christian identity were hopelessly lost (1999, 44). In that same year, columnist Cal Thomas and pastor Ed Dobson, who both had served as lieutenants to Falwell in the early days of the Moral Majority, published *Blinded by Might*, in which they argued that despite the Christian Right's efforts, "the moral landscape [in America] has become worse" (1999, 23). They included in that landscape Christian leaders themselves, who they proclaimed were morally compromised by their search for power. Other elites took up the debate in the Christian press, with Jerry Falwell, Ralph Reed, Charles Colson, and James Dobson exhorting evangelicals to stay in the political fray, win or lose. But the debate was largely about strategies, effectiveness, and personal piety, not basic cultural assumptions. Few leaders challenged the underlying idea that a war over cultural values was under way with two armies on the battlefield. The key question was whether the Judeo-Christian side ought to clear the field and hunker down in its own encampments.

Cracks in that culture-war narrative began to show in the early 2000s and accelerated in the 2010s. Organizations such as the National Association of Evangelicals (NAE) expanded their range of concerns from the old issues of abortion, human sexuality, and education to the environment and immigration—and the new issues came along with fresh perspectives on addressing human diversity. On the immigration issue, for example, the NAE was joined in 2012 by the Southern Baptist Convention, the Council for Christian Colleges and Universities (CCCU), World Relief, and dozens of self-described "influential signatories" in a centrist evangelical statement that called for protections of families and a path toward legal status for undocumented immigrants (Evangelical Immigration Table, n.d.). Many people and organizations from the old guard were conspicuously absent from the list. New voices prominently waded into other areas of societal diversity with an independent outlook. Russell Moore, who assumed leadership of SBC's ERLC in 2013, declared reparative therapy for gays and lesbians a "utopian" and "severely counterproductive" idea (Bailey 2014). Like many other new leaders, he has also repeatedly called on his fellow Christian conservatives—especially Southern Baptists—to repent of racism and seek reconciliation and has generally thrown cold water on the notion of a "culture war" as a pluralist response to diversity.

The 2016 election laid many of these differences bare. Moore (2016) questioned not only Trump's character but also the Republican Party's flirtations with "ethno-nationalist populism," which had replaced the "multiethnic, constitutionally-anchored, forward looking conservatism" that "many of us had hoped for." In contrast, Jerry Falwell Jr., president of the largest evangelical university (Liberty), enthusiastically invited Trump to stump on his campus and seemed to welcome harder-line messages about ethnicity, nationalism, interfaith relations, and sexuality in his comments on Muslims, refugees, and LGBT (lesbian, gay, bisexual, and transgender) concerns. Old culture warriors like James Dobson and Richard Land (Moore's immediate predecessor at the ERLC) declared they would hold their nose and vote for Trump to win a unified government under the Republican banner. Editorialists at *Christianity Today*, a leading evangelical magazine, were clearly far less supportive, and a diverse group of evangelicals, mostly left leaning but many with leadership positions at center-right evangelical organizations, signed a letter condemning Trump—and implicitly the Republicans—for giving "voice to a movement that affirms racist elements in white culture" ("A Declaration," n.d.). The NAE's monthly Evangelical Leaders Survey in late 2015 documented highest preferences for Republicans Marco Rubio, Ben Carson, and John Kasich (and barely registered Hillary Clinton or Donald Trump). The same survey conducted again in June 2016 revealed deep ambivalences when nearly four in ten leader-respondents were considering a vote for a third party or simply not voting for president (National Association of Evangelicals 2015, 2016). Countless other voices at churches, new media outlets, think tanks, advocacy groups, faith-based universities and seminaries, parachurch organizations, and nonprofits added to the cacophonous mix.

Faith, Pluralism, and the GOP: An Analysis of Platforms

If evangelical conservatism and the Republican Party have coevolved, how have these patterns of increasing fracture and restlessness among evangelical elites played out in GOP strategy? Here I turn to a data source—party platforms—that is sometimes maligned for its irrelevance because ordinary voters rarely pay attention to the platforms. But there is ample evidence that platforms, as statements of party principles and policy preferences, do indeed signal to the networks of highly attuned insiders about party direction and priority (Reinhardt and Victor 2012). And evangelical elites and their allies have been more than mere consumers of platforms. They have also participated fervently in designing platform language for both state parties (Conger 2000) and the national Republican Party (Layman 2001). Several evangelical groups monitor platform development, and evangelical activists such as Tony Perkins; David Barton, an activist and independent historian who subscribes to controversial views about the Christian roots of the American founding; and John Ashcroft, the former U.S. senator and attorney general; among many others, have served in various capacities on platform committees at national conventions.

As David Domke and Kevin Coe (2008) demonstrate, platforms provide a rare data resource for comparison over time that can reveal changes in religion-based cues in the Republican Party. They note, for example, that during the modern presidential era, the emergence of the Christian Right marks a split in platform language: the GOP is much more likely to invoke the Constitution or the judiciary in platforms after 1980 than in platforms from the pre–Christian Right period (which they pinpoint as 1932–1976). They argue that this pattern suggests that religious conservatives pushed the party to institutionalize their cultural agenda. Others have used platforms as a prism for understanding the influence of religious activism within the party. Geoffrey Layman's work on party activists notes that both the Democratic and Republican Parties shifted their platforms to focus on what he calls "moral and cultural issues" from 1972 to 1996, though of course the content of those platforms reflected the parties' different ideological perspectives on those issues (2001, ix). The GOP actively attempted to build and catalyze its bases of support in both economic and social conservative circles by asserting the rights of the unborn, seeking to expand religious prerogatives in schools and other public institutions, and combating burgeoning efforts to extend civil rights protections to same-sex couples.

Domke and Coe and Layman picked up on broad patterns across party platforms. But there were subtler variations between platforms that would send important cues to attentive readers. To identify those variations, we can examine whether the use of signaling words in one platform differs in systematic ways from the use of those same words in other years. For this kind of analysis, I used AntConc, a corpus linguistics program that isolates language patterns in a specific corpus (in this case, a text file of a party platform in a given year) by comparing to a reference corpus (in this case, a text file directory of all platforms from 1996 to 2016). Using a variety of statistical tests and analytical tools, AntConc determines whether observed differences between an individual platform and the entire corpus of platforms are nonrandom.

Table 4.1 provides the top twenty words and phrases that vary in one platform year compared to all others, using the log-likelihood statistic (for purposes of this analysis, I removed names of candidates and parties). Some of the differences are obviously time bound (e.g., Desert Storm in 1992, Bosnia in 1996) or retrospectives on recent policy initiatives (e.g., George W. Bush's initiative on AIDS/HIV, touted in the 2004 platform). Some platforms develop unique themes—terrorism in 2004, the environment in 2008—but none come close to 2016 in its distinctive and coherent vision. The language of that platform heavily invokes the institutional, constitutional, and bureaucratic—far more than even Domke and Coe's analysis identified in earlier years. The 2016 platform takes to task an unusual number of federal agencies—the Food and Drug Administration (FDA), the Federal Reserve, and the Veterans Administration (VA)—and bemoans the size of the federal workforce. The references to "amendment"—forty-four in total, far exceeding any of the other five platforms since 1996—mostly focus on a laundry list of concerns about abridgment of existing constitutional provisions but also include proposals for such mainstays as pro-life and balanced-budget amendments. The platform is unusual in its emphasis on the inalienability of rights. It is also set apart in its references to "religious" and "abortion."

We can see more clearly the movement toward the themes of the 2016 platform—and perhaps the imprint of evangelical pressure—through a qual-

TABLE 4.1   WORD VARIATIONS ACROSS GOP PLATFORMS, BY YEAR

2016	2012	2008	2004	2000	1996
banks	current	must	[variations on] terror	governor	we
religious	fiscal	health care	AIDS/HIV	administration	vetoed
powers	voter	UN	nations	Republican	[White] House/ House [of Rep]
mental [health]	unsustainable	should	working	new	Bosnia
inalienable/rights	service	energy	efforts	Russia	juvenile
amendment	EPA	climate	America	price	opposed
constitutional	twenty-[first]	fossil fuels/fuel	help	United [States]	theater
executive	cybersecurity	Washington	initiative	fees	embargo
current [adminis-tration/president]	severe	especially	Congress	let	restore
territories	[American] Indians	treatment	September [11]	weapons	congressional
[Federal] Reserve	federal	able	support	purpose	crime
officials	taxpayers	civic	million	surpluses	less
FDA	leaks	appreciate	Afghanistan	result	welfare
ISIS [Islamic State]	call	provider	relief	[last/past] eight [years]	renewal
abortion	Constitution	education	war	fellowship	Republican
discrimination	Obamacare	rule	homeland	heart	incomes
federal	pension	owe	Africa/African	missile	cut
workforce	systems	smarter	provided	next	drug
Veterans Administration	transparency	right	broadband	age	interests
state	ballots	ballot	Iraq	emerging	space

Note: For all words/phrases, $p < .05$.

itative lens. Consider simple searches of references to (1) religion in general, measured through the terms "religion" or "faith";[1] (2) the supernatural, specified as "god," "creator," "divine," and "providence"; and (3) specific religions, indicated by "Christian," "Muslim," "Islam," "Jewish," and so on. As displayed in Figure 4.1, the growing word/phrase counts suggest a heightened GOP awareness that support of evangelical elites (among other religious groups) may be softening and cannot be taken for granted. In 1996, the GOP platform referenced religion in general a mere fifteen times, largely with what had become boilerplate platform language about resisting taxation of faith-based groups and supporting religious liberty as an abstract principle. It also included a smattering of other references to God and divine providence. Just four years later—as we have seen, after a great deal of consternation among prominent evangelicals—the Republican platform had

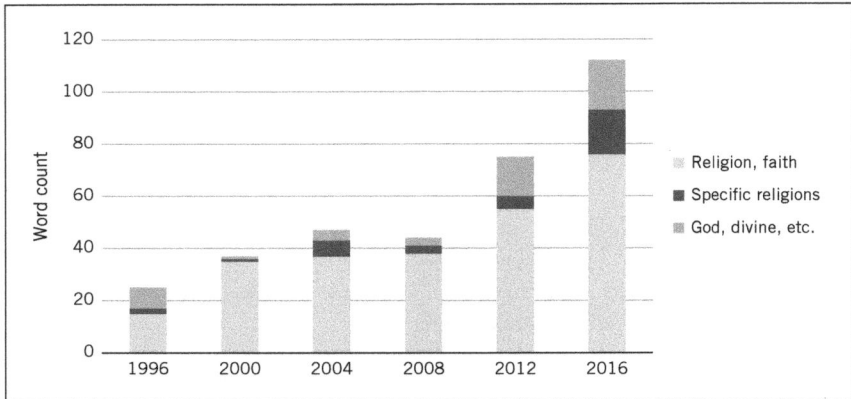

Figure 4.1 GOP platform language on religion, the supernatural, and specific faiths, 1996–2016

begun to increase its religion-based invocations. References to religion increased nearly fivefold from 1996 to the high-water mark in 2016.

The changes are not simply in quantity but also in quality, as well as in those substantive shifts we see the GOP signaling about pluralism. The most obvious external event pressuring platform committees was the appropriate reaction to terrorism in the wake of the September 11, 2001, attacks. The immediate response was conciliatory toward Muslims. The 2004 platform mentions "Muslims" or "Islam" only three times, and those references frame terrorism as a violation of the "fundamental tenets" of Islam, while portraying Muslim Americans as law-abiding citizens and lauding the efforts of Muslim leaders to build peace. A whiff of a more inclusive pluralism was still in the air. By 2016, however, the platform's tone had shifted considerably. All seven references to Islam were associated with radicalism, and terrorism itself was often defined as "Islamic" without the modifier "radical" (e.g., "regions associated with Islamic terrorists" or "support and sacrifice in the fight against Islamic terrorism").

The treatment of Islam and terrorism illustrates the broader changes in tone surrounding interfaith inclusion and religious liberty, as we see in the comparison of the 2000 and 2016 platforms. The 2000 platform emphasized public-private partnership, primarily through initiatives that would foster government support of the full range of faith-based organizations in civil society. The platform declared that "[Republicans] commit . . . to aiding and encouraging the work of charitable and faith-based organizations" in fighting poverty (Republican Party 2000). That theme is clear at various points of the document, including its support for charitable-choice provisions, enshrined in the 1996 welfare reform law, that allowed faith-based social services to compete for federal grants on an equal footing with other organizations and without challenging their religious identity. While some leaders were cautious in their support—Land is fond of saying that "along with the king's shekels will ultimately come the king's shackles" (2004, 200)—many evangelical elites had argued for the charitable-choice goals in the name of equal treatment and religious autonomy for all groups.

The 2016 platform contrasts sharply with its 2000 predecessor—and all intervening platforms as well—in the space and intensity it commits to a vision of religious liberty. Evangelical activists would certainly recognize its appeal to protect institutions, particularly schools and houses of worship. But that appeal is framed in partisan messages that reflect tensions over the concept of pluralism. For example, the platform declares that President Barack Obama and Democrats in Congress "refuse to control our borders but try to control our schools, farms, businesses, and even our religious institutions" (Republican Party 2016, i). Here the politics of immigration, which raises a host of questions about the proper response to ethnic diversity, is linked subtly to low-wage employment and anxieties about key institutions in the market and civil society, religion included. A similar dynamic is at play on sexual identity and marriage. The 2012 platform had already strongly declared the GOP's disapproval of same-sex marriage and the "homosexual rights agenda" (Republican Platform 2012), but the U.S. Supreme Court gave the platform committee more fodder in 2016, with the court's recent decision invalidating bans on same-sex marriage squarely in the GOP's sights: "In *Obergefell*, five unelected lawyers robbed 320 million Americans of their legitimate constitutional authority to define marriage as the union of one man and one woman" (Republican Party 2016, 11).

Unlike their 2000 platform, the Republicans in 2016 encapsulate their concerns in an entire section on religious liberty. The platform goes beyond a discussion of the "first freedom" as a mere negative liberty, a freedom to practice religious faith without interference from the state. Most of the discussion focuses on the failure of the federal government to accommodate and support the crucial role of religion within civil society. While "religion and morality are indispensable supports to a free society," it declares, government has "barred" faith-based institutions from getting contracts and "threaten[ed]" religious colleges and universities over personnel decisions that counter liberal orthodoxies. "Places of worship," it continues, "for the first time in our history have reason to fear the loss of tax-exempt status," an assertion coupled with a call to repeal the so-called Johnson Amendment, a legal provision dating to 1954 that forbids clergy and other nonprofit leaders from endorsing or opposing candidates at the risk of their tax-exempt status (Republican Party 2016, 11). A little later in the platform, in a discussion of foreign policy that is otherwise remarkably brief, the treatment of religious liberty is relatively expansive. Yet here the contrast with the 2004 platform over Islam is unmistakable. The platform suggests no redeeming qualities to the faith; every reference to "Muslim," "Islam," or "Islamic" is tied directly to "radical Islamic terrorism," which "poses an existential threat." As a response to that threat, the document demands a counteracting radicalism, a "radical rethinking of our human rights diplomacy" that places "standing up for repressed religious groups" alongside economic and security interests (Republican Party 2016, 52–53).

This brief analysis of platforms is suggestive, not definitive. The link between the GOP's commitments and evangelical elites is only circumstantial, although it is telling that evangelical culture warrior David Barton publicly revealed that the 2016 committee was given carte blanche (Peters 2016). Therefore, the shifts in platform tone provide insight into the partisan framing of competing concepts of pluralism. Taken together, the statistical and qualitative patterns in platforms over time reflect a Republican strategy of doubling down on one side of the culture wars, with an emphasis on Judeo-Christian heritage and repeated clarion calls about threats to the traditionalist vision of family and community. These ways of responding to diversity are not as strongly shared among evangelical elites as in the past, especially on questions of race and ethnicity and interfaith relations. But in its clearest statement to attentive publics—its platform—the GOP has walked a less inclusive path that only some prominent elites could fully embrace.

Conclusion: The Electoral Connection

Why has the Republican Party walked this path? I end with a straightforward speculation that picks up where I started with the evangelical voter. The GOP's electoral calculus helps explain this choosing of sides among evangelical elite visions of pluralism. The God gap persists (Smidt et al. 2010); the most important pattern in religion-based voting behavior has been continuity. White evangelical support for Republicans has been consistent over many election cycles, and their underlying preferences about family, human sexuality, interfaith relations, security, and culture have budged only at the margins. The GOP now has a long history of aggregating and mobilizing those preferences into electoral success. For Republican leaders, then, the winning strategy is to reinforce support for those evangelical elites who are least likely to disrupt underlying mass preferences. In the near term, there is very little electoral downside to losing those prominent evangelicals who have left the culture war.

In the longer term, the Republican Party faces some challenges that might bring a crackup of the relationship of evangelical elites and the party. Two groups might be able to *create* disruption—evangelical leaders with a different pluralistic vision who find a way to mobilize politically, or the Democratic Party through concerted outreach to evangelicals. The former has had halting success to this point, and the latter has been uneven in its effort. It is perhaps more likely that the disruption will happen without intention, as the result of demographic change, especially as a younger generation gathers electoral strength yet shows little interest in the cultural combat of the past few decades.

NOTE

1. The analysis of "faith" includes only those references that are related to religion. It excludes phrases such as "keep faith with the past," "faith in the future," or "acting in good faith."

REFERENCES

Bailey, Sarah Pulliam. 2014. "Evangelical Leader Russell Moore Denounces 'Ex-Gay Therapy.'" *Huffington Post*, October 28. Available at https://www.huffingtonpost.com/2014/10/28/russell-moore-ex-gay-therapy_n_6062474.html.

Balmer, Randall. 2014. "The Real Origins of the Religious Right." *Politico Magazine*, May 27. Available at http://www.politico.com/magazine/story/2014/05/religious-right-real-origins-107133.

Bawn, Kathleen, Martin Cohen, David Karol, Seth Masket, Hans Noel, and John Zaller. 2012. "A Theory of Political Parties: Groups, Policy Demands and Nominations in American Politics." *Perspectives on Politics* 10 (3): 571–597.

Cohen, Martin, David Karol, Hans Noel, and John Zaller. 2008. *The Party Decides: Presidential Nominations before and after Reform.* Chicago: University of Chicago Press.

Conger, Kimberly H. 2000. "Party Platforms and Party Coalitions: The Christian Right and State-Level Republicans." *Party Politics* 16:651–668.

"A Declaration by American Evangelicals concerning Donald Trump." n.d. *Change.org.* Available at https://www.change.org/p/donald-trump-a-declaration-by-american-evangelicals-concerning-donald-trump (accessed March 19, 2018).

Domke, David, and Kevin Coe. 2008. *The God Strategy: How Religion Became a Political Weapon in America.* New York: Oxford University Press.

Emerson, Michael, and Christian Smith. 2000. *Divided by Faith: Evangelical Religion and the Problem of Race in America.* New York: Oxford University Press.

Evangelical Immigration Table. n.d. "Influential Signatories." Available at http://evangelicalimmigrationtable.com/influential-signatories (accessed March 19, 2018).

Koger, Gregory, Seth Masket, and Hans Noel. 2009. "Partisan Webs: Information Exchange and Party Networks." *British Journal of Political Science* 39 (3): 633–653.

Land, Richard. 2004. *Real Homeland Security: The America God Will Bless.* Nashville, TN: Broadman and Holman.

Layman, Geoffrey. 2001. *The Great Divide: Religion and Cultural Conflict in American Party Politics.* New York: Columbia University Press.

Lipka, Michael. 2016. "Are Churches Key to Solving Social Problems? Fewer Americans Now Think So." Pew Research Center, July 18. Available at http://www.pewresearch.org/fact-tank/2016/07/18/are-churches-key-to-solving-social-problems-fewer-americans-now-think-so/.

Moen, Matthew C. 1992. *The Transformation of the Christian Right.* Tuscaloosa: University of Alabama Press.

Moore, Russell. 2016. "President Trump: What Now for the Church?" *Russell Moore* (blog), November 9. Available at http://www.russellmoore.com/2016/11/09/president-trump-now-church/.

National Association of Evangelicals. 2015. "Rubio Leads List for Evangelical Leaders; Many Undecided." October. Available at http://nae.net/rubio-leads-list-for-evangelical-leaders-many-undecided.

———. 2016. "Lesser of Two Evils, Third Party or Not Vote?" June. Available at http://nae.net/lesser-two-evils-third-party-not-vote.

Peters, Jeremy W. 2016. "G.O.P.'s Fight over Gay Rights Is One Trump Prefers to Sit Out." *New York Times*, July 11, p. A1.

Reinhardt, Gina, and Jennifer Victor. 2012. "Competing for the Platform: The Politics of Interest Group Influence on Political Party Platforms in the United States." Paper presented at the 108th annual meeting of the American Political Science Association, New Orleans, LA, 2012.

Republican Party. 2000. "2000 Republican Party Platform." Available at http://www.presidency.ucsb.edu/ws/index.php?pid=25849.

———. 2012. "We Believe in America: 2012 Republican Platform." Available at http://www.presidency.ucsb.edu/ws/?pid=101961.

———. 2016. "Republican Platform, 2016." Available at https://prod-cdn-static.gop.com/static/home/data/platform.pdf.

Rozell, Mark, and Clyde Wilcox. 1996. *Second Coming: The New Christian Right in Virginia Politics*. Baltimore: Johns Hopkins University Press.

Smidt, Corwin E., Kevin R. den Dulk, Bryan T. Froehle, James M. Penning, Stephen V. Monsma, and Douglas L. Koopman. 2010. *The Disappearing God Gap? Religion in the 2008 Presidential Election*. New York: Oxford University Press.

Thomas, Cal, and Ed Dobson. 1999. *Blinded by Might: Can the Religious Right Save America?* Grand Rapids, MI: Zondervan.

Weyrich, Paul. 1999. "The Moral Minority." *Christianity Today*, September 6, pp. 44–45.

Wilcox, Clyde. 2009. "Of Movements and Metaphors: The Coevolution of the Christian Right and the GOP." In *Evangelicals and Democracy in America*, edited by Steven Brint and Jean Reith Schroedel, 2:331–356. New York: Russell Sage.

Wuthnow, Robert. 2005. *America and the Challenges of Religious Diversity*. Princeton, NJ: Princeton University Press.

5

Divided over Rights

Competing Evangelical Visions for
Twenty-First-Century America

ANDREW R. LEWIS

The book of Mark records Jesus's aphorism that "if a house be divided against itself, that house cannot stand" (Mark 3:25, King James Version), and at the brink of civil war Abraham Lincoln (1982) applied this message to the American division over slavery. Despite these prophetic warnings, 2016 was a year of division in America. The presidential election between Donald Trump and Hillary Clinton bitterly divided Americans, with Trump winning decisively in the Electoral College and Clinton winning the popular vote. The election also divided American religion, especially evangelicalism. However, the evangelical division was different from the American political division. The election did not divide evangelical political sympathies; as exit polls showed, they supported Donald Trump at similar levels as they had supported prior Republican candidates, both in vote choice and turnout (Grant 2016; Smith and Martinez 2016). Rather, the election exposed an evangelical division over the proper way forward in a changing culture. Should evangelicals return to majoritarian, morality-based politics of the prior generation or pursue a minority, rights-based position? The division bared a fault line. The recent trend toward pluralism and respect for rights within evangelicalism was not without its detractors, who hoped for a return to an era in which Christianity was great again in American politics. And the questions remain: Will this evangelical political house remain divided, and, if so, for how long will it stand?

The Christian Right and Rights in the Contemporary Age

Christian Right politics gained momentum in the mid-twentieth century (Williams 2010; Claassen 2015), but it came to the fore in the 1980s with the election of Ronald Reagan and Jerry Falwell's Moral Majority (see, e.g., Wilcox and Larson 2006). The early themes of this movement were strongly majoritarian. The Christian Right rejected progressive cultural politics, instead emphasizing a return to a common Christian morality. It opposed American courts for removing religious values and symbols (e.g., prayer in schools and religious monuments) and legalizing a progressive cultural agenda (e.g., abortion and gay rights).

In the 1990s, many leaders advanced a second wave of Christian Right politics. Led by figures such as Ralph Reed of the Christian Coalition, this second wave sought to orient Christian Right politics within mainstream conservative politics (Moen 1992, 1994). It was more secular in its message, often arguing for pluralism alongside majoritarianism. Thus, in part the second wave sought to advance a rights culture of the Christian Right. It used the First Amendment as a potent weapon to gain equal access to public spheres and public arguments for religious citizens (Brown 2002). In the process, parts of the Christian Right became more professionalized, especially the lawyer corps, and more ingrained in the politics of liberalism—focusing on deliberation, compromise, and rights (Shields 2009; Wilson 2013; Lewis 2016, 2017).

In the past decade, the Christian Right has been soul searching, especially with its largest culture-war defeat to date—the rapid legalization of (and public support for) same-sex marriage. One religious demographer has written the obituary, proclaiming "the end of white Christian America" (Jones 2016). With the cultural writing on the wall, prominent Christian Right leaders and organizations have increasingly turned toward preserving broad individual rights, particularly the rights of religious freedom and free speech, shifting from a communitarian approach adopted when they were the moral majority. Evangelicals have sought to protect their own political rights, but they have also been willing to selectively stand up for the political rights of others, even political enemies, with an eye toward protecting their increasingly unpopular views. Nowhere is this more evident than free-speech law, where evangelical legal advocates have embraced some of the most liberal, individualistic notions of political free speech, for both allies and enemies, and the rank and file has also become more accepting (Lewis 2016, 2017). The same has been true for religious-liberty advocacy, where a focus on robust individual rights has sought exemptions from common good–oriented policies.

What is potentially troubling for the cohesion of the movement is that pursuing a rights-based strategy may serve to further integrate followers into the American rights culture. Among the evangelical public, religious-freedom arguments for allies have been shown to boost evangelicals' tolerance for disfavored groups (Djupe, Lewis, and Jelen 2016). Strikingly, rights advocacy for in-groups may promote rights extensions to out-groups. Yet not all evangelicals have been satisfied with this acceptance of minority politics and growing commitment to rights for all. The candidacy of Donald Trump exposed this division.

The Donald Trump Candidacy and Evangelical Tolerance

During the Republican primary, the Trump campaign made headlines for intolerant statements, actions, and policies. Following the terrorist attack in San Bernardino, California, in early December 2015, Trump called for an immediate halt to Muslim entry into the United States (Johnson 2015). While this proposal resonated with some on the right, others critiqued the position for being impractical and unwise and a violation of civil liberties. Much of the Republican Party's leadership came out against the ban, especially as articulated (Haberman 2015). There were mixed views among religious advocates, though many evangelical leaders quickly opposed the ban and criticized it for singling out a religion (Islam) for disfavor (Taylor 2015).

For example, evangelical leader Franklin Graham, son of the famed evangelist Billy Graham, supported Trump's proposal, arguing for security and warning of cultural threats. Graham (2015) posted a Facebook message to his readers supporting the ban and warning about the war on Islamic terror and the possibility of sharia law in the United States. Limiting rights was necessary. Russell Moore, head of the Southern Baptist Convention's advocacy arm, took a different position, sharply criticizing the proposal as "reckless, demagogic rhetoric" (Taylor 2015). In his critique, Moore (2015) wrote an op-ed, picked up by the *Washington Post*, declaring that "we should stand for religious liberty for everyone."

While nearly all evangelical leaders are for religious liberty generally and theoretically, especially for allies, the actual extension of religious liberty to disfavored groups has less support, as it always does. Of late, conservative Christian groups have increasingly become active in defending the religious freedoms of other religious minorities, including Muslims. In 2014, the Becket Fund for Religious Liberty brought a suit on behalf of Abdul Muhammed against the Arkansas Department of Corrections. Arkansas denied Muhammed the ability to wear in prison a half-inch beard in accordance with his Muslim faith. The Becket Fund and Douglas Laycock of the University of Virginia School of Law represented Muhammed in *Holt v. Hobbs*, a case that went before the U.S. Supreme Court. Several religious organizations joined the cause, filing amicus curiae briefs encouraging the court to rule in favor of Muhammed. These included evangelical and conservative

Christian organizations such as the National Association of Evangelicals, Alliance Defending Freedom, Prison Fellowship, World Vision, the International Mission Board of the Southern Baptist Convention, and the Lutheran Church–Missouri Synod. In a January 2015 unanimous ruling, the Supreme Court sided with Muhammed.

The next year, a diverse group of religious and civil rights groups came together to support a community of Muslims in New Jersey that had been repeatedly denied the ability to build a mosque, despite complying with zoning requirements. This coalition asked a U.S. district court to rule in favor of the Muslim community. Among the supporting groups were conservative Christian stalwarts—the Becket Fund, the National Association of Evangelicals, and Southern Baptist Convention's (SBC) Ethics and Religious Liberty Commission (ERLC), led by Russell Moore (Beckett Fund for Religious Liberty 2016). Some of the classic Christian Right groups were missing, though, including the American Center for Law and Justice and Alliance Defending Freedom.

The Russell Moore–led SBC participation in supporting the Muslim group spawned some controversy at the SBC's annual convention in June 2016. A Southern Baptist messenger from Arkansas made a motion that "all Southern Baptist officials or offices who support the rights of Muslims to build Islamic mosques in the United States be immediately removed from their position within the Southern Baptist Convention." A later motion asked the ERLC to remove its name from the amicus brief. Both motions were ruled out of order, exceeding the authority of messengers, but Moore later responded, "What it means to be a Baptist is to support soul freedom for everybody," receiving applause from the SBC audience. "Brothers and sisters, when you have a government that says 'we can decide whether or not a house of worship can be constructed based upon the theological beliefs of that house of worship,' then there are going to be Southern Baptist churches in San Francisco and New York and throughout the country that are not going to be able to build." With this defense, the SBC overwhelmingly supported the ERLC's position supporting the mosque (Gryboski 2016).

Though Moore secured a victory at the SBC convention, evangelical factions supporting limited tolerance for the rights of out-groups—especially Muslims—seemed to triumph in the presidential election. While some evangelicals were skeptical of Donald Trump, his policies, and his temperament, most supported the Republican nominee by Election Day, though they surely had diverse reasons.

Evangelical momentum toward Trump increased as he secured the Republican nomination. In June 2016, Trump convened an evangelical advisory board, led by Ralph Reed, architect of the Christian Right's 1990s evolution toward pluralism and professionalization. The advisory board included many prominent evangelical leaders from the 1980s and 1990s, such as James Dobson of Focus on the Family; Jerry Falwell Jr. of Liberty University; and Richard Land, formerly of the SBC's advocacy arm (Shellnutt and Eekhoff Zyistra 2016). Late in the campaign, Trump closed much of the polling gap with Clinton, primarily because disaffected Republicans came back to support the party's nominee (Bump 2016). These included many evangelicals. There were some holdouts, including Russell Moore and the prominent evangelical magazine *Christianity Today*. In October, Andy Crouch (2016), the executive editor of *Christianity Today*, published an editorial denouncing Trump: "[Trump] has given no evidence of humility or dependence on others, let alone on God his Maker and Judge. He wantonly celebrates strongmen and takes every opportunity to humiliate and demean the vulnerable. He shows no curiosity or capacity to learn. He is, in short, the very embodiment of what the Bible calls a fool."

Evangelicals such as Crouch and Moore opposed Trump in large part because of his disrespect for the rights of others. Despite their strong warnings, white evangelicals voted for Trump at overwhelming levels, motivated by distrust of Hillary Clinton, as well as the desire to protect their own rights—the right to religious liberty for dissenters of same-sex marriage and the right to life for the unborn (Bailey 2016). For this, they were willing to set aside Trump's statements about women, religious minorities, immigrants, and domestic and foreign enemies.

Rights, Tolerance, and Evangelical Support for Trump

In the 2016 campaign, there was a prominent divide among evangelicals over rights—particularly how much importance to attach to the rights of others. Evangelical leaders who opposed Trump often cited his intolerance for others, while those who endorsed him claimed that he was the most capable of defending evangelicals' rights. Tolerance for others, and its importance, thus is a demarcation point dividing strong evangelical support for Trump and reluctant evangelical supporters or those who vowed never to support him (Never Trumpers). Among elites, this division was often between old and new Christian Right leaders and activists and between established, "big-tent" organizations and more narrow, regionally focused ones. Yet what about the rank and file? Public-opinion surveys can provide some insights.

Evangelicals and Rights

Political rights and liberties are a central theme of American politics (Hartz 1955), though there is an academic debate whether they are *the* orienting concept of the American experience (Shain 1994; Smith 1993; Zuckert 1996). While rights are central to the American experience, liberals have been more attuned to individual rights, especially in the twentieth century, than conservatives—who often stood by the countervailing influences of community, morality, and order. As the twentieth century waned and the twenty-first century arrived, rights had become ubiquitous in American politics (Glendon 1991), even among evangelical Christians, who had long been communitarian holdouts (Jelen 2005; Djupe et al. 2014; Lewis 2017).

In June 2015, Steven Mockabee and I fielded an online survey to a sample of twelve hundred evangelicals, using Survey Sampling International (SSI) to secure the sample. We obtained the sample of evangelicals through a randomized screening process of asking respondents for either their affiliation with an evangelical religious tradition or the self-identification as a born-again Protestant Christian. While not a national random sample, the demographic characteristics of the evangelicals are quite similar to characteristics of national samples of evangelicals.

After the screening process, we asked individuals a variety of political and religious questions, including two items about their commitment to individual rights versus common morality. For this, we asked whether the respondents agreed or disagreed with the following two statements: (1) "Too often people only care about their individual rights, and not what's good for others" (individual rights); and (2) "Freedom means the ability to do what you want without worrying about what other people think" (freedom). Respondents were able to select options from "strongly disagree" to "strongly agree," with a "neutral" option. These were then recoded into a 0–4 scale, with lower scores being more supportive of the community and higher scores being more supportive of individual rights and freedom.

Despite evangelicals' increasing support for individual rights, at both the public-opinion and advocacy levels, their scores were still relatively low on these questions. For the individual-rights question, the mean was 1.12, effectively agreeing that people too often care about their individual rights and not what is good for others. The mean response for the freedom question was nearly a point higher (1.96), landing exactly halfway between doing what you want and caring about what others think. Surprisingly, these items are uncorrelated, with a correlation of −.087 and an alpha of .15. Individual rights and individual freedom appear to be distinct concepts for the evangelical public.

The evangelical responses to these questions expose a division within evangelical politics. On the whole, evangelicals seem to desire others to conform to a particular minority, while at the same time respecting their rights to act. Majoritarian impulses are embedded in a rights culture.

I created multivariate statistical models to help highlight how differences among evangelicals predict support for the individual-rights and freedom questions. The models use a variety of political, religious, and demographic independent variables. The variables are scaled 0–1 and listed in Figure 5.1, which shows the results of the model. For each variable, the coefficients are

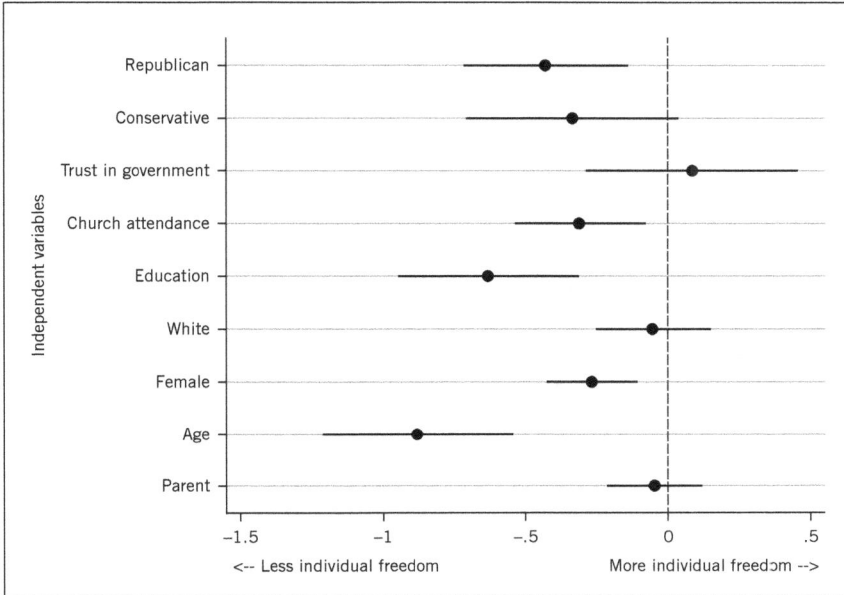

Figure 5.1 Linear regression model of evangelical support for individual freedom at the expense of others

Note: Variables are coded Democratic-Republican, liberal-conservative, and low-high. Standardized coefficients with 95 percent confidence intervals.

plotted with dots and horizontal lines to represent the confidence intervals. If the horizontal line does not cross the vertical line, the variable has a statistically significant effect.

The most interesting results come from the freedom question, the only model shown in Figure 5.1. More Republican and conservative evangelicals are less likely to support freedom at the expense of others, as are women, those who are older, and those who attend church more frequently. Surprisingly, more-educated evangelicals are also less likely to support broad claims to individual freedom, as one would expect more-educated individuals to adopt the disposition of liberalism and pluralism. For the individual-rights question (not shown), the only significant result is that men are more supportive of unfettered individual rights than women. On the whole, these big-picture questions suggest that while evangelicals may have been more supportive of individual rights, there remain overarching impulses toward community, morality, and exclusion.

These data show that there is very little evangelical division over the theoretical commitment to individual rights versus community morality; the evangelical base wants both individual rights and traditional morality.

Even in 2015, there were signals that political elites might be able to capitalize on these sentiments to restrict rights, especially among the most committed and most politically conservative evangelicals.

Evangelicals and Political Tolerance

While understanding support for individual rights and liberties in general can help us grasp the evangelical division over rights (or lack thereof), the Trump campaign suggests that the primary division is about the extension of political rights—tolerance for out-groups. Thus, the absence of major fault lines concerning the concepts of individual liberty and freedom is not surprising. But based on the elite disagreements, we should expect the fault lines to appear in regard to the rights and freedom of out-groups.

Since the mid-1970s, the General Social Survey (GSS) has asked a nationally representative sample of Americans a battery of questions that tap into tolerance for political minority groups—atheists, racists, communists, militarists, and homosexuals. The questions ask respondents if they favor members of these groups being able to make a speech in the respondent's community, teach in a college or university, and have books in support of their views in the library.[1] Scholars have long used this battery in what is called a "fixed group" approach to political tolerance (see, e.g., Gibson 1992; 2013, 46). While this battery of questions gauges political tolerance, it also provides some insight into people's willingness to extend tolerance to groups they are uncomfortable with, at least hypothetically. Examining this battery might expose fault lines among evangelicals regarding their commitment to rights.

Figure 5.2 uses these data to assess the political tolerance of evangelicals and non-evangelicals over time. I combined the three tolerance measures for the five groups, creating a tolerance scale calibrated 0–1—higher scores represent more tolerance for these minority groups. The scale holds together quite well with an alpha of .92.

Over the forty-year period, non-evangelicals (dashed line) consistently have higher levels of political tolerance than evangelicals (solid line). But the gap between these two groups has narrowed considerably, especially since the 1990s. In the mid-1990s, non-evangelicals (.6) were about .1 more tolerant than evangelicals (.5). In 2014, the tolerance gap was only .05, as evangelical tolerance increased at a greater rate over the period. Though they started at lower levels, evangelicals were about .2 more tolerant than they were in 1974, while non-evangelicals grew just under .1 more tolerant.

Though evangelicals have become increasingly tolerant, closing much of the tolerance gap with the general public, are there segments of the evangelical population that lag in their rates of political tolerance, making them

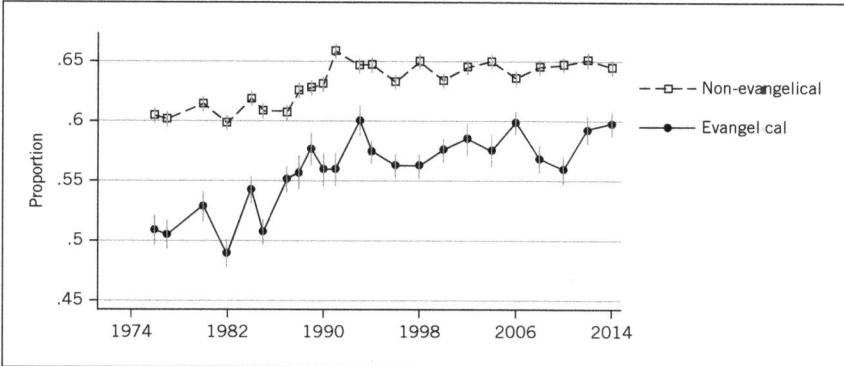

Figure 5.2 Increase in average political tolerance of evangelicals and non-evangelicals
Source: General Social Survey, 1975–2014.

more susceptible to Trump's overtures? A multivariate analysis can help identify potential fissures within evangelicalism.

Using the pooled data from 1975 to 2014, I examined the effect of religious, political, and demographic characteristics on political tolerance. Being religious consistently reduced tolerance, as evangelical Protestants, mainline Protestants, and black Protestants are less tolerant than seculars. No religious group is more tolerant than the unaffiliated. Higher levels of religious attendance also consistently linked to lower political tolerance. In regard to politics, Republicans are surprisingly more tolerant than Democrats in the pooled models, but those who are more conservative and have stronger antiabortion views are less tolerant. Trust also matters, as those who have a higher level of trust in both the government and people are more respectful of people's rights.

Demographic characteristics are also important. Men, white people, and younger individuals report higher degrees of political tolerance, but the greatest factor appears to be education. Higher levels of education strongly predict increased political tolerance over time. Education may be important in light of Trump's performance, as initial analyses suggested that lower education, more than income, was an important component of Trump support (Silver 2016).[2]

To assess the role of education in evangelical tolerance, I incorporated an interaction variable into the model that combined education and evangelical affiliation. As the last line in Figure 5.3 shows (I: Evangelicals and education),[3] the interaction is statistically significant and positive, as it is on the right of the vertical dividing line and does not cross it. Education is a

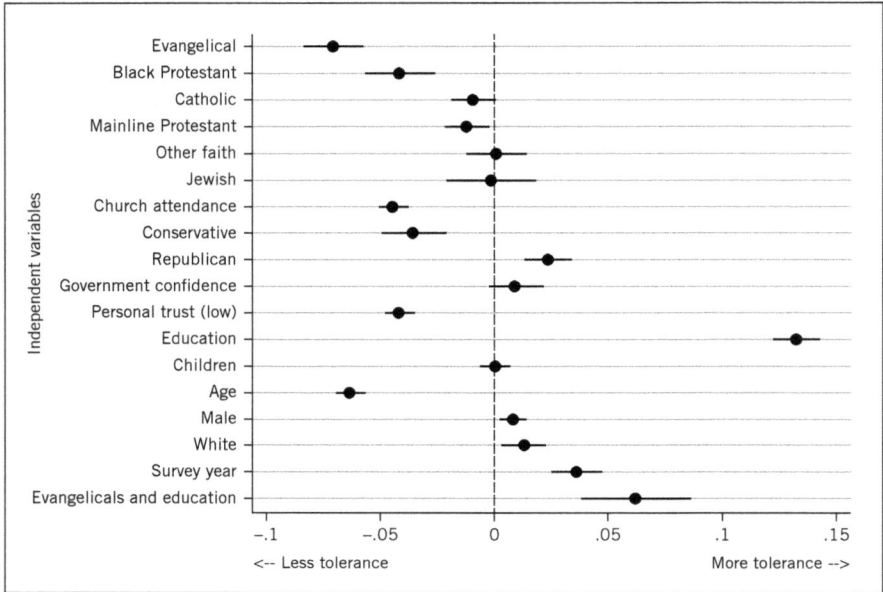

Figure 5.3 Linear regression model of support for greater political tolerance, including evangelical and education interaction
Source: General Social Survey, 1975–2014.
Note: Variables are coded Democratic-Republican, liberal-conservative, and low-high. Standardized coefficients with 95 percent confidence intervals.

particularly potent mediator for the political tolerance of evangelicals. Being more highly educated increases the political tolerance of evangelicals at a much greater rate than it does for non-evangelicals. It effectively helps close the gap between evangelicals and non-evangelicals. This relationship has increased in more recent years, with the coefficient for the interactive term more than doubling from the pre-2000 to post-2000 period. The predicted probabilities suggest that holding a college degree increases tolerance among evangelicals a bit more than among non-evangelicals. In the pre-2000 period graduate degrees are primarily responsible for the significant effects of the interaction term. This expands to both undergraduate and graduate degrees in the post-2000 period.

The outsized link between education and evangelical political tolerance might help explain the limited evangelical opposition to Trump and his policies. Elite evangelicalism has been most likely to support a rights-based culture, championing the rights of all and supporting the rights of others in federal court. Anti-Trump advocacy was concentrated among a younger, more educated evangelical segment, highlighted by Russell Moore and *Christianity Today*, while the previous generation's evangelical leaders were not nearly as concerned about Trump's denial of rights for others.

Evangelicals, Tolerance, and Support for Trump

When it became certain that Trump would be the Republican nominee for president, there remained numerous evangelical and Republican skeptics of the candidate. Statements of "Never Trump" proliferated across social media and within some religious and conservative websites. While most evangelicals warmed to Trump by the November general election, this early Never Trump period provides an opportunity to understand what types of evangelical Republicans were most wary of Trump and what his politics stood for. Within this context, my colleagues Paul Djupe, Jacob Neiheisel, and I fielded a survey in March 2016, using a census region and gender-balanced, national-convenience sample from SSI. Again, the demographic characteristics were similar to those of the national adult population. We first asked these one thousand respondents which remaining political candidate they would vote for if the election were held today. On the Republican side, this included Trump, Ted Cruz, Marco Rubio, and John Kasich. We then asked if the general election were between Trump and Hillary Clinton, would they vote for Clinton, Trump, or refrain from voting. This allows us to investigate which would-be Republican voters were considering defecting from supporting the presumptive Republican nominee for president in March 2016, choosing either Clinton or abstention. It also allows for an assessment of how support for the rights of others might have impacted the potential for defection.

In March 2016, 45 percent of eligible respondents were considering defecting from backing the Republican nominee if it were Trump. Of the 18 percent of the sample who identified as evangelical, 66 percent indicated support for a Republican primary candidate. One-third of those evangelicals indicated that they would defect from Trump if the election were held in March. This rate of defection is less than the average rate of Republican defection (45 percent), and multivariate models show that evangelical identity is associated with at least as much as, if not greater than, rates of loyalty to the GOP standard-bearer than party identification. Even in the early days, evangelicals were loyal partisans.

What types of evangelicals were most likely to defect from Trump at that early stage? On the surface, it does not appear to be the more tolerant evangelicals. In the survey we gauged people's level of political tolerance toward their least-liked political group, including Islamic fundamentalists, illegal immigrants, the Ku Klux Klan, Christian fundamentalists, atheists, gay rights activists, pro-life activists, and pro-choice activists. Political scientists have long utilized this approach to measure tolerance (see Gibson 1992, 2013; Sullivan, Pierson, and Marcus 1982). For all Republicans, the level of political tolerance is nearly identical for potential defectors and loyalists. Potential evangelical defectors were slightly more tolerant on average, though this failed to reach statistical significance.

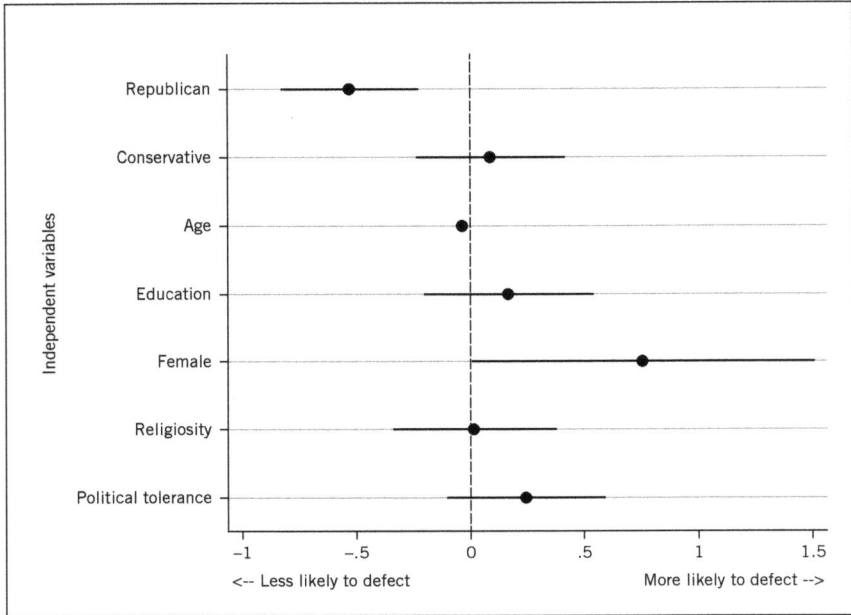

Figure 5.4 Logistic regression model predicting evangelical Republicans defecting from supporting Trump in March 2016

Note: Variables are coded Democratic-Republican, liberal-conservative, and low-high. Standardized coefficients with 95 percent confidence intervals.

Multivariate models provide further insight into the characteristics of potential evangelical loyalists and defectors. Figure 5.4 presents multivariate logistic regression model results that predict defection in March 2016. The model suggests that the most Republican evangelicals were the most loyal to Trump, likely because of their commitment to the party. Older evangelicals were also more likely to remain loyal, as were men. Women and younger evangelicals were more likely to defect. Ideology did not have a significant effect, and neither did religiosity or education.

Though it fails to meet standard levels of statistical significance, political tolerance (the last line in Figure 5.4) is also suggestive of defection, as the descriptive statistics indicated. Evangelicals with higher levels of tolerance for their least-liked group may have been more likely to defect from supporting Trump, though their defection fails to reach statistical significance ($p = .17$). Again, tolerance for out-groups seems to be a minor or weak dividing point among evangelicals.

Analyzing periods prior to the national presidential election provides for a greater opportunity to capture some of the possible fissuring of the evangelical political coalition. There may be a host of reasons for evangelicals to support the Republican rather than the Democratic candidate, but months earlier defection often seems more viable. With Trump as the candidate, women, younger evangelicals, and less committed partisans were more likely to defect, though different studies are needed to see if certain evangelicals became less committed partisans because of Trump. There is only statistically weak, suggestive support that increased levels of political tolerance promoted defection from Trump in the spring of 2016.

Related to the division over tolerance and the politics of Trump is evidence of an evangelical division over the institutional protector of rights—the U.S. Supreme Court. In the same 2015 SSI survey of evangelicals discussed previously, the sample was asked to rate the performance of the Supreme Court on a 0–10 scale, with higher scores indicating better performance. The mean score was almost exactly in the middle (4.98), though the standard deviation was quite high (2.30). In a multivariate model, again few variables stand out as significant (Figure 5.5). Conservatives are less supportive of the Supreme Court ($p < .001$), as are those who attend church more frequently ($p = .09$). Education, however, emerges as a key difference, as it did in the GSS tolerance models. More-educated evangelicals were much more likely to support the Supreme Court ($p < .001$), perhaps indicating a ripeness to defend the

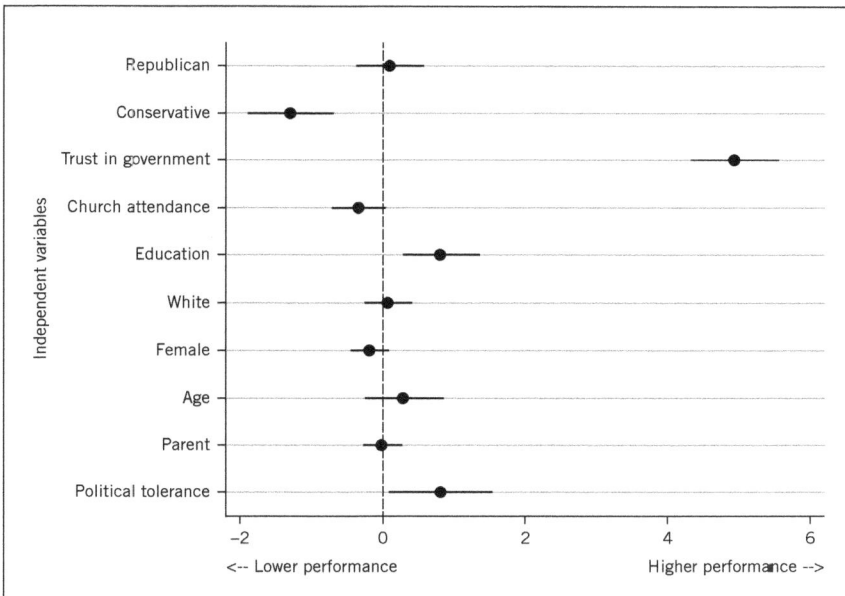

Figure 5.5 Linear regression model of evangelical views of the performance of the U.S. Supreme Court

Note: Variables are coded Democratic-Republican, liberal-conservative, and low-high. Scale is ranked low to high (0–10). Standardized coefficients with 95 percent confidence intervals.

institutional supports of rights and tolerance. In fact, evangelicals with higher levels of political tolerance were more supportive of the Supreme Court, as shown in the bottom of the figure ($p = .03$). Similarly, more-educated evangelicals are more supportive of judicial review, in a separate question that asks whether they support the ability of the court to overturn the will of the people. It is no coincidence that there is a similar profile of those evangelicals with greater political tolerance and more support for the courts. More-educated and more-tolerant evangelicals have adapted to a pluralistic, minority politics that seeks to protect rights and promote rights-protecting institutions. Evangelicals with less education (and perhaps a different generation) seem to want to recapture a previous era of Christian nationalism.

Conclusion

Though Donald Trump was elected with overwhelming support, ironically the white evangelical political house is as divided as it has been for the past several decades. Though the November exit polls showed unity on the surface, fissures are present beneath the surface. These divisions are socioeconomic and generational, and perhaps the enduring question is whether evangelicals will pursue a rights-focused minority politics, as Russell Moore has advocated ("New Southern Baptist Leader" 2014), or seize the political moment to return to the unachieved majoritarian politics of the 1980s and early 1990s. Had Hillary Clinton won the 2016 election, evangelicals would undoubtedly be pursuing a rights-based, minority-politics strategy, at least nationally. The Trump victory, however, has raised new questions. Should evangelical Republicans follow the course of several states, like Kansas, which have pursued Christian Right majoritarian governance, or should they be cautious given their waning cultural prospects and seek to secure rights in a pluralistic environment? Some diversity is to be expected among the states, as each operates in a different religious-political environment, but evangelical leaders and organizations are currently waging the struggle for the national strategy.

Donald Trump was able to maintain much of the rights-centric elements of conservative evangelicalism because of an open Supreme Court seat (perhaps the highest priority for conservative rights politics), negative partisanship, and out-group intolerance. Yet the fault lines remain, and tremors are escalating. Will the evangelical house remain divided, and, if so, for how long will it stand? It might depend on the implications of another one of Jesus's construction parables (Matthew 7:24–27). Will evangelical leaders, seeking to be wise, build their political house on the American political bedrock—rights? Or will they settle for the easier, but more tenuous, shifting sands of Christian nationalism? The next four years are likely to feature a battle for the evangelical political foundation rather than unity.

NOTES

1. Survey data are available from the GSS website, at http://gss.norc.org.
2. As more research has been conducted, some find that racial and gender animosity were also strong predictors of Trump support (e.g., Schaffner 2016).
3. "I" notes the interaction between independent variables, in this case evangelicals and education.

REFERENCES

Bailey, Sarah Pulliam. 2016. "The Deep Disgust for Hillary Clinton That Drives So Many Evangelicals to Support Trump." *Washington Post*, October 9. Available at https://www .washingtonpost.com/news/acts-of-faith/wp/2016/10/09/the-deep-disgust-for-hillary -clinton-that-drives-so-many-evangelicals-to-support-trump.
Becket Fund for Religious Liberty. 2016. "Christians, Jews, Sikhs, Hindus Defend New Jersey Mosque." May 11. Available at http://www.becketfund.org/amicus-brief-defends-new -jersey-islamic-society/.
Brown, Steven P. 2002. *Trumping Religion: The New Christian Right, the Free Speech Clause, and the Courts*. Tuscaloosa: University of Alabama Press.
Bump, Philip. 2016. "White Republicans Are Coming Home to Donald Trump, at Just the Right Time." *Washington Post*, October 30. Available at https://www.washingtonpost .com/news/the-fix/wp/2016/10/30/white-republicans-are-coming-home-to-donald -trump-at-just-the-right-time.
Claassen, Ryan L. 2015. *Godless Democrats and Pious Republicans? Party Activists, Party Capture and the "God Gap."* New York: Cambridge University Press.
Crouch, Andy. 2016. "Speak Truth to Trump: Evangelicals, of All People, Should Not Be Silent about Donald Trump's Blatant Immorality." *Christianity Today*, October 10. Available at https://www.christianitytoday.com/ct/2016/october-web-only/speak-truth-to -trump.html.
Djupe, Paul A., Andrew R. Lewis, and Ted G. Jelen. 2016. "Rights, Reflection, and Reciprocity: Implications of the Same-Sex Marriage Debate for Tolerance and the Political Process." *Politics and Religion* 9 (3): 630–648.
Djupe, Paul A., Andrew R. Lewis, Ted G. Jelen, and Charles D. Dahan. 2014. "Rights Talk: The Opinion Dynamics of Rights Framing." *Social Science Quarterly* 95 (3): 652–668.
Gibson, James L. 1992. "Alternative Measures of Political Tolerance: Must Tolerance Be 'Least-Liked'?" *American Journal of Political Science* 36 (2): 560–577.
———. 2013. "Measuring Political Tolerance and General Support for Pro–Civil Liberties Policies: Notes, Evidence, and Cautions." *Public Opinion Quarterly* 77:45–68.
Glendon, Mary Ann. 1991. *Rights Talk: The Impoverishment of Political Discourse*. New York: Free Press.
Graham, Franklin. 2015. Facebook post of December 9. Available at https://www.facebook .com/FranklinGraham/posts/1055176477871866 (accessed April 25, 2018).
Grant, Tobin. 2016. "Did White Evangelical Support for Trump Drop due to Lower Turnout?" *Religion News Service*, November 14. Available at http://religionnews.com/2016/11/14/ white-evangelical-support-for-trump-dropped-due-to-lower-turnout/.
Gryboski, Michael. 2016. "Russell Moore Takes on Critics at SBC for Supporting Religious Freedom for Muslims to Build Mosques." *Christian Post*, June 16. Available at http:// www.christianpost.com/news/erlcs-russell-moore-takes-heat-sbc-supporting-religious -freedom-muslims-build-mosque-165299.
Haberman, Maggie. 2015. "Donald Trump Deflects Withering Fire on Muslim Plan." *New York Times*, December 8. Available at https://www.nytimes.com/2015/12/09/us/politics/ donald-trump-muslims.html.

Hartz, Louis. 1955. *The Liberal Tradition in America: An Interpretation of Political Thought.* New York: Harcourt, Brace, and World.

Jelen, Ted G. 2005. "Political Esperanto: Rhetorical Resources and Limitations of the Christian Right in the United States." *Sociology of Religion* 66 (3): 303–321.

Johnson, Jenna. 2015. "Trump Calls for 'Total and Complete Shutdown of Muslims Entering the United States.'" *Washington Post,* December 7. Available at https://www.washingtonpost.com/news/post-politics/wp/2015/12/07/donald-trump-calls-for-total-and-complete-shutdown-of-muslims-entering-the-united-states.

Jones, Robert P. 2016. *The End of White Christian America.* New York: Simon and Schuster.

Lewis, Andrew R. 2016. "Learning the Value of Rights: Abortion Politics and the Liberalization of Evangelical Free Speech Advocacy." *Politics and Religion* 9 (3): 309–331.

———. 2017. *The Rights Turn in Conservative Christian Politics: How Abortion Transformed the Culture Wars.* New York: Cambridge University Press.

Lincoln, Abraham. 1982. "House Divided Speech." In *The Abraham Lincoln Encyclopedia,* edited by Mark E. Neely Jr., 152. New York: Da Capo Press. Available at https://www.nps.gov/liho/learn/historyculture/housedivided.htm.

Moen, Matthew C. 1992. *The Transformation of the Christian Right.* Tuscaloosa: University of Alabama Press.

———. 1994. "From Revolution to Evolution: The Changing Nature of the Christian Right." *Sociology of Religion* 55 (3): 345–357.

Moore, Russell. 2015. "Russell Moore: Why Christians Must Speak Out against Donald Trump's Muslim Remarks." *Washington Post,* December 8. Available at https://www.washingtonpost.com/news/acts-of-faith/wp/2015/12/07/russell-moore-people-who-care-an-iota-about-religious-liberty-should-denounce-donald-trump.

"New Southern Baptist Leader Calls for Fresh Approach in 'Increasing Post-Christian America.'" 2014. *CBS News,* April 18. Available at http://www.cbsnews.com/videos/new-southern-baptist-leader-calls-for-fresh-approach/.

Schaffner, Brian. 2016. "White Support for Donald Trump Was Driven by Economic Anxiety, but Also by Racism and Sexism." *Vox,* November 16. Available at http://www.vox.com/mischiefs-of-faction/2016/11/16/13651184/trump-support-economic-anxiety-racism-sexism.

Shain, Barry Alan. 1994. *The Myth of American Individualism: The Protestant Origins of American Political Thought.* Princeton, NJ: Princeton University Press.

Shellnutt, Kate, and Sarah Eekhoff Zyistra. 2016. "Who's Who of Trump's 'Tremendous' Faith Advisors." *Christianity Today,* June 22. Available at https://www.christianitytoday.com/ct/2016/june-web-only/whos-who-of-trumps-tremendous-faith-advisors.html.

Shields, Jon A. 2009. *The Democratic Virtues of the Christian Right.* Princeton, NJ: Princeton University Press.

Silver, Nate. 2016. "Education, Not Income, Predicted Who Would Vote for Trump." *FiveThirtyEight,* November 22. Available at http://fivethirtyeight.com/features/education-not-income-predicted-who-would-vote-for-trump/.

Smith, Gregory A., and Jessica Martínez. 2016. "How the Faithful Voted: A Preliminary 2016 Analysis." Pew Research Center, November 9. Available at http://www.pewresearch.org/fact-tank/2016/11/09/how-the-faithful-voted-a-preliminary-2016-analysis/.

Smith, Rogers M. 1993. "Beyond Tocqueville, Myrdal, and Hartz: The Multiple Traditions in America." *American Political Science Review* 87 (3): 549–566.

Sullivan, John L., James E. Piereson, and George E. Marcus. 1982. *Political Tolerance and American Democracy.* Chicago: University of Chicago Press.

Taylor, Jessica. 2015. "Citing Religious Liberty, Evangelical Leaders Blast Trump's Muslim Ban." *NPR,* December 9. Available at http://www.npr.org/2015/12/09/459086641/citing-religious-liberty-evangelical-leaders-blast-trumps-muslim-ban.

Wilcox, Clyde, and Carin Larson. 2006. *Onward Christian Soldiers: The Religious Right in American Politics*. Boulder, CO: Westview Press.

Williams, Daniel K. 2010. *God's Own Party: The Making of the Christian Right*. New York: Oxford University Press.

Wilson, Joshua C. 2013. *The Street Politics of Abortion: Speech, Violence, and America's Culture Wars*. Stanford, CA: Stanford University Press.

Zuckert, Michael P. 1996. *The Natural Rights Republic: Studies in the Foundation of the American Political Tradition*. South Bend, IN: University of Notre Dame Press.

6

Rethinking the State-Level Strategy

The Christian Right and Left in the States

KIMBERLY H. CONGER

On January 20, 2016, Donald Trump spoke to the chapel convocation at Liberty University in Lynchburg, Virginia. The five-decade-old bastion of conservative evangelical higher education has been a regular stop on the Republican presidential candidate route for several of the past election cycles. Liberty University provided an audience of more than ten thousand students to the candidate, who quoted a Bible passage by stating he was reading from "Two Corinthians." This small gaffe provides a lens through which to view both evangelicals' support for Donald Trump and the status of the Christian Right as a movement in the early twenty-first century. By seeking to connect his populist vision to the conservative social commitments of evangelicals, Trump followed the well-trod path of Republican candidates looking to shore up their voting base. But by making a mistake in his expression of solidarity with evangelical culture, Trump highlighted his problem among rank-and-file evangelical Republicans: Trump is not truly committed to the social and cultural conservatism and religious beliefs that drive the larger evangelical political movement.

This slip matters because he was talking to evangelical voters directly, not simply wooing the leadership of the religious and political movement. Evangelicals' support for Donald Trump raises many questions about the religious and political commitments of both the general demographic of evangelical voters and those who have aligned themselves with, and served in leadership for, the Christian Right movement. The president of Liberty, Jerry Falwell Jr., was a vocal supporter of Trump, as was Franklin Graham, son of the Reverend Billy Graham. Both of these men lead evangelical organizations—started by their respective fathers—that sit at the heart of the evangelical subculture and political Christian Right. But these men were the exception in the larger movement. Most Christian Right activists were either silent or only cautiously supportive of the Republican standard-bearer, who seemed an unlikely champion of conservative and religious family values. Does the election of Donald Trump, and the generous majority of white evangelicals who voted for him, signal important shifts both in the Christian Right and the white evangelical subculture?

In this chapter, I focus on white evangelicals ("evangelicals") as a political movement embodied by the Christian Right and its attendant organizations, issues, and policy proposals. I concentrate on state-level politics, where the movement and evangelical voters have fought some important cultural and ideological battles over the last decades. First, I examine the lay of the land of the Christian Right movement in the states—its history, the character of state political context, and the important rifts in the movement drawn into focus by the 2016 elections. Next, I dig deeper into the organizations and issues that animate the movement in the states and evaluate the impact that the movement has had in state politics over the past decade. Finally, I take a look forward to imagine how the Christian Right in the states might look after four years of a Trump administration and conclude by exploring the enduring influence of religious movements in American state politics.

The Lay of the Land

One of the challenges for both scholars and pundits who observe and analyze the political activity of American evangelicals has been the conflation of the body of evangelical voters as a whole and the social movement known as the Christian Right. While there is certainly significant overlap, as in many ideological movements, the flagship leaders and organizations take more visible and coherent stands on policy and issues than do rank-and-file voters. This is an important distinction in the current political climate when very few Christian Right leaders openly endorsed Donald Trump, but many exit polls suggest that Trump received more than 80 percent of evangelical votes ("Election 2016" 2016). Both groups reflect the resentment of liberal elites and visceral opposition to Hillary Clinton. But many visible leaders within the Christian Right movement were part of the #NeverTrump movement and expressed concern with the lack of conservative bona fides of the Republican candidate. This distinction between evangelical voters and the Christian Right movement is also important for understanding how these entities operate in state politics.

States in many ways reflect the institutions and structures of national government, but a number of variations make a world of difference in the interest community's ability to advocate for policy and influence political decision making. Most important, states exist within a federal system. They are required by the national government to fulfill responsibilities and are heavily dependent on the national government for their income. States vary in terms of their institutional procedures, election schedule, and informal rules of the political game in political parties and business organizations. More specifically, all but one state is required to pass a balanced budget, and some states have direct-democracy provisions or other mechanisms designed to represent citizens' opinions.

Beyond the variations of state political structures, religious bodies and organizations bring varying resources to their attempts to influence government behavior. For the Christian Right, the proportion of a state's population that self-identifies as evangelical is an important ingredient for the movement's ability to make an impact. This can be as low as 8 to 9 percent in states on the East Coast or as high as 52 percent in Tennessee (Pew Research Center, n.d.). The overall number of seculars in a state matters as well, because higher numbers of seculars likely means that evangelicals feel more threatened (Campbell 2006) and because the Christian Right movement faces more opposition. These political structures and religious resources have generally been in place for decades, but it took a precipitating event to coalesce them into a viable Christian Right movement.

The advent of the Christian Right as a political movement is a story that can be told in a number of ways. These stories demonstrate the multifaceted changes in society and religious engagement that brought the Christian Right as a political movement into supporters' consciousness, their churches, and finally the voting booth. For our purposes, however, it makes sense to explain the advent of the Christian Right movement as a reaction to local laws, specifically local laws barring discrimination against gays and lesbians and concerning the placement and operation of adult bookstores (Fetner 2008). The movement's agenda was expanded by a growing focus on picketing (local) abortion clinics and controversies over behavior and curriculum in (local) schools. The religiously motivated activists who now make up the Christian Right have long been involved with state and local politics, but it took the political acumen of evangelicals such as Ralph Reed to grow these opinions and activities into a viable movement.

This state-level strategy has borne fruit in the politics of many states, especially in state Republican parties. Measures of Christian Right influence in the states show an increase over time, with twenty-two states reporting strong influence of the Christian Right in Republican state politics by 2008 (Conger 2014). Those measures of influence have likely grown, as Republicans have taken control of many state legislatures and governors' mansions since 2010. But in a book about the evangelical "crackup," how might we evaluate the movement's prospects and influence in 2016? One of the ways

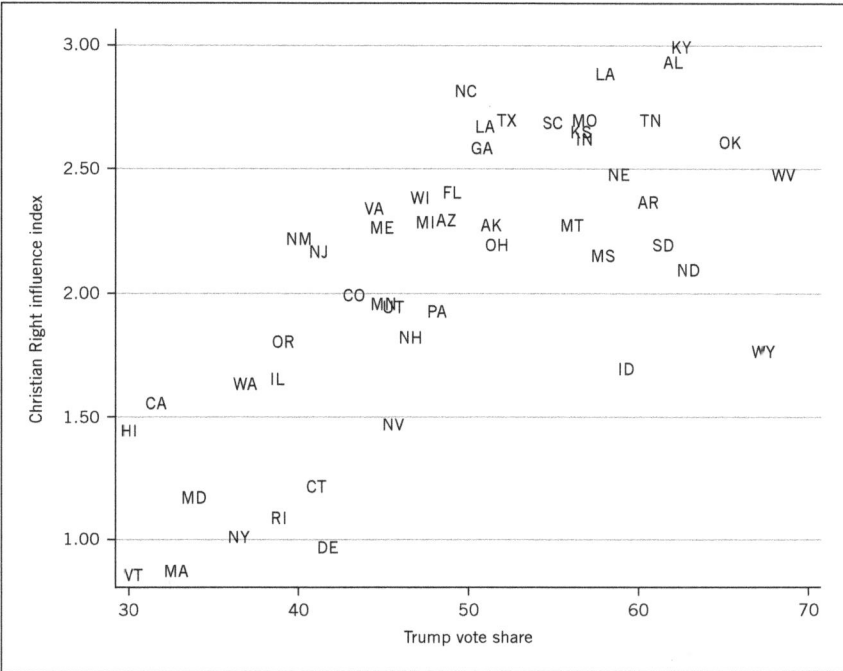

Figure 6.1 Influence of 2008 Christian Right voters in 2016 Trump vote, by state

we can evaluate the current state of the Christian Right in state politics is to compare the strength of the movement with the proportion of voters who voted for Donald Trump in 2016. This should help delineate both the impact of Christian Right presence on the Trump vote and help us understand what portion of evangelicals were attracted to, or at least not repelled by, Trump's message of economic populism and a return to American "greatness."

Figure 6.1 demonstrates that there is a significant relationship between the Christian Right's influence in state politics in 2008 and the proportion of Trump voters in the state in 2016. Overall, states with substantial Christian Right presence in 2008 gave Trump their electoral votes in 2016. The few outliers to the trend help clarify the story. Notice that the states where Trump got proportionally larger vote percentages than their Christian Right influence predicts—North Dakota, Wyoming, and West Virginia—are small conservative states with fewer evangelicals but more of the white working-class voters that were so important to Trump's winning coalition.

Much has been made in the postmortems of the 2016 election of the role of resentment among Trump voters. Evangelicals and the Christian Right may be good evidence for the role of cultural resentment. Because they tend to be more suburban and rural and to live in states in the middle of the country, many evangelicals feel like they are at best ignored and at worst ridiculed by a liberal political, business, and media elite residing on the coasts. While a quantitative explanation must wait for more scrutiny of exit and postelection polls, qualitative evidence suggests that this resentment and a long-standing dislike of Hillary Clinton (for similar reasons) and a deep concern over the trajectory of the Supreme Court were the primary ingredients for a Trump landslide among conservative evangelical voters. That reality made it hard for evangelical voters to heed Christian Right leaders' pleas to vote for a third-party candidate. This decision also makes sense in the context of the trajectory of the movement and subculture in American state politics. Evangelicals felt like they were losing ground. Presidential election results suggest that they may have been at least temporarily wrong.

State-Level Christian Right Organizations

The Christian Right at the state level has evolved over the years the movement has been active. Much of the movement's activity in the 1980s and 1990s was visible at the national level through Pat Robertson's campaign for president and the Republican takeover of the U.S. House. These victories affected the movement at the state level and state Republican parties by mobilizing activists and bringing newly engaged evangelicals into the system. This development was greatly enhanced by the organization and mission of the Christian Coalition, which was explicitly geared toward both aggregating efforts already under way at the state level and encouraging new state-level affiliates focused on state- and local-level politics. While the Christian Coalition is only a shell of its former self, a number of other organizations have imitated or tried to sustain its state-level focus, such as the Family Research Council and the older and more fundamentalist-oriented American Family Association. Most states have at least one organization that is an affiliate of one of these groups that serves as the focal point for seeking influence in state politics.

In many states, contemporary conservative politics consists of interplay between Christian Right organizations and religious conservative activists within the Republican Party establishment (Conger 2010a, 2010b, 2014; Green and Guth 1988). This division of labor among entities allows them to share an activist core and a grassroots constituency but to reach out to new supporters on both the religious and political margins. While many professional Christian Right activists report that their supporters are probably more motivated by national issues and personalities, they strive to channel this interest into activity about more immediate state-level issues.

In addition to the national Christian Right organizations, there are many organizations unique to their own states. For example, the Maine Christian Civic League was started by temperance activists in the early part of the twentieth century, the Traditional Values Coalition began in Southern

California in 1984, and Michigan's Citizens for Traditional Values began in 1993. These homegrown organizations continue to play a pivotal role in the Christian Right movement, and many new activists are mobilized and trained within them (Conger 2009).

The Christian Right Movement and Policy Opportunities in the States

As we have seen, one of the primary reasons for the Christian Right's focus on state politics is that many of the issues that are most important to them are inherently state-level issues. The regulations that determine abortion procedures are state-level medical licensing laws; the educational standards that affect the teaching of science and human reproduction are state-level laws; and the standards on which the Religious Freedom Restoration Act can be enforced (e.g., antidiscrimination laws) are entirely state governed. Even the battle over the provision of contraceptives by private companies under the Affordable Care Act had a state-level dimension because insurance companies are licensed and regulated by the states.

The exception that proves the rule is, of course, same-sex marriage. This issue was hotly debated in state legislatures and courts and placed on the ballot of many direct-democracy states for nearly two decades. Much of the Christian Right's visibility and power to mobilize was linked to the fact that rules governing marriage had traditionally been state-level laws. State laws vary dramatically in terms of marriage issues such as the age of consent and the process by which one obtains a marriage license. So the Christian Right's success in passing Defense of Marriage Acts and amendments to state constitutions demonstrated to evangelicals and other religiously motivated conservatives both the need for the movement and its ability to succeed. By at least 2010, however, most Christian Right activists believed that a Supreme Court decision on the issue was imminent. And while in many cases they joined national efforts to affect policy on the federal level, national politics once again proved to be infertile ground for the movement. The *Obergefell* decision, which legalized same-sex marriage across the United States, robbed many state-level organizations of an important rallying point that was used to introduce concerned citizens to the larger arena of Christian Right political efforts.

The resolution of the same-sex marriage question highlights one of the bigger challenges the movement faces on the state level. In all cases, citizens are more motivated to vote and participate in politics by news and controversy concerning national politics. This is in direct opposition to the fact that state and local politics make a much bigger difference in the everyday lives of most people. Since I first began interviewing religious conservative activists more than a decade ago, one of the constant descriptions of state-level work has included mobilizing people and convincing them to be active in less publicized, less glamorous state politics (Conger 2009, 2014). But it is also clear that state-level activists attempt to use attention given to national politics to shed light on state issues and raise citizen interest. One movement activist described their own organization as being less driven by national controversies, and therefore it was smaller and less well known and funded than other Christian Right organizations in the state that did focus on national issues.

New issues have emerged from the evangelical subculture—particularly from younger adherents—that are not currently part of the Christian Right portfolio, though they may become so in the future. These are the even more specifically local issues of human trafficking and adoption. For instance, in 2007, the Colorado adoption project, Project 1.27, made it a goal to make sure there were no children in the state foster system who were eligible to be adopted. Bringing together churches and parachurch organizations from across the state, they flooded the state system with people eager to be trained and certified to adopt these children. The project has been largely successful, though more children enter the foster system every year, and it remains to be seen whether the effort can be sustained over time (Israel 2013).

Threats to the Christian Right's Viability in the States

The advance of abortion restrictions in many states, shared with their allies in the pro-life movement, has been one of the few victories the Christian Right has had in politics during the Barack Obama administration. While many in the national movement saw the George W. Bush administration as a high point with an evangelical (in identity, if not affiliation) in the White House, state leaders of Christian Right organizations began to lose their enthusiasm much earlier in the administration. Bush's focus on the war on terror and homeland security crowded out many of the domestic-policy issues evangelicals hoped a Bush administration would address. This had a great impact on state-level policy priorities. Many activists within the party and even beyond expressed concern over the scope of the increases in the size of government and government spending during the Bush years (Conger 2009). This concern and the Great Recession added economic issues to the portfolios of many Christian Right activists at the outset of the Obama administration. The outgrowth of those economic concerns led to the advent of the Tea Party, a Republican movement whose roots in the existing religious-conservative milieu inside the Republican Party is generally overlooked (see Hayden 2010).

While it is certainly the case that the Tea Party's primary goal was and is economic (Deckman 2016), many people who identified as supporters of the Christian Right were identifying themselves as part of the Tea Party by mid-2010 (Clement and Green 2011; Williamson, Skocpol, and Coggin 2011). This shift reflects the disenchantment of evangelicals with the Christian Right as a movement after the end of the Bush administration, but it also reflects a growing sense of being "left behind," in this case by a housing bubble and the recession that followed its burst. This shift matters for our conversation about the Christian Right movement in the states because these newly energized Tea Party organizations, many of them based at the local and state levels, seemed to eclipse Christian Right organizations in their ability to mobilize and garner press attention. Observers point to the Tea Party movement as drawing away activists from the Christian Right. And others find a clear link between the Tea Party and Trump's economic populism. Thus, it seems that evangelicals' support of Trump may run through the Tea Party, not traditional Christian Right organizations. Though many Tea Party groups and candidates have faded from view, Christian Right organizations have deep roots and remain to contest policy at the state level.

One of the most interesting developments within both the Christian Right and the larger evangelical subculture that surrounds it has been the growing call to rethink religiously motivated activism in light of obvious policy defeats like same-sex marriage. Some advocate for the "Benedict Option" to withdraw into more separatist Christian communities, while others advocate for an abandonment of politics, though not the larger American culture (Dreher 2017). These calls are not new, because these types of critiques existed from the very earliest entry of religious conservatives into Republican politics. But the calls are coming from new and previously unlikely places, such as the head of the Southern Baptists' Ethics and Religious Liberty Committee, Russell Moore. Many visible evangelical leaders of religious and political organizations encouraged evangelical voters to distance themselves from Trump; others embraced him. These developments are important for the status of the Christian Right movement in the states because they both reflect and presage these organizations' ability to draw participation and impact the policy issues of concern. Much of this movement away from an explicitly electoral politics based on culture-war themes has been signaled by Christian Right leaders who did not support Trump. It remains to be seen how rank-and-file religious conservatives, many of whom voted for Trump, will respond to this new direction.

Christian Right Impact in the States

One important question about the Christian Right's orientation toward state politics over the last decade is whether it has borne fruit. Is there a measurable impact of the movement's efforts to influence state policy? As with most questions about influence, the evidence is mixed; abortion restrictions are a victory, while same-sex marriage is a loss. Is a conservative bent to state politics a result of the influence of the Christian Right movement and evangelical voters? Or is it the result of more muscular Republican majorities in state legislatures? Or is the movement, along with other conservative pressures, partly responsible for both the partisan and ideological move to the right in state politics? There are good arguments to make for all of these possibilities; here I concentrate on those changes in policy or politics that have clearly depended on Christian Right support.

Perhaps the most obvious impact that the movement has had on state politics is the significant increase in abortion restrictions across the nation. While this is a victory shared with the pro-life movement, the Christian Right has played a significant role both in writing the laws that tested the limits of state power to regulate abortion and in broadening the appeal of such legislation to a wide variety of conservatives. The strength of the movement in each state has been linked to increased abortion restrictions and seems to be mediated by Republican control of a state house (Bentele et al. 2013).

Less obvious, but no less important, has been the success of the movement in lowering the wall between religion and government at the state level. One study found that eighty-seven different laws have been passed at the state level since the mid-1990s that explicitly protect freedom of religion: "overt support for display of religious symbols in public settings, the facilitation of access to public funding for religious institutions, and the characterization of religion as embattled by a secular state" (Bentele et al. 2013, 504). The most famous of these laws may be the religious freedom act passed in Indiana in early 2015 that gave protections to people who objected to serving gays and lesbians in all forms of business endeavor if it was based on religious convictions (Wang 2015). The law was quite controversial, with many businesses in the state's capital, Indianapolis, posting signs declaring them to be hate-free zones. And the state's then-governor, Mike Pence, an outspoken religious conservative and currently vice president, asked for and received an amended bill that made clear that the law could not be used to discriminate against anyone (Cook, LoBianco, and Stanglin 2015). Most other state-level attempts to encode religious freedom or state support for religious organizations have attracted much less national controversy.

Finally, the Christian Right has been successful in influencing state-level legislative and executive decision making through lobbying. While lobbying is a ubiquitous activity among interest groups at both the national and state levels, it is one of the least-studied areas of Christian Right activism. Perhaps because of the explicit grassroots nature of the movement and its public attempts to impact elections and the Republican Party, its strategy and success in "insider" politics are less visible to pundits and scholars. While the scholarship that does exist concentrates primarily at the national level (Lugo et al. 2011; Robinson 2015), recent work has demonstrated not only that the movement is active in state-level lobbying but also that this lobbying activity can be linked to issues of special concern to the Christian Right, such as same-sex marriage and LGBT (lesbian, gay, bisexual, and transgender) rights (Conger and Djupe 2016). Other more qualitative work suggests that Christian Right lobbyists and advocacy organizations are playing a significant role in drafting bills for state legislators to introduce on issues important to the movement (Conger 2009). While we still lack robust measures of lobbying activity by the movement in state-level politics, it is clear that the movement has institutionalized itself in the states beyond electoral and Republican politics. Christian Right organizations are active not only in citizen mobilization but also in the standard policy advocacy of state-level politics.

What Is Next for the Christian Right in the States?

The future of the Christian Right movement at the state level relies greatly on the changes wrought to domestic policy by unified Republican government at the national level. But I suspect that the landscape for the movement in state politics and its incarnation in state-level organizations may look much the same four years from now. While candidate Trump had promised to abolish abortion, prosecute Hillary Clinton, and roll back many of the economic and civil rights changes produced by the Obama administration, President Trump is walking back or delaying many of those promises. Additionally, abortion restriction has proven much more effective at the state level than at the national level; and Trump has signaled he has no intention of trying to reverse the legality of same-sex marriage, which is a progressive policy change of much more recent vintage than the nearly forty-five-year-old *Roe v. Wade* decision. All in all, Christian Right activists and evangelical voters are likely to face a relatively unaltered landscape in terms of the social issues that motivate them and Republicans to retain control of a majority of state governments. This suggests that while incremental gains are certainly possible, wholesale change that radically increases or decreases the movement's relevance seems unlikely.

The areas where more substantial change in domestic politics seems possible—social welfare spending and civil rights legislation—are less central to the Christian Right's purposes, though not necessarily less central to evangelical voters' policy preferences. The challenge for the Christian Right movement in this context may be agenda building. If the attention of its constituents remains largely on national politics that has little social-issue content, and if they are satisfied with other aspects of a Trump presidency, the movement may struggle to remind its supporters of its relevance.

In this chapter, I examine the Christian Right movement in the contemporary politics of the American states. I begin by asking whether evangelicals' majority vote for Trump signaled a shift in the Christian Right and how a Trump administration might affect the future of the movement. Tracing evangelicals' support for Trump through the Tea Party during the Obama administration illuminates the roots of the split between voters who enthusiastically supported Trump and an evangelical leadership that was generally more circumspect. Because the condition of state politics will change very little, even within the bounds of the federal system, it is likely that the Christian Right movement will be in a similar position four years from today. It will be wielding power and influence in some states but largely fighting a rear-guard battle to hold back social change.

REFERENCES

Bentele, Keith Gunnar, Rebecca Sager, Sarah A. Soule, and Gary Adler. 2013. "Breaking Down the Wall between Church and State: State Adoption of Religious Inclusion Legislation, 1995–2009." *Journal of Church and State* 56 (3): 503–533.
Campbell, David E. 2006. "Religious 'Threat' in Contemporary Presidential Elections." *Journal of Politics* 68 (1): 104–115.
Clement, Scott, and John C. Green. 2011. "The Tea Party and Religion." Pew Research Center, February 23. Available at http://www.pewforum.org/2011/02/23/tea-party-and-religion.
Conger, Kimberly H. 2009. *The Christian Right in Republican State Politics*. New York: Palgrave Macmillan.
———. 2010a. "A Matter of Context: Christian Right Influence in U.S. State Republican Politics." *State Politics and Policy Quarterly* 10 (3): 248–269.
———. 2010b. "Party Platforms and Party Coalitions: The Christian Right and State-Level Republicans." *Party Politics* 16 (5): 651–668.
———. 2014. "Same Battle, Different War: Religious Movements in American State Politics." *Politics and Religion* 7 (2): 395–417.
Conger, Kimberly H., and Paul A. Djupe. 2016. "Culture War Counter-mobilization: Gay Rights and Religious Right Groups in the States." *Interest Groups and Advocacy* 5 (3): 278–300.
Cook, Tony, Tom LoBianco, and Doug Stanglin. 2015. "Indiana Governor Signs Amended 'Religious Freedom' Law." *USA Today*, April 2. Available at https://www.usatoday.com/story/news/nation/2015/04/02/indiana-religious-freedom-law-deal-gay-discrimination/70819106.
Deckman, Melissa. 2016. *Tea Party Women: Mama Grizzlies, Grassroots Leaders, and the Changing Face of the American Right*. New York: New York University Press.
Dreher, Rod. 2017. *The Benedict Option: A Strategy for Christians in a Post-Christian Nation*. New York: Penguin.
"Election 2016: Exit Polls." 2016. *CNN*, November 23. Available at https://www.cnn.com/election/2016/results/exit-polls.
Fetner, Tina. 2008. *How the Religious Right Shaped Lesbian and Gay Activism*. Minneapolis: University of Minnesota Press.
Green, John C., and James L. Guth. 1988. "The Christian Right in the Republican Party: The Case of Pat Robertson's Supporters." *Journal of Politics* 50 (1): 150–165.
Hayden, Erik. 2010. "Is the Tea Party Simply a Division of the Religious Right?" *The Atlantic*, October 6. Available at https://www.theatlantic.com/politics/archive/2010/10/is-the-tea-party-simply-a-division-of-the-religious-right/343918/.
Israel, Charlene. 2013. "Colo. Christians Answering the Prayers of Orphans." *Charisma News*, May 10. Available at https://www.charismanews.com/us/39427-colorado-christians-answering-the-prayers-of-orphans.

Lugo, Luis, Alan Cooperman, Erin O'Connell, and Sandra Stencel. 2011. "Lobbying for the Faithful: Executive Summary." Pew Research Center, May 15. Available at http://www .pewforum.org/2011/11/21/lobbying-for-the-faithful-exec/.

Pew Research Center. n.d. "Evangelical Protestants." Available at http://www.pewforum.org/ religious-landscape-study/religious-tradition/evangelical-protestant (accessed March 19, 2018).

Robinson, Zoë. 2015. "Lobbying in the Shadows: Religious Interest Groups in the Legislative Process." *Emory Law Journal* 64 (4): 1041–1102. Available at http://law.emory.edu/elj/ content/volume-64/issue-4/articles/lobbying-shadows-religious-groups-legislative .html.

Wang, Stephanie. 2015. "What the 'Religious Freedom' Law Really Means for Indiana." *Indianapolis Star*, March 29. Available at https://www.indystar.com/story/news/politics/ 2015/03/29/religious-freedom-law-really-means-indiana/70601584/.

Williamson, Vanessa, Theda Skocpol, and John Coggin. 2011. "The Tea Party and the Remaking of Republican Conservatism." *Perspectives on Politics* 9 (1): 25–43.

PART II

Religious Change and the Politics of Evangelicals

7

Organizational Divisions within the Evangelical Tradition

J. Tobin Grant
David Searcy

I n the early months of the Republican presidential primaries, some hoped that evangelicals would save the party from Donald Trump. In December 2015, Harry Enten, a political analyst at *FiveThirtyEight* (Nate Silver's popular blog), looked at the polls and concluded, "The GOP establishment doesn't need to win Iowa—it just needs Trump to lose. And the establishment may have to rely on an old frenemy to make that happen: born-again and evangelical Christians." The establishment's frenemy turned out to be unwilling or unable to defeat Trump.

One of the key reasons for this is that evangelicals are notoriously divided, decentralized, and disorganized. Evangelicals are united around some core beliefs related to the conversion experience, salvation, the Bible, and evangelism (Bebbington 1989). Those holding these shared beliefs created organizations, publications, and institutions that form the basis for a religious tradition that developed separately from both mainline Protestantism and historically black churches (Steensland et al. 2000). But evangelicals also share an ecclesiology that emphasizes the local congregation and sectarian denominations that hold distinctive beliefs and practices. Lydia Bean compares evangelicals to a "fleet of ships." According to Bean, "American evangelicalism is best described as a coalition: a decentralized movement of local churches, denominations, parachurch ministries, and entrepreneurial media empires. . . . Conservative Protestants have always been prone to fissuring and infighting, because *anyone* could lay claim to legitimate authority in a culture that valued scripture as the sole source of truth" (2014, 27).

This image of evangelicals differs from the view of public commentators, religious leaders, and many social scientists. Even the title of this book may be inaccurate since the study of a "crackup" among evangelicals implies that there was once a solid, unified evangelicalism. We argue that, in many ways, there was not.

We approach the organization of evangelicals by examining their *organizations*. Some of these congregations are independent and local, with no ties to other congregations. Others belong to denominations or associations. Some of these denominations form associations; others remain ardently distinct and independent. We find that these subtraditions within evangelicalism differ in both their religious and political behaviors.

An Organization-Based Classification

Our classification of evangelicals begins with the local congregation. Nearly all people who are religious are embedded in a local religious network. These networks are not limited to those in the same congregation, but congregations provide the framework for creating and sustaining these networks. Each congregation has its own religious leaders and its unique mix of beliefs and behaviors. In the religious market, the congregation is the place where most religious goods and services are distributed. In short, the local congregation is nearly always the most important organization in a person's lived religion.

In an ideal study of religion, we would be able to gather data on the local congregation. This is difficult in research using representative samples from the population (i.e., surveys that do not include additional data from congregations). As a result, researchers use denominations to classify people into religious groups. Denominations give researchers a rough estimate of the theology and practice found in local congregations.

Denominations are a valid means of classification because they are *organizations* of local congregations. In some denominations, there is a hierarchical ecclesial structure that creates, owns, and operates local congregations (e.g., the Episcopal Church). In others, the denomination may be a loose association (e.g., Southern Baptist Convention [SBC]). Nevertheless, we make the following assumption: *all else being equal, congregations within the same denomination will be more similar to each other than they are to congregations outside the denomination.* Congregations in a denomination provide similar religious goods and services; they share a common history; and they share a common brand in the religious market.

In most surveys in the United States, this approach may be used to distinguish only a few denominations. Catholics, for example, form one group. Among Protestants and other sectarian Christians, however, there are thousands of denominations (Mead, Hill, and Atwood 2010). As a result, denominations alone result in categories too small to be useful in most surveys of the national population.

To be useful to researchers, denominations need to be classified into larger groups. The methodology used by researchers to group denominations has evolved over time. Whether it is a blunt Protestant-Catholic-Jew formulation or something more nuanced, researchers categorize persons based on their denomination. We challenge how denominations are categorized, however. We now build on our previous assumption: congregations in the same denomination can be seen as the same type. When categorizing denominations into larger categories, we should look for organizations, networks, and other institutions that include denominations as members. We assume that denominations organize together with denominations most similar to themselves.

This organizational approach to categorizing denominations differs from current practice. These approaches are each valid in that they organize groups based on a set of clearly articulated criteria. For example, Tom W. Smith's (1990) FUND scale (short for "fundamentalism," a measure created within the General Social Survey) placed denominations on a fundamentalist-moderate-liberal scale based on theories of how religious groups related to society.

The most dominant method of classifying denominations in use today is RELTRAD (for "religious tradition," a somewhat different measure also created within the General Social Survey). This categorization classifies denominations based on their *shared historical development*. First introduced by Brian Steensland and colleagues (2000) and since revised (Woodberry et al. 2012; see also Stetzer and Burge 2016), RELTRAD sorts Protestant Christianity into three categories: evangelical, mainline, and historically black Protestant. Groups with similar histories are placed together; those whose developments diverged are put in different categories. Both RELTRAD and FUND are based on qualitative assessments of the theology, practices, and histories of denominations. They select characteristics that the researchers consider important and sort denominations based on these features. In contrast, we create a categorization that reflects how religious groups self-organize on the principle that groups that form organizational ties to each other are more similar than those that do not.

Our approach also allows us to vary group membership over time. It is not static. Groups that worked together in the past may not today; denominations that were separated may now be in communion with one another. When RELTRAD was first developed, many historically black denominations were separate from white denominations. Since then, there have been developments, including ecumenical groups that seek to address racial divides. The United Methodist Church (UMC), for example, is now in full communion with historically black Methodist churches, including the

African Methodist Episcopal Church (AME). While RELTRAD would view AME and UMC as parts of distinct traditions, our approach would have differentiated them twenty years ago but classify them as similar today. Similarly, the Community of Christ (formerly the Reorganized Church of Jesus Christ of Latter-day Saints) became a member of the National Council of Churches (NCC) in 2010, making it connected to mainline Protestantism. Among evangelicals, there was almost a split in the Council for Christian Colleges and Universities (CCCU) when two colleges affiliated with the Mennonite Church added "sexual orientation" to their statement on nondiscrimination; the situation resulted instead in Goshen College and Eastern Mennonite University leaving the CCCU. Our classification allows denominations and churches to have their classification changed when their organizational membership changes. We base this on the denomination's own organization: if they see themselves as being in communion, then we do, too.

Therefore, to classify denominations, we use a denomination's membership in ecumenical organizations. Some of these ecumenical organizations represent deep, meaningful connections between denominations. Many are akin to professional organizations (e.g., Evangelical Press Association) or represent one aspect of denominational presence (e.g., CCCU). Our aim was to find ecumenical organizations and other institutions that demonstrated a close relationship between denominations.

In sum, our classification begins with individuals who are part of congregations. These congregations may belong to denominations or associations. And these denominations organize into ecumenical groups. Assuming that these organizations indicate more similarity, we can classify people into religious categories based on these organizations.

Classifying Evangelicals

In this chapter, we use this organization-based approach to examine evangelicals. Our use of "evangelical" is nearly identical to the RELTRAD category of "evangelical Protestant," even though we base it on organizational ties rather than a group's history or shared beliefs. We consider evangelicals to be Christians whose congregation/denomination is *not* part of the Catholic Church, National Council of Churches, or Conference of National Black Churches. Evangelical denominations, instead, belonged to evangelical ecumenical groups. The broadest is the National Association of Evangelicals (NAE), but there are more narrow evangelical ecumenical groups, such as the CCCU and the Evangelical Christian Publishers Association (ECPA). We also include Baptists who are not members of the National Council of Churches (e.g., we do not include American Baptists); these are often members of the Baptist World Alliance and/or the North American Baptist Fellowship (NABF).

There are some Christians whom we place into the evangelical category who do not belong to one of these denominations. Most of these are Christians who belong to independent or nondenominational congregations. Some are members of denominations that are either too small or too sectarian to belong to broader associations. In these cases, we place them in this category as long as they are Christian and do not hold beliefs rejected by evangelicals.

While our category of "evangelicals" is nearly identical to the corresponding evangelical tradition using RELTRAD, we go further and examine the organizations within evangelicalism. We identify four types of evangelicals based on their organizational ties: sectarian Baptists, Pentecostals, other sectarian evangelicals, and nondenominational.

Baptists. Unlike other evangelicals, Baptists do not belong to the NAE. Some Baptists do have associations with other evangelical denominations through educational associations (e.g., CCCU) or professional associations (e.g., ECPA). We refer to this group as "sectarian Baptists" to differentiate them from American Baptists, National Baptists, and others who belong to the NCC. This includes the SBC and other Baptists not in the NCC. The SBC has long maintained that while it will cooperate with other groups on some issues, it will not commit itself to any organization that could compromise what it views at its "historic distinctives or the unique witness" of its message (Southern Baptist Convention 1996). Most of these associations are part of the Baptist World Alliance and the NABF. Notably the SBC is no longer a member of either alliance, but many of its churches are part of state or regional associations that remain in the NABF. The SBC Women's Missionary Union remains a member of both groups.

Pentecostals. We do not define Pentecostals by belief or behavior; we base our categorization on denominations in the Pentecostal/Charismatic Churches of North America (PCCNA, the successor of the Pentecostal Fellowship of North America). It includes historically black and historically white denominations; indeed, reconciliation is one of the purposes of the PCCNA. The organization includes Church of God in Christ (COGIC), Assemblies of God, and other major Pentecostal churches. For the purposes of this chapter, we examine only historically white denominations that have ties to other evangelicals. In a broader analysis of American religion, we would retain COGIC and other black Pentecostal churches in this category.

Sectarian. This is a catch-all category for denominations that are neither Pentecostal nor Baptist but are evangelical. Most of these denominations are members of the NAE, have colleges in the CCCU, and/or have publications in the ECPA. These include denominations that left mainline denominations

TABLE 7.1   DEMOGRAPHICS OF EVANGELICAL SUBTRADITIONS

	Baptists (%)	Pentecostals (%)	Sectarian (%)	Nondenominational (%)	All evangelicals (%)
White, not Latino	84	63	75	69	75
Northeast	6	13	11	9	9
Midwest	14	23	34	23	22
South	70	42	34	38	50
West	11	23	21	30	20
High school or less	48	52	39	34	43
Some college	34	35	34	39	35
College degree	18	13	26	27	21
N (weighted)	3,112	1,441	1,664	2,147	8,364

Source: Pew Research Center 2014.

(e.g., Presbyterian Church in America), refused to join ecumenical mergers (e.g., Lutheran Church–Missouri Synod), holiness churches (e.g., Nazarene), restorationist (e.g., Churches of Christ), and other sectarian denominations (e.g., Seventh-Day Adventist).

Nondenominational. Nondenominational congregations are a large and growing segment of evangelicals. But as the name suggests, they are not organized with other congregations. We include any Christian without a denomination in this category.

These are the four major subtraditions we identify, but there are others that could be explored. With sufficient variation in the sample, one might identify denominations that are fundamentalist or reformed, for example. We identified these four because we find that they are the largest we could classify within evangelicalism (see Table 7.1).

Comparing Four Evangelical Categories

We use the 2014 U.S. Religious Landscape Survey conducted by the Pew Research Center. The survey is useful for our study because it includes a large number of respondents ($N = 35,507$) and includes a wide range of political and religious questions, including specific denominational affiliation. This allows us to examine 8,364 evangelicals. Breaking down evangelical respondents into our four subtraditions reveals the following about composition:

- Baptists (37 percent)
- Pentecostal (17 percent)

- Sectarian (19 percent)
- Nondenominational (26 percent)

These religious groups differ in their social demographics. Baptists are the highest percentage white (not Latino) of the four groups and are primarily located in the South. Pentecostals are also more often located in the South, but they are also more geographically, racially, and ethnically diverse. Sectarian denominations have a greater presence in the Midwest. This is due, in part, to the Lutheran Church–Missouri Synod. It is also a reflection of the fundamentalist splits in northern evangelicalism that occurred in the 1920s. These denominations and nondenominational churches have much higher educational attainment than Baptists or Pentecostals. Nondenominational churches also differ from other evangelical churches in that they are more common in the West. These demographic differences are not necessarily the reason churches organize together, but it does support our claim that these groups have organized themselves into groups that differ from one another.

There are religious differences as well. Table 7.2 shows that while the vast majority of Baptists, Pentecostals, and nondenominational Christians self-identify as a "born-again" or "evangelical" Christian, this identification is lower among other sectarian denominations. This identity is particularly low among conservative Lutheran, Presbyterian, and Reformed denominations, which is consistent with the decision by Darren E. Sherkat (2014) to not place them with other evangelicals. On beliefs, the pattern is more complex. Across the board, Pentecostals are the most conservative in their religious beliefs. Baptists are more likely than sectarian or nondenominational Christians to see the Bible as the literal word of God, but on other beliefs nondenominational

TABLE 7.2   RELIGIOUS IDENTITY AND BELIEFS OF EVANGELICAL SUBTRADITIONS

	Baptists (%)	Pentecostals (%)	Sectarian (%)	Nondenomi- national (%)	All evangelicals (%)
Identify as born-again or evangelical	82	86	63	95	60
Bible is literal word of God	63	72	51	56	60
Other religions cannot lead to eternal life	66	71	57	69	66
Believe in Hell	91	93	82	88	89
No human evolution	60	65	54	63	60
N (weighted)	3,112	1,441	1,664	2,147	8,364

Source: Pew Research Center 2014.

TABLE 7.3   RELIGIOUS IDENTITY AND BELIEFS OF EVANGELICAL
SUBTRADITIONS

	Baptists (%)	Pentecostals (%)	Sectarian (%)	Nondenomi- national (%)	All evangelicals (%)
Attend worship weekly	54	66	57	61	58
Read scripture weekly	61	71	56	66	63
Share faith with others weekly	34	46	29	36	36
Speak in tongues weekly	6	25	7	14	11
Religion very important in life	79	84	74	81	79
N (weighted)	3,112	1,441	1,664	2,147	8,364

Source: Pew Research Center 2014.

Christians are similar to Baptists. Sectarian denominations are less religiously conservative, but these differences are not substantial.

Table 7.3 shows that religious identity differences extend to behavior. Pentecostals are consistently the most religiously active of the four groups. They report attending church, praying, sharing their faith with others, and reading the Bible more than other groups. Nondenominational Christians are also highly involved in these behaviors. All of the groups, however, report relatively high levels of religious commitment, including eight in ten reporting that religion is "very important" in their lives. Pentecostals are distinctive in the relatively high percentage who report "speaking in tongues" on a weekly basis. Nondenominational Christians, however, are also much more likely to speak in tongues than Baptists and those in other sectarian denominations.

Political Differences

What are the political differences between these evangelical subtraditions? While we do not believe that politics is the reason these subtraditions exist, we do expect there to be significant differences between the groups. Some of this will, of course, be due to differences in demographics. But there should also be differences that are linked to differences in theology, elite messages, and values (see Table 7.4).

Each group is majority Republican and conservative, with Baptists slightly more so than the others. They are also conservative on abortion policy, same-sex marriage, size of government, and views on immigration. However, there appear to be differences. Sectarian and nondenominational Christians are less conservative on social issues, particularly same-sex marriage. Nondenominational Christians, however, want a smaller government

TABLE 7.4   POLITICAL IDENTITIES AND BELIEFS OF EVANGELICAL
SUBTRADITIONS

	Baptists (%)	Pentecostals (%)	Sectarian (%)	Nondenomi- national (%)	All evangelicals (%)
Republican	61	49	53	56	56
Conservative	59	51	51	53	55
Oppose abortion in all/most cases	67	71	60	67	67
Against same-sex marriage	73	77	64	67	70
Immigration is change for worse	57	45	46	40	49
Prefer smaller government	70	58	67	72	68
N (weighted)	3,112	1,441	1,664	2,147	8,364

Source: Pew Research Center 2014.

that provides fewer services. Pentecostals are more populist: they are the most conservative on social issues, but they are the least supportive of a smaller government. Baptists hold the most consistently conservative positions. They are the most Republican, most conservative on social issues, and most supportive of smaller government. Baptists also stand out as the most anti-immigrant. When asked about the growing number of immigrants over the past fifty years, a majority of Baptists said it was "a change for the worse." While each group is more conservative than other religious groups in the U.S. population, there are political cracks between the subtraditions.

Of course, these political differences may reflect other differences. The groups come from different regions and differ in their racial and ethnic compositions. To help assess whether these differences stem from demographic composition or religious distinctiveness, we estimate models for four political attitudes. In addition to subtradition, the model includes party identification,[1] educational attainment,[2] region,[3] race/ethnicity,[4] and gender. For each model we present the predicted probabilities for the four subtraditions in Table 7.5. The predicted probabilities show the relative level of support on each issue, holding all other values at the same level. Thus, they do not show the typical person for the group, but they do allow us to show how the effect of being in each subtradition results in different political attitudes.

We find that while these groups are similar to each other, there are statistically significant differences across the evangelical subtraditions. These differences exist despite controlling for other variables, including partisanship, ideology, church attendance, and race. These differences do not fall along a consistent, ideological line with a single group always more moderate

TABLE 7.5   RELATIVE LEVELS OF POLITICAL ATTITUDES (CONTROLLING
FOR OTHER VARIABLES)

	Baptists	Pentecostals	Sectarian
Oppose abortion in all/most cases	0.76	0.82	0.74
	(0.72:0.78)	(0.79:0.84)	(0.71:0.76)
Against same-sex marriage	0.71	0.73	0.66
	(0.69:0.72)	(0.70:0.76)	(0.63:0.69)
Immigration is change for worse	0.53	0.48	0.49
	(0.51:0.55)	(0.45:0.51)	(0.46:0.52)
Prefer smaller government	0.73	0.70	0.74
	(0.71:0.75)	(0.67:0.73)	(0.72:0.76)

Source: Pew Research Center 2014.
Note: Predicted probabilities; 95 percent confidence intervals are in parentheses. Predicted probabilities
    estimated using CLARIFY. Estimates vary by subtradition while setting all other values at their mean for
    all evangelicals.

(or conservative) than the others. A group that is more conservative on one
issue may be more moderate on others. The result is a complex and intriguing picture of evangelical politics.

Pentecostals differ on two issues. They are more opposed to abortion
than the other three groups. They are also significantly less in favor of a
smaller government. On same-sex marriage and immigration, Pentecostals
hold similar attitudes as other denominations. For Pentecostals, economic
conservatism does not align neatly with social conservatism, at least not as
neatly as it does for some other evangelicals.

The other three groups each have one issue that differentiates them from
the others. Baptists are, all else being equal, similar to other evangelical
groups on abortion, same-sex marriage, and the size of government. On
these issues, the differences seen in Table 7.4 are largely due to their different
demographics and identities. But there is one issue on which Baptists stand
out from other evangelicals: immigration. Even after accounting for race,
ethnicity, partisanship, and ideology, Baptists are significantly more likely
to view the growth of immigration over the past fifty years as a turn for the
worse. Evangelicals in other sectarian denominations are likewise distinctive on one issue. Compared to other evangelicals, they are more supportive
of same-sex marriage. This is a relative—yet statistically significant—difference. Finally, nondenominational Christians are more positive about immigration. They are significantly less likely to see growing immigration as
negative.

The 2016 Election

Are the subtraditions within evangelicalism politically meaningful? We
show that there are real demographic, religious, and political differences

between the four subtraditions. However, in electoral politics these differences may pale in comparison to the similarities that unite them. Not every crack is a cleavage.

The 2016 election provides a unique opportunity to test for the differences between the four subtraditions. During the primary, several prominent evangelical voices spoke out against the nomination of Donald Trump. The "Never Trump" camp included Russell Moore, Albert Mohler, David French, Deborah Fikes, and others who would normally support a Republican candidacy. Pastor and best-selling author Max Lucado took a rare step into politics to decry Trump as too indecent to be president. Pastors from large nondenominational churches who have quietly supported Republicans in the past were absent from the campaign. Trump had his evangelical supporters, but they were notably more fundamentalist Baptists (e.g., Jerry Falwell Jr., Franklin Graham, and Robert Jeffress) and Pentecostals (e.g., Kenneth and Gloria Copeland, Jan Crouch, and Jentezen Franklin). Evangelicalism as a whole appeared to have a divide in leadership. But recognizing that there are subtraditions, we suspect that these leaders may reflect (or even lead) subtraditions in interesting ways.

Ideally, we would have used another large survey of voters and tested the effect of their evangelical subtradition on their vote. Unfortunately, such a data set was not available at the time of this study. Instead, we use the 2014 Pew Religious Landscape Study to determine the religious composition of each state. We use the percentage in each subtradition as a test for whether its presence in a state was electorally effective.[5] To be clear, analysis of state-level results cannot determine individual differences, but it can provide evidence for how election results change in states where certain religious groups are more prevalent.

Table 7.6 shows the relationship between Trump's vote and each religious group's share of the state's population. As expected, there is a positive relationship between the vote and evangelicalism. The highest correlation is the evangelical tradition as a whole. Among the four subtraditions, the percentage of Baptists is the most strongly related to the vote. This is consistent with the individual-level evidence from the Pew study—without any controls, Baptists are more closely aligned with conservative politics.

The table shows the relationship controlling for race (percentage white/not Latino), unemployment rate, and educational attainment (percentage with at least a bachelor's degree).[6] Controlling for education, unemployment, and race, the relationship between the vote and evangelicalism is reduced but still positive. The relationship is stronger for the evangelical tradition and Pentecostals than for Baptists and sectarians. Still, the correlations are statistically significant. The exception is nondenominational evangelicals. There is no longer a statistical relationship between the percentage nondenominational and the vote when we control for race and educational

TABLE 7.6   EFFECT OF EVANGELICALS ON STATE VOTE FOR TRUMP

	Correlation with Trump vote	Partial correlation controlling for race and college attainment	Partial correlation controlling for race, college attainment, and Romney vote
Percentage evangelical	0.67*	0.37*	< 0.01
Percentage Baptist	0.56*	0.26*	< 0.01
Percentage Pentecostal	0.47*	0.39*	< 0.01
Percentage sectarian	0.48*	0.20*	0.05
Percentage non-denominational	0.43*	0.12	−0.11*

Sources: Pew Research Center 2014; Federal Election Commission 2013.

Note: Coefficients show correlation between a state's vote percentage for Donald Trump and the percentage of adult population in each religious group, using the religious composition of each state in the Pew Research Center (2014) data. Partial correlation coefficients are relationships controlling for percentage of the population that is white/not Latino, percentage of adults with at least a bachelor's degree, and percentage of the vote received by Mitt Romney in 2012. Data include District of Columbia. Utah was excluded because it was an outlier due to the high support for independent candidate Evan McMullen.

* $p < .05$.

attainment. These results demonstrate the strength of the relationship between evangelicalism and the election outcome.

The final set of correlations adds the state's vote for Mitt Romney as an additional control. Despite popular perceptions that the 2016 election results were unusual, the 2012 and 2016 election results were highly correlated. Taking into account the Romney vote, Trump still did worse the greater a state's educational attainment and the higher the unemployment rate. Evangelicals, however, had no effect on the state election outcome above and beyond what would be expected based on past voting results. There is one important exception: nondenominational evangelicals. States with more nondenominational evangelicals were less supportive of Trump. What does this mean? By controlling for the 2012 vote result, we are taking into account the long-term voting pattern of the state. There is a relationship between evangelical presence in states and support for the GOP, but there was no change in this relationship in 2016. Nondenominational evangelicals, however, may have deviated from their historical pattern. States with more nondenominational evangelicals were less supportive of Trump than they were of Romney.

Together, these results suggest that there may have been significant cracks between subtraditions of evangelicals. Trump did better in states with more Baptists, but this may have been due to race and educational differences. Pentecostalism has the strongest relationship with Republican voting once other factors are taken into account. The real story may be nondenominational evangelicals. States with more nondenominational evangelicals gave Trump less support than they gave Romney four years earlier. This could be due to nondenominational evangelicals being more prominent in states that would otherwise have opposed Trump, but it could also mean a widening political crack within evangelicalism.

Implications and Discussion

We began by taking a new approach to studying evangelicals and other religious groups. We view people as part of local religious networks that are located in congregations. These congregations are often part of denominations and associations. There are then ecumenical organizations that form ties between churches and denominations. By taking seriously how religious groups self-organize, we create a new way of classifying people into religious categories.

Evangelicals are notoriously disorganized, but there are organizations that represent relationships between churches. Using these organizations, we identify four subtraditions within evangelicalism based solely on the current organizational ties of different denominations. Our analysis supports this classification because it finds demographic, religious, and political differences between these four subtraditions. Even when controlling for other variables—including partisanship, ideology, religious belief, and church attendance—there were statistically significant differences on political attitudes.

What should we make of these differences? Our interpretation is that evangelicals remain a conservative religious tradition, but within it there are some political issues that are likely to cause groups to look a bit askew at others. Each subtradition is mostly made up of those who identify as Republican and as conservative. On political issues, their members are more likely than not to take the more conservative position. Most important, there does not appear to be one group that stands out as consistently different in every aspect of its politics. And on three of the four issues we examine, only one group stands out from the others. Views of immigration are the most divisive, with Baptists most negative toward immigration and nondenominational evangelicals most positive.

We suspect (but cannot prove yet) that these differences explain some of the disagreement and debate among evangelicals during the 2016 presidential election. The prominent evangelical leaders who supported Donald Trump were often fundamentalist Baptists and Pentecostals. Trump's message on immigration would be particularly appealing to Baptists. Pentecostals would also appreciate his economic populism. But for nondenominational evangelicals, Trump was promoting a vision that was too populist on economics and too anti-immigrant. These differences were unlikely to be great enough for a split among evangelicals, but it would explain why we saw far more Baptists and Pentecostals publicly backing Trump.

Future researchers should consider taking these differences into account when conducting their research. It is not simply that Baptists do not join into ecumenical groups with Pentecostals; they also do not attend church at the same rate, have quite the same political opinions, or have the same religious beliefs as Pentecostals. Lumping all these groups together is sometimes necessary because of data limitations. But it is our hope that this categorization scheme becomes another tool in the toolbox of scholars of religion. Our belief is that this scheme has the potential to give us new insights into the ways in which religion influences politics.

NOTES

1. Party identification is a seven-point ordinal measure (1 = strong Democrat, 2 = weak Democrat, 3 = independent-leaning Democrat, 4 = independent, 5 = independent-leaning Republican, 6 = weak Republican, and 7 = strong Republican).

2. Educational attainment is an eight-point ordinal measure: 1 = less than high school (grades 1–8 or no formal schooling); 2 = high school incomplete (grades 9–11 or grade 12 with no diploma); 3 = high school graduate (grade 12 with diploma or GED certificate); 4 = some college, no degree (includes some community college); 5 = two-year associate degree from a college or university; 6 = four-year college or university degree/bachelor's degree (e.g., B.S., B.A., A.B.); 7 = some postgraduate or professional schooling, no postgraduate degree (e.g., some graduate school); and 8 = postgraduate or professional degree, including master's, doctorate, medical, or law degree (e.g., M.A., M.S., Ph.D., M.D., J.D., graduate school).

3. Four regions based on state of residence: South, Midwest, Northeast, and West.

4. Categories are white non-Hispanic/Latino, black non-Hispanic/Latino, Hispanic/Latino, and other.

5. We recognize the danger of the ecological fallacy. We emphasize that this is not a test for why individuals voted for Trump. We can test only whether having a greater proportion of evangelicals leads to a higher vote for Trump.

6. While we did not include it in the table, we also ran correlations between our religious subtraditions and the control variables. Evangelicalism is negatively correlated with educational attainment (–0.66). The correlation is higher for Baptists (–0.58) and Pentecostals (–0.54) than for sectarians (–0.37) and nondenominational evangelicals (–0.45). This reflects the demographic data we present in Table 7.1.

REFERENCES

Bean, Lydia. 2014. *The Politics of Evangelical Identity: Local Churches and Partisan Divides in the United States and Canada*. Princeton, NJ: Princeton University Press.

Bebbington, David. 1989. *Evangelicalism in Modern Britain: A History from the 1730s to the 1980s*. Grand Rapids, MI: Baker Book House.

Enten, Harry. 2015. "The GOP Establishment May Need Religious Voters to Stop Donald Trump." *FiveThirtyEight*, December 7. Available at https://fivethirtyeight.com/features/the-gop-establishment-may-need-religious-voters-to-stop-donald-trump/.

Federal Election Commission. 2013. "Federal Elections, 2012: Election Results for the U.S. President, the U.S. Senate, and the U.S. House of Representatives." Available at https://transition.fec.gov/pubrec/fe2012/federalelections2012.shtml.

Glock, Charles Y., and R. Rodney Stark. 1965. "The New Denominationalism." In *Religion and Society in Tension*, 86–122. New York: Rand McNally.

Manza, Jeff, and Clem Brooks. 1997. "The Religious Factor in U.S. Presidential Elections, 1960–1992." *American Journal of Sociology* 103:38–81.

Mead, Frank S., Samuel S. Hill, and Craig D. Atwood. 2010. *Handbook of Denominations in the United States*. 13th ed. Nashville, TN: Abingdon Press.

Pew Research Center. 2014. "How Americans Feel about Religious Groups." Available at http://www.pewforum.org/files/2014/07/Views-of-Religious-Groups-07-27-full-PDF-for -web.pdf.

Sherkat, Darren E. 2014. *Changing Faith: The Dynamics and Consequences of Americans' Shifting Religious Identities*. New York: New York University Press.

Smith, Tom W. 1990. "Classifying Protestant Denominations." *Review of Religious Research* 31:225–245.

Southern Baptist Convention. 1996. "Resolution on Southern Baptists and Ecumenism." Available at http://www.sbc.net/resolutions/459/resolution-on-southern-baptists-and -ecumenism.

Steensland, Brian, Jerry Z. Park, Mark D. Regnerus, Lynn D. Robinson, W. Bradford Wilcox, and Robert D. Woodberry. 2000. "The Measure of American Religion: Toward Improving the State of the Art." *Social Forces* 79 (1): 291–318.

Stetzer, Ed, and Ryan P. Burge. 2016. "Reltrad Coding Problems and a New Repository." *Politics and Religion* 9 (1): 187–190.

Woodberry, Robert D., Jerry Z. Park, Lyman A. Kellstedt, Mark D. Regnerus, and Brian Steensland. 2012. "The Measure of American Religious Traditions: Theoretical and Measurement Considerations." *Social Forces* 91 (1): 65–73.

8

Subcultural Identity and the Evangelical Left

Comparing Liberal Young Evangelicals
to Other Young Liberals

JEREMIAH J. CASTLE

Any analysis of a potential "crackup" among evangelicals has to consider the case of young evangelicals. Over the past three presidential election cycles, a number of popular and journalistic accounts have suggested that young evangelicals are becoming more liberal on a variety of issues and may be moving away from the GOP (e.g., FitzGerald 2008; Harris 2008; Jones 2013; Kirkpatrick 2007; Krattenmaker 2013; Mendenhall 2006; T. Williams 2016; cf. Carroll 2002; Carter 2012). Academic researchers are just beginning to study these journalistic accounts in greater depth. While scholars have found evidence that young evangelicals are liberalizing on some issues, such as gay marriage and premarital sex (Farrell 2011; Putnam and Campbell 2010), academics have generally failed to find evidence of consistent, large-scale liberalization among young evangelicals (Castle 2015; Pelz and Smidt 2015; Smith and Johnson 2010).

While liberal young evangelicals are more rare than some accounts in the media would lead us to believe, it is nevertheless important to gain a better understanding of the sources and consequences of their political attitudes. How does their faith influence their attitudes? Are they different from other young liberals, and if so, how? Studying these questions may yield important insights into the nature of evangelicalism itself.

In this chapter, I draw on research characterizing the evangelical tradition as a subculture to develop a framework for understanding the political attitudes of liberal young evangelicals. When I label evangelicalism a subculture, I mean that the tradition is *engaged* in the larger culture, but it has *beliefs and values that are in tension with those of the larger culture* (e.g., C. Smith 1998). This evangelical subculture is united by a variety of commonly held beliefs, including the literal truth of the Bible, an emphasis on evangelism, and a strong commitment to cultural conservatism. I develop the idea that, nested within this broad evangelical subculture, there is a narrower liberal evangelical subculture, which, I argue, remains bound by many of the norms of the larger evangelical subculture.

If my argument is right, we would expect to find important differences between liberal young evangelicals and liberal young people from other traditions. I test for three such differences. First, I hypothesize that liberal, committed evangelicals tend to be more conservative than their non-evangelical counterparts on cultural issues such as abortion and LGBT (lesbian, gay, bisexual, transgender) rights. Second, I argue that liberal, committed evangelicals tend to emphasize noncultural issues on which the evangelical tradition's public image is not as clearly defined. Emphasizing noncultural issues provides a means of reducing the tension between seemingly conflicting social identities. I show that committed, liberal young evangelicals tend to downplay the salience of cultural issues like abortion and instead focus on issues that do not conflict with the public image of evangelicalism, such as the environment and government help for the poor. Finally, I predict that liberal young evangelicals will be more likely than other young liberals to vote Republican. Thus, this chapter suggests that even the small subculture of highly committed, liberal young evangelicals is bound in some ways by the norms of the evangelical subculture. This suggests that the mere existence of liberal evangelicals is not enough to signal an evangelical crackup, as the evangelical subculture continues to exert a considerable impact on the political behavior of its members.

Theorizing Liberal Evangelicals

Before we can understand liberal evangelicals, we must have some theoretical framework for understanding evangelicalism itself. First and foremost, scholars have defined evangelicalism as a religious tradition that unites a set of denominations with historical and theological ties (e.g., Leege and Kellstedt 1993; Smidt, Kellstedt, and Guth 2009). In an attempt to explain the distinctiveness of evangelicals, some scholars characterize evangelicalism as a subculture that is engaged with mainstream culture but also holds unique values that contrast with the norms of mainstream culture (Oldfield 1996; Smith 1998). Duane M. Oldfield (1996) lists among those values biblical literalism, a unique vision for the family, and a conservative approach to sexual behavior. Although not writing within the framework of this subcultural theory, Corwin E. Smidt (2007) adds theological exclusivism, a born-again experience, and an emphasis on evangelism. This theoretical perspective has two advantages over the more traditional "three Bs" perspective on religion. First, subcultural theory provides a unified picture of religion that encompasses beliefs, behaving, belonging, and identity. Second, subcultural theory provides a useful lens for explaining a number of differences in the behavior of evangelicals. For example, Christian Smith (1998) argues that evangelicalism's status as a subculture helps explain its success in retaining members as other denominations shrink. Elsewhere, I argue that subcultural theory can help us understand public opinion among evangelicals (Castle 2015).

The basis for believing that the evangelical subculture might constrain the political attitudes of adherents is rooted in public opinion theory. Researchers understand that public opinion as expressed in political surveys is the result of individual respondents sampling from the available considerations on a given issue (Zaller 1992). The evangelical subculture and the values that it promotes should help insulate evangelicals from trends in public opinion by both introducing new considerations consistent with the norms of the tradition and undermining some secular considerations that go against the core values of the faith. However, the subculture's effects should be strongest among those who are more engaged in the subculture and on issues that are more closely related to the core values of the evangelical tradition (Castle 2015).

This subcultural theory of evangelicalism can help us understand several aspects of the political behavior of liberal young evangelicals. First, it can help explain the (lack of) prevalence of liberal evangelicals. Political scientists have repeatedly found that social-group identity is an important aspect of the formation of partisan and ideological identification (Campbell et al. 1960; Green, Palmquist, and Schickler 2002). As modernism and cultural liberalism became more prominent forces in American culture throughout the twentieth century, the parties became more divided along cultural lines (Hunter 1991; Layman 2001; Leege et al. 2002). Since the rise of the Christian Right in the 1970s and 1980s, the evangelical subculture has become inextricably linked with conservatism and the Republican Party (Adkins et al. 2013; Campbell, Green, and Layman 2011; Castle et al. 2016; McDermott 2009; D. Williams 2010). Given the importance of social-group identity to American politics broadly, and the importance of conservative identity to evangelicalism, it is no surprise that liberal evangelicals remain uncommon.

A second major change that affects patterns of ideology among evangelicals is the increasing importance of religious commitment. At one time in American history, the two major political parties were divided primarily along the lines of religious tradition (Berelson, Lazarsfeld, and McPhee 1954; Green 2010; Kleppner 1970). However, the wave of modernism and cultural liberalism mentioned previously also caused the religious cleavage to shift. Between the 1970s and the 1990s, the Republican Party increasingly became the party of the religiously committed from a variety of traditions, and the Democratic Party increasingly became the party of seculars and the less religiously committed (Hunter 1991; Layman 2001; Wuthnow 1988). Given this increasing association between religious commitment and ideology, my subcultural theory suggests that liberal evangelicals should be concentrated among evangelicals with lower levels of religious commitment.

Nevertheless, in recent years American politics has seen a revival of sorts among politically liberal evangelicals. Perhaps the most visible face of this movement has been Jim Wallis, the founder of the evangelical group Sojourners. Wallis, Tony Campolo, Ronald Sider, and others have written numerous books that present a considerably more liberal viewpoint than that of the New Christian Right. The next generation of these liberal evangelicals, including best-selling author Shane Claiborne, has likewise garnered mainstream attention for breaking political stereotypes of evangelicals. How does the prevalence of these liberal evangelical elites and groups fit into my subcultural account of evangelicalism?

I argue that this liberal movement is itself a subculture, nested within the broader evangelical subculture (hereafter, where possible, I refer to the "evangelical tradition" instead of the "evangelical subculture" to reduce confusion). Understanding liberal evangelicals as a subculture is useful for a variety of reasons. On the one hand, it highlights that these liberal evangelicals are distinctive from their conservative counterparts. Liberal evangelicals have a somewhat different set of theological influences (including many of the authors discussed previously). Their religious, political, and social beliefs also may be different from those of their more conservative counterparts in a variety of ways. At the same time, though, the "subculture" label highlights the fact that liberal evangelicals are bound by many of the same core theological, social, and political commitments as the larger evangelical tradition. The differences, while important, are largely variations in emphasis. For example, evangelicals of all stripes likely agree on the importance of the Bible, but liberal evangelicals are probably more likely than their more conservative cousins to emphasize Jesus Christ's teachings on social justice and stewardship. In short, the notion of a liberal evangelical subculture captures both the shared commitment to certain core values and the distinctive aspects of how their faith affects their political beliefs.

This characterization of a liberal evangelical subculture can generate predictions of where we might find evidence of continued distinctiveness among liberal evangelicals and other liberals. In particular, we would expect that evangelicalism might constrain the liberal evangelical subculture the most on cultural issues like abortion, same-sex marriage, and stem-cell research, which have been central to evangelical identity (Hunter 1991; Layman 2001; Martin 2005). For these reasons, we would expect that even liberal evangelicals should remain more conservative on cultural issues than liberals from other faiths.

The evangelical tradition has put much less emphasis on noncultural issues. My subcultural theory suggests that the evangelical tradition allows, and may even reward, liberalization on noncultural issues (Castle 2015). If evangelicalism was distinctive on every political issue, the costs of membership might become too high and/or evangelicals' ability to mobilize in the presence of embattlement might suffer. In addition, if it were to emphasize distinctiveness on every issue, the broad subculture might risk becoming too "countercultural" and losing some of its ability to stay engaged in society. Thus, a more successful strategy for evangelicalism may be allowing liberalization on noncultural issues.

In particular, the literature suggests that economic attitudes may be one area in which liberal evangelicals are less distinctive from other liberals. While some scholars have suggested that the "Protestant ethic" predisposes evangelicals to conservative economic attitudes (Barker and Carman 2000; Guth et al. 2006; Hargrove 1989; Jelen, Smidt, and Wilcox 1993; Johnstone 1988; Weber 1930), other scholars have found that evangelicals may support antipoverty efforts, especially when directed toward the "deserving poor" or hosted by local congregations (Pyle 1993; Will and Cochran 1995; Wilson 1999; Wuthnow 1994). This ambiguity in evangelical attitudes toward social-welfare programs led one recent reviewer of the literature to conclude that religious influence on economic attitudes is "contested and complicated" (Wilson 2009, 195), suggesting at least the potential for liberal attitudes to be present within the liberal evangelical subculture.

Likewise, attitudes toward the environment may be an area primed for liberalization. Traditionally, scholarship has suggested that important evangelical theological commitments, including biblical literalism and premillennialism (a belief that the world will be ruled by an Antichrist until Christ comes to summon the faithful in the Rapture), predispose evangelicals to environmental conservatism (Guth et al. 1995; Wilcox and Robinson 2010). However, evangelical leaders, including the late Billy Graham and Rick Warren, have spoken in favor of preserving the environment, and a recent analysis of evangelical periodicals suggests that opinions on the issue among elites are becoming increasingly diverse (Danielsen 2013). The ambiguity of the views of evangelical elites on the environment should lead us to expect that this is another area in which liberal evangelicals might not be as distinctive from other liberals.

Finally, subcultural theory can help us understand issue salience among liberal evangelicals. Given the fact that evangelicalism and political liberalism are not currently a dominant pairing in American politics, liberal evangelicals may be more likely to experience cognitive dissonance as a result of belonging to seemingly contradictory social groups. Cognitive dissonance is the psychological tension individuals feel as a result of holding a set of seemingly conflicting beliefs or attitudes at the same time (Festinger 1957; *Merriam-Webster* 2016). According to cognitive-dissonance theory, when individuals feel inconsistency between multiple identities, they will experience motivation to resolve that tension to increase their level of psychological comfort (Festinger 1957). We would expect the drive to resolve dissonance to be particularly strong in the context of modern American politics, where various social groups play a powerful role in forming attitudes toward the parties and policies (e.g., Campbell et al. 1960; Green, Palmquist, and Schickler 2002; Kinder and Kam 2009). Thus, cognitive-dissonance theory predicts that we should see evidence of liberal evangelicals taking a variety of steps to relieve the dissonance or tension between their identity as liberals and their identity as evangelicals.

One such step toward relieving cognitive dissonance described by Leon Festinger (1957) is attempting to reduce the salience of issues associated with cognitive dissonance. One strategy that evangelicals might use to accomplish this goal is downplaying those issues in which the values of political liberalism and evangelicalism seem most at odds. Abortion and same-sex marriage are two such issues. Therefore, theory suggests that liberal young evangelicals should tend to deemphasize "culture-wars" issues and instead focus their political attention on noncultural issues like the environment or income inequality, where the dissonance between evangelicalism and political liberalism is less strong.

Liberal, Committed Evangelicals in Perspective

Just how widespread are liberal evangelicals? And just how large a role does religious commitment play in the ideology of young evangelicals? Answering these questions is key to understanding just how widespread the liberal evangelical subculture is. Therefore, I turn to weighted data from the 2012 Cooperative Congressional Election Survey (CCES), a national Internet-based sample (Ansolabehere and Schaffner 2013). Research comparing previous CCES studies to other national samples shows that the CCES is a reasonably close approximation of the American electorate, although perhaps slightly more politically knowledgeable (Ansolabehere 2006, 2010; Rivers 2006; Vavreck and Rivers 2008). The 2012 CCES data are ideal because they contain most of the relevant religious and political variables and have a sample size of more than fifty-four thousand, making the sample large enough to facilitate very precise comparisons across religious traditions and age categories. In both the CCES data and the Pew Religious Landscape Study data I use later, evangelicals are measured by a set of denomination codes that were collapsed into the now-standard religious-tradition scheme (e.g., Layman 2001; Layman and Green 2005; Steensland et al. 2000).

To facilitate an easy comparison, I divided evangelicals into two categories based on their frequency of church attendance: those who attend services once or twice a month or more and those who attend a few times a year or fewer. Figure 8.1 shows the relationship between ideology and frequency of church attendance among evangelicals between the ages of eighteen and twenty-nine. The data show that just 16 percent of evangelicals in this age group identify as liberal, while a whopping 55 percent of them identify as conservative (this difference is statistically significant at $p < .05$). Consistent with my theoretical expectations, liberal evangelicals are even more rare among those who attend church monthly or more often: 9 percent of monthly attendees identify as liberal; 19.5 percent of young evangelicals who attend a few times a year or fewer (this difference is statistically significant at $p < .05$) identify as liberal. The 9 percent figure is also notable when contrasted with the 65 percent of the group who identify as conservative. Thus, the data suggest that, in the aggregate, liberal evangelicals are both relatively rare and disproportionately concentrated among the less committed. While it is im-

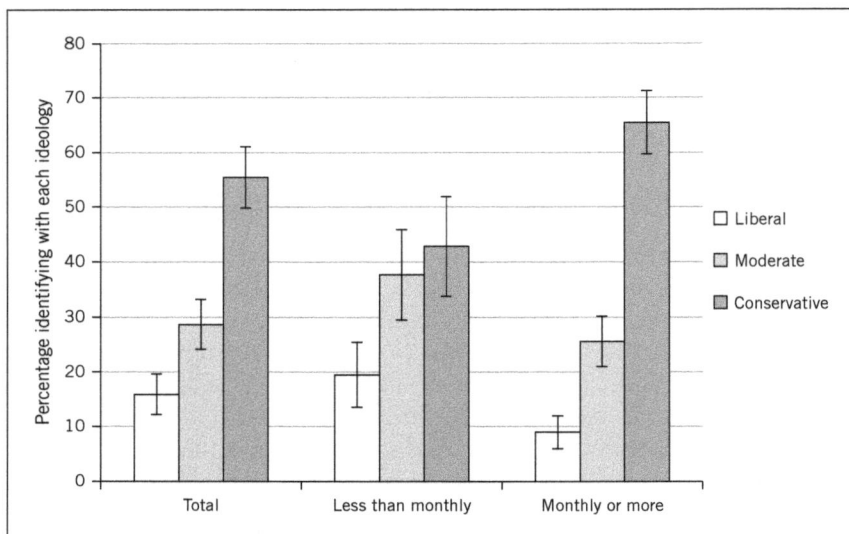

Figure 8.1 Relationship between church attendance and ideology among 18- to 29-year-old evangelicals
Source: Weighted 2012 CCES data (see Ansolabehere and Schaffner 2013).
Note: Error bars represent an 85 percent confidence interval, meaning that overlapping intervals create a 95 percent test. Uncorrected χ^2: 46.91. Design-based F: 9.19, $p < .001$.

portant to study the liberal, committed young evangelicals, it is also important for readers to recognize that such individuals constitute a very small subset of the total population of young evangelicals.

Issue Attitudes among Liberal, Committed Evangelicals

Studying public opinion among liberal young evangelicals is particularly important for understanding how this group relates to the larger evangelical tradition. By understanding liberal evangelicals as a subculture, we recognize that even liberal young evangelicals are bound by many of the same constraints as the broader evangelical tradition. To test my hypothesis that liberal evangelicals should prove distinctively conservative on cultural issues, I turn to data from both the 2012 CCES and the 2007 Pew Religious Landscape Study because the data are recent, and the large samples make it possible to retain statistical precision when limiting the data to small groups like liberal young evangelicals.[1]

Figure 8.2 shows public opinion on abortion among self-identified liberals who attend church a few times a year or more and are from the four largest Christian religious traditions in the United States: evangelical Protestantism, mainline Protestantism, Catholicism, and black Protestantism. Among those who attend a few times a year or more, the results are striking: While 26 percent of liberal young evangelicals believe that abortion should be illegal in all circumstances, just 2 percent of mainline Protestants, 8 percent of black Protestants, and 12 percent of Catholics are in agreement. The difference is statistically significant ($p < .05$) for black and mainline Protestants. The fact that liberal evangelicals are not statistically different from Catholics can be attributed to the small sample size of liberal evangelicals. The relative difference in the point estimates suggests that with a slightly larger sample we would see a statistically significant effect. Overall, the results on abortion provide some support for my theory: even liberal young evangelicals remain comparatively more conservative on cultural issues.

Another cultural issue that presents an opportunity to test my hypothesis is gay marriage, which has been a defining issue for millennials (e.g., Putnam and Campbell 2010), and even evangelicals have become more liberal on this issue over time (Castle 2015; Pelz and Smidt 2015). How do liberal young evangelicals compare to their peers in other traditions? Respondents were asked whether they would support or oppose a constitutional amendment banning gay marriage. Figure 8.2 shows that among those liberal young evangelicals who attend church a few times a year or more, 32 percent supported banning gay marriage. This is comparable to the figure for black Protestants (41 percent) and well above that for mainline Protestants (8 percent) and Catholics (13 percent). Liberal evangelicals are significantly more conservative on this issue than liberal mainline Protestants and

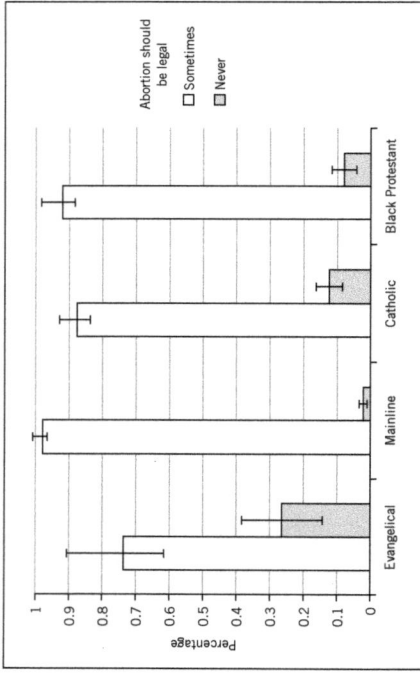

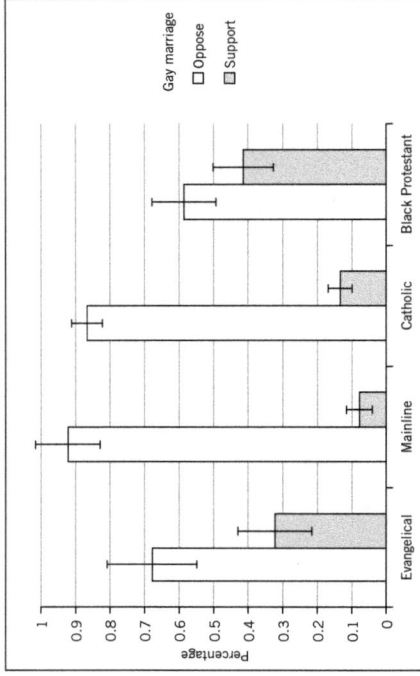

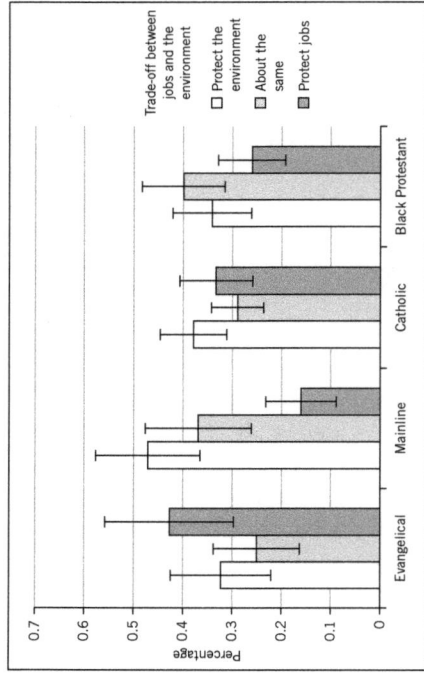

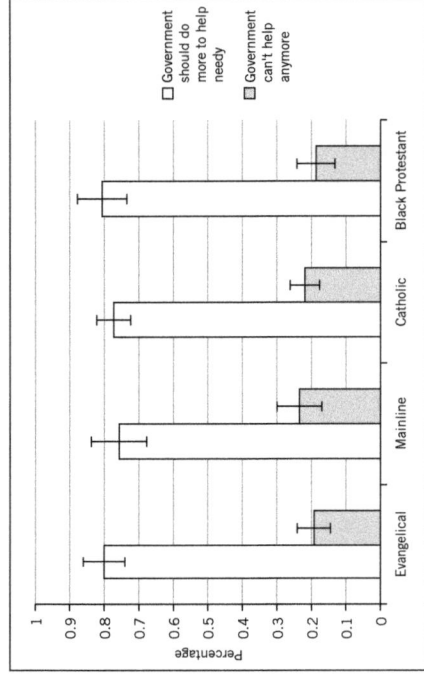

Figure 8.2 Attitudes on issues of abortion, gay marriage, the environment, and welfare among 18- to 29-year-olds attending church a few times a year or more, by religious tradition

Source: Weighted 2012 CCES data (abortion, gay marriage, environment; see Ansolabehere and Schaffner 2013); weighted 2007 Pew Religious Landscape Study (welfare).

Catholics ($p < .05$). Thus, while support for gay marriage among liberal young evangelicals is much higher than anyone might have expected during the peak of the Christian Right, it remains true that they are more conservative on this issue than liberal young people from other faiths.

I predicted that liberal evangelicals may be less distinctive on noncultural issues. Figure 8.2 shows attitudes on the environment among young evangelicals. Specifically, the question asked respondents about the trade-offs between jobs and the environment. The scale has been condensed into three categories (from the original five) to facilitate a clearer comparison. Among liberals who attend church a few times a year or more, the percentage of evangelicals who would prioritize helping the environment even if it costs some jobs (32 percent) was comparable to that of Catholics (38 percent) and black Protestants (34 percent), although all groups still lagged behind mainline Protestants (47 percent). None of these differences were statistically significant. That said, the conservative influence of the larger evangelical tradition was still apparent when looking at who would prioritize jobs over protecting the environment: 43 percent of evangelicals, 16 percent of mainline Protestants, 33 percent of Catholics, and 26 percent of black Protestants said we should protect jobs first (evangelicals were statistically different from mainline Protestants: $p < .05$). Overall, evangelicals seem somewhat less distinctive in regard to attitudes on the environment.

Finally, Figure 8.2 shows social welfare attitudes among the four largest Christian religious groups. Respondents were asked to choose between two statements drawn from the 2007 Pew Religious Landscape Study: "The government should do more to help needy Americans, even if it means going deeper into debt," or "The government today can't afford to do much more to help the needy." Figure 8.2 shows that liberal young evangelicals' attitudes on social welfare are not distinctive from the attitudes of other liberals. Among liberal evangelicals who attend church a few times a year or more, 81 percent say that the government should give more help to the needy. This figure shows that evangelicals are similar to monthly-attending liberals from other large traditions: 76 percent of mainline Protestants, 78 percent of Catholics, and 81 percent of black Protestants. As my theory predicted, liberal young evangelicals are quite similar to other young liberals in their attitudes toward welfare.

Are Liberal Evangelicals Distinctive? A Multivariate Analysis

Do the bivariate findings hold once we control for partisanship and the relevant demographic factors? To answer this question, I set up a series of regression models using the 2007 Pew Religious Landscape Study data. The sample consists of liberals from select faith traditions who attend church once or twice a month or more. The model type was chosen according to the dependent variable: ordered logistic regression for the abortion item and logistic regression for attitudes on homosexuality, welfare, and the environment. Independent variables that I control for include party identification, gender (a dummy variable for females), income, education, age (dummy variables for ages thirty to forty-nine, fifty to sixty-four, and sixty-five-plus, with eighteen to twenty-nine as the comparison category), race/ethnicity (dummy variables for black, Asian, Hispanic, and mixed/other, with white as the comparison category), and region (a dummy variable for those who live in the South). Finally, I include a simple dummy variable for evangelicals (with select non-evangelicals as the comparison category).[2]

The results, available via the online supplementary materials, indicate that even after controlling for a variety of demographic factors, liberal, frequently attending evangelicals remain distinctive from liberal, frequently attending members of other faiths on cultural issues. Focusing first on the model for abortion attitudes, the results show that liberal, committed evangelicals were more conservative than their non-evangelical counterparts ($p < .01$). Since ordered logistic regression coefficients are difficult to interpret, Figure 8.3 shows the effects in terms of the predicted probability of giving a particular response.[3] The predicted probability of responding that abortion should be legal in all cases was .21 for evangelicals and .28 for non-evangelicals. Differences were also apparent at the most conservative end of the abortion spectrum. The probability of responding that abortion should be illegal in all cases for evangelicals was .12 and .09 for non-evangelicals. These results indicate that liberal, committed evangelicals are distinctive from other religiously committed liberals in their attitudes about abortion.

The data suggest that evangelicals are even more unique concerning their attitudes on homosexuality. In the Pew data, the question asks respondents to indicate whether homosexuality should be "accepted" or "discouraged" by society. The data show that liberal, committed evangelicals were less supportive of homosexuality than their non-evangelical counterparts ($p < .001$). To put this effect in context, Figure 8.3 shows that the probability of a liberal, committed evangelical saying that society should discourage homosexuality was .16, compared to .08 for non-evangelicals. Of course, this distinctiveness of liberal evangelicals on cultural issues is consistent with my theoretical expectation that the evangelical tradition's emphasis on cultural conservatism still shapes the attitudes of liberal evangelicals.

The multivariate models also support my hypothesis that religiously committed liberal evangelicals are less distinctive than religiously committed liberals from other traditions on noncultural issues. In terms of their attitudes on social welfare, once demographic and party differences are accounted for, evangelicals are not statistically different from members of any of the other traditions. The predicted probabilities help drive this point

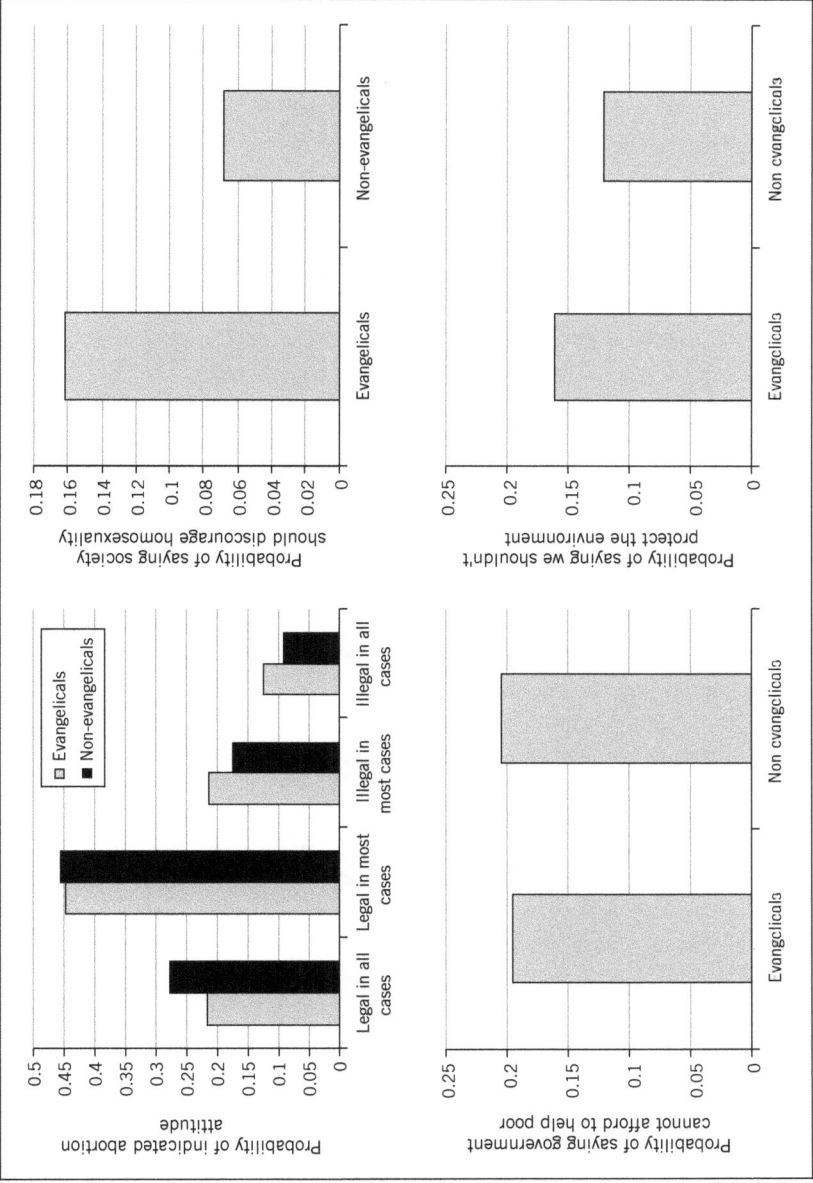

Figure 8.3 Predicted probabilities from regression models

Source: 2007 Pew Religious Landscape Study.

home: the predicted probability of a liberal, committed evangelical declaring that the government cannot afford to help the poor (.19) was nearly identical to the probability for non-evangelicals (.20). Considering attitudes toward the environment, liberal evangelicals are more conservative on the environment than liberal non-evangelicals once other differences are accounted for ($p < .05$). However, the predicted probabilities suggest that the substantive size of the effect is quite small. The predicted probability of a liberal young evangelical declaring that we should not protect the environment at the expense of jobs (.16) was only slightly greater that of non-evangelicals (.12). In short, while liberal evangelicals are still distinctive from other liberals in terms of their attitudes on cultural issues, liberal evangelicals are quite similar to their non-evangelical peers on noncultural issues.

Issue Salience in the Liberal Evangelical Subculture

Another implication flowing from my understanding of liberal evangelicalism as a subculture is that liberal evangelicals may tend to emphasize noncultural issues. To test this hypothesis, I turn to the Public Religion Research Institute's (PRRI) 2012 Millennial Values Survey data, which include a series of measures of issue salience.[4] For each issue, respondents were asked whether they would consider it a "critical issue," "one among many," or "not that important."

Table 8.1 shows the percentage of respondents selecting "critical issue" by ideology for evangelicals and non-evangelicals ages eighteen to twenty-four.[5] While the sample size for liberal evangelicals is much smaller than ideal (a further testament to their rarity), the data nonetheless reveal interesting patterns when comparing liberal evangelicals to other young liberals. On noncultural issues, the two groups are quite similar. Comparable proportions of liberal young evangelicals and liberal young non-evangelicals thought that the environment (50 percent and 46 percent, respectively), the gap between the rich and the poor (53 percent and 57 percent), and national security (26 percent and 25 percent) were important issues. However, on cultural issues, the divisions between the two groups were much larger. While 24 percent of liberal young evangelicals labeled abortion a critical issue, just 16 percent of liberal young non-evangelicals did the same. This finding reinforces my argument that the broader evangelical tradition's emphasis on cultural issues extends to the liberal evangelical subculture. On the issue of gay marriage, the results are even more interesting: while 24 percent of young non-evangelical liberals considered gay marriage a critical issue, among young evangelical liberals the figure was just 14 percent. This disparity is consistent with my argument that the cognitive dissonance that

TABLE 8.1   ISSUE SALIENCE AMONG 18- TO 24-YEAR-OLDS

	Evangelicals			Non-evangelicals		
	Liberal (%)	Moderate (%)	Conservative (%)	Liberal (%)	Moderate (%)	Conservative (%)
Abortion	23.5	34.0	50.3	16.4	14.4	25.7
Gay marriage	14.1	32.6	30.6	23.9	13.8	21.4
Education	55.9	59.0	42.8	64.1	55.7	53.8
Immigration	29.4	32.6	41.0	26.8	30.3	43.0
Federal deficit	52.9	61.8	67.0	48.8	55.5	57.8
Jobs and unemployment	73.5	81.9	66.5	77.8	79.6	74.9
National security	26.5	39.6	41.0	24.9	35.5	44.3
Growing gap between the rich and the poor	52.9	39.6	23.1	56.6	41.4	31.9
Environment	50.0	37.50	16.8	46.1	33.6	28.4
N	34	144	173	523	769	370

Source: Public Religion Research Institute Millennial Values Survey, 2012, available at http://www.thearda
.com/Archive/Files/Descriptions/MILVAL12.asp.
Note: Percentage reflects respondents labeling the issue a "critical issue." Response options for each item
included "critical issue," "one among many," and "not that important."

liberal evangelicals experience leads them to downplay issues like gay marriage.

Liberal Young Evangelicals and the 2012 Presidential Vote

So far in this chapter, I argue that liberal evangelicals are distinctively more conservative than their liberal peers from other traditions on cultural issues but are quite comparable on noncultural issues such as the environment and welfare. I also show that, at least in terms of cultural issues, liberal young evangelicals appear to have different priorities than other young liberals. One final question that warrants investigation is whether liberal evangelicals are distinct from other liberals in terms of their vote choice. On the one hand, we have seen that the liberal evangelical subculture allows for liberal positions on the environment and government-funded social welfare programs, and we have seen that liberal evangelicals have a very different set of issue priorities than their more conservative counterparts. So it is plausible that liberal evangelicals do not behave that differently than other liberals in the voting booth. On the other hand, scholars dating back to Oldfield (1996) have noted the close association between the broader evangelical subculture and political conservatism and the Republican Party. Given that close

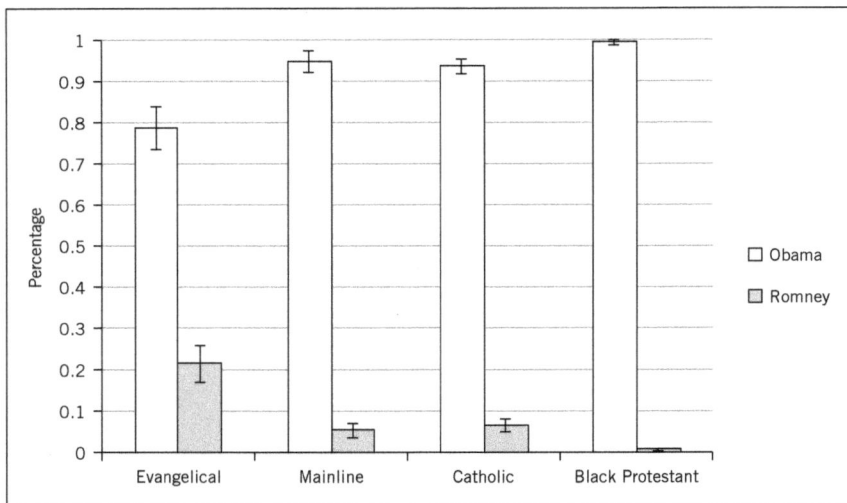

Figure 8.4 Presidential vote among 18- to 29-year-olds attending church a few times a year or more, by religious tradition, 2012
Source: Weighted 2012 CCES data (see Ansolabehere and Schaffner 2013).

association, it would not be surprising that the broader evangelical subculture may constrain even liberal evangelicals.

To answer this question, I again turn to the 2012 CCES data, which asked respondents which candidate for president they voted for in 2012. Here, I use the data for all liberals who attend church a few times a year or more (rather than limit the data to those ages eighteen to twenty-nine). I make this change because even with the CCES's large sample size, when the data are limited to liberal young evangelicals who voted, cell sizes become too small to engage in reliable analysis. The results, shown in Figure 8.4, once again indicate that liberal evangelicals are distinctive from other liberals. About 21 percent of liberal evangelicals who attend church a few times a year or more voted for Mitt Romney. Liberal evangelicals were significantly ($p < .05$ in all cases) more likely to vote for Romney than were mainline Protestants (5 percent), Catholics (6 percent), and black Protestants (nearly 0 percent). The results are particularly striking because Mitt Romney was a less-than-ideal candidate to many evangelicals: he was a Mormon, he was once pro-choice, and he struggled to use the same faith-based language that George W. Bush had on the campaign trail (Bruns 2012). In short, if ever there was a time for liberal evangelicals to stick with the liberal candidate, this may have been it. Nevertheless, about one in five liberal evangelicals who attend church a few times a year or more voted for the Republican Party's candidate. The results provide yet more evidence for my contention that liberal evangelicals remain distinctively more conservative than liberals from other traditions, at least in some areas.

Conclusion

One of the themes of most analyses of evangelical politics over the last four decades has been the increasing connection between membership in the evangelical subculture and political conservatism. This analysis helps us understand the implications of that connection for the 16 percent of young evangelicals who identify as political liberals. Conceptualizing liberal evangelicals as a subculture helps us understand how liberal evangelicalism relates to the larger evangelical tradition. Specifically, I stress the fact that the liberal subculture is still bound by many of the norms and values of the dominant evangelical subculture. This theoretical account helps explain why liberal evangelicals continue to hold relatively conservative attitudes on cultural issues, as well as why liberal evangelicals tend to prioritize noncultural issues.

The findings have numerous implications for the larger discussion of an evangelical crackup. While liberal evangelical elites like Jim Wallis and Shane Claiborne provide an important alternative voice to the Christian Right, the data suggest that their ideas are not leading to an increase in the percentage of evangelicals who identify as liberal. In other work, I show that the percentage of young evangelicals who identify as liberal has not changed significantly over time (Castle 2015). In short, despite the talk of an evangelical crackup, the data indicate that most young evangelicals will continue to identify as conservatives for the foreseeable future. Furthermore, the evidence presented here suggests that even if the proportion of liberal, committed evangelicals begins to grow, such individuals will likely remain comparatively more conservative on cultural issues as a result of the evangelical subculture's continuing influence. The evidence also suggests that liberal young evangelicals will primarily emphasize noncultural issues such as welfare and the environment, leaving the battlefield of the culture wars for their more conservative counterparts. Overall, this analysis suggests that at the mass level, there are few signs of the type of deep crackup that would undermine the evangelical tradition's political influence. Instead, if anything, the diversity of opinion on noncultural issues that is allowed by the evangelical subculture might actually help the evangelical tradition endure in today's polarized political era.

NOTES

1. An interactive tool with data from the Pew Religious Landscape Study is available at http://www.pewforum.org/religious-landscape-study. For a report on the 2007 survey, see Pew Forum on Religion and Public Life 2008.

2. Only evangelical Protestants, mainline Protestants, black Protestants, Catholics, Jews, and the unaffiliated are included in this model. The sample size for other faiths was too small to engage in reliable analysis.

3. For all of the probabilities discussed, respondents were assumed to be age eighteen to twenty-nine, female, non-southern, and white non-Hispanic (other variables were held at their means). Probabilities were calculated in Stata using prvalue (Long and Freese 2006).

4. The survey is available at http://www.thearda.com/Archive/Files/Descriptions/MILVAL12.asp.

5. Unfortunately, the PRRI data did not include the full battery of religious-tradition variables. Rather, it used a truncated set of labels that did not distinguish between Protestant traditions. Therefore, for this data set I define "evangelicals" as "Protestants" or "Just Christians" who (1) were not African American and (2) described themselves as born-again Christians. I continue to use the label "evangelicals" to maintain the continuity of my narrative, but readers should be aware that when using the PRRI data, the measure was not achieved through the traditional religious-tradition battery.

REFERENCES

Adkins, Todd, Geoffrey C. Layman, David E. Campbell, and John C. Green. 2013. "Religious Group Cues and Citizen Policy Attitudes in the United States." *Politics and Religion* 6 (2): 235–264.

Ansolabehere, Stephen. 2006. "Cooperative Congressional Election Study Common Content, 2006." Available at https://dataverse.harvard.edu/dataset.xhtml?persistentId=hdl:1902.1/14002.

———. 2010. "Guide to the 2006 Cooperative Congressional Election Study." Available at https://dataverse.harvard.edu/file.xhtml?fileId=2139077&version=RELEASED&version=.0.

Ansolabehere, Stephen, and Brian Schaffner. 2013. "CCES Common Content, 2012." Available at http://hdl.handle.net/1902.1/21447.

Barker, David C., and Christopher Jan Carman. 2000. "The Spirit of Capitalism? Religious Doctrine, Values, and Economic Attitude Constructs." *Political Behavior* 22 (1): 1–27.

Berelson, Bernard R., Paul F. Lazarsfeld, and William N. McPhee. 1954. *Voting*. Chicago: University of Chicago Press.

Bruns, Alex. 2012. "Mitt Romney and Evangelical Voters: An Arranged Marriage." *PBS NewsHour*, July 10. Available at http://www.pbs.org/newshour/rundown/mitt-romney-and-evangelical-voters-an-arrainged-marriage/.

Campbell, Angus, Philip E. Converse, Warren E. Miller, and Donald E. Stokes. 1960. *The American Voter*. Unabridged ed. Chicago: University of Chicago Press.

Campbell, David E., John C. Green, and Geoffrey C. Layman. 2011. "The Party Faithful: Partisan Images, Candidate Religion, and the Electoral Impact of Party Identification." *American Journal of Political Science* 55 (1): 42–58.

Carroll, Colleen. 2002. *The New Faithful: Why Young Adults Are Embracing Christian Orthodoxy*. Chicago: Loyola University Press.

Carter, Joe. 2012. "The Myth of the Liberal Young Evangelical." *Patheos*, October 5. Available at http://www.patheos.com/blogs/joecarter/2012/10/the-myth-of-the-liberal-young-evangelical/.

Castle, Jeremiah J. 2015. "Rock of Ages: Subcultural Religious Identity and Public Opinion among Evangelical Millennials." Ph.D. diss., University of Notre Dame.

Danielsen, Sabrina. 2013. "Fracturing over Creation Care? Shifting Environmental Beliefs among Evangelicals, 1984–2010." *Journal for the Scientific Study of Religion* 52 (1): 198–215.

Farrell, Justin. 2011. "The Young and the Restless? The Liberalization of Young Evangelicals." *Journal for the Scientific Study of Religion* 50 (3): 517–532.

Festinger, Leon. 1957. *A Theory of Cognitive Dissonance*. Stanford, CA: Stanford University Press.

FitzGerald, Frances. 2008. "The New Evangelicals." *New Yorker*, June 30. Available at https://www.newyorker.com/magazine/2008/06/30/the-new-evangelicals.

Green, Donald, Bradley Palmquist, and Eric Schickler. 2002. *Partisan Hearts and Minds: Political Parties and the Social Identities of Voters*. New Haven, CT: Yale University Press.

Green, John C. 2010. *The Faith Factor: How Religion Influences American Elections*. Westport, CT: Praeger.

Guth, James L., John C. Green, Lyman A. Kellstedt, and Corwin E. Smidt. 1995. "Faith and the Environment: Religious Beliefs and Attitudes on Environmental Policy." *American Journal of Political Science* 39 (2): 364–382.

Guth, James L., Lyman A. Kellstedt, Corwin E. Smidt, and John C. Green. 2006. "Religious Influences in the 2004 Presidential Election." *Presidential Studies Quarterly* 36 (2): 223–242.

Hargrove, Barbara. 1989. *The Sociology of Religion: Classic and Contemporary Approaches*. Arlington Heights, IL: Harlan Davidson.

Harris, Dan. 2008. "Are Young Evangelicals Skewing More Liberal?" *ABC News*, February 10. Available at http://abcnews.go.com/Politics/Vote2008/story?id=4269824&page=1.

Hunter, James Davison. 1991. *Culture War: The Struggle to Define America*. New York: Basic Books.

Jelen, Ted G., Corwin E. Smidt, and Clyde Wilcox. 1993. "The Political Effects of the Born-Again Phenomenon." In *Rediscovering the Religious Factor in American Politics*, edited by David C. Leege and Lyman A. Kellstedt, 199–215. Armonk, NY: M. E. Sharpe.

Johnstone, Ronald L. 1988. *Religion in Society: A Sociology of Religion*. Englewood Cliffs, NJ: Prentice-Hall.

Jones, Robby. 2013. "Religious Progressives Hold Stronger Appeal among Millennials." *Progressive Christianity*, July 23. Available at https://progressivechristianity.org/2013/07/23/religious-progressives-hold-stronger-appeal-among-millennials/.

Kinder, Donald R., and Cindy D. Kam. 2009. *Us versus Them: Ethnocentric Foundations of American Public Opinion*. Chicago: University of Chicago Press.

Kirkpatrick, David. 2007. "The Evangelical Crackup." *New York Times Magazine*, October 28. Available at http://www.nytimes.com/2007/10/28/magazine/28Evangelicals-t.html.

Kleppner, Paul. 1970. *The Cross of Culture: A Social Analysis of Midwestern Politics, 1850–1900*. New York: Free Press.

Krattenmaker, Tom. 2013. *The Evangelicals You Don't Know: Introducing the Next Generation of Christians*. Lanham, MD: Rowman and Littlefield.

Layman, Geoffrey C. 2001. *The Great Divide: Religious and Cultural Conflict in American Party Politics*. New York: Columbia University Press.

Layman, Geoffrey C., and John C. Green. 2005. "Wars and Rumours of Wars: The Contexts of Cultural Conflict in American Political Behavior." *British Journal of Political Science* 36 (1): 61–89.

Leege, D., and L. Kellstedt, eds. 1993. *Rediscovering the Religious Factor in American Politics*. Armonk, NY: M. E. Sharpe.

Leege, David C., Kenneth D. Wald, Brian S. Krueger, and Paul D. Mueller. 2002. *The Politics of Cultural Differences: Social Change and Voter Mobilization Strategies in the Post–New Deal Period*. Princeton, NJ: Princeton University Press.

Long, J. Scott, and Jeremy Freese. 2006. *Regression Models for Categorical Dependent Variables Using Stata*. 2nd ed. College Station, TX: Stata Press.

Martin, William. 2005. *With God on Our Side: The Rise of the Religious Right in America.* New York: Broadway Books.

McDermott, Monika L. 2009. "Religious Stereotyping and Voter Support for Evangelical Candidates." *Political Research Quarterly* 62 (2): 340–354.

Mendenhall, Vanessa. 2006. "Are Young Evangelicals Leaning Left?" *PBS NewsHour,* November 21.

Merriam-Webster. 2016. "Cognitive Dissonance." Available at http://www.merriam-webster .com/dictionary/cognitive%20dissonance.

Oldfield, Duane M. 1996. *The Right and the Righteous.* Lanham, MD: Rowman and Littlefield.

Pelz, Mikael L., and Corwin E. Smidt. 2015. "Generational Conversion? The Role of Religiosity in the Politics of Evangelicals." *Journal for the Scientific Study of Religion* 54 (2): 380–401.

Pew Forum on Religion and Public Life. 2008. *U.S. Religious Landscape Survey.* Washington, DC: Pew Forum on Religion and Public Life.

Putnam, Robert D., and David E. Campbell. 2010. *American Grace: How Religion Divides and Unites Us.* New York: Simon and Schuster.

Pyle, Ralph E. 1993. "Faith and Commitment to the Poor: Theological Orientation and Support for Government Assistance Measures." *Sociology of Religion* 54 (4): 385–401.

Rivers, Douglas. 2006. "Sample Matching: Representative Sampling from Internet Panels." YouGovPolimetrix White Paper. Available at http://www.websm.org/uploadi/editor/ 1368187057Rivers_2006_Sample_matching_Representative_sampling_from_Internet _panels.pdf.

Smidt, Corwin E. 2007. "Evangelical and Mainline Protestants at the Turn of the Millennium: Taking Stock and Looking Forward." In *From Pews to Polling Places: Faith and Politics in the American Religious Mosaic,* edited by J. Matthew Wilson, 29–52. Washington, DC: Georgetown University Press.

Smidt, Corwin E., Lyman A. Kellstedt, and James L. Guth. 2009. "The Role of Religion in American Politics: Explanatory Theories and Associated Analytical and Measurement Issues." In *The Oxford Handbook of Religion and American Politics,* ed. Corwin E. Smidt, Lyman A. Kellstedt, and James L. Guth, 3–42. New York: Oxford University Press.

Smith, Buster G., and Byron Johnson. 2010. "The Liberalization of Young Evangelicals: A Research Note." *Journal for the Scientific Study of Religion* 49 (2): 351–360.

Smith, Christian. 1998. *American Evangelicalism: Embattled and Thriving.* Chicago: University of Chicago Press.

Steensland, Brian, Jerry Z. Park, Mark D. Regnerus, Lynn D. Robinson, W. Bradford Wilcox, and Robert D. Woodbury. 2000. "The Measure of American Religion: Toward Improving the State of the Art." *Social Forces* 79 (1): 291–318.

Vavreck, Lynn, and Douglas Rivers. 2008. "The 2006 Cooperative Congressional Election Study." *Journal of Elections, Public Opinion, and Parties* 18 (4): 355–366.

Weber, Max. 1930. *The Protestant Ethic and the Spirit of Capitalism.* Translated by Talcott Parsons. New York: Scribner.

Wilcox, Clyde, and Carin Robinson. 2010. *Onward Christian Soldiers? The Religious Right in American Politics.* 4th ed. Boulder, CO: Westview Press.

Will, Jeffry A., and John K. Cochran. 1995. "God Helps Those Who Help Themselves? The Effects of Religious Affiliations, Religiosity, and Deservedness on Generosity toward the Poor." *Sociology of Religion* 56 (3): 327–338.

Williams, Daniel K. 2010. *God's Own Party: The Making of the Christian Right.* New York: Oxford University Press.

Williams, Timothy J. 2016. "Evangelicals Aren't Always Conservatives." *New Republic,* October 17. Available at https://newrepublic.com/article/137839/evangelicals-arent-always -conservatives.

Wilson, J. Matthew. 1999. "'Blessed Are the Poor': American Protestantism and Attitudes toward Poverty and Welfare." *Southeastern Political Review* 27 (3): 421–437.

———. 2009. "Religion and American Public Opinion: Economic Issues." In *The Oxford Handbook of Religion and American Politics*, edited by Corwin E. Smidt, Lyman A. Kellstedt, and James A. Guth, 191–216. New York: Oxford University Press.

Wuthnow, Robert. 1988. *The Restructuring of American Religion*. Princeton, NJ: Princeton University Press.

———. 1994. *God and Mammon in America*. New York: Free Press.

Zaller, John. 1992. *The Nature and Origins of Mass Opinion*. Cambridge: Cambridge University Press.

9

The Rise of Latino Evangelicals

J. Benjamin Taylor
Sarah Allen Gershon
Adrian D. Pantoja

The Latino evangelical community has long been considered a swing demographic in American politics. However, since the 2004 presidential election, attention on this key demographic group has been more concentrated because of Latinos' gradual shift toward the Democratic Party in elections. Luis Lugo and Allison Pond's (2007) report detailing their findings about the evolution of Latino religious affiliations and the related political implications noted that, without movement among evangelical Latinos to the GOP, Republicans would have trouble in future elections. This is also well known to Republican leaders. The Republican Party explicitly described outreach to the Latino community predicated on faith-based organizations and policies in their 2012 "Growth and Opportunity Project" (Barbour et al. 2013), though Donald Trump's 2016 victory has put those plans on hold. Furthermore, the political impact the Latino community could have is not lost on evangelical leaders. In a 2013 interview with *U.S. News and World Report*, Richard Land, president of the Southern Evangelical Seminary, summarized the views of many evangelical leaders regarding the status of Latinos and comprehensive immigration reform:

> If you want the conservative movement to be a national movement that can win elections, it is going to have to include Hispanics. . . . Hispanic voters are more culturally conservative unless they are driven away by [charged] language. They are family oriented, religiously oriented, culturally oriented toward other conservative values. (Quoted in Fox 2013)

Since the 2006 immigration reform push from the George W. Bush administration, evangelical churches and organizations have made a concerted effort to get their congregants and fellow church members to mobilize in support of issues and policies favored by the Latino community. As noted in Land's comments, there is clearly a political objective to this mobilization.

In the years since these reports, Latino voters have generally remained solidly Democratic,[1] but the political implications of rising evangelicalism among Latinos in the United States remain unclear. As in the Anglo evangelical movement, there is a segment of Latino evangelical leaders who identify with and support conservative political causes (e.g., National Hispanic Christian Leadership Conference) (Linthicum 2016), but there are also Latino evangelical leaders who align themselves with social-justice-oriented actions and partner organizations (e.g., National Latino Evangelical Coalition and Esperanza) (Jenkins 2015). Regardless of ideological point of view, the Latino population represents a significant growth opportunity in the near future for evangelical churches and organizations satisfying both their temporal and spiritual goals (Cortés 2013; Menjívar 1999; NAMB Research Workgroup 2009; Wong, Rim, and Perez 2008). Given this expected growth, what are the political behavior and attitudinal ramifications of the rise of evangelicalism among Latinos in the United States?

Answering this question has implications for both political science and practical politics in the United States. By 2050, the United States will be a "majority-minority" country for the first time in its history, and Hispanics will constitute the largest ethnic minority group and a significant proportion of the electorate (Humes, Jones, and Ramirez 2011; Krogstad 2014).[2] Latino church participation (as it does for other ethnic groups) will likely shape the political incorporation of this growing group. Churches produce civic skills that make participation in politics more likely (Djupe and Gilbert 2009; Verba et al. 1993; Wald and Calhoun-Brown 2011), but members of evangelical churches, unlike their Catholic and mainline Protestant brethren, have a particular political point of view that comes with their missionary and community service. Evangelicals are generally more politically and religiously conservative (e.g., see Layman 1997, 2001). As evangelical churches make entries into this growing community, it will be crucial to see if Latinos finally become the constituency Republicans have been claiming they could be for a generation (Ross 2012). This political evolution is not guaranteed. It may be that Latino evangelicals follow the path of African Americans who, even among the most religious, remain solidly tied to the Democratic Party. Indeed, Trump's immigration policies may drive a permanent wedge between Latino evangelicals and the Republican Party.

In this chapter, we examine the state of the literature at present and describe what the future may hold for research in this area. First, we discuss the ways evangelical churches and organizations interact with Latino immigrants coming into the United States. Next, we examine how evangelicalism affects the identities and attitudes of Latinos. Finally, we highlight what we know about the ways evangelicalism affects partisanship and voting behavior among Latinos in the United States.

Evangelicalism and Immigration in the United States

Perhaps one of the reasons evangelical leaders are so focused on the Latino community—and immigration reform as an issue—is their mission work with newly arrived immigrants. During the lead-up to the 2010 census, evangelical churches played a critical mediating role trying to link immigrant populations and the government to ensure accurate reporting (e.g., see Banks 2011; Preston 2009). Beyond demystifying access to government services in the United States, churches can be important players in maintaining transnational ties between immigrants and their home countries, which are extremely important in the political socialization process for new immigrants (DeSipio 2007; Jones-Correa 1998; Pantoja 2005). For instance, those who have more robust transnational ties with their home country are more likely to seek citizenship in the United States (Gershon and Pantoja 2014). Thus, keeping transnational ties alive is part of the objective for religious institutions assisting immigrants in the United States.

The immigration process is one of the places evangelical organizations can make first impressions on the Latino community. Like their Catholic peers, evangelical churches have myriad networks that include groups and missionary organizations that serve both spiritual purposes and temporal goals. Assisting new immigrants with finding housing, work, and social and language services is common among evangelical and Catholic organizations alike (Menjívar 1999, 2003). For the Catholic Church, an organization more than two millennia old with a political agenda that cuts across partisan lines in the United States, these tasks are simply part of a general community engagement process (Baia 1999; Menjívar 2003). What we find in evangelical organizations is something slightly different.

Both evangelical and Catholic organizations work to create networks between immigrants and their home countries to help facilitate the ease of transition (Hagan and Ebaugh 2003; Wuthnow and Offutt 2008). However, evangelical organizations also put a focus on how their religious identities connect with what being "American" means (Wong, Rim, and Perez 2008). These behaviors build an attachment both to the organization helping with the immigration transition and to a more specific political understanding in the United States. Though discussing politics happens within both Catholic and evangelical churches (Menjívar 1999), the distinct focus on the religious and personal goals of evangelical organizations opens the doors to more conservative politics as immigrants become acculturated. Fundamentally, the religious experience of Catholics and evangelical Latinos is simply different, which gives rise to differences in understanding the church's role in politics even as the organizations seek similar social goals (Berggren and Rae 2006; Menjívar 2003).

Understanding that evangelical organizations can serve both their spiritual and political goals through the immigration process highlights some of the impetus behind their support of immigration reform. However, beyond knowing some of the details about how these organizations support immigrant communities, the ways in which evangelical experiences (for both immigrants and nonimmigrants) translate into political attitudes requires a more in-depth consideration of how evangelicalism generates differences in (Latino) political attitudes more broadly.

The Impact of Evangelicalism on Ideology and Attitudes

Christianity and American identity are closely linked for many, particularly among the very religious (Jacobs and Theiss-Morse 2013). This is also true for evangelical Latinos, particularly Latino immigrants. Research demonstrates that Latino immigrants who are affiliated with evangelical churches are more likely than other Latinos to say being Christian is important for being American. Furthermore, evangelical Latino immigrants are more likely to adopt "American" as their primary identity in the United States (Taylor, Gershon, and Pantoja 2014). This is important because the primary identifying nomenclature varies widely among Latinos in the United States (Bedolla 2005; Mohamed 2013; Oboler 1995). If shaping the political awareness of immigrants to whom they minister is part of the mission for some evangelical organizations, then helping shape a particular version of American identity is likely a critical first step.

Evangelical Christianity is a belief system generally emphasizing both biblical teaching as absolute truth and the need to spread the gospel of Jesus Christ (Woodberry and Smith 1998). Engaging with this content and developing social networks where this message is a source of discussion and bonding lead its adherents to find social and moral issues more salient as well as to take more conservative issue positions (Brown 2015; Djupe and Gilbert 2009). While there is some ideological variation within the evangelical movement (Smidt 1988), most evangelicals are more conservative on social issues and consider moral issues fundamentally important in American politics (Kohut et al. 2001). One of the main reasons evangelical organizations have made the Latino community a target for growth is that their numbers are sizable and there is a belief that Latinos share these fundamental attitudinal orientations (NAMB Research Workgroup 2009).

The notion that Latinos may share a concern for socially conservative or traditional values and be motivated by policies linked to those values has not escaped the attention of scholars, commentators, or politicians (e.g., see Barbour et al. 2013; de la Garza et al. 1992; Leal et al. 2005; National Journal 2006; Wong 2015). In their analysis of the first Latino National Political Survey (LNPS), Rodolfo de la Garza and colleagues (1992) found that Latinos self-identified ideologically as moderate to conservative regardless of country of origin. Recent research shows a more mixed picture, with some finding conservatism more prevalent (Alvarez and Bedolla 2003; Funk and Martínez 2014, chap. 9), while others find Latinos more liberal on balance (Bowler and Segura 2012). A 2016 survey of fifteen hundred Latinos in Los Angeles County by the Pat Brown Institute and Latino Decisions showed that 40 percent said they were liberal (somewhat to very); 33 percent were moderate; and a mere 22 percent said they were conservative (somewhat to very). The preference for liberal is not surprising given that the survey was taken during a time when the Republican Party nominee was running on an anti-immigrant platform. There is, of course, an ongoing debate whether their self-ideological placement aligns with policies associated with these ideologies (Barreto and Segura 2014). Regardless of the ideology of the Latino population generally, we know that when Latinos attend evangelical churches, their political ideology and policy preferences tend to be conservative (Kelly and Morgan 2008; Pantoja 2010). All of this strongly suggests that evangelical Latinos and the larger Latino community may exhibit important differences on policy and social issues.

While the extent to which Latinos are *actually* conservative remains unclear, attitude changes among Latinos mirror American attitudes generally. For instance, Pew Research shows that between 2006 and 2009 Latinos were generally opposed to recognizing same-sex marriage in the United States (Funk and Martínez 2014). These attitudes began to change in favor of same-sex marriage in 2012 and 2013, which reflects the evolution on same-sex marriage attitudes present in the broader American public during the same time period. Of note, however, is the extent to which evangelical Latinos do not exhibit these attitude shifts. Using Pew Research data, Christopher G. Ellison and colleagues (2011) show that in 2006, evangelical Latinos were 84 percent less likely than the Catholic majority to support same-sex marriage. These data also revealed that mainline Protestant Latinos were more than twice as likely as Catholic Latinos to support same-sex marriage.

The impact of evangelicalism on Latino attitudes is not confined to social issues like same-sex marriage. In fact, evangelical Latinos differ from the wider Latino community on a host of issues (e.g., see Wong 2015). Despite the predominance of the Catholic Church and Catholicism being a crucial cultural cornerstone in Latino communities—which has a strict doctrine against abortion access—evangelical Latinos are more likely than their Catholic counterparts to support restricting abortion access (Bartkowski et al. 2012; Kelly and Morgan 2008; Wong 2015). These findings match survey data from Pew showing that 54 percent of Catholic Latinos believe abortion should always or mostly be illegal (51 percent of Anglo Catholics share this view). However, 70 percent of evangelical Latinos believe that all or most abortions should be illegal (76 percent of Anglo evangelicals share this view) (Lipka and Gramlich 2017; Pew Research Center 2014). Evangelical Latinos are less likely than non-evangelical Latinos to express interest in overcoming gender discrimination through public policy in the United States (McKenzie and Rouse 2013). Furthermore, on more general social issue concerns, Latinos who identify with evangelical denominations favor more socially conservative education policies such as teaching creationism and allowing prayers in public schools (Espinosa 2008). These ideological placements and issue positions highlight important aspects of being an evangelical Latino in the United States that set this group of people apart from the larger Latino community.

Partisanship, Political Behavior, and Latino Evangelicals

The research on ideology and attitudes highlights an interesting paradox: Latinos are generally inclined to take conservative positions on social issues, but they are also more likely to be Democrats than Republicans. It is precisely this paradox that has caused the Republican Party such distress since Reagan's famous admonition: "Latinos are Republicans; they just don't know it yet" (Ross 2012).

Even though, as a whole, the Latino population is generally more religious than other demographic groups in the United States (Funk and Martínez 2014), succeeding generations of Latinos have become less religious (see Gershon, Pantoja, and Taylor 2016). For instance, in the 2006 LNS, 22 percent of first-generation respondents report never attending church or doing so only on major holidays. Among 2.5- and third-generation Latinos, this percentage increases to 34 and 33 percent, respectively. This matches the trends and behavior of other ethnic groups in the United States (Navarro-Rivera, Kosmin, and Keysar 2010). Among those who do identify as religious, the Latino population in the United States is predominantly Catholic (Pew Research Center 2007). However, the percentage of Catholic identifiers among Latinos continues to decrease, which is demonstrated by Pew's 2014 report, which shows that in 2010, 67 percent of Latinos identified as Catholic, but by 2013, 55 percent did so (Funk and Martínez 2014).

Latino millennials tend to display lower levels of religiosity than previous generations of Latinos, which may suggest an increase in secularism over time. In the 2016 Pat Brown Institute/Latino Decisions survey, 20 percent of Latinos sixty-five years and older said they "almost never" or "never" attend religious services. Among Latinos eighteen to thirty-four years old, that figure increases to 36 percent. The decline in Catholicism is also evident in that survey, with 77 percent of persons sixty-five years and older self-identifying as Catholic and 52 percent of Latinos eighteen to thirty-four years old identifying as Catholic, a twenty-five-point drop. The extent to which religiosity matters to and affects Latino political behavior is important because this is often the trait specifically identified as the path for values-based political action.

The Latino community is quite diverse, and this diversity—predicated on one's ancestral nation of origin—is crucial to consider when looking at voting patterns among Latinos (e.g., see de la Garza 2004). However, religious identification affects the ways Latinos exercise their political power in elections. Evangelical Latinos are more likely than their Catholic and mainline Protestant counterparts to identify as Republicans (Gibson and Hare 2012; Kelly and Morgan 2008; Lee and Pachon 2007; McDaniel and Ellison 2008). Furthermore, Nathan J. Kelly and Jana Kelly (2005) find that evangelicalism significantly increases the odds of identifying as Republican, particularly for Latinos whose home-country heritage is outside Mexico, Cuba, or Puerto Rico.

Beyond partisan identification, evangelical Latinos are routinely shown to be more likely than other Latinos to vote for Republicans. In fact, Robert Suro and colleagues (2007) suggest that a higher percentage of Latino evangelicals identify as Republicans than do Anglo evangelicals. Their point is that one is more likely to find non-Republican, evangelical Anglos than non-Republican, evangelical Latinos. Illustrative of this point, outreach to and mobilization of the Latino evangelical community are considered one of the reasons President Bush won reelection in 2004, as Latino evangelicals supported Bush over John Kerry 58 to 33 percent, respectively (Leal et al. 2005). As demonstrated in Figure 9.1, neither Mitt Romney nor Donald Trump was able to replicate the success of the 2004 Bush campaign, winning just 27 and 26 percent, respectively, of the Latino vote nationally (Ansolabehere and Schaffner 2017; Linthicum 2016). However, Romney was able to win about 45 percent of self-identified evangelical Latino voters, while Trump garnered only 38 percent.[3] Romney and Trump's inability to generate more support among evangelical Latinos is one of the reasons their showing among Latino voters was so poor.

Curiously, Romney's poor showing among Latinos is widely cited as a significant contributor to his 2012 loss (e.g., see Barbour et. al 2013), whereas Trump was still able to win the Electoral College. One explanation, based on early analyses, is Trump's use of racial and economic competition to prime voting among white voters—particularly in the Midwest—to offset losses from other voting blocs, particularly Latinos (Griffin and Teixeira 2017). Upcoming elections will certainly test the long-held theory that Republican electoral success depends on significant contributions from the growing evangelical Latino community.

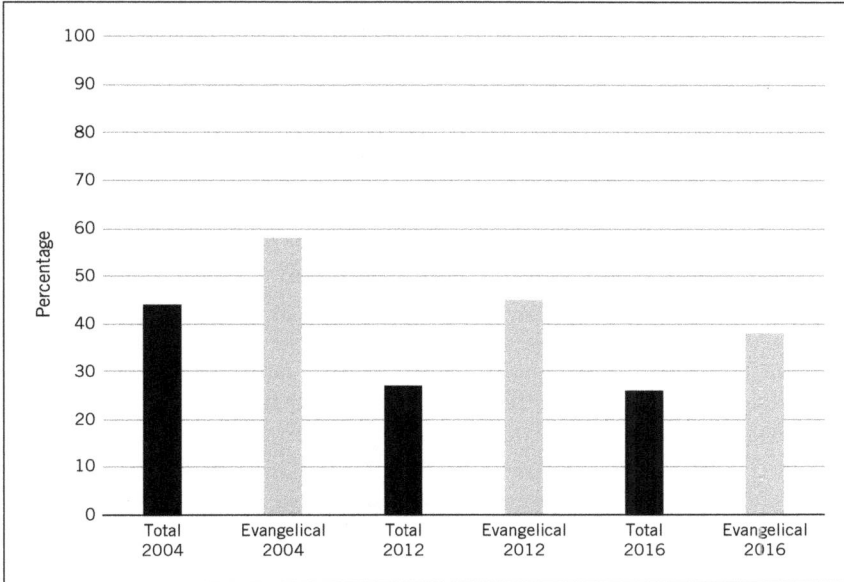

Figure 9.1 Latino vote percentages for Republican presidential candidates, 2004, 2012, and 2016
Source: Leal et al. 2005 (2004 data); Linthicum 2016 (2012 data); Cooperative Congressional Election Survey, 2016 (2016 data; see Ansolabehere and Schaffner 2017).

Does Evangelicalism Produce Unique Political Behavior among Latinos?

The ability of evangelical churches to push Latino congregants to political action more broadly in American politics remains unclear (Leal 2010). Some scholars find the parallels between Anglo evangelical churches and Latino evangelical congregations dubious, noting that Latino evangelical churches simply do not produce political engagement in the same way that Anglo evangelicals do (Djupe and Neiheisel 2012; Ramírez 2005). Perhaps a better parallel is African American churches. Historically, one of the qualities on which African American churches rely to generate political activity is homogeneity, which creates an environment rich with linked fate-based social capital (see Dawson 2003; Wald and Calhoun-Brown 2011). According to the Pew Research Center (2009), 59 percent of African Americans report going to historically black Protestant churches where almost all churchgoers are African American. Among Catholic Latinos, 66 percent report having all Latino congregations while, among evangelicals, 58 percent report attending services in all Latino congregations (48 percent of mainline Latinos report the same thing) (Pew Research Center 2014). Thus, we see similar ethnic contexts among these minority groups but not the same behavioral implications for politics.

At present, there is simply a dearth of research exploring the behavioral implications of Latino evangelicalism compared to that in the Anglo and African American communities. For what research does exist, scholars find that Latino Catholics are more politically engaged than Latino Protestants in the 1990s (Jones-Correa and Leal 2001), while some find minimal or nonexistent denominational differences for participation (Lee, Pachon, and Barreto 2002). Even in scholarship where there is evidence of statistically different findings on vote preference (i.e., evangelical Latinos supported President Bush at higher levels than other Latinos in 2004), there are null effects on broader questions of participation, such as the likelihood of being mobilized (Lee and Pachon 2007). Yet the fact remains that more research is needed to determine whether affiliation with evangelicalism has a mobilizing or demobilizing effect on Latinos. We suspect turnout will vary across electoral contexts. Candidates' religious identities and positions on immigration, one of the most salient issues for Latinos, could lead to variations in turnout among evangelically oriented Hispanics.

Conclusion

It was anticipated that, for the Republican Party to be competitive in future presidential elections, Republican candidates would need to win something near or better than 47 percent of the Latino vote nationally (Damore and Barreto 2015). These forecasts assumed that the share of the non-Hispanic white electorate supporting the Democratic candidate would be unchanged from the previous election. Nonetheless, given what research demonstrates about the political behavior and attitudes of evangelical Latinos, it makes sense that a disproportionate share of that 47 percent should be made up of these voters. Yet early reports on vote choice among Latinos estimate that GOP nominee Donald Trump earned between 19 percent (Sanchez and Barreto 2016) and 26 percent (Ansolabehere and Schaffner 2017) of the vote among Latinos. Mitt Romney's tepid support from Latinos in 2012 looks remarkable compared to the support in these estimates, which confirm prior findings indicating that Trump's comments and issue positions were generally unfavorable among Latinos (see Damore 2016a; Pantoja 2016). If this trend continues, it appears a crackup is indeed a possibility.

When thinking about what the future holds for evangelical Latinos and research in this area, there are several things to consider. One interesting question is whether we should continue to consider Latino evangelicals as a distinct group, which—as we demonstrate—much of the literature does. Perhaps we can consider a panethnic evangelicalism where evangelical identity supersedes being Latino. We do not have a definitive answer at this time, but we believe there are three possible pathways scholars should explore over time.

To include Latinos in a panethnic evangelical group, it seems the forces of assimilation would need to remain strong enough so that the concept of "whiteness" extends to Hispanics. If this happens, their ethnic or racial identity loses salience, and they will be another group that simply sees itself as American. Conversely, if Latinos remain a racialized group (as seen and treated by white people)—like African Americans—their evangelicalism will be separate from that of white evangelicals, and it would not make sense to include them in a panethnic evangelical category. A third possibility is segmented assimilation. In this scenario, Latinos who are seen and treated as white (colorism) and who have high socioeconomic status (e.g., education, income, home ownership) assimilate into the mainstream, which would make their evangelicalism more important than being Latino. However, Afro-Latinos/Mestizo-Latinos with lower socioeconomic status would remain distinct. The former will likely worship at white evangelical churches. The latter will be in predominantly Hispanic churches, which reinforces the divisions between Latino evangelicalism and a broader understanding of evangelicalism that might otherwise emerge.

At present, it seems that conceptualizing Latino evangelicalism as distinct from white or African American evangelicalism continues to be warranted. It certainly is the case that evangelical spiritual and evangelistic goals are being met within the Latino community; there is a growing Latino evangelical population in the United States. Yet this growth has not yet clearly contributed to a massive shift from Democratic to Republican votes. Though evangelical Latinos are more conservative, more likely to call themselves Republican, and more likely to hold socially conservative attitudes, there is one issue that unites many Latinos: immigration reform. Evangelical Latino leaders and organizations have made immigration reform a keystone issue for the foreseeable future. It is clear that unless and until the Congress—particularly the Republican Party—begins to negotiate in good faith on this issue, the cascading waves of new Latino Republicans on which conservative leaders have been waiting will not arrive. This is borne out in polling data from 2016, in which the pressing concern for immigration reform overrode all other concerns in representative samples of Latino voters (Damore 2016b).

Research into the political implications of the rise in evangelicalism among Latinos has been hampered by the limited data available concerning Latino political attitudes and religious affiliation. Beyond the LNS, select Pew Research studies, and the 2012 and 2016 American National Election Studies, there simply are not many data sets with large Latino samples that ask questions on relevant political attitudes as well as religious affiliation. Given the lack of solid data, researchers have been cut short even while asking pertinent questions. For instance, Paul A. Djupe and Jacob R. Nei-heisel (2012) explore the impact of religion on political participation, finding that Catholic and non-Catholic Latino churchgoers do participate in politics differently; however, because of data limitations, they are not able to evaluate the impact of evangelical churches on political behavior. They point out, as do others, that scholars are not able to say much about the variation in po-litical messages and political talk within various Latino religious traditions at this time. Cecilia Menjívar (1999, 2001, 2003) and Gastón Espinosa (2007, 2008) are able to overcome these limitations with qualitative and historical analyses. However, for these findings to be examined on a broader scale, the field requires diverse surveys that drill down further into what types of reli-gious services Latinos attend, how they worship, and what their attitudes are about American politics.

Since 2004, the most fervent prayer among some Republican and conser-vative leaders was that Latino voters would begin moving more decidedly to their party in elections. At present, the chances for this look bleak. Despite various immigration-reform efforts, Republican presidents and leaders in Congress have not been able to capitalize on the ideological and attitudinal similarities they share with the evangelical Latino community. Perhaps, if Republicans pass an expansive comprehensive immigration-reform package in the next two years, the inroads with the evangelical Latino community will be made deeper and more meaningful. However, Trump's executive or-ders on immigration may drive a permanent wedge between the GOP and Latino evangelicals—particularly leaders of Latino evangelical organizations (Dias 2017). This may mark a turning point in the political identity of Lati-nos. Thus, regardless of the religious identities, Latinos (like African Amer-icans) will likely remain steadfast Democrats.

NOTES

1. Their remaining Democratic is attributed in part to the hard-line stance Republicans and conservative commentators have taken on immigration reform at the federal level (e.g., see Bolton 2013; Elliott and Altman 2015; Peters and Parker 2015).

2. We use the terms "Latino" and "Hispanic" interchangeably.

3. The 2016 exit-poll data for the Latino population has been called into question (Latino Decisions 2016), so we use the CCES conducted during the 2016 election cycle. The main point is that GOP candidates are losing their share of both the overall Latino vote and the evangelical Latino vote over time.

REFERENCES

Alvarez, R. Michael, and Lisa García Bedolla. 2003. "The Foundations of Latino Voter Par-tisanship: Evidence from the 2000 Election." *Journal of Politics* 65 (1): 31–49.
Ansolabehere, Stephen, and Brian F. Schaffner. 2017. "CCES Common Content, 2016." Avail-able at https://dataverse.harvard.edu/dataset.xhtml?persistentId=doi%3A10.7910/DVN/GDF6Z0.

Baia, Larissa Ruiz. 1999. "Rethinking Transnationalism: Reconstructing National Identities among Peruvian Catholics in New Jersey." *Journal of Interamerican Studies and World Affairs* 41 (4): vi, 93–109.

Banks, Adelle M. 2011. "Hispanic Groups Divided over 2010 Census." *Christianity Today*, April 30. Available at http://www.christianitytoday.com/ct/2009/aprilweb-only/117-42.0.html.

Barbour, Henry, Sally Bradshaw, Ari Fleischer, Zori Fonalledas, and Glenn McCall. 2013. "Growth and Opportunity Project." Available at https://gop.com/growth-and-opportunity-project.

Barreto, Matt A., and Gary Segura. 2014. *Latino America: How America's Most Dynamic Population Is Poised to Transform the Politics of the Nation*. New York: PublicAffairs.

Bartkowski, John P., Aida I. Ramos-Wada, Chris G. Ellison, and Gabriel A. Acevedo. 2012. "Faith, Race-Ethnicity, and Public Policy Preferences: Religious Schemas and Abortion Attitudes among U.S. Latinos." *Journal for the Scientific Study of Religion* 51 (2): 343–358.

Bedolla, Lisa García. 2005. *Fluid Borders: Latino Power, Identity, and Politics in Los Angeles*. Berkeley: University of California Press.

Berggren, D. Jason, and Nicol C. Rae. 2006. "Jimmy Carter and George W. Bush: Faith, Foreign Policy, and an Evangelical Presidential Style." *Presidential Studies Quarterly* 36 (4): 606–632.

Bolton, Alexander. 2013. "Immigration Reform Hinges on Rubio Proposals for Border Security." *The Hill*, June 9. Available at http://thehill.com/homenews/senate/304311-immigration-reform-hinges-on-rubio-proposals-for-border-security.

Bowler, Shaun, and Gary Segura. 2012. *The Future Is Ours: Minority Politics, Political Behavior, and the Multiracial Era of American Politics*. Washington, DC: CQ Press.

Brown, Candy Gunther. 2015. "Conservative Evangelicalism: Safeguarding Theology and Transforming Society." In *Handbook of Global Contemporary Christianity: Themes and Developments in Culture, Politics, and Society*, edited by Stephen Hunt, 49–74. Leiden, Netherlands: Brill.

Cortés, Luis, Jr. 2013. "Building the Church in Hispanic Populations." National Association of Evangelicals, June 21. Available at http://nae.net/building-the-church-in-hispanic-populations/.

Damore, David F. 2016a. "The Policy Priorities of Latino Voters in Battleground States." Latino Decisions, July 27. Available at http://www.latinodecisions.com/blog/2016/07/27/the-policy-priorities-of-latino-voters-in-battleground-states/.

———. 2016b. "10 Reasons Why Immigration Politics Will Affect the Latino Vote." Latino Decisions, February 16. Available at http://www.latinodecisions.com/blog/2016/02/16/10-reasons-why-immigration-politics-will-affect-the-latino-vote/.

Damore, David F., and Matt Barreto. 2015. "The Latino Threshold to Win in 2016." Latino Decisions, July 17. Available at http://www.latinodecisions.com/blog/2015/07/17/the-latino-threshold-in-2016-to-win/.

Dawson, Michael C. 2003. *Black Visions: The Roots of Contemporary African-American Political Ideologies*. Chicago: University of Chicago Press.

de la Garza, Rodolfo O. 2004. "Latino Politics." *Annual Review of Political Science* 7 (1): 91–123.

de la Garza, Rodolfo O., Louis DeSipio, F. Chris Garcia, John Garcia, and Angelo Falcon. 1992. *Latino Voices: Mexican, Puerto Rican, and Cuban Perspectives on American Politics*. Boulder, CO: Westview Press.

DeSipio, Louis. 2007. "Transnational Politics and Civic Engagement: Do Home-Country Political Ties Limit Latino Immigrant Pursuit of U.S. Civic Engagement and Citizenship?" In *Transforming Politics, Transforming America: The Political and Civic*

Incorporation of Immigrants in the United States, edited by Taeku Lee, 126. Charlottesville: University of Virginia Press.

Dias, Elizabeth. 2017. "Donald Trump's Inaugural Pastor Creates 'Safe Haven' for Immigrants." *Time*, March 1. Available at http://time.com/4686592/donald-trump-immigration-sam-rodriguez-church/.

Djupe, Paul A., and Christopher P. Gilbert. 2009. *The Political Influence of Churches*. Cambridge: Cambridge University Press.

Djupe, Paul A., and Jacob R. Neiheisel. 2012. "How Religious Communities Affect Political Participation among Latinos." *Social Science Quarterly* 93 (2): 333–355.

Elliott, Philip, and Alex Altman. 2015. "The Republican 2016 Field Takes a Hard Right on Immigration." *Time*, August 20. Available at http://time.com/4005245/republican-president-immigration/.

Ellison, Christopher G., Gabriel A. Acevedo, and Aida I. Ramos-Wada. 2011. "Religion and Attitudes toward Same-Sex Marriage among U.S. Latinos." *Social Science Quarterly* 92 (1): 35–56.

Espinosa, Gastón. 2007. "'Today We Act, Tomorrow We Vote': Latino Religions, Politics, and Activism in Contemporary U.S. Civil Society." *Annals of the American Academy of Political and Social Science* 612:152–171.

———. 2008. "The Influence of Religion on Latino Education, Marriage, and Social Views in the United States." *Marriage and Family Review* 43 (3–4): 205–225.

Fox, Lauren. 2013. "Evangelicals Could Be Key to GOP Immigration Push." *US News and World Report*, March 11. Available at http://www.usnews.com/news/articles/2013/03/11/evangelicals-could-be-key-to-gop-immigration-push.

Funk, Cary, and Jessica Hamar Martínez. 2014. "The Shifting Religious Identity of Latinos in the United States." Pew Research Center, May 7. Available at http://www.pewforum.org/2014/05/07/the-shifting-religious-identity-of-latinos-in-the-united-states/.

Gershon, Sarah Allen, and Adrian D. Pantoja. 2014. "Pessimists, Optimists, and Skeptics: The Consequences of Transnational Ties for Latino Immigrant Naturalization." *Social Science Quarterly* 95 (2): 328–342.

Gershon, Sarah Allen, Adrian D. Pantoja, and J. Benjamin Taylor. 2016. "God in the Barrio? The Determinants of Religiosity and Civic Engagement among Latinos in the United States." *Politics and Religion* 9 (1): 84–110.

Gibson, Troy, and Christopher Hare. 2012. "Do Latino Christians and Seculars Fit the Culture War Profile? Latino Religiosity and Political Behavior." *Politics and Religion* 5 (1): 53–82.

Griffin, Robert, and Ruy Teixeira. 2017. "The Story of Trump's Appeal." Democracy Fund Voter Study Group, June 11. Available at https://www.voterstudygroup.org/reports/2016-elections/story-of-trumps-appeal.

Hagan, Jacqueline, and Helen Rose Ebaugh. 2003. "Calling upon the Sacred: Migrants' Use of Religion in the Migration Process." *International Migration Review* 37 (4): 1145–1162.

Humes, Karen R., Nicholas A. Jones, and Roberto R. Ramirez. 2011. "Overview of Race and Hispanic Origin: 2010." *2010 Census Briefs*, March. Available at https://www.census.gov/content/dam/Census/library/publications/2011/dec/c2010br-02.pdf.

Jacobs, Carly M., and Elizabeth Theiss-Morse. 2013. "Belonging in a 'Christian Nation': The Explicit and Implicit Associations between Religion and National Group Membership." *Politics and Religion* 6 (2): 373–401.

Jenkins, Jack. 2015. "The Explosive Growth of Evangelical Belief in Latinos Has Big Political Implications." *ThinkProgress*, June 16. Available at https://thinkprogress.org/the-explosive-growth-of-evangelical-belief-in-latinos-has-big-political-implications-c71a9a0a5009.

Jones-Correa, Michael. 1998. *Between Two Nations: The Political Predicament of Latinos in New York City.* Ithaca, NY: Cornell University Press.

Jones-Correa, Michael, and David L. Leal. 2001. "Political Participation: Does Religion Matter?" *Political Research Quarterly* 54 (4): 751–770.

Kelly, Nathan J., and Jana Morgan Kelly. 2005. "Religion and Latino Partisanship in the United States." *Political Research Quarterly* 58 (1): 87–95.

Kelly, Nathan J., and Jana Morgan. 2008. "Religious Traditionalism and Latino Politics in the United States." *American Politics Research* 36 (2): 236–263.

Kohut, Andrew, John C. Green, Scott Keeter, and Robert C. Toth. 2001. *The Diminishing Divide: Religion's Changing Role in American Politics.* Washington, DC: Brookings Institution Press.

Krogstad, Jens Manuel. 2014. "With Fewer New Arrivals, Census Lowers Hispanic Population Projections." Pew Research Center, December 16. Available at http://www.pewresearch.org/fact-tank/2014/12/16/with-fewer-new-arrivals-census-lowers-hispanic-population-projections-2/.

Latino Decisions. 2016. "The Rundown on Latino Voter Election Eve Polling and Latino Exit Polls." November 9. Available at http://www.latinodecisions.com/blog/2016/11/09/the-rundown-on-latino-voter-election-eve-polling-and-latino-exit-polls/.

Layman, Geoffrey. 1997. "Religion and Political Behavior in the United States: The Impact of Beliefs, Affiliations, and Commitments from 1980 to 1994." *Public Opinion Quarterly* 61 (2): 288–316.

———. 2001. *The Great Divide: Religious and Cultural Conflict in American Party Politics.* New York: Columbia University Press.

Leal, David L. 2010. "Religion and the Political and Civic Lives of Latinos." In *Religion and Democracy in the United States: Danger or Opportunity?*, edited by Alan Wolfe and Ira Katznelson, 308–352. Princeton, NJ: Princeton University Press.

Leal, David L., Matt A. Barreto, Jongho Lee, and Rodolfo O. de la Garza. 2005. "The Latino Vote in the 2004 Election." *PS: Political Science and Politics* 38 (1): 41–49.

Lee, Jongho, and Harry P. Pachon. 2007. "Leading the Way: An Analysis of the Effect of Religion on the Latino Vote." *American Politics Research* 35 (2): 252–272.

Lee, Jongho, Harry P. Pachon, and Matt Barreto. 2002. "Guiding the Flock: Church as a Vehicle of Latino Political Participation." Paper presented at the annual meeting of the American Political Science Association, Boston, MA, August 29–September 1.

Linthicum, Kate. 2016. "Evangelicals Are the Kind of Latinos the GOP Could Be Winning: But Probably Not with Donald Trump." *Los Angeles Times*, May 23. Available at http://www.latimes.com/politics/la-na-pol-evangelical-latinos-20160523-snap-htmlstory.html.

Lipka, Michael, and John Gramlich. 2017. "5 Facts about Abortion." Pew Research Center, January 26. Available at http://www.pewresearch.org/fact-tank/2017/01/26/5-facts-about-abortion/.

Lugo, Luis, and Allison Pond. 2007. "¡Here Come 'Los Evangélicos'!" Pew Research Center, June 6. Available at http://www.pewforum.org/Politics-and-Elections/Here-Come-Los-Evanglicos.aspx.

McDaniel, Eric L., and Christopher G. Ellison. 2008. "God's Party? Race, Religion, and Partisanship over Time." *Political Research Quarterly* 61 (2): 180–191.

McKenzie, Brian D., and Stella M. Rouse. 2013. "Shades of Faith: Religious Foundations of Political Attitudes among African Americans, Latinos, and Whites." *American Journal of Political Science* 57 (1): 218–235.

Menjívar, Cecilia. 1999. "Religions Institutions and Transnationalism: A Case Study of Catholic and Evangelical Salvadoran Immigrants." *International Journal of Politics, Culture, and Society* 12 (4): 589–612.

———. 2001. "Latino Immigrants and Their Perceptions of Religious Institutions: Cubans, Salvadorans and Guatemalans in Phoenix, Arizona." *Migraciones Internacionales* 1 (1): 65–88.

———. 2003. "Religion and Immigration in Comparative Perspective: Catholic and Evangelical Salvadorans in San Francisco, Washington, D.C., and Phoenix." *Sociology of Religion* 64 (1): 21–46.

Mohamed, Heather Silber. 2013. "Can Protests Make Latinos 'American'? Identity, Immigration Politics, and the 2006 Marches." *American Politics Research* 41 (2): 298–327.

NAMB Research Workgroup. 2009. "Evangelism and Church Planting in North America: An Internal Study of the North American Mission Board." Previously available at http://www.namb.net/workarea/DownloadAsset.aspx?id=8589966766.

National Journal. 2006. "Evangelical Hispanics Turning Away from GOP." *NBC News*, September 7. Available at http://www.nbcnews.com/id/14713664/ns/politics-national_journal/t/evangelical-hispanics-turning-away-gop/.

Navarro-Rivera, Juhem, Barry A. Kosmin, and Ariela Keysar. 2010. "U.S. Latino Religious Identification, 1990–2008: Growth, Diversity and Transformation." Trinity College Digital Repository. Available at http://digitalrepository.trincoll.edu/facpub/9/.

Oboler, Suzanne. 1995. *Ethnic Labels, Latino Lives: Identity and the Politics of (Re)Presentation in the United States.* Minneapolis: University of Minnesota Press.

Pantoja, Adrian D. 2005. "Transnational Ties and Immigrant Political Incorporation: The Case of Dominicans in Washington Heights, New York." *International Migration* 43 (4): 123–146.

———. 2010. "The Effects of Being Born-Again Christian on Latino Socio-political Attitudes." *Journal of Religion and Society* 12. Available at https://dspace2.creighton.edu/xmlui/bitstream/handle/10504/64587/2010-16.pdf.

———. 2016. "Latino Voters Eager to Turnout against Trump and the GOP in 2016." Latino Decisions, April 27. Available at http://www.latinodecisions.com/blog/2016/04/27/latino-voters-eager-turnout-against-trump-and-the-gop-in-2016/.

Peters, Jeremy W., and Ashley Parker. 2015. "Rubio's History on Immigration Leaves Conservatives Distrustful of Shift." *New York Times*, November 15, p. 24.

Pew Research Center. 2007. "Changing Faiths: Latinos and the Transformation of American Religion." April 25. Available at http://www.pewforum.org/2007/04/25/changing-faiths-latinos-and-the-transformation-of-american-religion-2/.

———. 2009. "A Religious Portrait of African-Americans." January 30. Available at http://www.pewforum.org/2009/01/30/a-religious-portrait-of-african-americans/.

———. 2014. "The Shifting Religious Identity of Latinos in the United States." May 7. Available at http://www.pewforum.org/2014/05/07/the-shifting-religious-identity-of-latinos-in-the-united-states/.

Preston, Julia. 2009. "Latino Leaders Use Churches in Census Bid." *New York Times*, New York edition, p. 1.

Ramírez, Daniel. 2005. "Public Lives in American Hispanic Churches: Expanding the Paradigm." In *Latino Religions and Civic Activism in the United States*, edited by Gaston Espinosa, Virgilio Elizondo, and Jesse Miranda, 177–195. Oxford: Oxford University Press.

Ross, Janell. 2012. "Mitt Romney Latino Loss Shows Republicans 'Have Been Their Own Worst Enemy.'" *Huffington Post*, November 11. Available at http://www.huffingtonpost.com/2012/11/11/mitt-romney-latino-loss-republican_n_2104966.html.

Sanchez, Gabriel, and Matt A. Barreto. 2016. "In Record Numbers, Latinos Voted Overwhelmingly against Trump: We Did the Research." *Washington Post*, November 11. Available at https://www.washingtonpost.com/news/monkey-cage/wp/2016/11/11/in-record-numbers-latinos-voted-overwhelmingly-against-trump-we-did-the-research/.

Smidt, Corwin. 1988. "Evangelicals within Contemporary American Politics: Differentiating between Fundamentalist and Non-fundamentalist Evangelicals." *Western Political Quarterly* 41 (3): 601–620.

Suro, Roberto, Gabriel Escobar, Gretchen Livingston, Shirin Hakimzadeh, Luis Lugo, Sandra Stencel, John C. Green, Gregory A. Smith, Dan Cox, and Sahar Chaudhry. 2007. "Changing Faiths: Latinos and the Transformation of American Religion." Available at http://www.pewforum.org/files/2007/04/hispanics-religion-07-final-mar08.pdf.

Taylor, J. Benjamin, Sarah Allen Gershon, and Adrian D. Pantoja. 2014. "Christian America? Understanding the Link between Churches, Attitudes, and 'Being American' among Latino Immigrants." *Politics and Religion* 7 (2): 339–365.

Verba, Sidney, Kay L. Schlozman, Henry E. Brady, and Norman H. Nie. 1993. "Race, Ethnicity, and Political Resources: Participation in the United States." *British Journal of Political Science* 23 (4): 453–497.

Wald, Kenneth D., and Allison Calhoun-Brown. 2011. *Religion and Politics in the United States*. 6th ed. Lanham, MD: Rowman and Littlefield.

Wong, Janelle S. 2015. "The Role of Born-Again Identity on the Political Attitudes of Whites, Blacks, Latinos, and Asian Americans." *Politics and Religion* 8 (4): 641–678.

Wong, Janelle, Kathy Rim, and Haven Perez. 2008. "Protestant Churches and Conservative Politics: Latinos and Asians in the United States." In *Civic Hopes and Political Realities: Immigrants, Community Organizations, and Political Engagement*, edited by S. Karthick Ramakrishan and Irene Bloemraad, 271–299. New York: Russell Sage Foundation.

Woodberry, Robert D., and Christian S. Smith. 1998. "Fundamentalism et al: Conservative Protestants in America." *Annual Review of Sociology* 24:25–56.

Wuthnow, Robert, and Stephen Offutt. 2008. "Transnational Religious Connections." *Sociology of Religion* 69 (2): 209–232.

10

We Find Truth by Talking

*Comparing Authority in Evangelicalism
and the Emergent Church*

RYAN P. BURGE

The history of Protestant American Christianity is marked by movements and countermovements. The most easily distinguishable of these swings occurred during the 1950s, 1960s, and 1970s. The 1950s saw the peak of American religiosity (Grant 2008), with mainline Protestants and evangelicals sharing a quarter of the American population (R. Jones 2016). During the height of the "Red Scare" and McCarthyism, members of Congress passed several pieces of legislation that were meant to inoculate Americans against the atheistic allure of communist ideology. These statutes inserted "under God" in the Pledge of Allegiance (1954), added "In God We Trust" to currency (1956), and included the National Anthem as a necessary component of sporting events (Kruse 2016). In reaction to the spread of nationalized religiosity, the 1960s saw the rise of the "free love" movement, the proliferation of the drug culture, and the widespread use of contraceptives (Putnam and Campbell 2012, 91–95). This was followed by two decades of one of the most significant movements in recent political history: the ascendancy of the Religious Right. A number of charismatic pastors took advantage of the widespread adoption of televangelism and nationwide fund-raising to launch a movement that aimed to counter the liberalizing American culture by advocating for a return to family values on behalf of a "moral majority" in the United States (Armstrong 2010).

What may be the most interesting, surprising facet of the Religious Right is that the movement has not seen an organized and sustained reaction to it in the nearly four decades since its creation. While there has been some research to indicate that the strong marriage between evangelical Christianity and Republican politics has driven some moderate Christians to leave the faith entirely (Hout and Fischer 2002; Patrikios 2008), these unattached Christians never coalesced in a recognizable way until the last decade. A few of these evangelical "refugees" have joined together in a loose collective that has been dubbed "the emergent church" by observers. While the group is small (Burge and Djupe 2016), many evangelical leaders see this phenomenon as a potential threat to mainstream evangelicalism. In this chapter, I describe the basic outline of the emergent church movement (ECM), explain the potential it has to pose a serious challenge to evangelicalism, and detail why it may be destined to fail because of its most closely held principles.

Each year the Family Research Council hosts a summit of socially conservative activists in Washington, D.C. The meeting typically consists of keynote speeches by prominent conservative politicians and commentators and is designed to energize and educate voters on a host of Republican issues. In 2013 Art Ally, one of the featured speakers at the meeting, made headlines when the subject of his breakout session was revealed to be what he labeled the three adversaries to America: communism, Islam, and ECM. Ally stated, "The Emergent Church has watered down biblical Christianity" and "(is) weakening further our church community" (Pulliam-Bailey 2013).

In an incident that has become well known in evangelical circles, one of the leading voices of the ECM, Rob Bell, released a video that promoted his then-unreleased book *Love Wins*. In the teaser video, Bell makes reference to Mahatma Gandhi and questions whether human beings can know for certain that Gandhi went to Hell after his death (Bell 2011b). This video quickly created a backlash in the evangelical community, with John Piper, a conservative evangelical pastor, famously tweeting, "Farewell Rob Bell" (Menzie 2011). Piper was joined by Al Mohler, president of the Southern Baptist Theological Seminary, who called Bell's book "theologically disastrous" (Meacham 2011).

These religious elites are not alone in their critique of the ECM but have joined a chorus of its opponents who are troubled by the movement on several fronts. As has been described, the most vocal of these critics have often been evangelical leaders who feel that the ECM is not just another form of rebranded Christianity but a type of spirituality that they believe borders on heresy (Burke and Taylor 2008). This opposition stems from the belief that the emergent church was created to pick off younger evangelicals who were critical of an evangelicalism that is all too often intolerant and ultraconservative (DeYoung and Kluck 2008).

Dimensions of the Emergent Church Challenge

The emergent church developed in a way that mirrors how the group has evolved over time: in an organic, largely leaderless fashion. In the early 1990s a small group of youth pastors held a series of meetings in which the conversation continued to return to their belief that the tried-and-true methods of outreach and evangelism were no longer working with the next generation of teenagers who were coming-of-age (Gibbs and Bolger 2005). A series of discussions coalesced around the understanding that this generation of children born in the late 1970s was entering adolescence in a post-Christian world and that this would have a profound impact on the way that the evangelical establishment must approach them (Kimball 2003). In its beginning stages, the ECM was embraced by evangelical leadership. However, when some of the early leaders in the movement began to push for a fundamental rethinking of many of the central tenets of evangelicalism, a chasm began to form between the two groups, and many mainline denominations began to embrace the kind of change advocated by the ECM (Burge and Djupe 2015; T. Jones 2009).

As the new millennium began to take shape, the ECM started to position itself as a place of refuge for young people who grew up in a conservative evangelical church and felt stifled by its homogeneity and perceived lack of authenticity (Marti 2009). In fact, many members of the ECM tell remarkably similar stories of how they came of age in a church that they never truly felt a part of and struggled with the decision of whether to merely leave the Christian tradition of their parents and find a new denomination or to leave Christianity entirely (Hempton 2008). These "deconversion" stories often contain a section in which adherents of the ECM say that when they first discovered the movement, there was a sense of relief knowing that they were not alone in their struggles with evangelical Christianity (Bielo 2012; Chia 2011). What attracts these young people to emergent Christianity is a focus on relativism, inclusivism, and a belief that conversation is the greatest exercise in spiritual formation.

Relativism

While evangelicals often criticize the ECM on a number of fronts, many of their points of departure stem from the emergent emphasis on a subjective interpretation of the Bible and Christian doctrine. Many emergent scholars find the roots of emergent Christianity in the postmodern philosophy of Jacques Derrida and Stanley Fish, who contend that any interpretation of the Bible is filtered through the reader's culturally constructed paradigm and is therefore unique to the individual (McKnight 2007). Tony Jones, the former leader of the Emergent Village, writes, "The emergent Christians are attempting another tack, one that steers between the Scylla of secularism and the Charybdis of fundamentalism. It's what might be called the postmodern posture: an attempt to both maintain one's distinctive identity while also being truly open to the identity of the other" (2009, 39).

Many outside observers have noted that because of emergent Christians' emphasis on constantly reevaluating and reconsidering their faith, "defining the emergent church is like nailing Jell-O to a wall" (DeYoung and Kluck 2008, 16–17). Evangelical theologians struggle with how to engage the emergent position because emergent leaders have been consistently evasive in interviews and purposely describe their personal theology in vague statements that are hard to pin down (Taylor 2011). This frustration is encapsulated on the back cover of the book *Why We're Not Emergent: By Two Guys Who Should Be*, which states, "Here's the Truth—There *Is* Truth," in bold letters. One of the most prominent emergent theologians, Brian McLaren, refuted this claim, "because the answer lies beyond both absolutism and relativism" (McLaren and Campolo 2006, 38).

The emergent approach to biblical authority and truth is diametrically opposed to the pervasive belief in evangelicalism that the Bible is literally true (Sproul et al. 2009). For example, Rev. Jerry Falwell, who was one of the most influential pastors in the Religious Right movement, was fond of saying, "The entire Bible, from Genesis to Revelation, is the inerrant Word of God, and totally accurate in all respects" (Ice 2009, 1). This stands in opposition to the overwhelming belief by the ECM that there is no objective understanding of the Bible, but instead everyone is limited by his or her own personal experience and bias. Rob Bell writes, "The idea that everybody else approaches the Bible with baggage and agendas and lenses and I don't is the ultimate in arrogance" (2009, 54).

Inclusivism

If the emergent church places a great deal of emphasis on its desire to understand the scripture from a variety of viewpoints, then it logically follows that the ECM would focus its effort on trying to include a large variety of diverging voices in its gatherings. Instead of focusing on ways to create their own social identity, emergent communities are interested in finding areas of common concern and agreement with other faith communities (Burke, Grenz, and Pepper 2003). One social scientist contends that the ECM has attempted to "decenter" itself from the Western, male-dominated style of Christianity and encourages an inclusive understanding of faith to include those who have often been marginalized by this approach, including women and minorities (Chia 2011, 139).

In addition, the ECM is quick to describe a faith that does not belong specifically to one type of Protestant Christian but instead focuses on revealing a faith that is already present in everyday life. There are many instances of emergent speakers arguing that Christian missionaries are not bringing Jesus to foreign populations. They instead state that the "truth is everywhere and available to everyone" (Bell 2011a, 78). If this is the case, then the role of a missionary is not to bring Jesus to a foreign population but to "[point] out to the people there the creative, life-giving God who is already in their midst" (Bell 2009, 88).

One interesting consequence of this belief is that the ECM struggles with the concept of authority and leadership. For instance, one observer notes, "Many emergent pastors seem to find the very notion of clergy slightly embarrassing" (Worthen 2013, 256). Thus, some prominent emergents believe that the best types of leaders are those "who refuse leadership" (Rollins 2008). Evangelical leadership, however, is clearly delineated and focused on lines of authority. Nancy Ammerman describes the structure as "a biblically legitimated expert provid[ing] unquestioned and respected leadership for those less able to care for themselves" (1987, 128). The ECM focus on inclusion bristles at the idea of one person dictating theology to the membership. Instead, the ECM believes that its theology and practice evolve and progress through their intentional focus on dialogue and conversation. While some critics, such as Scot McKnight (2007) have doubted whether the ECM is truly welcoming to political conservatives, some scholarship has provided support for the ECM's insistence on inclusion (Burge and Djupe 2015).

Faith through Conversation

Lloyd Chia, a social scientist writes, "The emerging church uses the metaphor of conversation to describe itself" (2011, 61). Possibly the most important and influential work in emergent theology, *A New Kind of Christian*, takes place almost completely as a conversation between a high school biology teacher who has embraced emergent theology and a middle-aged pastor who is struggling with orthodox evangelicalism (McLaren 2008). Brian D. McLaren and Tony Campolo (2006) write about the ECM's view of the world in a conversational style between the two authors; and a compilation by Leonard Sweet and colleagues presents five perspectives on the ECM and contains thoughts by other ECM leaders in the margins of each page (Sweet et al. 2003).

This approach to conversation is infused through all parts of the ECM worship experience. In a typical evangelical service, the pastor speaks in a monologue style that often concludes with an altar call and invitational hymn, which McLaren describes as "selling God as if God were selling vinyl siding, replacement windows, or a mortgage refinancing service" (2009, 8). Instead, the emergent approach begins with a committee meeting during the week to work on sermon preparation. This results in a collaborative effort that is delivered during the worship service by one member of the congregation. This "progressional dialogue," as it has been called, is then transitioned into a time devoted to discussion, questions, and answers from the membership (T. Jones 2009, 38; Wollschleger 2011). While evangelical services give a few minutes to their altar calls, the emergent approach is an open-ended one that focuses on dialogue, debate, and "pushing listeners to reflection" on the biblical text and its application (Marti and Ganiel 2014, 115–116).

These times of dialogue are crucial to the ECM. According to Phyllis Tickle, "When one asks an emergent Christian where ultimate authority lies, he or she will sometimes choose to say either 'in Scripture' or 'in the Community.' More often though, he or she will run the two together and respond, 'in Scripture and the community'" (2012, 151). The result of this emphasis is that the role of the clergy is greatly diminished and the theology of the congregation bends and evolves as a direct result of the shifting theology of the community members.

Taken in total, emergent theology stands in stark opposition to traditional evangelical theology. Emergents are reluctant to indicate that there is one objective way to read the Bible and understand Christ's teaching, while evangelicals are known for their strong adherence to an established canon of orthodox thought. While many evangelicals are quick to draw sharp contrasts between their social group and outsiders, the ECM encourages a diversity of viewpoints and seeks out individuals from diverse backgrounds to join the religious community. Both of these points come together in the ECM's pursuit of faith through conversation. While the writing of emergent leaders paints this coherent picture of the movement, the real question is if those ideals have managed to find their way into the personal theology of members of other Christian communities.

Data

When considering the most likely population to be exposed and internalize the teachings of the ECM, it would seem that members of the clergy would be the most aware and receptive to this new way of thinking. A large body of previous research has indicated that clergy serve important roles in opinion formation among their congregations (Olson 2000; Quinley 1974; Stark 1971). While pastors are admittedly not perfect representatives of what their parishioners believe, they can serve as an early indication of a shift in the theology of local church communities. To this end, a survey was conducted among American clergy in a number of Christian traditions, including the Southern Baptist Convention, the United Methodist Church, the Reformed Church in America, the Presbyterian Church (USA), and clergy from the Greek Orthodox Church. This survey was distributed using the Qualtrics Panels, and 411 clergy responded to at least one question. It is important to point out that while this sample does contain several important Christian denominations, it does not accurately represent all of American Christianity. It seems likely that because of the somewhat unstructured nature of the ECM, these churches are not denominationally affiliated; previous scholarship has indicated that many of the most prominent ECM gatherings were initially sponsored by established denominations, and some are still linked to groups such as Lutherans, Baptists, and Presbyterians (Chia 2011, 203–204). The overall strength of these data is that they do contain a significant sample size, as well as a number of questions that tap into an overall belief in emergent values.

Analysis

In the survey, participants could check a box next to a few possible descriptors, such as "evangelical," "orthodox," and "emergent." For purposes of this study those who checked the "emergent" box (approximately 6 percent of this sample) are compared with the remainder of the sample that did not identify as emergent. To determine how these two samples differ theologically, the survey contained a battery of questions that attempted to measure the theological conservatism of the sample: the Bible is literally true, Jesus will return to earth in bodily form, Jesus was born of a virgin, there is an objective standard of right and wrong established by God's word, and men are given authority over women. Respondents were given five response options ranging from strongly disagree (1) to strongly agree (5). The means for the two samples are displayed at the top of Figure 10.1 as dot plots. Each of these group means was significantly different at the .05 level.

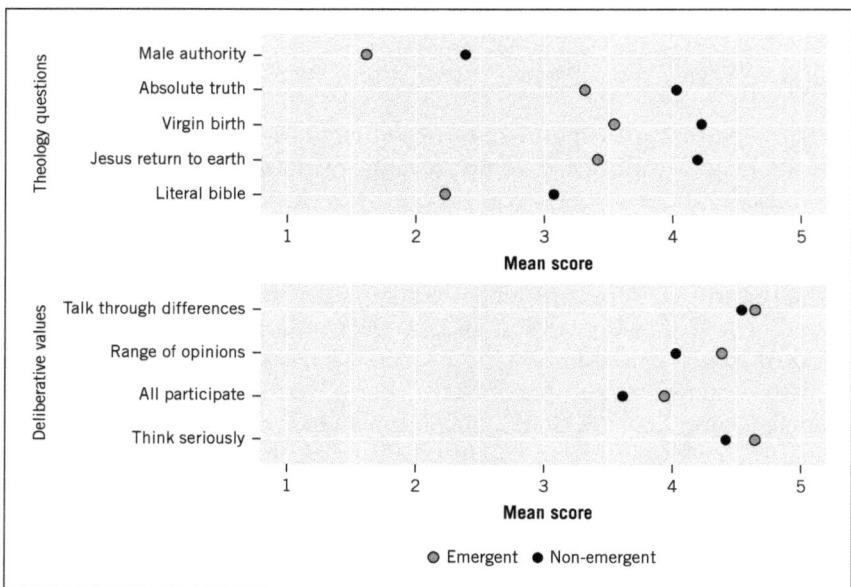

Figure 10.1 Emergent versus non-emergent responses to theology and deliberation questions

On each of these five questions, the portion of the sample that self-identified as emergent was more theologically liberal. For each question, the means between the samples were approximately three-quarters of a point apart on a five-point scale. Taken in total, these results provide support for the belief that emergent Christians are more theologically liberal than their non-emergent counterparts, and this difference is carried through across a wide range of Christian theology, including eschatology, truth, and the roles of women in society. This comports with the general perception of qualitative scholars of the movement who have noted its theological flexibility (Chia 2011; Marti and Ganiel 2014).

In addition to their openness to considering different approaches to Christian theology, the ECM places a great deal of emphasis on the role of dialogue in shaping its faith community. The survey included several questions to determine how eager clergy were to focus on true deliberation happening in their congregations. This deliberative-values battery contained the following statements regarding church-conducted forums: "We would explicitly encourage participants to think seriously about the views of others," "it would be essential that all those present participate," "it would be essential that a range of views are presented," and "it would be essential for participants to learn how to talk through their differences." Forums that encourage serious dialogue and openness would seem to be in line with how emergents see the role of the church (McLaren 2015), and these results indicate that emergent pastors are more committed to deliberation than their non-emergent colleagues. Of the four statements displayed here, all but "talk through their differences" have statistically different means at the .05 level. These three statements all indicated that emergent clergy are more committed to dialogue and openness during adult forums and would encourage participation and contemplation among the participants. These results seem to align with the ECM's approach to worship services that are more participatory in nature and provide a great deal of freedom for laity to debate theological and social issues with each other and the clergy (Wollschleger 2011).

One way in which the ECM has actively encouraged this inclusive dialogue is by advocating for an organizational model that puts less emphasis on identifiable clergy and instead seeks to generate a "flat" organizational model that stands in stark opposition to the traditional church hierarchy (T. Jones 2011, 22). A section of the survey attempted to assess if clergy had a strong view of religious authority or favored a more inclusive model of leadership. Five items were summed to create a scale of religious authority ($\alpha = .66$): "The more clergy can step out of the way of the congregation the better," "it is important for the congregation to construct their own salvation," "the Gospel is what the congregation makes of it," "the church must adapt to a postmodern culture in order to spread the Gospel," and "I believe there are many valid interpretations of the Bible." The religious-authority scale runs from zero (low view of religious authority) to one (a stronger belief in religious authority) (mean = .67).

Figure 10.2 uses the religious-identification labels mentioned previously to compare the religious-authority means of each of these groups. The vertical dashed line indicates the religious-authority mean for the entire sample, and the capped line indicates the 95 percent confidence intervals for each mean. As is apparent, labels that conventionally are associated with conservative theology, including "fundamentalist" and "evangelical," have a higher view of religious authority. However, as one moves to the lower portion of the histogram, labels like "liberal" and "emergent" show low views of religious authority. For example, emergents have on average 20 percent lower views of religious authority than conservatives and 15 percent lower authority scores than evangelicals.

One of the most intriguing questions regarding the ECM is whether the political ideology of its supporters is orthogonal to the Republican Party's. To test this relationship, a regression model was specified using a seven-point scale of party identification as the dependent variable, with higher values indicating more Republican affiliation. A variable that indicated support of the ECM was included along with a number of control variables. This model included measures based on gender, race, number of years in ministry (a proxy for age), education, and the size of the community of the pastor's church. In addition, there was a scaled variable of religious conservativism

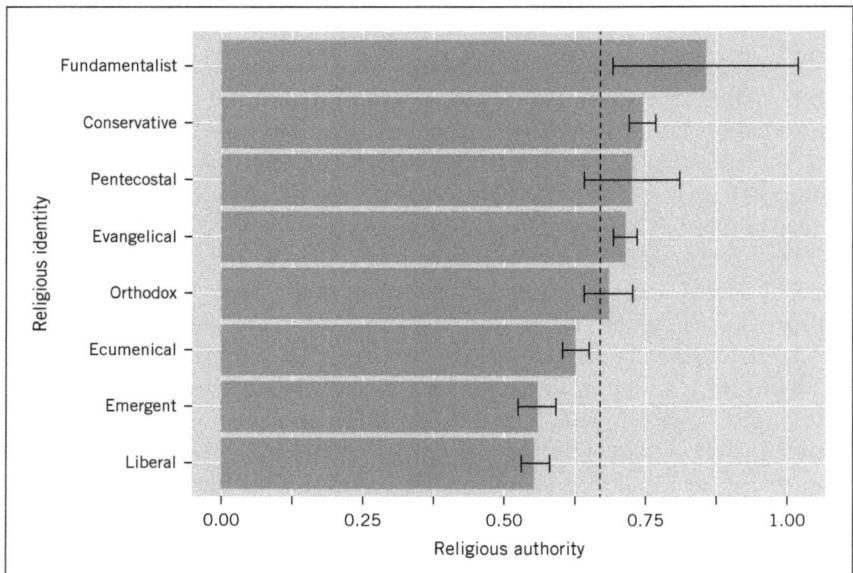

Figure 10.2 Religious-authority means by religious identity

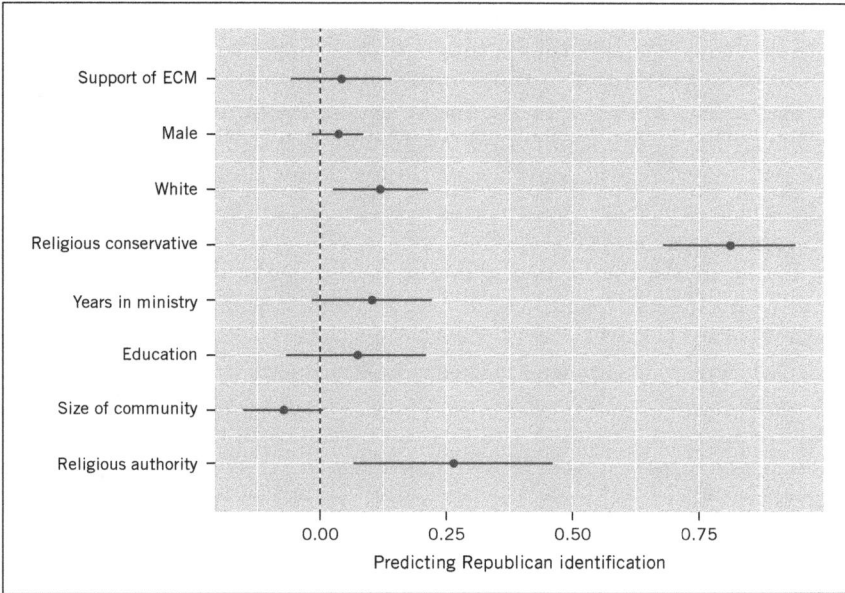

Figure 10.3 Coefficient plot predicting Republican Party identification

($\alpha = .94$) and a scaled variable for religious authority. Figure 10.3 displays the results in a coefficient plot. In this plot, variables that intersect with the vertical dashed line are not statistically significant, variables to the right of the line predict a stronger Republican affiliation, and variables to the left predict more Democratic leanings. The relationship between supporting the ECM and supporting the Republican Party is inconclusive in this analysis, as the coefficient cannot be determined to differ from zero. However, those who hold more conservative religious theology and those who hold a higher view of religious authority are more likely to describe themselves as Republican. These results comport with a great deal of previous literature that indicates a strong linkage between religious and political conservatism, and the religious-authority measure provides an additional angle for support for Republican politics (Green 1996; Green, Rozell, and Wilcox 2000).

Conclusion

Modern American evangelism has enjoyed a nearly forty-year dominance on the Christian landscape. This grip may be loosening, however, as a number of forces have begun to chip away at the demographic margins evangelicals have enjoyed. These fractures seem to be occurring on two fronts: individuals becoming unattached to evangelicalism entirely but finding a religious

home in another Protestant tradition or now seeing themselves as unaffiliated (R. Jones 2016). But it appears that the emergent church is well positioned to attract some of these individuals who are disillusioned with
evangelicalism but not Christianity in general. A number of studies have
concluded that young people are much more supportive of rights for gays
and lesbians (Kinnaman and Lyons 2012; R. Jones 2016), and the emergent
approach to inclusivity and tolerance is well suited to welcome these spiritual
refugees (Burge and Djupe 2015).

However, while the emergent critique of evangelicalism may be palatable
to some disaffected Christians, it may be likely that it was never set up to
succeed in the first place because of the general aims of the movement. The
fact that many of the earliest leaders of the emergent movement went out of
their way to not call themselves leaders (T. Jones et al. 2005) or to even identify as emergent (McLaren and Campolo 2006, 249) makes it difficult to
present a coherent message to Christians who are considering leaving their
current evangelical church. The fact that there was no recognized ECM national leadership, along with the emergent belief that there should be little to
no leadership at the local church level (T. Jones 2011), makes it impossible for
an emergent community to appear organized and coherent to those who
may be interested in the movement's approach to Christianity.

While the Religious Right has evolved slowly into more nondenominational megachurches, it still holds together as generally recognizable evangelical Christianity (Loveland and Wheeler 2003). The same, however,
cannot be said for emergent Christianity. For example, one of earliest leaders
of the ECM stated in 2008, "I can't defend or even explain theologically what
is now known broadly as 'the emerging church' anymore, because it has
developed into so many significantly different theological strands. Some I
strongly would disagree with" (Scaramanga 2008). This may be both the
greatest strength and the greatest weakness of the ECM.

The emergent movement might be seen by history as the so-called canary
in the coal mine, a pioneering group that tried to split the difference between
the liberalism of mainline Christianity and the conservative dogma of evangelicalism. While the GOP has catered to right-leaning Christians by continuing to campaign on the appointment of pro-life judges to the Supreme
Court (Benen 2016), even President Donald Trump has indicated that gay
marriage is a settled matter and his administration will not challenge its
legality (Stokols 2016). In addition, many evangelical leaders have become
vocal critics of the position of the Republican Party on allowing refugees to
seek asylum in the United States (Shellnutt 2017). ECM's most widely re-
garded theologian, Brian McLaren (2017), has been vocally opposed to the
presidency of Donald Trump, possibly in hopes of reaching younger evangelicals who bristle at their tradition's strong support of his administration.
If a group is still explicitly Christian, as the ECM is, but also presents a mes-

sage of welcoming and inclusion, the GOP may not be able to count on the evangelical vote in future electoral cycles.

REFERENCES

Ammerman, Nancy. 1987. *Bible Believers*. New Brunswick, NJ: Rutgers University Press.

Armstrong, Karen. 2010. *The Case for God*. New York: Anchor.

Bell, Rob. 2009. *Velvet Elvis: Repainting the Christian Faith*. Grand Rapids, MI: Zondervan.

———. 2011a. *Love Wins: A Book about Heaven, Hell, and the Fate of Every Person Who Ever Lived*. New York: HarperCollins.

———. 2011b. Promotion for *Love Wins: A Book about Heaven, Hell, and the Fate of Every Person Who Ever Lived*. Available at http://www.youtube.com/watch?v=ivwfcBNICf4&feature=youtube_gdata_player.

Benen, Steve. 2016. "Trump's Promise: 'I Will Appoint Judges That Will Be Pro-Life.'" *MSNBC*, May 11. Available at http://www.msnbc.com/rachel-maddow-show/trumps-promise-i-will-appoint-judges-will-be-pro-life.

Bielo, James S. 2012. "Belief, Deconversion, and Authenticity among U.S. Emerging Evangelicals." *Ethos* 40 (3): 258–276.

Burge, Ryan P., and Paul A. Djupe. 2015. "Emergent Church Practices in America: Inclusion and Deliberation in American Congregations." *Review of Religious Research* 57 (1): 1–23.

———. 2016. "Emergent Fault Lines: Clergy Attitudes toward the Emergent Church Movement." *Journal of Religious Leadership* 15 (1): 5–30.

Burke, Spencer, Stanley J. Grenz, and Colleen Pepper. 2003. *Making Sense of Church: Eavesdropping on Emerging Conversations about God, Community, and Culture*. Grand Rapids, MI: Zondervan/Youth Specialties.

Burke, Spencer, and Barry Taylor. 2008. *A Heretic's Guide to Eternity*. San Francisco: Jossey-Bass.

Chia, Lloyd. 2011. "Emerging Faith Boundaries: Bridge-Building, Inclusion, and the Emerging Church Movement in America." Ph.D. diss., University of Missouri.

DeYoung, Kevin L., and Ted A. Kluck. 2008. *Why We're Not Emergent: By Two Guys Who Should Be*. Chicago: Moody.

Gibbs, Eddie, and Ryan K. Bolger. 2005. *Emerging Churches: Creating Christian Community in Postmodern Cultures*. Grand Rapids, MI: Baker Academic.

Grant, J. Tobin. 2008. "Measuring Aggregate Religiosity in the United States, 1952–2005." *Sociological Spectrum* 28 (5): 460–476.

Green, John C. 1996. *Religion and the Culture Wars: Dispatches from the Front*. Lanham, MD: Rowman and Littlefield.

Green, John C., Mark J. Rozell, and Clyde Wilcox. 2000. *Prayers in the Precincts: The Christian Right in the 1998 Elections*. Washington, DC: Georgetown University Press.

Hempton, David. 2008. *Evangelical Disenchantment: Nine Portraits of Faith and Doubt*. New Haven, CT: Yale University Press.

Hout, Michael, and Claude S. Fischer. 2002. "Why More Americans Have No Religious Preference: Politics and Generations." *American Sociological Review* 67 (2): 155–190.

Ice, Thomas. 2009. "The Falwell Legacy: The Bible, the Blood, and the Blessed Hope." Available at http://digitalcommons.liberty.edu/pretrib_arch/17.

Jones, Robert P. 2016. *The End of White Christian America*. New York: Simon and Schuster.

Jones, Tony. 2009. *The New Christians: Dispatches from the Emergent Frontier*. San Francisco: Jossey-Bass.

———. 2011. *The Church Is Flat: The Relational Ecclesiology of the Emerging Church Movement*. Minneapolis, MN: JoPa Group.

Jones, Tony, Doug Pagitt, Spencer Burker, Brian McLaren, Dan Kimball, Andrew Jones, and Chris Seay. 2005. "Our Response to Critics of Emergent." Available at http://emergent -us.typepad.com/emergentus/2005/06/official_respon.html.

Kimball, Dan. 2003. *The Emerging Church: Vintage Christianity for New Generations*. Grand Rapids, MI: Zondervan/Youth Specialties.

Kinnaman, David, and Gabe Lyons. 2012. *UnChristian: What a New Generation Really Thinks about Christianity . . . and Why It Matters*. Grand Rapids, MI: Baker Books.

Kruse, Kevin M. 2016. *One Nation under God: How Corporate America Invented Christian America*. New York: Basic Books.

Loveland, Anne C., and Otis B. Wheeler. 2003. *From Meetinghouse to Megachurch: A Material and Cultural History*. Columbia: University of Missouri Press.

Marti, Gerardo. 2009. *A Mosaic of Believers: Diversity and Innovation in a Multiethnic Church*. Bloomington: Indiana University Press.

Marti, Gerardo, and Gladys Ganiel. 2014. *The Deconstructed Church: Understanding Emerging Christianity*. New York: Oxford University Press.

McKnight, Scot. 2007. "Five Streams of the Emerging Church." *Christianity Today*, January 19. Available at http://www.christianitytoday.com/ct/2007/february/11.35.html.

McLaren, Brian D. 2008. *A New Kind of Christian: A Tale of Two Friends on a Spiritual Journey*. San Francisco: Jossey-Bass.

———. 2009. *More Ready Than You Realize: The Power of Everyday Conversations*. Grand Rapids, MI: Zondervan.

———. 2015. *We Make the Road by Walking: A Year-Long Quest for Spiritual Formation, Reorientation, and Activation*. New York: Jericho Books.

———. 2017. "Being Church in the Trump Years (Part 1)." February 17. Available at https:// brianmclaren.net/being-church-in-the-trump-years-part-1/.

McLaren, Brian D., and Tony Campolo. 2006. *Adventures in Missing the Point: How the Culture-Controlled Church Neutered the Gospel*. Grand Rapids, MI: Zondervan/Youth Specialties.

Meacham, Jon. 2011. "Pastor Rob Bell: What If Hell Doesn't Exist?" *Time*, April 14. Available at http://content.time.com/time/magazine/article/0,9171,2065289,00.html.

Menzie, Nicole. 2011. "Has John Piper's 'Farewell, Rob Bell' Prediction Come to Pass?" *Christian Post*, September 23. Available at http://www.christianpost.com/news/has-john -pipers-farewell-rob-bell-prediction-come-to-pass-56382/.

Olson, Laura R. 2000. *Filled with Spirit and Power: Protestant Clergy in Politics*. Albany: State University of New York Press.

Patrikios, Stratos. 2008. "American Republican Religion? Disentangling the Causal Link Between Religion and Politics in the US." *Political Behavior* 30 (3): 367–389.

Pulliam Bailey, Sarah. 2013. "Newest 'Values Voters' Adversary to America: The Emergent Church." *Religion News Service*, August 27. Available at http://www.religionnews.com/ 2013/08/27/newest-values-voters-adversary-to-america-the-emergent-church/.

Putnam, Robert D., and David E. Campbell. 2012. *American Grace: How Religion Divides and Unites Us*. New York: Simon and Schuster.

Quinley, Harold E. 1974. *The Prophetic Clergy: Social Activism among Protestant Ministers*. New York: John Wiley and Sons.

Rollins, Peter. 2008. "The Leader Is Needed in Order to Refuse Leadership." *Peter Rollins* (blog), April 4. Available at http://web.archive.org/web/20160524225648/http:// peterrollins.net/2008/04/the-leader-is-needed-in-order-to-refuse-leadership/.

Scaramanga, Url. 2008. "R.I.P. Emerging Church." *CT Pastors*, September. Available at http:// www.christianitytoday.com/pastors/2008/september-online-only/rip-emerging-church .html.

Shellnutt, Kate. 2017. "Evangelical Experts Oppose Trump's Plan to Ban Refugees." *Christianity Today*, January 25. Available at http://www.christianitytoday.com/ct/2017/january-web-only/evangelical-experts-oppose-trump-plan-to-ban-refugees-syria.html.
Sproul, R. C., Joel R. Beeke, Sinclair B. Ferguson, W. Robert Godfrey, Ray Lanning, John MacArthur, Derek W. H. Thomas, and James White. 2009. *Sola Scriptura: The Protestant Position on the Bible*. Edited by Don Kistler. 2nd ed. Orlando, FL: Reformation Trust.
Stark, Rodney. 1971. *Wayward Shepherds, Prejudice and the Protestant Clergy*. New York: Harper and Row.
Stokols, Eli. 2016. "Trump Says He's 'Fine' with Legalization of Same-Sex Marriage.'" *Politico*, November 13. Available at http://politi.co/2fQe7pw.
Sweet, Leonard, Andy Crouch, Brian D. McLaren, Erwin Raphael McManus, Michael Horton, and Frederica Matthewes-Green. 2003. *The Church in Emerging Culture: Five Perspectives*. El Cajon, CA: Zondervan/Youth Specialties.
Taylor, Justin. 2011. "MSNBC: Martin Bashir's Interview with Rob Bell." *TGC*, March 15. Available at https://blogs.thegospelcoalition.org/justintaylor/2011/03/15/msnbc-martin-bashirs-interview-with-rob-bell/.
Tickle, Phyllis. 2012. *The Great Emergence: How Christianity Is Changing and Why*. Grand Rapids, MI: Baker Books.
Wollschleger, Jason. 2011. "Off the Map? Locating the Emerging Church: A Comparative Case Study of Congregations in the Pacific Northwest." *Review of Religious Research* 54 (1): 69–91.
Worthen, Molly. 2013. *Apostles of Reason: The Crisis of Authority in American Evangelicalism*. New York: Oxford University Press.

11

The Political Networks of Evangelicals, 1992–2016

PAUL A. DJUPE
JACOB R. NEIHEISEL
ANAND E. SOKHEY

Because of the high boundaries that evangelicals are often encouraged to place between themselves and the secular world, we have strong theoretical notions about both the form and function of their social environments. Thus, in many ways it is particularly surprising—and more than a little troubling—how little evidence we have concerning the structure and composition of evangelicals' interpersonal networks.

The boundaries we typically associate with evangelicals are rooted in an emphasis on theological purity, congregational social engagement (Iannaccone 1994), and behavioral limitations; these lead to the widespread assumption that evangelicals' networks are generally characterized by "strong ties." Strong ties can be denoted by a number of factors (e.g., greater intimacy; more frequent interaction; multiple, overlapping-relationships) and are often associated with the promotion of communication (for a discussion, see Lazer et al. 2015).

Of course, networks that feature such connections are also famous for being insular—for promoting information that shields people from disagreement (Granovetter 1973; Huckfeldt et al. 1995). That is, when scholars talk generally about "strong" networks, they often mean ones that reinforce agreeable information, a meaning that we adopt here. This all makes sense given the political implications that typically turn from such networks: attitude polarization and opinion extremity (e.g., Djupe and Calfano 2009; Levitan and Visser 2009; Putnam and Campbell 2010; Sunstein 2002), both of which are essential for the creation and sustenance of political movements like the Christian Right.

In this chapter, we evaluate the degree to which we might reasonably call evangelical networks "strong" compared to those of other religious groups. How much political disagreement do evangelicals encounter in their social environment? To answer this question, we look at rates of interpersonal agreement by religious group, drawing on nationwide studies of the United States that include batteries designed to measure core social networks. We then consider the consequences of exposure to disagreement, focusing on how disagreement is linked to support for Christian Right groups. Contrary to popular and scholarly perception, we find evangelicals' networks to be unremarkable in their levels of agreement. We also find evidence that exposure to difference seems to *strengthen* evangelicals' positive opinions toward Christian Right groups.

If there is a coming crackup, the social sciences tell us that one strong indicator may be social chinks in the armor—that is, the diversification of social ties as more and more evangelicals admit of greater degrees of religious and political diversity within their interpersonal networks. At the same time, as we find evidence that exposure to disagreement seems to actually strengthen opinions toward Christian Right groups, we note that social processes may play out in unanticipated ways. Exposure to disagreement is only half the battle, which reminds us that assuming any one set of effects for a large group is likely misguided.

Religious Networks, Political Diversity, and Opinion Extremity

Religion is a social institution. Religious organizations provide opportunities for social engagement but also a set of norms prescribing the ways in which adherents should interact with others and in which others are acceptable social companions. Religion's opportunities and norms both compete with the larger society for the attention of adherents. The social fact of religion makes it difficult to study either aspect of the religious experience in isolation, which is not to say that there have not been studies. Early research on recruitment into nontraditional or New Age faiths, where social ties and norms are evolving, served to underscore the importance of social ties to the decision of whether to join a particular religious group (see, for instance, Lofland and Stark 1965). Subsequent work placed social networks at the center of religious life more generally (see Everton 2015 for a review), helping encourage the adoption of beliefs and behaviors normative to the group (e.g., Cavendish, Welch, and Leege 1998; Cornwall 1987; Welch 1981). In general, conformity to group norms has repeatedly been found to track with the nature of the networks formed within religious organizations; dense, reinforcing networks—where friends of friends are friends—help promote adherence to behavioral rules through social monitoring (Everton 2015; for similar discussions of mechanisms outside the religious context, see, e.g., Sinclair

2012). Over time, such conformity pressures are expected to result in highly agreeable social environments (for relevant discussions on the survival of disagreement, see Huckfeldt, Johnson, and Sprague 2004).

Although most, if not all, religious groups are widely believed to lead to the creation and maintenance of tight-knit social ties among frequent church attenders (Putnam and Campbell 2010, 436), "theologically strict groups, that is, those whose beliefs place high demands on people's time, money, and behavior," are thought to aid in the construction of especially dense networks among their followers (Everton 2015, 8; see also Wald, Owen, and Hill 1990). Relative to religious communities that offer more lenient interpretations of the faith, strict churches simply demand more from their members (Iannaccone 1994); such religious organizations encourage regular attendance at religious services and discourage socialization outside the group or engagement with the secular world (Sherkat and Wilson 1995). For instance, Sean F. Everton points out that members of "high tension groups," or "sects," including those who attend churches affiliated with the Southern Baptist, Assemblies of God, or Seventh-Day Adventist denominations, have denser networks than those affiliated with other denominations (2015, 9–10). (Most coding schemes would characterize all three such denominations as evangelical.)

Of course, others have highlighted the dense—and expectedly agreeable—nature of evangelicals' social environments. As Charles Y. Glock and Rodney Stark pointed out in their canonical study, those who belong to evangelical denominations reported having more "close friends" who were members of the same congregation. According to their surveys, "more conservative (religious) groups tend to resemble moral communities," wherein the "congregation serves as a *primary source of informal social relations*" (Glock and Stark 1965, 163; emphasis in original). For instance, almost half of those who belonged to what Glock and Stark called sects—members of denominations such as the Assemblies of God, the Church of God, and the Church of the Nazarene—reported that four or more of their closest friends attended the same church. Similarly, members of evangelical denominations were also more likely to indicate that they did not personally know someone of the Jewish faith (Glock and Stark 1966).

The Political Implications of Strong Ties

Strong tie–rich environments hold a number of political implications. Just as church-based networks may promote uniformity in religious belief and widespread agreement on the main tenets of the faith, we might expect evangelicals' social environments to promote political conformity and connections to opportunities for political activism (see Djupe and Gilbert 2009; Rosenstone and Hansen 1993). Robert D. Putnam and David E. Campbell summarize the process as follows: "Social interaction among like-minded co-religionists reinforces and even hardens one's beliefs, even if the process is subtle" (2010, 437). For evidence, they point out that there are close connections between religiosity and partisanship among those deeply embedded in social networks comprising other religious identifiers (cf. Djupe and Gilbert 2009; Sokhey and Mockabee 2012).

Of course, if church-based networks (and in this case, evangelicals' networks) are dominated by agreement, then the dismissal of them as potential sources for reasoned debate and deliberation makes sense. Indeed, religious networks have often been treated as social spaces in which "talk is needed to count numbers and build up courage, but after that they march against the enemy" (Tocqueville 1969, 193). Insular networks do more than just reinforce and strengthen opinions among the faithful. Such homogeneity might actually cause movement toward the views of the most extreme elements within the network (Everton 2015; Wojcieszak 2011). It is not surprising, then, that militaristic metaphors have been used to describe the willingness of the faithful—and evangelicals in particular—to confront the political world as part of a unified front. Dense, agreeable networks of coreligionists are typically thought to be central to stories about evangelicals (and others) mobilizing for political action.

Given existing work, perhaps the modal expectation is that interpersonal agreement is going to strengthen opinions and pave the way for political action. In turn, this implies that the complement—disagreement—is going to moderate opinions and stand as a barrier to participation (Mutz 2006). However, it is also possible that exposure to disagreement strengthens opinions, serving to clarify differences via something akin to social categorization (e.g., Tajfel and Turner 1979; Seyle and Newman 2006). Indeed, the presence of disagreement may actually prove a benefit, not by moderating opinion but by motivating individuals to search for support. In this way, social discord may help connect individuals to the interest groups that best represent them (Djupe 2011; Djupe and Lewis 2015; Djupe and Neiheisel 2008).

Data

Are evangelicals' social networks becoming more politically diverse? How does disagreement among evangelicals link to their voting for Republican candidates and support for the Christian Right? To address these and other questions, we need studies that contain items on interpersonal networks.

Social-network data are somewhat hard to come by in omnibus data-gathering efforts like the General Social Survey and the American National Election Studies. However, we use what is available (the 1992 Comparative National Elections Project [CNEP]; 2000 American National Election

Studies [ANES]; and the 2008–2009 ANES) and then supplement these with our original panel data sets collected in 2012 and 2016.[1] In each, survey respondents were asked to generate names of discussion partners, though the wording of these "name generators" varied considerably. Some asked about discussion of important matters, while others asked some variation of discussion about "politics, campaigns, and elections." Those differences do produce somewhat different, though not tremendously different, networks (see Klofstad, McClurg, and Rolfe 2009; Sokhey and Djupe 2014).

In addition to differences in name generators across these studies, we also see differences in the measurement of network characteristics. Of central interest to us, of course, is disagreement. Across studies we see this concept operationalized quite differently, whether through comparing party affiliation, matching on candidate choice, or capturing respondents' subjective level of disagreement with their named alters. It is worth noting that these measures are only modestly correlated, and the differences in what they measure are important for gauging both political choice and behavior (Klofstad, Sokhey, and McClurg 2013). The ANES asked only about church connections in nonfamily relationships (though there is tremendous overlap in family and church relationships—see Djupe and Gilbert 2009; Djupe and Sokhey 2014), while our original studies are the only ones to include questions suitable to gauge close ties when defined as the degree to which the discussion partners "know each other."

Importantly, the surveys include very different measures of religious affiliation. The ANES includes a denominational approach to capturing religious traditions (Steensland et al. 2001), while the others most often use a general religious-tradition question ("Are you a Protestant, Catholic, Jew, etc.") combined with a follow-up question about born-again/evangelical identification (to differentiate among Protestants). The latter approach is often called the Pew method (following Green 2007). Just as in the case of network measurement of disagreement, it is worth noting that these two approaches produce slightly different estimates of what evangelicals look like (Hackett and Lindsay 2008). That said, we are less concerned with these differences in terms of religious and social network measurement and more with the fact that the political and network implications of evangelicals have gone largely unstudied.

Disagreement over Time

We begin by looking at network disagreement over time, focusing on a measure based on the unity of presidential-candidate choice, which has the benefit of being available in all studies. With this measure, disagreement means an ego and alter not agreeing about their presidential-candidate choice. Figure 11.1 displays levels of candidate disagreement in political networks from 1992 to 2016. Disagreement is so much higher in 1992 because of Ross Perot

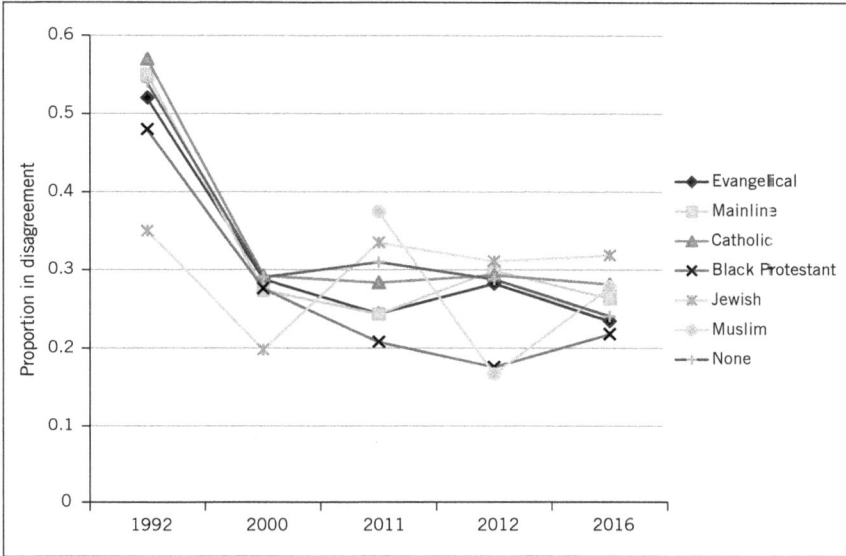

Figure 11.1 Candidate-based disagreement in evangelical (and other) networks, 1992–2016

and the size of the networks included.[2] After 1992, respondents average disagreeing with just under one discussant (25 percent in these networks translates to just under one discussant). There is some small variation among religious traditions, which is generally insignificant. In 1992 and 2000, Jewish networks were more homogeneous; in 2012 and 2016, they were on the high end of disagreement (using very small samples). Disagreement in black Protestant networks is always on the low end, which highlights the political homogeneity of the black vote as well as the continued racial-friendship segregation of Americans (e.g., Cox, Navarro-Rivera, and Jones 2016).

In sum, despite strong expectations about the insularity of evangelical networks, we find that they are effectively indistinguishable from the pack. White evangelicals are in the mix, perhaps closer to black Protestants, who are also evangelical in their religious beliefs and behaviors but at the same time indistinguishable from mainline Protestants and Catholics. We have omitted confidence intervals from the graph for legibility, but they almost all overlap, suggesting that networks at this high level of aggregation are nearly uniformly diverse.

Disagreement and the Vote

Of course, similar networks need not mean that they operate in the same way. For example, it is possible that evangelicals' religious beliefs provide greater cognitive defenses to fend off dissonant messages. While a sensible proposition, there is mixed support in the literature. Higher religious commitment promotes resistance to the reception of political information from clergy (Djupe and Gilbert 2009), and evangelicals with less attitude strength have been shown to be receptive to elite messages (Djupe and Gwiasda 2010). At the same time, higher religiosity has been linked to the adoption of messages from select denominational elites in regard to the topic of immigration (Wallsten and Nteta 2016).

Here, we are concerned with the vote choice among evangelicals exposed to disagreement: Are they resistant? We picked mainline Protestants as a comparison group since they are now demographically similar and display considerably less religiosity (e.g., 25 percent lower in church attendance).[3] Figure 11.2 shows how vote choice shifts among evangelicals and mainline Protestants given exposure to disagreement over the presidential candidates in their networks from 1992 to 2016. In each election, evangelicals' support for the Republican presidential candidate drops considerably when disagreement is present in their networks. Throughout this period, a network full of disagreement drops evangelical support for the Republican candidate by twenty to twenty-five points.[4]

Since evangelicals have higher scores on religiosity measures relative to those of mainline Protestants, this is suggestive evidence that religiosity is not a barrier to influence. However, we can also test this notion directly. Figure 11.3 displays evidence from 2012 and 2016 about how network disagreement among evangelicals is linked to a Republican vote, conditional on church attendance. In these two election years the Republican base of support lived in an echo chamber. High-attending evangelicals with no reported network disagreement voted almost unanimously for the Republican candidate. However, disagreement erodes a good deal of this support: high attenders who are surrounded by disagreement have a less than 40 percent chance of voting for Romney (a probability that is a bit lower in 2016).

If the Republican bastion is high-attending evangelicals—which was quite the opposite of Trump's support early in the primaries (Layman 2016)—then it would be natural to think that low-attending evangelicals are simply less reliable Republican voters. On the one hand, that was true in 2012: politically insulated low attenders were likely (at a lower level) to vote for Romney, and they followed their networks to choose other candidates when options presented themselves.

On the other hand, low attenders displayed the exact opposite pattern in 2016: their support for Trump *increased* with their exposure to disagreement in the network. Despite stereotypes, these cells are not empty: 32 percent of evangelicals in 2012 attended less than once a month or never, and this figure climbed to 37 percent in 2016. This finding, in particular, is consistent with the expectations of inoculation theory (McGuire 1961), as exposure to

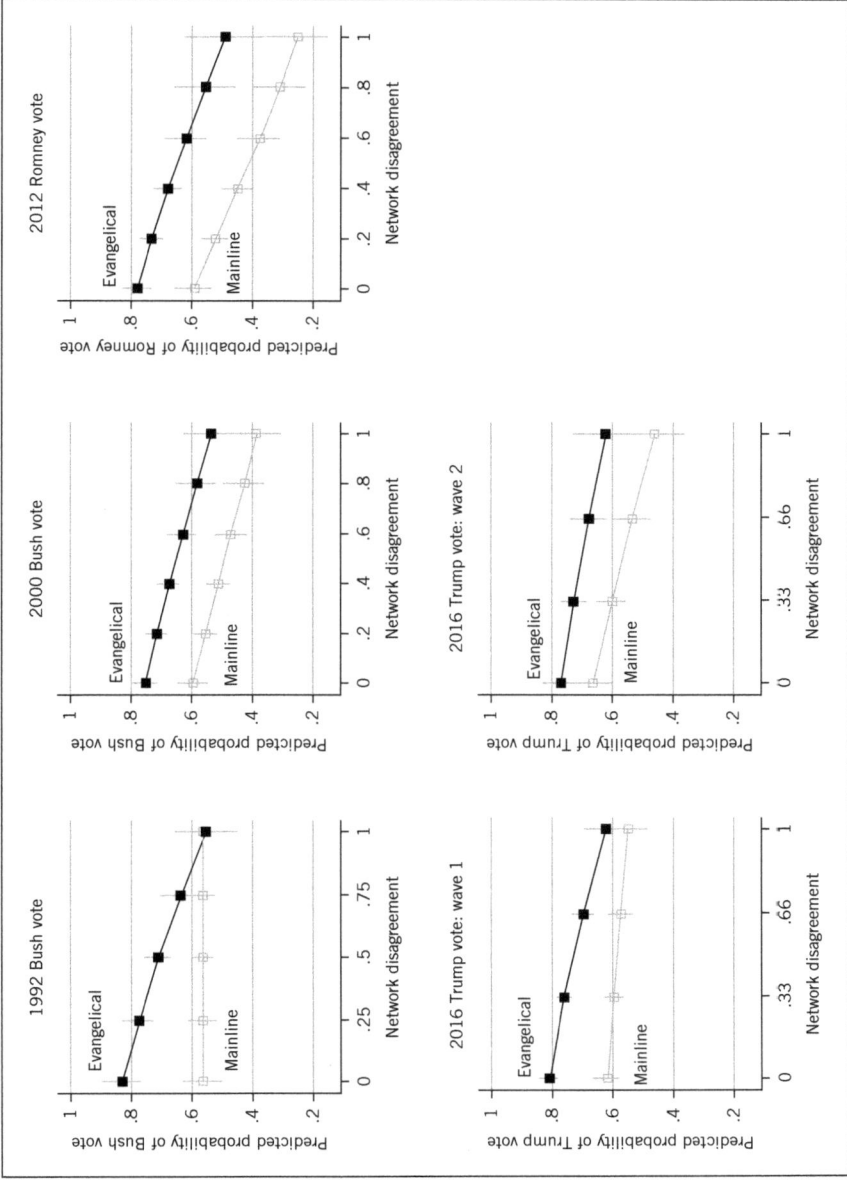

Figure 11.2 Disagreement effects on white evangelical vote choice, 1992–2016

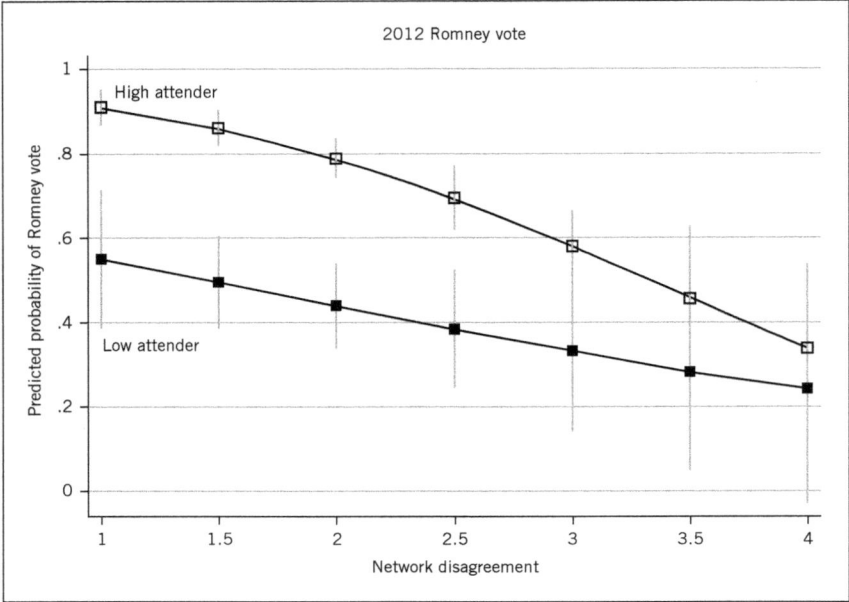

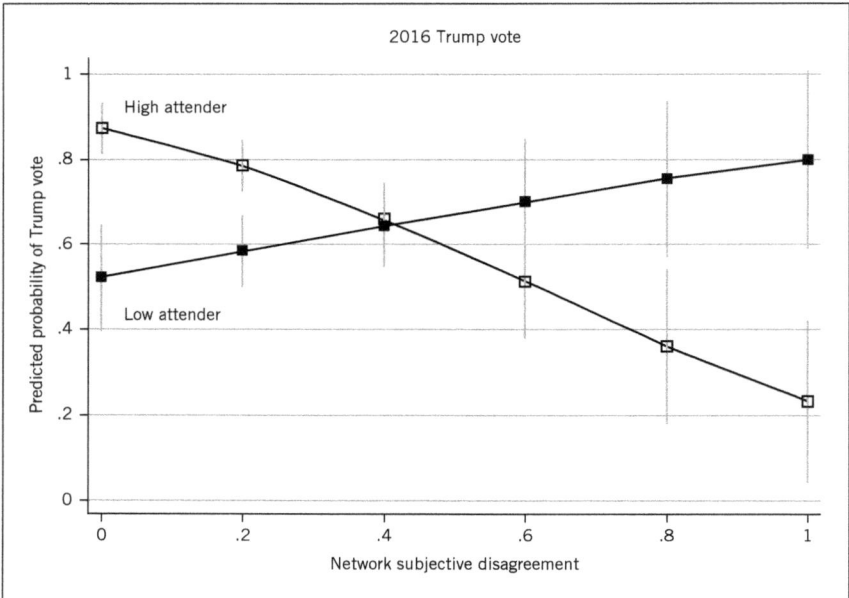

Figure 11.3 Evangelical Republican vote shift based on church attendance and disagreement, 2012 and 2016

disagreement can apparently encourage some individuals to double-down on their initial candidate decision and aid in resisting efforts at persuasion (see also Wojcieszak 2011; for additional discussion of polarization in deliberative settings, see Myers and Mendelberg 2013).

One other data point helps reinforce this pattern—low attenders exposed to more social disagreement were also more likely to report that their opinions are in the majority; high attenders reduced their majoritarian status when exposed to more disagreement. This was a new measure in 2016, so we do not have comparative data from 2012. But it shows from another vantage point that the social experience of disagreement may be only conditionally effective at persuasion.

We should exercise caution in attempting to apply more general social-scientific explanations for opinion extremity in the face of disagreement to the particular case of 2016. The pattern that we observe regarding low attenders' propensity to increase support for Trump in high-disagreement social situations may be unique to the circumstances surrounding Trump's candidacy. That is, those without much of an attachment to a religious institution may have reacted to assaults from peers regarding the apparent hypocrisy inherent in supporting a candidate whose comments about women appeared anathema to their own religious beliefs by engaging in motivated reasoning and latching on to their political identity as evangelicals even more tightly (see also Patrikios 2013). We do have a bit of evidence to suggest this very thing happened. Low attenders felt more warmly (fifteen points more) toward Christian fundamentalists when they experienced more disagreement than when they experienced none.

This begs the question of what allows disagreement to permeate evangelical networks. In our 2012 data, the presence of disagreement varied by neither gender nor attendance. Instead, older evangelicals had less disagreement in their networks—twenty-year-olds had about ten percentage points more disagreement than eighty-year-old evangelicals. Education does more work: those with a graduate degree have twenty points more disagreement than those without a high school education. Together these measures capture social mobility that would enlarge social opportunities. Moving freely creates opportunities to interact with a much wider range of people who may bring political disagreement to share (e.g., Huckfeldt and Sprague 1995).

It is interesting to note that these same factors do not correlate with network disagreement among evangelicals in our 2016 data. Gender, age, education, attendance, and other variables are not related to variation in network disagreement in either the pre- or postelection waves of the survey. However, disagreement in reported networks declined by five points among evangelicals from wave one (mid-September) to wave two (November 15) ($p = .05$), while the rest of the sample did not change over this time period. This suggests that forces unique to evangelicals were at work late in the election.

One of those forces may have been the clarity of signals in evangelical congregations. These organizational contexts were perceived to be the most supportive of Trump earlier in the campaign, and those signals only intensified by the time Election Day rolled around, going up from 54 percent to 62 percent supportive. Mainline Protestants showed a similar gain (though at a lower threshold—from 47 to 56 percent), but this was not linked to disagreement in networks. Given evangelicals' religiosity, it is not surprising that perceived support in the congregation for Trump is linked to lower disagreement in the network (controlling for wave-one disagreement). Changes in evangelicals' networks did not entail a greater focus on church networks or on the aspects overlapping with the workplace or family. Rather, the only other attribute that changed is the concentration of perceived expertise, which went up (the concentration of expertise did not increase among other religious traditions).

These changes are broadly consistent with Robert P. Jones's argument in *The End of White Christian America* (2016) that cultural resentment among "White Christian America" (essentially white Protestants) leads to support for the Republican Party and opposition to immigration and other progressive causes. What is different about our evidence is the ability to see how campaigns may affect the clarity of the message that helps unify congregations and, in turn, members' social networks. Resentment is not static but can be activated in campaigns through religious organizations and networks (see also Cramer 2016).

Connection to the Christian Right

Just how support for Trump would affect sentiment toward the Christian Right was a hotly debated topic in some circles this election cycle. The appearance of Jerry Falwell Jr. endorsing Trump while standing next to a cover of *Playboy* magazine told the tale. As one writer for conservative web magazine the *Federalist* put it, "Naturally, endorsing a candidate like Trump has its pitfalls for Christians, and by pitfalls I mean Grand Canyon-sized pockets of greed, adultery, fornication, and misogyny" (Sammons 2016). Others warned that a Trump win and religious support for him would undermine Christian witness both at home (Crouch 2016) and abroad (Shellnutt 2016). This suggests that support for the Christian Right might look different than it has before. At the same time, Falwell did stand with Trump, as did other Christian Right leaders such as Tony Perkins of the Family Research Council.

Evangelicals have a higher rate of support for Christian Right organizations than other religious traditions, which leads researchers to assume that high levels of religiosity drive up support for the movement. But people need motivation to learn about organizations, which suggests a logical, if peculiar link between interest-group support and social facts on the ground. That is, people need discord to motivate learning about organizations (Djupe 2011; Djupe and Lewis 2015); thus, those who feel different from their congregation or disagree with their discussion partners would be more motivated to have opinions about relevant interest groups. For this reason, Paul A. Djupe and Jacob R. Neiheisel characterized supporters of the Christian Right in an Ohio election as "lone wolves" rather than platoon leaders (2008, 58). That is, mobilization from organizations is unlikely to radiate through their networks if their interest is motivated by social disagreement.

We see this play out in two ways in 2016.[5] The most straightforward demonstration of this logic is shown in the top panel of Figure 11.4. It shows that, among evangelicals, exposure to greater disagreement in the network boosts "support [for] conservative Christian groups active in politics, such as the Christian Coalition, American Family Association, or Focus on the Family." But evangelicals are not just reacting to their networks. Christian Right support is also a reaction to the congregation. The top panel shows that the boost in support for the Christian Right from high attendance is about the same as experiencing a network full of disagreement. The bottom panel of Figure 11.4 shows that support for the Christian Right is strongly linked to congregational solidarity as well. Trump supporters express only tepid support for the Christian Right when their congregation is not full of other Trump supporters. The same applies to non-Trump evangelicals—they actually express greater support for the Christian Right when their congregation is not full of Trump voters. The Christian Right may have paid a (small) price for backing the Republican candidate to the extent there were evangelicals not voting for Trump (20–40 percent according to Burge 2017).

More broadly, these results are consistent with the view that Christian interest groups are extensions of their congregational experiences driven by the genial cues to which people exposed to social disagreement are open. Thus, the combination of social disagreement and contextual solidarity strongly shapes popular connections to relevant interest groups and movements.

Ryan Claassen commented in his thoughtful set of suggestions for this chapter that it is possible that Figure 11.4 is simply an artifact of the #Never-Trump movement. That is, the non-Trump voters in congregations without perceived support for Trump who show support for the Christian Right are actually ultraconservatives. While we included attendance in the model that generated the results in Figure 11.4, we can also address this by assessing whether the religiosity of evangelicals who were not Trump supporters and did not perceive support for Trump in the congregation varies from the religiosity of others. In results not shown, we find no difference in religiosity (a combination of attendance and religious importance) between Trump and non-Trump voters at any point in perceived congregational support for Trump.

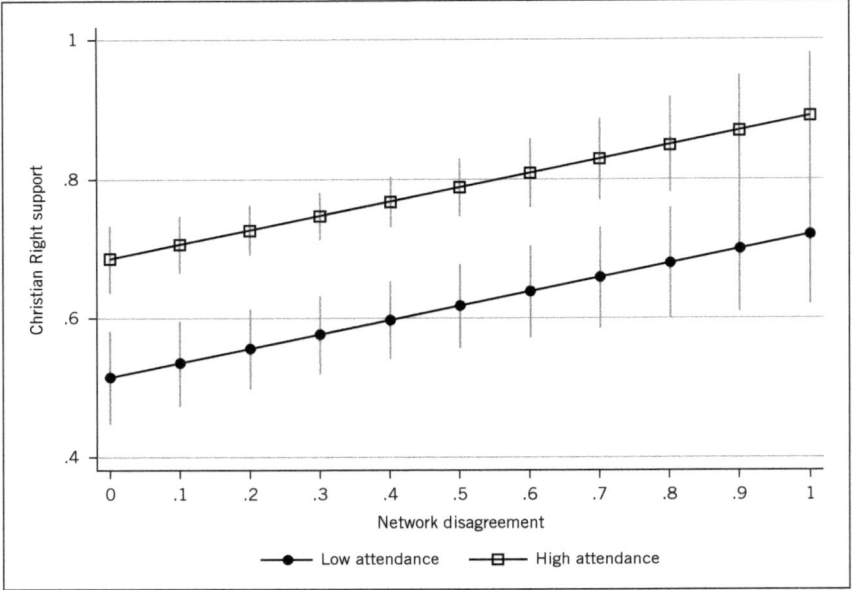

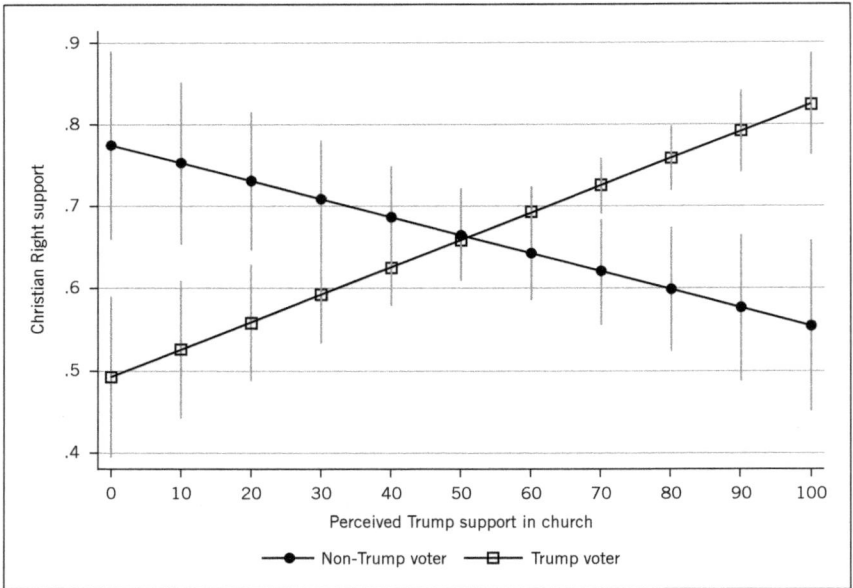

Figure 11.4 Effect of network disagreement, church attendance, and church solidarity on support for the Christian Right

Put another way, if the #NeverTrump hypothesis is correct, then evangelical liberals would not show more support for the Christian Right when exposed to disagreement (since that is the domain of the ultraconservatives). This is a testable notion, and the results are revealing. Figure 11.5 shows the interaction between ideology and network disagreement. Strong conservatives show consistently high support for the Christian Right, but support for the movement varies among liberals. Liberal evangelicals without disagreement in their network are strong opponents of the Christian Right, but those exposed to considerable disagreement show equivalent support for the Christian Right as strong conservatives do. This is not conclusive proof that #NeverTrump did not matter (since we do not have exposure to the movement in the data), but it is suggestive that the social dynamics in congregations and networks were operating to shape views of the Christian Right.

These patterns also suggest that movements have a different status from electoral choice, and of course we should not ignore the possibility that 2016 may have been somewhat of an outlier in history (though we have found these patterns repeatedly across the years). Because of their scope, elections are difficult to ignore, and therefore they permeate social contexts and networks. As networks tend to reflect contexts, evangelical high attenders exposed to disagreement are less likely to follow the Republican standard. However, movements (and their interest groups) can be a refuge for those

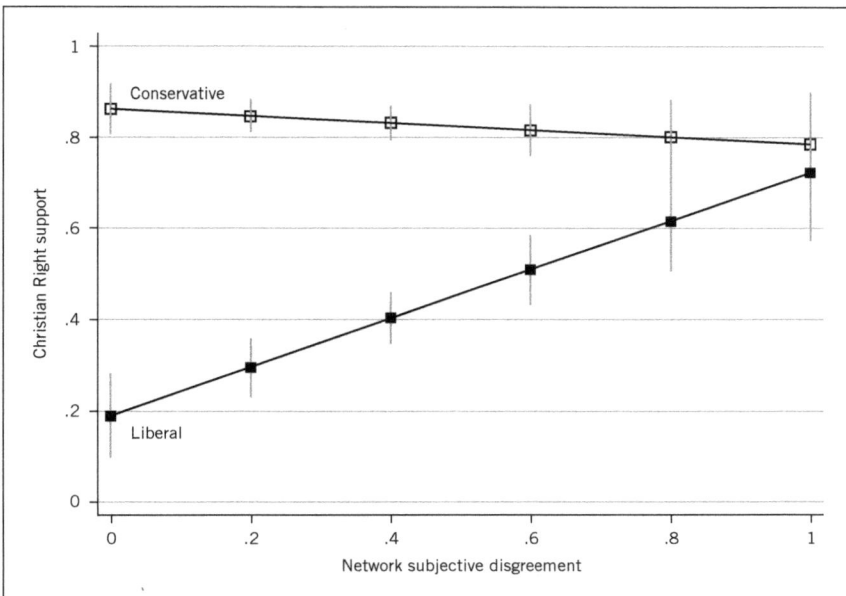

Figure 11.5 Interaction between ideology and network disagreement

exposed to social disagreement—they provide identity and arguments to shield their attitudes. In this way, support for interest groups and movements may reflect different social patterns than electoral choice does. That could be especially true in 2016, when evangelicals felt under siege by the broader culture—more evangelicals thought Christians encountered discrimination than Muslims or LGBT (lesbian, gay, bisexual, transgender) people (Cox and Jones 2017).

Conclusion

In this chapter we endeavor to chart the contours of evangelicals' social and organizational environments. Our findings undermine widely held perceptions of both the structure and the composition of evangelicals' social networks. At least over the time period under examination, evangelical networks exhibit characteristics that are not broadly consistent with expectations of political homogeneity derived from theories that focus on the stringency of the faith tradition as a determinant of adherents' social surroundings. Rather, evangelicals' networks are not unique and host as much disagreement as any other religious tradition. Black Protestants, Catholics, and mainline Protestants' social networks are similar in composition to those in evidence among evangelical Protestants. Thus, treating congregations *across religious traditions* as essentially undifferentiated units would appear to be justified (e.g., Mutz and Mondak 2006; Scheufele et al. 2004).

At the same time, there are some indications that those who would seek to organize evangelicals for action in the political arena may soon find themselves victims of their own success (Djupe, Neiheisel, and Conger 2018). Interest-group entrepreneurs who want to tap into existing religious networks to mobilize so-called values voters are likely to find an increasingly educated group of supporters that is more connected to the outside world than ever before. Since the 1980s, staffing the front lines of the culture wars in the form of conservative Christian legal organizations (Bennett 2017) has required evangelicals to engage with the largely secular legal arena. Even though numerous law schools are affiliated with religious denominations, and evangelical Christians certainly have the option of seeking out a religiously focused legal education, involvement in the legal system itself ensures contact with a diverse group of others. In many ways, then, mounting a professional challenge to the extant political system necessitates greater involvement with views that deviate from those held by members of the Christian Right. Such involvement, as we show here, may in turn precipitate attitudinal changes among rank-and-file members of conservative Christian (and other) organizations as the natural course of social influence processes.

As we also show here and elsewhere (see Djupe 2011; Djupe and Lewis 2015; Djupe and Neiheisel 2008), strong ties among those who might support the aims of the Christian Right may actually work at odds with organizational efforts at building a robust grassroots network of committed activists. At first blush it might seem obvious that strongly tied networks of like-minded individuals provide a powerful base on which to construct an organization that would be the envy of any in Washington circles. After all, the "law of group polarization" (Sunstein 2002; see also Sunstein 2000) dictates that conversations that take place among those who agree in echo chambers encourage opinion extremity—conditions that would seem ripe for mobilization by entrepreneurial organizational elites. Instead, it is those who face disagreement who are most supportive of Christian Right groups.

While seemingly counterintuitive, this finding is grounded in more than a half century of theorizing regarding the social conditions that make individuals susceptible to persuasion from mass-mediated sources and elite influence more generally. As Rüdiger Schmitt-Beck (2003) points out, those who lack anything in the way of a social network represent something of an "open flank" through which elite communication can have an outsized impact on attitudes (see also Druckman and Nelson 2003). Formulated in such a way, previous work suggests that the degree of opinion change is the result of a lack of resistance to elite messaging. Here, however, we suggest another possible mechanism: those without a social-support structure are motivated to actively seek out connections with interest groups in an effort to compensate for the absence of a political-support network.

What, then, does this mean for future relations between evangelicals and the Republican Party? If evangelicals' networks look (essentially) similar to those of other groups, then perhaps the status quo can hold—a crackup in this cozy relationship is not on the immediate horizon. But when exposed to disagreement, evangelicals are not immune to countervailing political arguments. Thus, researchers should continue to be on the lookout for new sources of diversity, especially among younger evangelicals (see Chapter 12).

Moreover, the strength of network effects on the vote and support for the Christian Right suggests how difficult it is to lead this group. There were quite visible rifts between evangelical leaders and adherents during the 2016 campaign (more during the primaries than during the general election cycle). On the one hand, those rifts may signal that there is nothing inevitable about the connection between evangelicals and the Republican Party. On the other hand, given the evidence presented in this chapter, evangelicals are well insulated from any pressure from elites, which provides considerable momentum to their political behavior for the time being.

NOTES

This chapter's authors are listed alphabetically.

1. The General Social Survey has included several network batteries since 1987 but has included questions about politics inconsistently.

2. The 1992 CNEP first asked about five total discussion partners—up to four were gener-ated with an "important matters" prompt, and a fifth discussant was solicited with an explicitly political prompt. The combination of these factors, as well as the presence of Ross Perot in the race (who drew 19 percent of the vote), serves to increase the amount of disagreement present in respondent networks. The more names elicited, the more likely disagreement is to enter a network (Huckfeldt, Johnson, and Sprague 2004).

3. Specifically, they are only 2.5 percent different in education, a year apart in average age, and equivalent in female composition. Thus, the only major difference we see in this sample is in their religiosity.

4. Interpersonal disagreement as captured by candidate choice is highly sensitive to measurement choices. Such measures can be built through prioritizing agreement and let-ting everything else be considered disagreement (i.e., disagreement = nonagreement). This is, generally, an approach more associated with Robert Huckfeldt and John Sprague (1995). Diana C. Mutz (2006) argues that capturing explicit disagreement should be the priority; by this logic, someone who is not sure about his or her vote does not necessarily disagree with someone who has picked a candidate. In the end, both measures of partisan disagreement are correlated with—but are not the same thing as—subjective, general disagreement ("How often do you disagree about politics?").

5. We tested for the following effects in a model that controls for partisanship, gender, age, and education. The dependent variable is constructed from respondent answers to the follow-ing question: "I support conservative Christian groups active in politics, such as the Christian Coalition, American Family Association, or Focus on the Family." It is coded from strongly disagree (1) to strongly agree (7), which was condensed to a 0–1 range.

REFERENCES

Bennett, Daniel. 2017. *Defending Faith: The Politics of the Christian Conservative Legal Move-ment*. Lawrence: University Press of Kansas.
Burge, Ryan P. 2017. "The 2016 Religious Vote (for More Groups Than You Thought Possible)." *Religion in Public*, March 10. Available at https://religioninpublic.blog/2017/03/10/the -2016-religious-vote-for-more-groups-than-you-thought-possible/.
Cavendish, James C., Michael R. Welch, and David C. Leege. 1998. "Social Network Theory and Predictors of Religiosity for Black and White Catholics: Evidence of a 'Black Sacred Cosmos'?" *Journal for the Scientific Study of Religion* 37 (3): 397–410.
Cornwall, Marie. 1987. "The Social Bases of Religion: A Study of Factors Influencing Religious Belief and Commitment." *Review of Religious Research* 29:44–56.
Cox, Daniel, and Robert P. Jones. 2017. "Majority of Americans Oppose Transgender Bath-room Restriction." PRRI. Available at http://www.prri.org/research/lgbt-transgender -bathroom-discrimination-religious-liberty/.
Cox, Daniel, Juhem Navarro-Rivera, and Robert P. Jones. 2016. "Race, Religion, and Political Affiliation of Americans' Core Social Networks." PRRI, August 3. Available at https:// www.prri.org/research/poll-race-religion-politics-americans-social-networks.
Cramer, Katherine J. 2016. *The Politics of Resentment: Rural Consciousness in Wisconsin and the Rise of Scott Walker*. Chicago: University of Chicago Press.
Crouch, Andy. 2016. "Speak Truth to Trump." *Christianity Today*, October 10. Available at http://www.christianitytoday.com/ct/2016/october-web-only/speak-truth-to-trump .html.
Djupe, Paul A. 2011. "Political Pluralism and the Information Search: Determinants of Group Opinionation." *Political Research Quarterly* 64 (1): 68–81.
Djupe, Paul A., and Brian R. Calfano. 2009. "Justification Not by Faith Alone: Clergy Gen-erating Trust and Certainty by Revealing Thought." *Politics and Religion* 2:1–30.

Djupe, Paul A., and Christopher P. Gilbert. 2009. *The Political Influence of Churches*. New York: Cambridge University Press.

Djupe, Paul A., and Gregory W. Gwiasda. 2010. "Evangelizing the Environment: Decision Process Effects in Political Persuasion." *Journal for the Scientific Study of Religion* 49 (1): 73–86.

Djupe, Paul A., and Andrew R. Lewis. 2015. "Solidarity and Discord of Pluralism: How the Social Context Affects Interest Group Learning and Belonging." *American Politics Research* 43 (3): 394–424.

Djupe, Paul A., and Jacob R. Neiheisel. 2008. "Christian Right Horticulture: Grassroots Support in a Republican Primary Campaign." *Politics and Religion* 1 (1): 55–84.

Djupe, Paul A., Jacob R. Neiheisel, and Kimberly H. Conger. 2018. "Are the Politics of the Christian Right Linked to State Rates of the Nonreligious? The Importance of Salient Controversy." *Political Research Quarterly*, April 26. Available at http://journals.sagepub .com/doi/abs/10.1177/1065912918771526.

Djupe, Paul A., and Anand E. Sokhey. 2014. "The Distribution and Determinants of Socially Supplied Political Expertise." *American Politics Research* 42 (2): 199–225.

Druckman, James N., and Kjersten R. Nelson. 2003. "Framing and Deliberation: How Citizens' Conversations Limit Elite Influence." *American Journal of Political Science* 47 (4): 729–745.

Everton, Sean F. 2015. "Networks and Religion: Ties That Bind, Loose, Build Up, and Tear Down." *Journal of Social Structure* 16 (10): 1–34.

Glock, Charles Y., and Rodney Stark. 1965. *Religion and Society in Tension*. Chicago: Rand McNally.

———. 1966. *Christian Beliefs and Anti-Semitism*. New York: Harper and Row.

Granovetter, Mark. 1973. "The Strength of Weak Ties." *American Journal of Sociology* 78:1360–1380.

Green, John C. 2007. *The Faith Factor: How Religion Influences American Elections*. Westport, CT: Praeger.

Hackett, Conrad, and D. Michael Lindsay. 2008. "Measuring Evangelicalism: Consequences of Different Operationalization Strategies." *Journal for the Scientific Study of Religion* 47 (3): 499–514.

Huckfeldt, Robert, Paul Allen Beck, Russell J. Dalton, and Jeffrey Levine. 1995. "Political Environments, Cohesive Social Groups, and the Communication of Public Opinion." *American Journal of Political Science* 39 (4): 1025–1054.

Huckfeldt, Robert, Paul E. Johnson, and John Sprague. 2004. *Political Disagreement: The Survival of Diverse Opinions within Communication Networks*. New York: Cambridge University Press.

Huckfeldt, Robert, and John Sprague. 1995. *Citizens, Politics, and Social Communications: Information and Influence in an Election Campaign*. New York: Cambridge University Press.

Iannaccone, Laurence R. 1994. "Why Strict Churches Are Strong." *American Journal of Sociology* 99:1180–1211.

Jones, Robert P. 2016. *The End of White Christian America*. New York: Simon and Schuster.

Klofstad, Casey, Scott D. McClurg, and Meredith Rolfe. 2009. "Measurement of Political Discussion Networks: A Comparison of Two Name Generator Approaches." *Public Opinion Quarterly* 73 (3): 462–483.

Klofstad, Casey, Anand Edward Sokhey, and Scott D. McClurg. 2013. "Disagreeing about Disagreement: How Conflict in Social Networks Affects Political Behavior." *American Journal of Political Science* 57 (1): 120–134.

Layman, Geoffrey. 2016. "Where Is Trump's Evangelical Base? Not in Church." *Washington Post*, March 29. Available at https://www.washingtonpost.com/news/monkey-cage/wp/ 2016/03/29/where-is-trumps-evangelical-base-not-in-church/.

Lazer, David, Anand Edward Sokhey, Michael Neblo, Kevin Esterling, and Ryan Kennedy. 2015. "Expanding the Conversation: Multiplier Effects from a Deliberative Field Experiment." *Political Communication* 32 (4): 552–573.

Levitan, Lindsey Clark, and Penny S. Visser. 2009. "Social Network Composition and Attitude Strength: Exploring the Dynamics within Newly Formed Social Networks." *Journal of Experimental Social Psychology* 45 (5): 1057–1067.

Lofland, John, and Rodney Stark. 1965. "Becoming a World-Saver: A Theory of Conversion to a Deviant Perspective." *American Sociological Review* 30:862–875.

McGuire, William J. 1961. "Resistance to Persuasion Conferred by Active and Passive Prior Refutation of the Same and Alternative Counterarguments." *Journal of Abnormal and Social Psychology* 63:326–332.

Mutz, Diana C. 2006. *Hearing the Other Side: Deliberative versus Participatory Democracy.* Cambridge: Cambridge University Press.

Mutz, Diana C., and Jeffery J. Mondak. 2006. "The Workplace as a Context for Cross-Cutting Political Discourse." *Journal of Politics* 68:140–155.

Myers, C. Daniel, and Tali Mendelberg. 2013. "Political Deliberation." In *The Oxford Handbook of Political Psychology*, 2nd ed., edited by Leonie Huddy, David O. Sears, and Jack S. Levy, 699–734. New York: Oxford University Press.

Patrikios, Stratos. 2013. "Self-Stereotyping as 'Evangelical Republican': An Empirical Test." *Politics and Religion* 6 (4): 800–822.

Putnam, Robert D., and David E. Campbell. 2010. *American Grace: How Religion Divides and Unites Us.* New York: Simon and Schuster.

Rosenstone, Steven J., and John Mark Hansen. 1993. *Mobilization, Participation, and Democracy in America.* New York: Macmillan.

Sammons, Eric. 2016. "Christians' Support for Trump Undermines Their Public Witness." *The Federalist*, October 12. Available at http://thefederalist.com/2016/10/12/christians -support-trump-undermines-public-witness/.

Scheufele, Dietram A., Matthew C. Nisbet, Dominique Brossard, and Erik C. Nisbet. 2004. "Social Structure and Citizenship: Examining the Impacts of Social Setting, Network Heterogeneity, and Informational Variables on Political Participation." *Political Communication* 21:315–338.

Schmitt-Beck, R. 2003. "Mass Communication, Personal Communication and Vote Choice: The Filter Hypothesis of Media Influence in Comparative Perspective." *British Journal of Political Science* 33:233–259.

Seyle, D. Conor, and Matthew L. Newman. 2006. "A House Divided? The Psychology of Red and Blue America." *American Psychology* 61 (6): 571–580.

Shellnutt, Kate. 2016. "Global Evangelical Leaders: Trump's Win Will Harm the Church's Witness." *Christianity Today*, November 15. Available at http://www.christianitytoday .com/gleanings/2016/november/global-evangelical-leaders-trump-win-will-harm -churchs-witn.html.

Sherkat, Darren E., and John Wilson. 1995. "Preferences, Constraints, and Choices in Religious Markets: An Examination of Religious Switching and Apostasy." *Social Forces* 73 (3): 993–1026.

Sinclair, Betsy. 2012. *The Social Citizen: Peer Networks and Political Behavior.* Chicago: University of Chicago Press.

Sokhey, Anand E., and Paul A. Djupe. 2014. "Name Generation in Ego-centric Network Data: Results from a Series of Experiments." *Social Networks* 36 (1): 147–161.

Sokhey, Anand E., and Stephen Mockabee. 2012. "Reexamining Political Discussion and Disagreement in Church Networks: An Exit Poll Assessment." *Politics and Religion* 5 (2): 253–279.

Steensland, Brian, Jerry Z. Park, Mark D. Regnerus, Lynn D. Robinson, W. Bradford Wilcox, and Robert D. Woodberry. 2000. "The Measure of American Religion: Toward Improving the State of the Art." *Social Forces* 79 (1): 291–318.

Sunstein, Cass R. 2000. "Deliberative Trouble? Why Groups Go to Extremes." *Yale Law Journal* 110 (1): 71–119.

———. 2002. "The Law of Group Polarization." *Journal of Political Philosophy* 10:175–195.

Tajfel, Henri, and John C. Turner. 1979. "An Integrative Theory of Intergroup Conflict." In *The Social Psychology of Intergroup Relations*, edited by William G. Austin and Stephen Worchel, 33–47. Monterey, CA: Brooks/Cole.

Tocqueville, Alexis de. 1969. *Democracy in America*. Translated by George Lawrence. New York: Doubleday.

Wald, Kenneth D., Dennis E. Owen, and Samuel S. Hill. 1990. "Political Cohesion in Churches." *Journal of Politics* 52 (1): 197–215.

Wallsten, Kevin, and Tatishe M. Nteta. 2016. "For You Were Strangers in the Land of Egypt: Clergy, Religiosity, and Public Opinion toward Immigration Reform in the United States." *Politics and Religion* 9 (3): 566–604.

Welch, Kevin W. 1981. "An Interpersonal Influence Model of Traditional Religious Commitment." *Sociological Quarterly* 22:81–92.

Wojcieszak, Magdalena. 2011. "Deliberation and Attitude Polarization." *Journal of Communication* 61 (4): 596–617.

12

Sowing the Seeds of Discord?

*Social Sources of Division among White
Evangelical Protestants*

Daniel A. Cox
Paul A. Djupe
Robert P. Jones
Juhem Navarro-Rivera

C oming after the highly successful ballot measure campaigns of 2004–
2006 and two George W. Bush terms in the White House, it was a bold
claim that there was an ongoing "evangelical crackup" (Kirkpatrick
2007; see also Cox 2007; Pew Research Center 2010; Wald and Calhoun-
Brown 2007). Yet it was easy then and even easier now to point to divisions
"over the evangelical alliance with the Republican Party, among approaches
to ministry and theology, and between the generations" (Kirkpatrick 2007;
see also Barna Group 2007; Fitzgerald 2008). These provocative claims are
still in dispute as academics wrestle with the presence, coherence, and trajectory of evangelicals in American politics. Among the more important questions is why there appears to be growing social and political diversity within
evangelical ranks, particularly among younger evangelicals. In this chapter,
we take up the question of the diversification of white evangelicals, focusing
on key sources of exposure to diverse information: social network diversity,
increasing resources that would enable more engagement with the world,
and connections to the Republican Party itself. However, we suspect that the
problem may lie within. Evangelical youth may be diversifying their views
in reaction to the embattled political style pursued by many evangelical leaders. That is, the evangelical marriage to the Republican Party may have sown
the seeds of discord that might serve to undercut its effectiveness going forward.

Into the Republican Fold

Few social groups have demonstrated such a profound and enduring influence over the American political system as white evangelical Protestants, who for more than thirty years have shaped the tenor of political debates, particularly around issues of sexual morality, such as abortion, contraception, sex education, and gay and lesbian rights (Green et al. 1996). They have also shaped debates at the local level, influencing local and state political races and issues, such as evolution, although their ability to influence political outcomes has varied considerably and is often overstated (Deckman 2004).

Their political influence is amplified by their strong partisan voting preferences. Few social groups of this size are as politically cohesive as white evangelical Protestants. Just over 80 percent of white evangelicals sided with Donald Trump in 2016.[1] Nearly eight in ten (78 percent) white evangelicals supported former Massachusetts governor Mitt Romney, the Republican candidate in the 2012 presidential election. Only African Americans have stronger partisan attachments than white evangelical Protestants (93 percent voted for Obama); however, they accounted for only 13 percent of all voters in 2012 ("Election 2012" 2012).

The strong evangelical support for Trump in 2016 and Romney in 2012 was hardly an anomaly. Republican presidential candidates have been able to rely on strong evangelical support for at least a quarter of a century. As early as the election of 1988, white evangelical Protestant voting preferences already skewed heavily toward Republican candidates. In the 1988 election, 69 percent of white evangelical Protestants voted for George H. W. Bush. Since that time, no Republican candidate has received less than 70 percent of the white evangelical vote.

The patterns of Republican voting in presidential elections predate a shift in partisan identity evident during this period. Although the overwhelming number of white evangelical Protestants voted Republican in 1988, fewer than half identified as Republican (35 percent) or said they leaned toward the Republican Party (14 percent). By the time Mitt Romney was the GOP's nominee, roughly seven in ten either identified as Republican (50 percent) or leaned toward the GOP (19 percent).[2]

However, there are signs that opinion on some social issues, such as same-sex marriage, is fracturing along generational lines. A recent survey found that 47 percent of young white evangelical Protestants favor allowing gay and lesbian couples to marry legally, a rate significantly higher than among white evangelicals overall (Cooper et al. 2016). There are also signs that younger white evangelical Protestants are more tolerant of social and cultural out-groups. Our goal is to determine to what extent the social environment among white evangelical Protestants, particularly among younger evangelicals, might contribute to these attitudinal differences and what this might portend for the future of this culturally and politically important constituency.

The Social Basis of Politics

Our question concerns the sources of diversity within a religious community. This is not the typical approach to considering issue attitudes in public-opinion research, which looks for variation across groups. Instead, we turn to classic considerations in the political-tolerance literature, which is likewise concerned in part with the exposure to, and willingness to consider, diverse sources of information. Education is perhaps the most important universal force broadening horizons and encouraging tolerance (Mill [1869] 1975); however, only enrollment past high school is thought to have liberalizing effects, including shifting commitments to value diversity (Golebiowska 1995).

But formal education is, fortunately, not the only way in which people are encouraged to consider the interests of others. A higher level of socioeconomic status (SES) and now technological resources allow people to leave their communities to interact with a greater diversity of people and ideas. Of course, interaction with people who do not share your interests is the essential experience that overcomes narrowness and enlarges the bounds of citizenship. Particularly essential is actual social contact with those who are different and objects of prejudice. Gordon Allport's (1954) contact hypothesis has received overwhelming support in the social sciences, with elaboration of the conditions under which such contact is likely to be efficacious (see Pettigrew and Tropp 2006). Contact is most effective in reducing prejudice under optimal conditions: the groups share status, they seek coincident goals, they cooperate, and they have perceived support from social institutions (Allport 1954).

From the group's perspective, though, the diversity of members' ties is a potential problem. On the one hand, diverse ties allow the group's message to disseminate to a wider audience (Granovetter 1973), but it also allows the community's views to seep into the group, undercutting group consensus. These forces discussed so far are parts of a whole because resources help broaden the form and content of social networks that can change the character of a group.

But that is not necessarily the entire story among groups, such as evangelicals. While evangelicals were once described as embattled and thriving (Smith 1998), tensions have revealed themselves. New leaders, even new movements like the emergent church (see Chapter 10), have developed since the early 1990s in reaction to what is perceived as a dominant style within evangelicalism. For instance, the emergent church began as a renewal movement among youth pastors who saw that a strident, exclusive, political evangelicalism was not winning over youth (Gibbs and Bolger 2005). New evangelical leaders like Rick Warren were seeking a new, more inclusive evangelicalism that deemphasized the importance of boundaries with the world and instead emphasized engagement (see Djupe and Calfano 2013).

This is not to say that a more inclusive evangelicalism has come to dominate societal perceptions or social reality. Instead, there is some research to suggest that evangelical and Republican identities have become fused, so that saying one is to mean the other as well (Patrikios 2013), part of which could be the result of long-run sorting (Djupe, Neiheisel, and Sokhey 2018). Of course, there is a solid basis for this perception in closely aligned voting patterns, the party activist corps, the party leadership, and the issue agenda of the Republican Party in the past three decades as we discuss earlier (e.g., Layman 2001; see also Chapter 2). This implies that information supplied by Republicans, in part because of evangelical influence, should reinforce typical evangelical opinions about out-groups, religion, and political issues.

However, if there is a coming generational divide, then millennials should be more turned off by a Christian conservative–dominated form of evangelicalism and more open to groups and opinions formerly outside the group. Whether this is a function of expanded resources social-network diversity or a reaction against the perceived core of the religious tradition remains to be seen.

Thus, we look for and expect four sets of forces to act on the diversity of opinion we see among evangelicals: (1) an expanded SES resource base among the young may act to diversify their opinions as they are exposed to a broader array of ideas and people; (2) more diverse social networks may accomplish the same thing by supplying persuasive information directly; (3) being surrounded by Republican discussion partners should foreclose taking unorthodox evangelical stances; and (4) millennials are likely to reject that orthodoxy when surrounded by it, since they are exposed to more diversity than their parents have been, but they may be more likely to adopt that orthodoxy when exposed to the wider world, since they are far less liberal than the rest of society.

Data and Design

Assessing the impact of social interactions and relationships presents an abundant array of challenges. A single individual may have six or seven relevant attributes that one might conceivably measure, but that same person might have engaged in hundreds of distinct interactions with dozens of different people, each representing a unique relationship. Moreover, these relationships are not stable but evolve considerably over time (Sokhey, Baker, and Djupe 2015); the degree of influence particular people have over an individual will grow or shrink as the relationship changes. Social influence is subsequently quite difficult to measure.

One method that has become increasingly common for measuring social influence is social-network analysis. Central to the social-network perspective is the idea that an actor's behavior and attitudes are at least partly a function of the different types of people surrounding him or her—the individual's social network (Marsden 1990; see also Chapter 11).

We draw on the Public Religion Research Institute (PRRI) 2013 American Values Survey, a nationally representative survey of more than twenty-three hundred adults that was conducted online using GFK's Knowledge Panel. A portion of the survey was modeled after the egocentric network used in the General Social Survey (GSS); respondents were asked to name people with whom they "discussed important matters" in the previous six months regardless of the nature of the relationship or the frequency of interaction. The first step in this approach, often referred to as "the name generator," is to have respondents record the names of all the people in their network.[3] Next, respondents are asked to provide relevant information for each member of their previously identified network.

The current study design differs from the GSS social-network battery in a few important respects. First, the survey was self-administered online, providing a more efficient and cost-effective way to collect the social-network data. The current study also allowed for up to seven alters, instead of five as in the GSS. Once respondents recorded the names of each alter, they moved to a new screen that asked them to "describe a few characteristics of the people with whom you discuss important matters." Five distinct categories of information were asked of each alter: relationship to respondent (e.g., parent, spouse), gender, race, religious identity, and 2012 vote for president.

Descriptive Results

The uniqueness of white evangelical Protestants' profiles lies in the presumed homogeneity of their social networks. In some respects that is true. White evangelicals are more likely than members of other major Christian groups to have friends and family whose religious identity is similar to their own. Overall, more than three-quarters (76 percent) of white evangelical Protestants' friends and family are *also* white Protestants. About 71 percent of the social networks of Catholics are other Catholics, while 63 percent of the people in white mainline Protestant networks are other white Protestants.[4] Of course, these figures among Protestants reflect denominational homophily (Mennonites with Mennonites) and not a generic preference to associate with Protestants.

The social networks of white evangelical Protestants are also more Republican. Americans on average have about one person in their network who voted for Mitt Romney in 2012. In contrast, white evangelical Protestants average nearly two Romney voters in their networks. Overall, white evangelical Protestants report that 51 percent of the friends and family members in their networks voted for Mitt Romney in 2012, nearly twice as many as the percentage of Romney voters in Americans' social networks (28 percent).

Among those who reported voting in the 2012 elections, white evangelical Protestants again have the most distinctively Republican network. About one-third (32 percent) of the friends and family members of Catholics who voted in 2012 are Romney supporters, as are 40 percent of the discussants of white mainline Protestants. A majority (55 percent) of the people in the networks of white evangelical Protestants voted for Mitt Romney in 2012. Notably, while the networks are more unified, none of these religious groups has networks composed of only their own members.

There are few differences among evangelicals in the composition of their social networks by age, which is problematic for the generational thesis we are advancing. As we develop later, network composition is one important facet, but usage or reaction to the same network may vary as well. There are some differences by gender, party affiliation, and church attendance. These differences yield some insight into the extent of the impact of networks on the views of white evangelical Protestants and into the future of white evangelical Protestants in the GOP.

The main difference between the networks of younger (twenty-nine years and younger) and older white evangelical Protestants is the percentage of their networks who have an alter from church (13.5 percent and 36 percent, respectively).[5] In other aspects, their networks are similar in their political outlook (majority of Romney voters) and the percentage who are white Protestants (more than three-fourths). Further, there is not a tremendous amount of other forms of diversity in their social networks. They do not differ in the extent to which their networks are composed of Republicans—both average 58 percent Republican. Nor do they differ in the amount of nonreligious discussants (19 percent for those under twenty-nine and 15 percent for those older; $p = .54$). There is a statistically very marginal difference in the non-Christian network presence (14 percent for those under twenty-nine and 8 percent for those older; $p = .22$). And there is no difference in the nonwhite presence in their networks—just 7 percent (younger than twenty-nine) and 5 percent (older than twenty-nine) of white evangelical networks have a nonwhite person. A combination of these three measures into a diversity index comes close to producing a significant difference ($p = .17$, in the expected direction of more diversity in younger evangelical networks).

An analysis of the networks of white evangelical Protestants by region shows that those in the Midwest and the South have the most distinctive Republican networks. About eight in ten networks of southern and midwestern white evangelicals consist of other white Protestants, but the number is significantly lower among bicoastal white evangelicals (those living in the West or Northeast), among whom 66 percent of their friends and family are also white Protestants. White evangelicals in the South and the Midwest also have the most Republican networks. More than half of the friends and family members of southern (54 percent) and midwestern (51 percent) white evangelicals voted for Mitt Romney in 2012. Fewer than half (47 percent) of the friends and family members of white evangelicals in the Northeast and the West voted for Romney.

The composition of white evangelical Protestant networks is also a product of their members' high levels of church attendance. Those who attend religious services at least once a week average four persons in their networks, fully one more person on average than those who attend religious services a few times a month or fewer. White evangelical Protestants who attend religious services more frequently are nearly six times more likely to have friends from their church in their networks than those who attend less frequently (17 percent and 3 percent, respectively). Frequent attenders have more contact with Romney supporters (2.1 persons) than those who attend less frequently (1.4 persons).

White evangelical Protestants are the largest religious tradition in the Republican coalition (even if they are not a majority of the GOP). They represent the core of the southern, Christian conservative base of the GOP, and their geographic concentration is a boon to their influence. They are also important players in the Tea Party movement.[6] It would seem like a great deal of this uniquely Republican profile comes from their social networks. White evangelical Protestants are more socially connected than the average American, and their networks are more likely to be filled with other white Protestants. Moreover, their friends and family are also more likely to agree with them politically (but see Chapter 11). This is especially true among evangelicals who are more active in church, as measured by attendance. These white evangelical Protestants have more Romney voters and church friends in their networks. To an extent, their influence in the Republican Party hinges on how people respond to their networks—if they respond in similar ways, their networks can reinforce solidarity, but it is possible that the responses of those who took the survey are conditional, as we have suggested may be the case for younger evangelicals.

Group Boundaries

We begin with feelings toward groups, as groups are some of the most fundamental ways in which politics is organized in society (Madison 1787; Truman 1951) as well as within people's heads (e.g., Brady and Sniderman 1985). Feelings toward groups help individuals triangulate their own opinions, help them understand elite cues, and serve as a reflection of where their sympa-

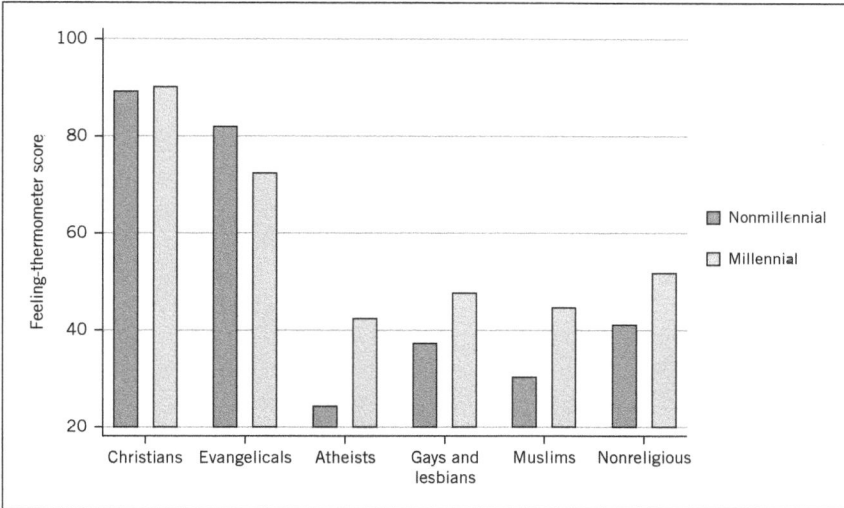

Figure 12.1 Evangelicals' feeling-thermometer scores of in-groups and out-groups by millennial status
Source: Cox, Navarro-Rivera, and Jones 2013.

thies lie. Here we examine the difference between how they feel toward Christians and evangelicals and how they feel toward traditional evangelical out-groups—atheists, Muslims, gays and lesbians, and the nonreligious.

Figure 12.1 shows those results broken down by millennial status (younger than twenty-nine versus those older). It is notable that there is no difference between millennials and their elders in evaluations of Christians—both near ninety points on the thermometer—but there is a nine-point drop among millennials in their feelings toward "evangelicals." This is our first evidence that younger evangelicals adopt a less embattled mentality than their elders.

Feelings toward the out-groups are quite low across the board, with significant differences between millennials and their elders. The average rating among millennials is more than forty and is well over that for their elders. The gap is about twenty points in the case of atheists and a bit lower for the other groups. Taken together, while all white evangelicals have warmer feelings about their own group than out-groups, younger evangelicals express much less antipathy to other social and religious groups than do their older coreligionists.

Our models examine the gap between feelings toward evangelicals and these four out-groups. Again, we focus on the effects of Republican acquaintances, network diversity, millennial status, and resources that may affect the diversity of information to which individuals are exposed. There is statistically marginal evidence that men and married evangelicals show a lower gap between their feelings toward evangelicals and atheists, but the only statistically crisp evidence is the monstrous effect of being a millennial, ratifying that the results from Figure 12.1 are not statistical artifacts. In fact, across the board, while there are only a few, sporadic significant effects from resources such as income, the one that stands out clearly and consistently is the radically smaller gap in group ratings by millennials, which hovers around a thirty-point drop. That is, millennials' feelings toward out-groups are thirty points closer to their feelings toward evangelicals than those of their elders.

There is evidence that having more Republican discussion partners promotes a greater gap in group ratings, too. For all but relative ratings of atheists, those with a homogeneous network of Republicans show a twenty-point greater gap. This is not an effect of Republican identification (which is insignificant in all cases but the relative rating of gays and lesbians) but a reflection of information flow (see Huckfeldt et al. 1995). And evangelicals' discussions with Republicans reinforce the group's boundaries with traditional out-groups. Other metrics of network diversity fail to find statistical purchase. It is unsurprising that knowing a nonreligious person or a non-Christian would ease prejudice against these out-groups, but members of such out-groups make up a very small proportion of evangelicals' networks. Given the numbers of Republicans and other evangelicals in their networks, that we find effects here suggests that these interactions are high impact.

Religious Valuation

Some evidence that may help us make sense of the differences between millennials and their elders is presented in Figure 12.2, which shows the average responses of the two age groups to a set of questions about the value of religion in society as an agent of socialization. There is little agreement with the statement that "Religion causes more problems in society than it solves" and that "under God" should be removed from the Pledge of Allegiance, but millennials are more likely to agree with both. However, there is quite a bit of support for the ideas that religious values are good for kids, that you have to believe in God to be moral, and that you should be tolerant of others. Millennials are a bit less likely to agree with the statement "It is important for children to be brought up in a religion so they can learn good values" and agree equally with the other two statements.

But this is not quite the evidence we are after because it does not explain the gulfs between millennials and their elders in group evaluations. The models help show that more negative views of the social value of religion are generated from within evangelicalism. That is, millennials react more negatively and see less value in religious socialization when they have *more homogeneous networks*. This is clearly not in accord with a straightforward social-contact approach, which would suggest that homogeneity drives in-

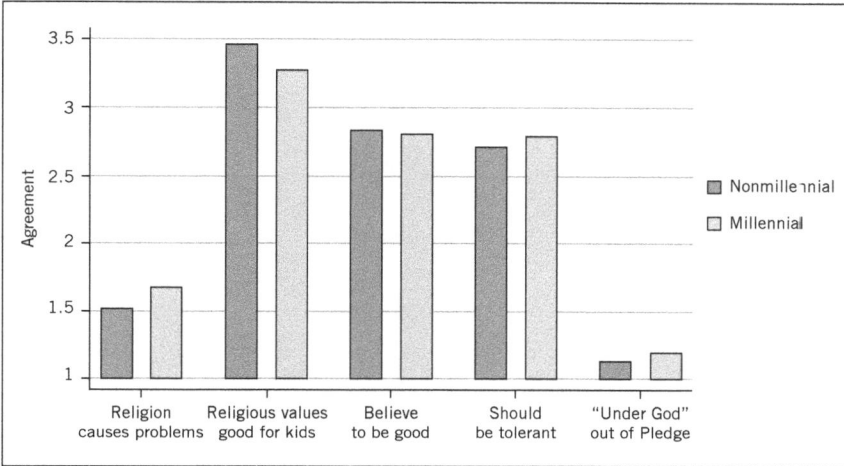

Figure 12.2 Attitudes of millennials and their elders on the value of religion in society
Source: Cox, Navarro-Rivera, and Jones 2013.

group love and out-group derogation. Instead, it suggests whiffs of rebellion when millennials are firmly embedded in the group.[7]

The interaction terms show some distinguishable effects, and the results are graphed in Figure 12.3, which shows the marginal effect of being a millennial rather than an older person. Through most of the range of network diversity, the effect of being millennial does not distinguish millennials from their elders—the confidence intervals overlap with zero. However, the evidence is clear that when their networks *do not* contain non-Christians, the religiously unaffiliated, and nonwhites (low diversity), they are more likely to agree that religion causes more problems, agree that "under God" should be removed from the Pledge, and disagree that religious values are good for kids.[8] Notably, evangelicals have highly homogeneous networks in the ways we are measuring them here. This end of the scale is by far where most all evangelicals, including millennials, are located. Therefore, we have gathered some evidence that is suggestive about why young evangelicals are different from their elders—they are reacting negatively to the embattled, political subculture of their parents.

Being a Republican and being surrounded by Republicans helps buttress an embattled mentality and reinforce the perceived value of religion in society. The interactions support separable effects in half of the models, and an example of how they work is shown in Figure 12.4. We can see that Republicans are more likely to disagree that religion causes problems and that non-Republicans are pulled to the same attitude by a network full of Republican discussants.

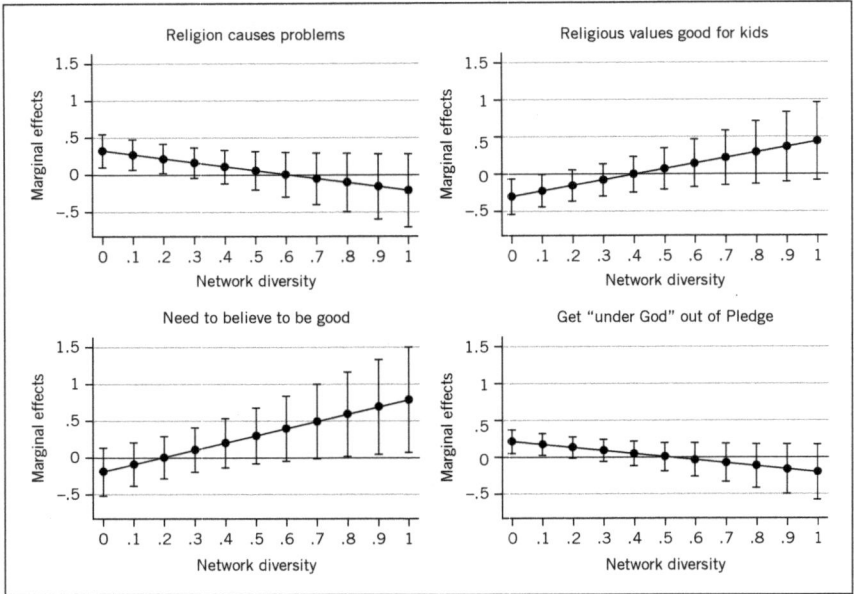

Figure 12.3 Marginal effects of millennial status on the value of religion in socialization across levels of network diversity

Source: Cox, Navarro-Rivera, and Jones 2013.
Note: 90 percent confidence intervals.

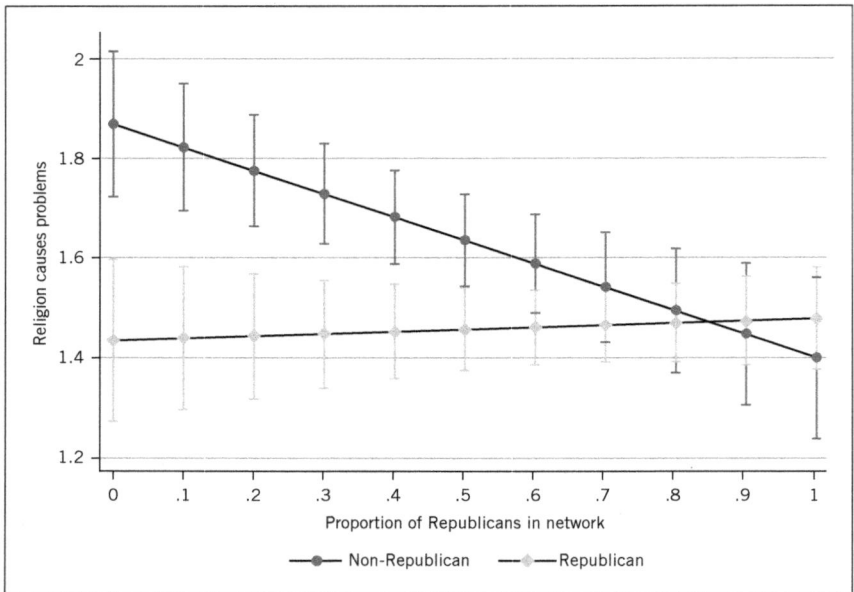

Figure 12.4 Informational pull of Republican social networks among evangelicals
Source: Cox, Navarro-Rivera, and Jones 2013.
Note: 90 percent confidence intervals.

Issue Attitudes and the Vote

It is important to understand how this evidence contributes to attitudes and behaviors closely connected to government control, such as political attitudes and vote choice. We examine a small selection of attitudes and the 2012 vote using essentially the same model as before, but now we have added two former dependent variables—a more or less relevant feeling thermometer and two religious-valuation variables.

Generally, the evidence is consistent with that of the earlier models but is less statistically crisp, in part because the measures are not as relevant. For instance, while we use a feeling thermometer toward gays and lesbians, which predicts much more support for gay marriage, we do not have relevant feeling thermometers for the other models (and use atheists instead). Positive feelings toward atheists provide marginal evidence of affecting the vote (against Romney) and opposition to abortion restrictions. The religious-valuation variables are both insignificant at conventional levels in all models but do offer statistically imprecise evidence that one or the other (they are not strongly correlated) affects issue attitudes and the vote in the way we would suspect—believing religion leads to more problems in society, for instance, is linked to a more liberal stance on abortion.

The dominant explanation, of course, is being a Republican and being surrounded by Republicans. In most cases, they act independently, working to reinforce more conservative stands and vote choice. But on the vote they interact, such that non-Republicans are brought in line with and resemble other Republicans. It is interesting to observe in Figure 12.5 that the tipping point for non-Republicans, where the probability of voting for Romney is better than 50 percent, comes *before* the network is majority Republican.[9] This suggests the power of the fused identity of evangelical-Republican (Patrikios 2013) and the common commitments in the evangelical community to voting Republican (see, e.g., Huckfeldt and Sprague 1995 for the social inferences people make about their discussion partners).

Conclusion

Over the last twenty years, the Republican Party's largest and generally most reliable constituency has been white evangelical Protestants. Therefore, when we see signs of a crackup, it is worth continually monitoring sources and the extent of seismic activity. Over the last decade, the most conservative leadership has fallen apart; formerly powerful organizations are mere shells of their former entities. A new generation of leaders has arisen that is not as united in its issue agenda, has taken stands that align with the Democratic Party in some instances (or with the broader faith community), and generally has adopted a more inclusive tone. New movements, such as the emergent

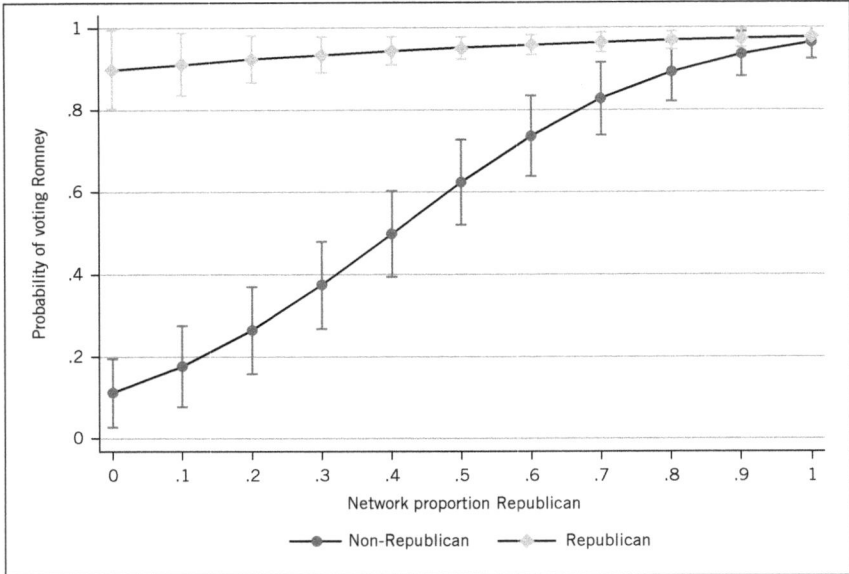

Figure 12.5 Interactive effects of being a Republican and network Republicanism on the Romney vote
Source: Cox, Navarro-Rivera, and Jones 2013.
Note: 90 percent confidence intervals.

church, have arisen that are hard to call renewal movements in the same ways as previous movements that breathed life into evangelicalism. Moreover, there are scattered signals that former juggernauts of the religious economy may not be invincible growth machines; for example, the Southern Baptist Convention membership reached a plateau by 2000 and then began to decline (see Jones 2016).

Spurred by this collection of evidence, we sought to investigate the internal workings of evangelicalism, assessing the sources of diversity as they bear on the political orientations of, especially, younger, millennial evangelicals. In contrast to the embattled mentality that has been central to the religious tradition's approach to society (Smith 1998), we looked for evidence of cosmopolitanism through a diversification of social networks, increased resources that might diversify experience and social ties, and a diversification in exposure to political ideas. Our efforts to identify differences in the extent of such exposure between young and older evangelicals are not particularly overwhelming. There is marginal evidence that younger evangelicals are more cosmopolitan than their elders.

However, we also allowed younger evangelicals to react differently to their surroundings, and here is where we found some differences to be hiding. On several dimensions, younger evangelicals are reacting negatively to their social environments. When they have more diverse networks, their politics looks like that of their elders—embattled. When they are surrounded by evangelicals, however, they react in ways that make them more open to new political ideas—religion is problematic, they are less warm to evangelicals, and they are warmer to traditional out-groups. And through that openness they are able to take somewhat more liberal stands on divisive social issues.

For now, these differences are not large, and their application to the vote is weak. The dominant force is social enclosure by Republicans, which serves to hem in non-Republicans. But as young evangelicals grow older, move, and begin to exercise more discretion in their social ties, their political choices may grow to match their political orientations. Put differently, a political movement surely cannot be sustained primarily on social pressure. Alternatively, these signs of youthful rebellion may subside over time and once the millennials have children, or they could drive millennials out of the church altogether if disagreement grows too great (see Djupe, Neiheisel, and Sokhey 2018).

NOTES

A previous version of this chapter was delivered at the 110th Annual Meeting of the American Political Science Association, Washington, DC, August 28–31, 2014. The authors are listed in alphabetical order.

1. There is considerable debate over how to define evangelicalism; see Chapter 7 and Djupe and Burge 2017.

2. Data come from the Pew Research Center's 1987–2012 Values Survey, available at http://www.people-press.org/2012/04/15/1987-2012-values-survey-combined-dataset.

3. The prompt read, "We are interested in the sort of political information and opinions people get from each other. Can you give me the FIRST names of the three people you talked with most about the events of the past election year? These people might be from your family, from work, from the neighborhood, from church, from some other organization you belong to, or they might be from somewhere else."

4. The survey did not ask if the discussant was an evangelical, simply a Protestant.

5. It should be noted that the survey followed common protocol, which is not to ask for a church affiliation for discussants independent of family, work, or other ties. Thus, this percentage represents networks with a discussant who is known only through a common church tie.

6. Daniel Cox and Robert Jones (2010) found that 47 percent of Americans who identified as part of the Tea Party movement also claimed membership in the Christian Right.

7. From this perspective, one could see the value of the Amish *rumspringa* or Mormon mission, where exposure to the outside world is what reinforces commitment to the group.

8. The only exception is in the third panel—millennials are more likely to agree that one needs to believe in order to be moral when they have more homogeneous networks.

9. Recall that evangelical networks, millennial or not, are 59 percent Republican—44 percent of their networks have less than a majority of Republicans. We do not have the sample size to see if the interactive effects hold specifically among millennials.

REFERENCES

Allport, Gordon. 1954. *The Nature of Prejudice*. Reading, MA: Addison-Wesley.

Barna Group. 2007. "A New Generation Expresses Its Skepticism and Frustration with Christianity." September 21. Available at https://www.barna.com/research/a-new-generation-expresses-its-skepticism-and-frustration-with-christianity.

Brady, Henry E., and Paul M. Sniderman. 1985. "Attitude Attribution: A Group Basis for Political Reasoning." *American Political Science Review* 79 (4): 1061–1078.

Cooper, Betsy, Daniel Cox, Rachel Lienesch, and Robert P. Jones. 2016. "Beyond Same-Sex Marriage: Attitudes on LGBT Nondiscrimination Laws and Religious Exemptions from the 2015 American Values Atlas." Public Religion Research Institute, February 18. Available at http://www.prri.org/research/poll-same-sex-gay-marriage-lgbt-nondiscrimination-religious-liberty.

Cox, Dan. 2007. "Young White Evangelicals: Less Republican, Still Conservative." Pew Research Center, September 28. Available at http://pewforum.org/Politics-and-Elections/Young-White-Evangelicals-Less-Republican-Still-Conservative.aspx.

Cox, Daniel, and Robert P. Jones. 2010. "Religion and the Tea Party in the 2010 Elections." Public Religion Research Institute, October 5. Available at http://www.prri.org/research/religion-tea-party-2010.

Cox, Daniel, Juhem Navarro-Rivera, and Robert P. Jones. 2013. "In Search of Libertarians in America." Available at https://www.prri.org/research/2013-american-values-survey.

Deckman, Melissa M. 2004. *School Board Battles: The Christian Right in Local Politics.* Washington, DC: Georgetown University Press.

Djupe, Paul A., and Ryan P. Burge. 2017. "Bud Was Right: 'Measurement Error Is Sin.'" *Religion in Public*, March 22. Available at https://religioninpublic.blog/2017/03/22/measurement-error-is-sin/.

Djupe, Paul A., and Brian R. Calfano. 2013. "Religious Value Priming, Threat, and Political Tolerance." *Political Research Quarterly* 66 (4): 768–780.

Djupe, Paul A., Jacob R. Neiheisel, and Anand E. Sokhey. 2018. "Reconsidering the Role of Politics in Leaving Religion: The Importance of Affiliation." *American Journal of Political Science* 62 (1): 161–175.

"Election 2012: President Exit Polls." 2012. *New York Times*, November 6. Available at https://www.nytimes.com/elections/2012/results/president/exit-polls.html.

Fitzgerald, Frances. 2008. "The New Evangelicals." *New Yorker*, June 30. Available at https://www.newyorker.com/magazine/2008/06/30/the-new-evangelicals.

Gibbs, Eddie, and Ryan Bolger. 2005. *Emerging Churches: Creating Christian Community in Postmodern Cultures.* Grand Rapids, MI: Baker Books.

Golebiowska, Ewa A. 1995. "Individual Value Priorities, Education, and Political Tolerance." *Political Behavior* 17:23–48.

Granovetter, Mark. 1973. "The Strength of Weak Ties." *American Journal of Sociology* 78: 1360–1380.

Green, John C., James L. Guth, Corwin E. Smidt, and Lyman A. Kellstedt. 1996. *Religion and the Culture Wars: Dispatches from the Front.* Lanham, MD: Rowman and Littlefield.

Huckfeldt, Robert, Paul Allen Beck, Russell J. Dalton, and Jeffrey Levine. 1995. "Political Environments, Cohesive Social Groups, and the Communication of Public Opinion." *American Journal of Political Science* 39:1025–1054.

Huckfeldt, R. Robert, and John Sprague. 1995. *Citizens, Politics and Social Communication: Information and Influence in an Election Campaign.* Cambridge: Cambridge University Press.

Jones, Robert P. 2016. *The End of White Christian America.* New York: Simon and Schuster.

Kirkpatrick, David D. 2007. "The Evangelical Crackup." *New York Times*, October 28. Available at https://www.nytimes.com/2007/10/28/magazine/28Evangelicals-t.html.

Layman, Geoffrey C. 2001. *The Great Divide: Religious and Cultural Conflict in American Party Politics.* New York: Columbia University Press.

Madison, James. 1787. "The Federalist No. 10: The Union as a Safeguard against Domestic Faction and Insurrection (Continued)." *Daily Advertiser,* November 22. Available at http://avalon.law.yale.edu/18th_century/fed10.asp.

Marsden, Peter V. 1990. "Network Data and Measurement." *Annual Review of Sociology* 16:435–463.

Mill, John S. (1869) 1975. *On Liberty.* Reprint, New York: Norton.

Patrikios, Stratos. 2013. "Self-Stereotyping as 'Evangelical Republican': An Empirical Test." *Politics and Religion* 6 (4): 800–822.

Pettigrew, Thomas F., and Linda Tropp. 2006. "A Meta-analytic Test of Intergroup Contact Theory." *Interpersonal Relations and Group Processes* 90 (5): 751–783.

Pew Research Center. 2010. "Growing Number of Americans Say Obama Is a Muslim." August 18. Available at http://pewforum.org/Politics-and-Elections/Growing-Number-of-Americans-Say-Obama-is-a-Muslim.aspx.

Smith, Christian. 1998. *American Evangelicalism: Embattled and Thriving.* Chicago: University of Chicago Press.

Sokhey, Anand E., Andy Baker, and Paul A. Djupe. 2015. "The Dynamics of Socially-Supplied Information: Examining Discussion Network Stability over Time." *International Journal of Public Opinion Research* 27 (4): 565–587.

Truman, David B. 1951. *The Governmental Process: Political Interests and Public Opinion.* New York: Alfred A. Knopf.

Wald, Kenneth D., and Allison Calhoun-Brown. 2007. *Religion and Politics in the United States.* Lanham, MD: Rowman and Littlefield.

PART III

Legal, Constitutional Battles and Morality Politics

13

Evangelicals and Local Efforts to Display "In God We Trust"

Joshua L. Mitchell
J. Tobin Grant

n the so-called culture war, most of the fighting occurs in local skirmishes. Religious conservatives have succeeded when they have focused on grassroots organizing (Rozell and Wilcox 1996) and local elections (Deckman 2004). This chapter focuses on efforts by evangelical activists to convince local governments to display the national motto: "In God We Trust." The symbol was created during the nationalism of the Civil War and has since been repeatedly used as a reaction to perceived threats to Christian national identity. As one of the few religious symbols sanctioned by the U.S. Supreme Court, the national motto provides a constitutional means for local governments to express support for Christian nationalism. For Republican political entrepreneurs, efforts to promote the national motto may offer costless, yet symbolically potent, ways to avert an "evangelical crackup."

Historical Symbolism of "In God We Trust"

With apologies to Harold Lasswell (1936), politics is more than who gets what when and how. Policies that drive our politics are often symbolic, representing political meanings beyond the literal meaning of the policy text (Edelmann 1964). Political symbols are important because they connect individuals to the "larger political order" and help facilitate collective action (Elder and Cobb 1983, 1). But political symbols are tricky and difficult to control because the meaning of any symbol may vary according to the person perceiving it (Elder and Cobb 1983, 10). A policy may represent meanings that are subjective regardless of the actual "who gets what when and how."

Some of the most important symbols in the politics of evangelicals and other religious conservatives involve America's civil religion. As Robert Bellah defines it, America's civil religion includes behaviors, rituals, and symbols that reflect a "public religious dimension" or a "religious orientation that the great majority of Americans share" (1967, 3–4). But like other political symbols, their meaning is subjective. For example, the public display of the Ten Commandments is viewed by some as an acknowledgment of the law's religious heritage but is seen by others as the establishment of a state religion. Such symbols have almost no substantive effect—they involve few public funds and involve no regulations. But as symbols, they may buttress those who view America as a Christian nation and may discourage those who see the nation as a secular state.

Unlike other religious symbols, placing "In God We Trust" in public spaces is not viewed as an unconstitutional establishment of religion. In 1956, President Dwight Eisenhower signed a joint resolution making "In God We Trust" the national motto of the United States. The House and the Senate each adopted the resolution unanimously and without debate. In 1970, the U.S. Court of Appeals for the Ninth Circuit ruled the motto constitutional because it was a patriotic statement, not a theological one, with no particular religious meaning (Aronow v. United States, 432 F.2d 242, 243). A 1996 ruling by the U.S. Court of Appeals for the Ninth Circuit stated that the motto and its printing on U.S. currency "clearly have a secular purpose":

> The motto symbolizes the historical role of religion in our society, formalizes our medium of exchange, fosters patriotism, and expresses confidence in the future. The motto's primary effect is not to advance religion; instead, it is a form of "ceremonial deism" which through historical usage and ubiquity cannot be reasonably understood to convey government approval of religious belief. (Gaylor v. United States, 595 F.3d 1364)

Other mottos have been similarly used. Ohio's motto, "With God All Things Are Possible," is a quote from the Bible (Matthew 19:26 NIV). Like the national motto, it is legally viewed as a statement with no specific religious meaning. It is prominently displayed at the state capitol and may be included on license plates.

The recent promotion of "In God We Trust" represents the latest in a series of efforts to use the phrase as a symbol of America's Christian heritage. The phrase originated in 1864. Responding to a request from a clergyman, the U.S. Treasury and the U.S. Mint sought the recognition of God on U.S. currency to express that the United States was a Christian nation (Fisher and

Mourtada-Sabbah 2002). The phrase was coined (pun intended) to fit on currency. It is a very brief statement that comes not from the Bible but from a stanza in the "Star-Spangled Banner" (Kulwinski 2008). Congress approved, but did not require, the phrase to be placed on U.S. currency.

The phrase became an issue four decades later when President Theodore Roosevelt wanted to redesign the currency. With the goal of boosting the artistic value of American coinage and to make U.S. currency more like that of classical Greece, Roosevelt proposed to remove the statement from currency (Fisher and Mourtada-Sabbah 2002). Clergy and churches took public positions against the removal. Roosevelt deferred to Congress, which almost unanimously voted to keep "In God We Trust" on the currency.

The debate over the phrase demonstrated that Congress saw it as affirming that America was a Christian nation. Congressional committees reported that the phrase expressed a religious commitment—specifically a "Christian patriotism"—that was necessary for the survival of any republic (quoted in Fisher and Mourtada-Sabbah 2002, 677). The congressional debate further emphasized that the phrase was both general enough to be supported by all churches and religions (including "Hebrews") and would aid in Christian missionary efforts (Fisher and Mourtada-Sabbah 2002). Roosevelt, in defending his position, argued that placing the phrase on currency was "in effect irreverence, which comes dangerously close to sacrilege" ("Roosevelt Dropped" 1907, 1).

The phrase also became the subject of congressional debate as part of the response to communism (Fisher and Mourtada-Sabbah 2002). In 1951, the Senate placed "In God We Trust" above its south entrance. In 1952, President Eisenhower declared a National Day of Prayer. In the following years, Congress added the phrase "under God" to the Pledge of Allegiance, added "so help me God" to oaths of office for federal judges, and required "In God We Trust" on all currency (Puro, Schultz, and Vile 2005).

Once it became the national motto, "In God We Trust" soon became more than a weapon in the Cold War. In 1962, it was first used in a battle in the culture wars when the U.S. Supreme Court first ruled against mandatory school prayer (Engel v. Vitale, 370 U.S. 421). The U.S. House responded by inscribing "In God We Trust" above the Speaker's chair in the chamber. The next year, the Supreme Court ruled again on the issue (Abington Township School District v. Schempp, 374 U.S. 203 (1963)). This time, some members proposed requiring that the inscription be placed above the bench in the Supreme Court ("In God We Trust Is Urged" 1963, 43). Chief Justice Earl Warren objected, stating the addition of the national motto would, like any other phrase, change the architectural design of the chamber ("Warren Opposed" 1963, 30). Congress did not pursue the issue further.

The courts have concluded that "In God We Trust" is a generic expression of religion and patriotism. But the historical record suggests that it has been understood as a symbol of *Christian* nationalism. It originated as an effort to affirm that the United States was a Christian nation. It was overwhelmingly reaffirmed as a Christian national symbol when President Roosevelt attempted to remove it from currency. In the 1950s, Congress adopted it as the national motto as one of the many symbolic policies meant to contrast a God-fearing America with its enemy, a godless Soviet Union. In the 1960s, Congress used the motto as a symbolic response to decisions by the Supreme Court that removed mandatory prayer from schools. In each case, the phrase was used to express not only patriotism but also the view that the United States is Christian nation.

"In God We Trust" in Current Politics

Over the past fifteen years, there has been an effort to have the national motto endorsed and displayed by *local* governments. Unlike the Ten Commandments or other religious symbols, "In God We Trust" can be displayed without violating the U.S. Constitution under current Supreme Court rulings. It is not a religious text per se; it is the national motto. While activists and politicians may see the motto as an expression of Christian nationalism, they can argue that *legally* it is less like the Ten Commandments and more like the Pledge of Allegiance. The courts have determined that it is a generic statement that does not establish a religion.

But the picture is different at the local level. In Congress, there are religious conservatives who will fight for Christian patriotic symbols. The same may not be said of a city council, county board, or other local government. Officials in localities may oppose the public display of such symbols out of principle. Others would vote for a measure brought by a colleague, but many may not see this as a priority. That is, there needs to be a policy entrepreneur who is willing to bring the policy to the local board.

Whether out of conviction or political expediency, Congress has promoted the public display of "In God We Trust." In 2006, the Senate voted to affirm "In God We Trust" as the official national motto. In 2011, the House followed suit, voting 396–9 in affirmation. At the urging of religious conservatives, Congress voted to engrave "In God We Trust" in the U.S. Capitol Visitor Center. As with previous votes, the measure passed with near unanimity (in the House, the vote was 410–8). Legislators who put the national motto up to a vote find few who will vote against it.

But the picture is different at the local level. In Congress, there are religious conservatives who will fight for Christian patriotic symbols. The same may not be said of a city council, county board, or other local government. Officials in localities may oppose the public display of such symbols out of principle. Others would vote for a measure brought by a colleague, but many may not see this as a priority. That is, there needs to be a policy entrepreneur who is willing to bring the policy to the local board.

A movement to have local governments display "In God We Trust" started with the initiative of one such policy entrepreneur. In 2001, Jacquie Sullivan, a Bakersfield, California, city council member, led an effort to have her city display the national motto. Here is how Sullivan (currently in her sixth term) describes this on her city council biography page:

In early 2001, while listening to the local Christian radio station, Jacquie heard on the news that there was a small group, back east, pro-
testing that *in god we trust* was displayed on a public building. She
thought, "They are working to take down our motto, I will work to put
it up," and so she did! On 2/20/2002, Jacquie led the Bakersfield City
Council to "Vote Yes" to proudly and prominently display the national
motto, *in god we trust*, in their City Council Chambers, at City Hall.
Jacquie considers this to be her most important accomplishment since
she has been in elected office. (City of Bakersfield, n.d.)

In 2004, Sullivan founded the nonprofit organization In God We Trust
America, Inc., which has pushed local governments to display "In God We
Trust" on public property. Since this nonprofit's creation, more than six hundred local governments in twenty-nine states have adopted these initiatives,
with several additional adoptions occurring each year.

There are far more localities that have not approved the display of the
national motto. There are more than thirty-one hundred counties, more
than nineteen thousand incorporated places, and thirty-nine thousand local
governments in the United States (U.S. Census 2007). Less than 2 percent of
local governments have voted to display the national motto. However, where
and when these adoptions take place tell us about the politics of this symbolic policy.

Figure 13.1 shows the annual number of municipalities that have adopted
a policy to promote the national motto. There are times when the policies
were more likely to be adopted. Prior to 2010, only one or two dozen municipalities adopted such a policy each year. Then came a period of frequent
adoptions (2010–2011). After another period of relative dormancy, a second
period of high adoption started in 2014. These spikes in adoption can be seen
even within years. There are months with high activity in which the policy
spreads quickly to neighboring governments, who also decide to promote
the motto.

The adoption of "In God We Trust" policies has been a regional phenomenon. Often adoption occurs but does not spread to nearby governments. As
shown in Figure 13.2, the majority of states have had a small number of
municipalities adopt these policies. Occasionally, however, there have been
"hot spots" in which adoptions occur quickly throughout a region. The result
is that the vast majority of municipality adoptions have occurred in six
states: California, Arkansas, North Carolina, Missouri, Texas, and Virginia.

Prior to 2010, most adoptions occurred in California. This began in 2001
when Jacquie Sullivan led Bakersfield to promote the national motto. Other
municipalities near Bakersfield then adopted similar policies. A few years
later, there were more adoptions in Orange County, a longtime home of

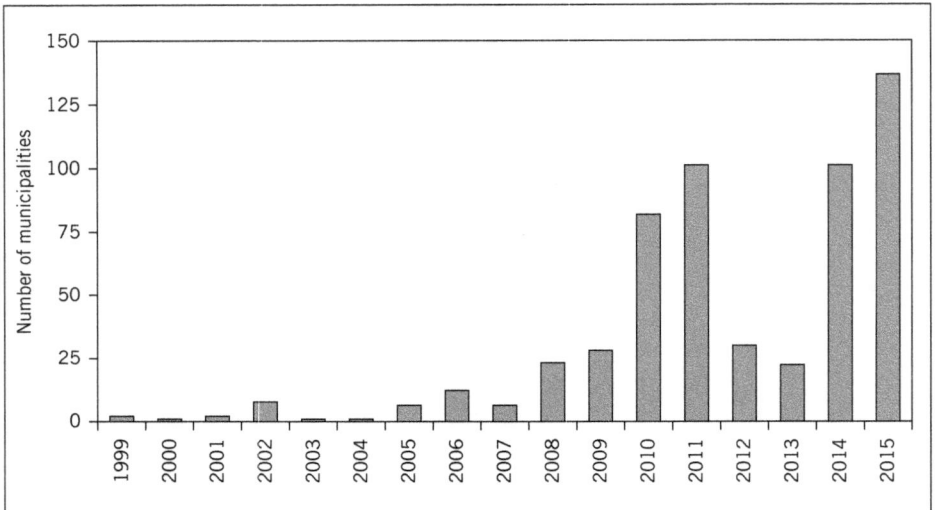

Figure 13.1 Annual number of municipalities adopting "In God We Trust" policies, 1999–2015

Source: In God We Trust America 2017.

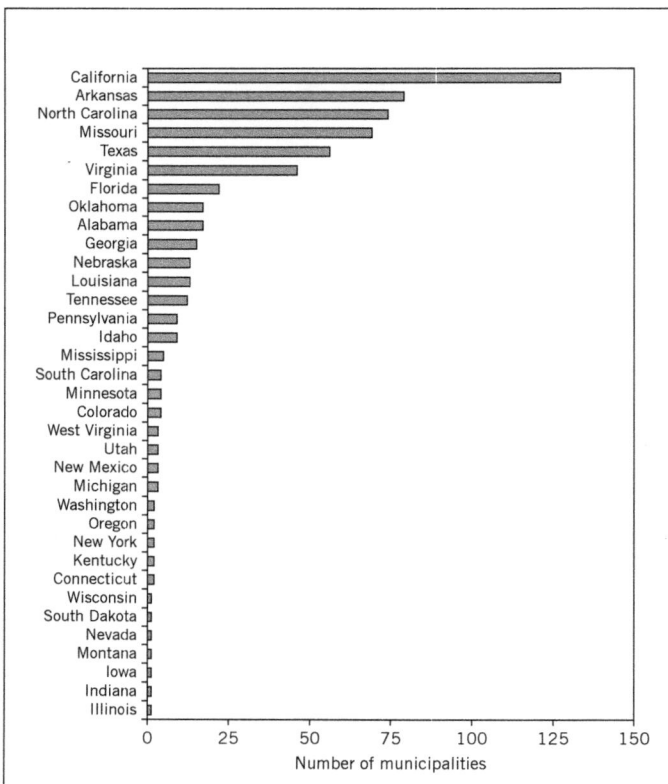

Figure 13.2 Number of municipalities adopting "In God We Trust" policies by state

Source: In God We Trust America 2017.

conservative evangelical politics. By 2010, sixty-nine municipalities in California had adopted an "In God We Trust" policy.

The spikes in adoptions in 2010, 2011, 2014, and 2015 were "outbreaks" within states. In 2010, sixty municipalities in Arkansas adopted an "In God We Trust" policy; and in 2011, forty-two cities and counties in Missouri. Two years later Virginia was the hotspot. In 2015 (the last year with complete data) there were fifty-three adoptions in North Carolina. Florida and Texas had smaller, regional outbreaks that occurred in different regions of each state at different times.

The story of "In God We Trust" policy adoption shows the power of local and regional politics. Nationwide, there are relatively few municipalities that have taken the time to promote the national motto. But in those relatively rare cases in which a city council member, county board official, or local activist convinces a municipality to adopt a policy, there is a chance that other municipalities in the region will follow suit. Policy adoption quickly spreads within the hotspot. Later, more municipalities in the state may adopt the policy but not at the same high rate. The result is that there are some regions of the country in which many municipalities display and promote the national motto.

Conclusion

What difference does it make if a local government decides to display or promote "In God We Trust"? One answer is that it is inconsequential. It costs little to implement; it is a generic nod to monotheism; and it will do nothing to the state of our economy. But another answer is that it symbolizes something great. For proponents, it acknowledges that the United States as a nation recognizes God and, albeit implicitly, that America is a Christian nation. For opponents, it is this very meaning that makes it dangerous; by promoting this motto, local governments are promoting a religion and the view that the state should be religious.

The national motto is a symbol, but a powerful one. Importantly, it is a symbol that can be promoted by those espousing Christian nationalism with the cover provided by the Supreme Court. One of the most important aspects of evangelical politics is Christian nationalism. Many evangelicals, particularly those active within conservative politics, hold the belief that the United States was founded as a Christian nation and should remain so. Ensuring that "In God We Trust" remain the national motto and be promoted at the local level is one way to show that America continues to be the Christian nation evangelicals believe it is. Unlike other religious symbols, the national motto is a constitutional expression of religion in government. Unlike a cross or crèche, the motto is not the symbol of a particular religion. Legally, it is a generic statement with no sectarian meaning. History shows, however, that the motto has been promoted and defended in times when there have been threats to Christian nationalism. Municipalities can promote "In God We Trust" and display it publicly to show that, at least locally, the government trusts in God. The fact that "In God We Trust" is the national motto provides municipalities with a justification—both legal and historical—that America is God's nation. Accordingly, against the backdrop of a possible evangelical crackup, promotion of the national motto represents a way of consolidating evangelical support.

At the national level, there is no battle over the motto. It was created without controversy. When it was questioned by President Roosevelt, it was resoundingly supported. It was adopted as the national motto unanimously and without much debate. In 2002, 2006, and 2011, Congress voted to uphold the national motto, despite there being no effort to change it. When the House of Representatives took up the matter in 2011, the only opponents objected to taking time away from other matters to debate something uniformly accepted.

We find that "In God We Trust" policies have been adopted in regional outbreaks. Activists or entrepreneurial politicians in a state promote the policy. When it is adopted, other nearby municipalities may follow suit as the motto becomes part of the regional agenda. We find that there may be sudden movements in a state in which dozens of municipalities adopt promotion policies. These have resulted in regions in California, Missouri, Arkansas, Virginia, North Carolina, and Texas in which one may find many cities and counties with the motto displayed publicly.

There remain other regions of the country where these "In God We Trust" initiatives have not been adopted. In some states, such as Mississippi and South Carolina, there have been relatively few adoptions despite having many communities that would likely approve. Adoptions have not been a nationwide phenomenon; they are regional events. This is the way culture wars are fought; they are not so much a national war than a series of local skirmishes.

REFERENCES

Bellah, Robert. 1967. "Civil Religion in America." *Daedalus* 96 (1): 1–21.
City of Bakersfield. n.d. "Jacquie Sullivan—Councilmember." Available at http://www .bakersfieldcity.us/gov/elected_officials/jacquie_sullivan.htm (accessed March 26, 2018).
Deckman, Melissa M. 2004. *School Board Battles: The Christian Right in Local Politics*. Washington, DC: Georgetown University Press.
Edelman, Murray J. 1964. *The Symbolic Uses of Politics*. Champaign: University of Illinois Press.
Elder, Charles D., and Roger W. Cobb. 1983. *The Political Use of Symbols*. New York: Cambridge University Press.
Fisher, Louis, and Nada Mourtada-Sabbah. 2002. "Adopting 'In God We Trust' as the U.S. National Motto." *Journal of Church and State* 44 (4): 671–692.

In God We Trust America. 2017. "Cities and Counties Whose Elected Officials Have, 'Voted Yes' to Legally Display Our National Motto, In God We Trust, in Their Chambers." Available at http://www.ingodwetrust-america.org/wp-content/uploads/2018/01/VictoryReport.pdf.

"In God We Trust Is Urged for the Court." 1963. *New York Times*, June 26, p. 43.

Kulwinski, Paul. 2008. "Trust in God Going Too Far: Indiana's 'In God We Trust' License Plate Endorses Religion at Taxpayer Expense." *Valparaiso University Law Review* 43:1317–1374.

Lasswell, Harold. 1936. *Who Gets What, When, How.* New York: Whittlesey House.

Puro, S., D. Schultz, and J. R. Vile. 2005. "The Encyclopedia of Civil Rights in America." *Library Journal* 130 (8): 117–118.

"Roosevelt Dropped 'In God We Trust.'" 1907. *New York Times*, November 14, p. 1.

Rozell, Mark J., and Clyde Wilcox. 1996. "Second Coming: The Strategies of the New Christian Right." *Political Science Quarterly* 111 (2): 271–294.

U.S. Census Bureau. 2007. "Local Governments and Public School Systems by Type and State: 2007." Available at https://www.census.gov/data/tables/2007/econ/gus/govorgtab03ss.html.

"Warren Opposed to Inscription of 'In God We Trust' for Court." 1963. *New York Times*, November 13, p. 30.

14

A Match Made in Heaven?

Linking Christian Legal Advocacy
with Conservative Politics

DANIEL BENNETT

In February 2016, U.S. Supreme Court justice Antonin Scalia unexpectedly died while on vacation in Texas. The news of the seventy-nine-year old justice's death sent shockwaves through the legal and political world. In addition to leaving the Supreme Court without its most outspoken (and longest-tenured) conservative voice, Scalia's death also set up an explosive battle between President Barack Obama and the Republican Senate to fill the sudden vacancy, all in the midst of a presidential election campaign.

The political reaction to Scalia's death was both swift and predictable. Within minutes of the news reaching media outlets, partisan lines in the sand were drawn. Then-presidential candidate and Texas senator Ted Cruz (2016) called on the Senate "to ensure that the next President names his replacement," and Senate Majority Leader Mitch McConnell said, "This vacancy should not be filled until we have a new president" (Everett and Thrush 2016). Even though President Obama pledged that he would "fulfill [his] constitutional responsibilities" (Politi 2016) and select a nominee to succeed Scalia, the Republican position was clearly and forcefully articulated: Barack Obama must not be allowed to fill Scalia's seat on the court.

Attorneys with Christian conservative legal organizations (CCLOs)—interest groups committed to defending Christian conservative concerns in the legal realm—were similarly quick to call for postponing any hearings on a nominee until after the next president was sworn in. Jay Sekulow (2016a), chief counsel with the American Center for Law and Justice (ACLJ), argued that this call is not unusual: "Historical precedent strongly favors letting the people decide something so vitally important at the ballot box." Casey Mattox (2016b) of Alliance Defending Freedom (ADF) made a similar argument about the wisdom of giving American voters a clear voice in this process, challenging, "Let's settle this on the field"—specifically, the election in November. And First Liberty's (FL) Kelly Shackelford said, "Anything the Senate does before January 20, 2017, to consider a nominee would undermine democracy by denying the American people a voice in the future of their country" (quoted in First Liberty 2016). In the aftermath of Justice Scalia's death, conservatives from across the spectrum—from institutional elites to conservative-cause lawyers—had coalesced around a simple argument: let the people choose the next Supreme Court justice.

Not surprisingly, President Obama was not persuaded by this line of reasoning. In March Obama nominated Judge Merrick Garland to fill the court's vacancy, lauding Garland as a brilliant jurist and touting his previous bipartisan support inside and outside the Senate (Shear, Davis, and Harris 2016). This nomination did not satisfy conservative actors, however; nor did it cause them to reevaluate their position. Indeed, several CCLOs—including the American Center for Law and Justice (2016), Alliance Defending Freedom (2016), and Liberty Counsel (LC) (2016)—quickly issued press releases opposing the nomination. Notably, not one of these releases mentioned Garland by name. Instead, they simply reiterated their shared position, preaching patience and deference to the next president. And while this strategy ultimately proved successful with the election of Donald J. Trump as president, it was certainly not without risks (see Everett 2016).

This episode highlights the obvious and inherent connection between CCLOs and conservative politics (and the Republican Party) in the United States. But this connection to partisan politics is in many ways uncomfortable for CCLOs: as legal interest groups, their specialties and emphases are often different from those of other conservative interest groups, let alone the Republican Party. Furthermore, CCLOs engaging in too much partisan activity may jeopardize their status as 501(c)3 nonprofit organizations. And while President Trump may prove to be an ally of the Christian legal movement in many respects, his off-the-cuff and controversial style of governing does not lend itself well to the measured and strategic advocacy of many in the Christian legal movement (Bennett 2017a). Thus, while issue overlap with the GOP may come naturally to CCLOs—especially on social issues— broad, vocal support for the Republican Party is not necessarily a given.

In this chapter I examine the relationship between Christian legal advocacy and conservative politics in the United States, with a specific focus on the connections between CCLOs and the Republican Party. Using these groups' press releases, interviews with movement attorneys, and various media accounts of these groups' activities, I argue that while every CCLO is in a sense connected to conservative politics more broadly, some of these groups are clearly more connected than others. I begin by offering a broader perspective on the Christian legal movement in the United States, identifying how CCLOs have emerged as key players in conservative law and politics. I then offer some background on the issues central to CCLO advocacy, with specific attention to issues that fall outside the traditional purview of this movement. Finally, I proceed in-depth on two areas where the interests of CCLOs and the Republican Party have clearly collided: President Obama and his policy agenda and the 2016 Republican presidential-nomination contest. Ultimately, while the goals of the GOP and those of CCLOs inevitably overlap in many ways, some CCLOs are more prone to cultivate these connections than others. Even so, the relationship between Christian legal advocacy and conservative politics in the United States remains a relatively strong one.

A Brief History of CCLOs and the Christian Legal Movement

Defining the Christian legal movement is, in some sense, a difficult task. On the one hand, it could include interest groups dedicated to advancing and defending the multi-issue agenda of Christian conservatives in the legal realm. On the other hand, it could include support structures for this movement, such as law schools, networks and professional associations, and other elite institutions (Epp 1998). I adopt the former definition for this movement, focusing on legal interest groups interested in the goals of the so-called Christian Right in the United States.

The emergence and ascendance of the Christian Right in American politics is well documented, in this book and elsewhere (Green et al. 1996). While there are various explanations for the movement's growth, many identify the outcome of *Roe v. Wade* as a foundational moment for Christians and political engagement in the United States. Many Christians interpreted the Supreme Court's decision in 1973 as some sort of call to arms, including Francis Schaeffer (1975), who cited the evils of abortion and its recent legal legitimation as reason to take up ideological arms in an effort to transform a culture in decline. Alternatively, Kevin Kruse (2015) suggests that the roots of the contemporary Christian Right can be traced much earlier to corporate interests, who sought to connect traditional Christian morality with opposition to Franklin D. Roosevelt's New Deal policies. Whatever the specific origin, the influence of the Christian Right—while arguably waning in recent years—has left an indelible mark on the American political landscape.

While the Christian Right, as a movement, originally tended toward more traditional political activity (such as lobbying, electioneering, and grassroots mobilization), legal advocacy soon became a critical part of the community's multipronged strategy. Elites in the Christian Right came to support the establishment of legal advocacy groups primarily to counter the success and prominence of liberal groups like the American Civil Liberties Union, whose work the Christian Right generally viewed as anathema to traditional values and morality. Pat Robertson lent his institutional muscle and resources to two CCLOs in the 1980s and 1990s, establishing the National Legal Foundation (NLF) and the ACLJ. Jerry Falwell would eventually come to support LC in the late-1990s, using his empire to transform the fledgling group into a bona fide legal powerhouse. And a host of Christian Right elites—including James Dobson, D. James Kennedy, and Bill Bright—came together to establish ADF in 1994, citing the necessity of Christian legal advocacy as another front in the culture wars (Alliance Defending Freedom, n.d). For the most part, CCLOs of all stripes have these kinds of explicit connections to American evangelicalism.

As stated earlier, CCLOs are multi-issue organizations dedicated to pursuing the interests of Christian conservatives primarily through the legal realm (Bennett 2014). As legal advocacy groups, CCLOs are expected to make litigation and related activity central to what they do, which distinguishes them from other Christian Right interest groups, such as the Family Research Council and Concerned Women for America. Additionally, as groups affiliated with the Christian Right, CCLOs are expected to pursue a range of issues in their legal advocacy; just as the Christian Right takes on a broad issue agenda, so too should CCLOs. This sets CCLOs apart from other legal interest groups focused on only one issue, such as Americans United for Life. Last, CCLOs are unapologetically Christian in their mission statements and foundational documents, which distinguishes them from other legal interest groups concerned with religious liberty from a different or interfaith perspective, such as the Becket Fund for Religious Liberty.

Table 14.1 introduces the CCLOs at the heart of the Christian legal movement. All but two have clear ties to evangelical Protestantism, with the Thomas More Law Center (TMLC) and Thomas More Society (TMS) having conservative Catholic foundations—in the case of the TMLC, Catholic businessman (and Domino's Pizza founder) Thomas Monaghan has spent millions of dollars to support the group over the years. CCLOs are geographically dispersed, including groups from the Midwest (TMS), Southeast (LC), Southwest (ADF), and West Coast (Freedom of Conscience Defense Fund [FCDF]). Some groups, like ADF, the ACLJ, and LC, maintain offices in multiple locations across the country, while others are geographically limited. They vary considerably with regard to financial resources—while half maintain annual revenue of around two million dollars, groups like ADF and the ACLJ have tens of millions of dollars to spend on legal advocacy. ADF employs more than forty staff counsel and maintains a network of about two thousand allied attorneys, while NLF and the Center for Law and Religious Freedom (CLRF) employ a total of two attorneys. Despite these differences,

TABLE 14.1   CHRISTIAN CONSERVATIVE LEGAL ORGANIZATIONS IN THE
UNITED STATES

Organization	Founded	Headquarters	President/ chief counsel	Recent revenue
Alliance Defending Freedom (ADF)	1994	Scottsdale, AZ	Michael Farris	$39.9 million
American Center for Law and Justice (ACLJ)	1990	Virginia Beach, VA	Jay Sekulow	$16.3 million*
Center for Law and Religious Freedom (CLRF)	1980	Springfield, VA	Kim Colby	$153,000
First Liberty (FL)	1997	Plano, TX	Kelly Shackleford	$8.4 million
Freedom of Conscience Defense Fund (FCDF)	2012	San Diego, CA	Charles LiMandri	$1.3 million
Liberty Counsel (LC)	1989	Orlando, FL	Mat Staver	$4.2 million
National Legal Foundation (NLF)	1985	Virginia Beach, VA	Stephen Fitschen	$83,000
Pacific Justice Institute (PJI)	1997	Sacramento, CA	Brad Dacus	$1.7 million
Thomas More Law Center (TMLC)	1998	Ann Arbor, MI	Richard Thompson	$1.9 million
Thomas More Society (TMS)	1997	Chicago, IL	Thomas Brejcha	$2.1 million

* Does not include revenue from the ACLJ dba (doing business as) Christian Advocates Serving Evangelism
  ($45.9 million).

CCLOs are fundamentally connected by two things: a shared commitment
to the Christian faith and a conservative reading of law and policy grounded
in that faith commitment.

"Political" Advocacy in the Christian Legal Movement

For reasons mentioned earlier, CCLOs are legally limited in their advocacy
for political causes. Federal law dictates that a 501(c)3 organization must not
engage in explicit political advocacy, as doing so would jeopardize the group's
tax-exempt status. These limitations notwithstanding, CCLOs frequently engage in clear and unmistakable efforts to influence policy and shape outcomes in the political system, all the while remaining within the parameters
of their status as nonprofit organizations. And while these collective efforts
are largely overshadowed by more traditional legal advocacy for religious
liberty, the traditional family, and the sanctity of life, some CCLOs are more
likely to engage in advocacy that can only be described as political in nature.

In analyzing the issues central to individual CCLOs' agendas, I collected
more than six thousand press releases—from the early 2000s through De-

cember 31, 2014—from these groups and coded them by general topic.[1] These
releases should be seen as providing a clear window into what CCLOs value
in their advocacy and how they spend their time and resources as legal interest groups. As seen in Table 14.2, three issues stand out as the most prevalent
and make up more than three-quarters of CCLOs' activities discussed in
these press releases: religious freedom and establishment, the traditional
family, and the sanctity of life. Nevertheless, some issues prevalent in
CCLOs' press releases defied easy categorization, requiring two separate categories: *other legal issue* and *other nonlegal issue*.[2] The press releases coded
in this way draw attention to issues, advocacy, and announcements outside
the traditional purview of CCLO advocacy.

Of particular relevance to this chapter is CCLOs' attention to issues political in nature, which can be found in these "other" categories. Table 14.3 breaks

TABLE 14.2   CCLO PRESS RELEASES, BY THE ISSUES

Issue	Number of releases	Percentage of total
Religious liberty and establishment	2,411	39.7
Traditional marriage and the family	1,213	20.0
Sanctity of life	1,079	17.8
Christmas	239	3.9
Other speech	173	2.8
Obscenity	73	1.2
Other legal	402	6.6
Other nonlegal	486	8.0

TABLE 14.3   OTHER LEGAL AND NONLEGAL ISSUES IN CCLO PRESS
RELEASES

CCLO	Number of releases with other legal issues (%)	Number of releases with other nonlegal issues (%)
Alliance Defending Freedom	99 (3.7)	62 (2.3)
American Center for Law and Justice	75 (14.1)	125 (23.5)
First Liberty	3 (0.6)	53 (11.3)
Liberty Counsel	75 (5.9)	155 (12.3)
Pacific Justice Institute	49 (15.3)	13 (4.0)
Thomas More Law Center	95 (18.0)	59 (11.2)
Thomas More Society	6 (2.0)	19 (6.2)

down these categories by organization, leading to some interesting observations. First, while ADF and LC are responsible for the most press releases in this movement, neither organization makes a great deal of noise about other legal issues; the same can be said for ADF and its attention to other nonlegal issues. Second, the ACLJ and the TMLC are proportionally much more active on these other issues than their fellow CCLOs, suggesting that they are more comfortable going out of their way to highlight issues not normally central to the movement's agenda. And third, CCLOs are, across the board, more likely to issue releases on other nonlegal issues than legal ones. Ultimately, while a handful of issues dominate this movement's advocacy (as seen through group press releases), there is a good amount of attention paid to issues not fitting this mold.

In these two categories there are, not surprisingly, a number of specific topics toward which CCLOs have directed the public's attention, topics that do not neatly fit with CCLOs' mission statements. Given these groups' ideological leanings, it is not surprising that some of these topics trend toward the political. But what are these issues? And, more important, what do they suggest about the relationship between CCLOs and conservative politics (and the Republican Party) in the United States?

In discussing two political themes commonly appearing in CCLO advocacy, first I explore how CCLOs have responded to President Obama's time in office—unsurprisingly, their responses have been overwhelmingly negative and critical. And second, I examine the extent to which CCLOs have commented on (or even have been involved with) the past several national elections in the United States. By focusing in-depth on these two themes, I highlight the degree to which CCLOs are connected to (and overwhelmingly supportive of) conservative and Republican Party politics. This focus also shows that CCLOs react to these types of issues in various ways, suggesting that these groups are not monolithic in their engagement with politics, even when those politics are undeniably conservative.

In-Depth: Opposition to President Obama

In October 2010, following a contentious battle over health-care reform and with the midterm elections weeks away, Senator Mitch McConnell detailed the Republican Party's strategy in the time leading up to the next presidential election: "The single most important thing we want to achieve is for President Obama to be a one-term president" (Kessler 2012). Of course, McConnell suggested the GOP would gladly cooperate with President Obama should he abandon his push for liberal policy initiatives and instead take a more conciliatory approach to presidential leadership. But the broader point was made: for Republicans in Congress (and in general), the best way to counter Obama's vision for the country was to become, as Democratic Party officials complained, the party of "no" (Nicholas 2009).

Not surprisingly, CCLOs generally embraced President Obama's policies with the same degree of warmth. In the aftermath of the 2008 election, several CCLOs issued press releases noting the consequences of Obama's victory. One ADF release acknowledged the challenges ahead: "ADF is ready to go to court to fight a vast number of leftist policies promised by the new administration and Congress" (Alliance Defending Freedom 2008). Similarly, while LC noted the historical importance of Obama's election, it also warned of its dangers: "We have just witnessed an historic election. America elected the first black president in her history. The enormity of this event cannot be overestimated. The majority of Americans looked beyond race to elect Barack Obama. They also looked beyond the content of his character and his left-wing agenda. . . . Obama is left of left" (Liberty Counsel 2008). And after the 2012 election, FL linked Obama's reelection with increasing challenges for people of faith: "In light of yesterday's election results, more than ever, [First Liberty] is fully committed to protecting and advancing religious liberty, our first freedom, in America" (First Liberty 2012).

Judging by these releases, it is clear that CCLOs were less than enthusiastic about President Obama's back-to-back electoral victories. But it was not simply Obama's election and eventual reelection that drew the ire of CCLOs—it was his policies that sustained most of their opposition and, for the most part, their unflinching criticism. By consistently critiquing President Obama and his administration on a number of fronts, CCLOs reinforce conservative arguments against Obama's policies, leadership, and performance as president.

Consider, for example, CCLOs' opposition to Obama's signature legislative achievement: the Affordable Care Act (ACA). While many Christian legal groups routinely characterized the ACA as posing serious problems for religious liberty—especially the law's requirements for contraceptive coverage—some highlighted other, traditionally conservative objections to the law. The ACLJ, for example, routinely characterized the law as "an unconstitutional power-grab by the federal government—[and] a clear violation of the Commerce Clause" (American Center for Law and Justice 2010b). The TMLC wrote that its case was, at its heart, about the power of federal government under President Obama: "Our case is about the constitutional limits of our federal government. Everyone agrees the health care system needs reform. But that doesn't mean Congress is allowed to violate the Constitution in the process" (Thomas More Law Center 2010a). And LC argued that Obama had no respect for the established constitutional order in shepherding the ACA through Congress: "It is unbelievable that the President would disregard the Constitution and the rule of law to push a narrow political agenda that most Americans have rejected" (Liberty Counsel 2010b). Like other conservative political groups, CCLOs found no shortage of ammunition in criticizing the ACA.

Some CCLOs also voiced their opposition to the Obama administration's lawsuit challenging a controversial immigration law from Arizona (see Arizona v. United States, 567 U.S. 387 (2012)). The TMLC pledged its support for the Arizona law, accusing the Obama administration of failing to protect American citizens from violence stemming from illegal immigration (Thomas More Law Center 2010b). And the ACLJ was quick to portray Obama's legal challenge as problematic: "Instead of spending taxpayer funds to challenge Arizona's constitutional right to protect its borders and its citizens, the Obama Administration should secure Arizona's borders and the borders of other states. Arizona clearly has the constitutional authority to protect and defend its borders" (American Center for Law and Justice 2010a). And while LC's Mat Staver acknowledged the legislation was probably not constitutional given the federal government's power over immigration policy, he decried the Obama administration for its supposed failures on immigration: "I sympathize with Arizona. The Arizona law is a cry for help because the federal government has not done its job of securing the borders" (quoted in Liberty Counsel 2010a).

Christian legal groups have criticized President Obama in a variety of other contexts as well. For example, LC was pleased when Goodwin Liu, one of Obama's nominees to the Ninth Circuit Court of Appeals, withdrew from consideration after being stonewalled in the Senate. "Judges should be fair and impartial," an LC press release noted, "not radical ideologues" (Liberty Counsel 2011). And Jay Sekulow (2016c) of the ACLJ has continually spoken out against the Obama administration for what he considers to be a general aura of corruption: "Pres. #Obama's Admin. does NOT play by the rules because it believe it's above them." Indeed, Sekulow (2016d) voiced his opposition up until the end of Obama's presidency: "Pres. #Obama will undoubtedly bypass the #Constitution to solidify his legacy in his last days. We must say no." Regardless of substantive issue, CCLOs have consistently been critical of President Obama and his administration from beginning to end.

One instance in which Christian legal groups found time to congratulate President Obama was his handling of the 2011 mission that killed Osama bin Laden. The ACLJ issued a release praising the U.S. military for carrying out the raid, as well as both Obama and George W. Bush for their "dedication in bringing Osama bin Laden to justice" (American Center for Law and Justice 2011). Likewise, while the TMLC did acknowledge Obama's role in the mission, it noted that the real congratulations should belong with the military and intelligence communities, whose interrogation programs began under President Bush (Thomas More Law Center 2011).

But Osama bin Laden's death was a rare moment of alignment between President Obama and CCLOs. Obama has been a steady target for conservatives since his inauguration in 2009. The Republican Party has (with few exceptions) made consistent opposition to Obama and his policies a kind of litmus test for its membership, in Congress and elsewhere. The organizations at the center of the Christian legal movement have generally gone along with this opposition, although some groups have been more vocal and active than others—the ACLJ, LC, and TMLC have been particularly outspoken in their criticism. While there is surprising diversity among CCLOs in their individual strategies and tactics in their advocacy (Bennett 2017a), one thing they can mostly agree on is opposition to Barack Obama.

In-Depth: Presidential Elections

While CCLOs were effectively unanimous in their opposition to President Obama and his vision for America, they were less cohesive in terms of their preference for those challenging him and his legacy. It is true, of course, that CCLOs cannot engage in explicit political endorsements because of regulations on nonprofit organizations and political activity. What is permissible, however, are these groups discussing candidates in a way that refrains from making an explicit endorsement, as well as their attorneys speaking out on and in defense of certain candidates. This behavior has exposed schisms within the Christian legal movement on the electoral front, with candidate preferences varying across attorneys and organizations. Ultimately, this behavior lends further support to the argument central to this chapter: CCLOs embrace the goals and preferred outcomes of the Republican Party in a variety of ways.

In the run-up to the 2008 presidential election, CCLOs had little to say about the two major party candidates—this is not surprising, considering the restrictions placed on 501(c)3 organizations concerning electioneering. And while LC issued a press release highlighting the need for conservative ideas and alternatives following Barack Obama's victory over John McCain (Liberty Counsel 2008), while also criticizing Obama's position on abortion following his inauguration (Liberty Counsel 2009), other CCLOs were less vocal during this period. In 2012, the ACLJ's Jay Sekulow endorsed eventual GOP nominee Mitt Romney fairly early in the cycle (Luo 2007), and after Obama's reelection First Liberty (2012) argued for a proactive, aggressive defense of religious freedom. But, again, other CCLOs were generally quiet on this front during this time.

While Christian legal groups are prohibited from electioneering and making endorsements, CCLO attorneys are clearly free to do as they like as private citizens. And during the Republican primaries in 2016, most movement lawyers who took a public stance on a candidate tended to be supportive of people not named Donald Trump. LC's Mat Staver (2016) took to Twitter during the primaries to highlight stories favorable to Ted Cruz. The ACLJ's Jordan Sekulow (2015) was an early backer of Jeb Bush. And ADF's

Casey Mattox (2016a) voted for Marco Rubio in his state's primary election, while acknowledging an affinity for Cruz as well. The sheer number of candidates seeking the Republican nomination for president gave CCLO attorneys plenty of options, and Trump was hardly the first choice for many.

About a month before he was officially nominated as the presidential candidate for the Republican Party, Trump held a meeting with several hundred evangelical activists—including Tony Perkins, James Dobson, Franklin Graham, and Mike Huckabee—to discuss the issues important to them and reassure them about his candidacy. Also attending this meeting was Kelly Shackelford of First Liberty. Shackelford asked Trump what kinds of judges he would nominate as president, leading Trump to praise the legal work and the vision of groups like the Federalist Society and the Heritage Foundation, groups with sterling credentials in the conservative legal community (Ward 2016). This line of reasoning no doubt proved attractive to CCLO lawyers, especially when compared to the prospect of a Supreme Court with multiple vacancies to be filled by Hillary Clinton.

Just weeks before Election Day, LC's Anita Staver (2016) authored an opinion piece connecting the Supreme Court to the outcome of the presidential election: "During the next four years, America could be transformed into a safe and prosperous home for future generations. Or our precious liberties could be decimated by a single black-robed individual with the stroke of a pen." Without explicitly endorsing Trump, Staver seemed to suggest that a Clinton presidency would be more likely to lead to the latter, unfavorable outcome. Similarly, Matt Bowman (2016a, 2016b), senior counsel for ADF, issued a series of tweets following Trump's victory, praising the outcome of the election for its probable effect on the future of the court. For CCLO lawyers, the future of the Supreme Court provided motivation enough to root for a GOP presidential victory in 2016, even with a flawed candidate like Donald Trump at the top of the ticket.

On June 8, 2016, during his daily radio broadcast, Jay Sekulow responded to a caller asking why the ACLJ had not been more forceful in endorsing Trump for president, especially considering the danger that a potential Clinton administration posed for the country. Sekulow's (2016b) response was in line with the political challenges facing nonprofit organizations like the ACLJ: "We do not endorse candidates on this broadcast. The ACLJ cannot do that, we will not do that. Our job is to simply lay out the evidence."

That said, the group has not been completely absent from electoral politics. After the Republican and Democratic Party's platforms were finalized in the lead-up to each party's convention, the ACLJ's Wesley Smith compared the platforms on the group's website. While not explicitly endorsing one platform over the other, the tone, tenor, and framing of the comparison made it clear that Smith (2016)—and, by extension, the ACLJ—preferred the Republican Party's platform. For example, Smith stated, "The Republicans call for an end to the 'Iran Nuclear Deal.' The Democrats applaud the Iran Deal and claim that it prohibits Iran from ever acquiring nuclear weapons, even though much of the text of the agreement remains secret." Further, Smith wrote, "The Republicans call for a pay raise for military personnel. The Democrat Platform does not mention this issue." Smith concludes, "For those who believe that national security and support of our military is important, we hope that you find this information helpful."

But the clearest example of the ACLJ's ties to Republican politics is Jay Sekulow's service on President Trump's legal team. Since his elevation to the team—which was formed to handle the inquiry into whether members of the Trump campaign had colluded with Russian entities—Sekulow has made regular appearances on television to defend the administration, the campaign, and Trump himself. Despite the occasional misstep, this is a job Sekulow is well suited for, considering his experience in the spotlight and tenacious personality (Bennett 2017b). But relative to other actors in the Christian legal movement, such direct engagement with elected officials is essentially unheard of.

Despite not overtly endorsing political candidates or actively campaigning against others, the ACLJ has developed a reputation within the Christian legal movement for walking perilously close to that line; an attorney affiliated with another CCLO told me that the ACLJ could well be jeopardizing its tax-exempt status, for example. For the most part, this kind of activity is not normal in Christian legal advocacy. Instead, CCLOs direct their organizational resources to work within the boundaries of 501(c)3 advocacy and leave the commentary on politics and elections to their attorneys, who are free to speak as private citizens. And over the course of the last several elections—but especially in 2016—these attorneys have not been passive (though not necessarily aggressive) in their support for the various Republican nominees and candidates for president.

Conclusion

After the *Obergefell v. Hodges* decision, in which the Supreme Court held bans on same-sex marriage to be unconstitutional, a county clerk in Kentucky named Kim Davis faced a choice: issue licenses to both different- and same-sex couples or face legal trouble. Choosing the former, Davis would eventually spend several days in jail for violating a federal judge's order to issue licenses to both sets of couples. This saga piqued the media's interest and captured the attention of several GOP candidates for president; Mike Huckabee went as far as appearing with Davis at a rally after her release from jail. Also appearing onstage with Davis and Huckabee that day was Mat Staver, founder and chairman of LC, which had provided Davis with legal representation throughout the ordeal (Weigel, Phillip, and Larimer 2015).

Connections between CCLOs and Republican politics are not always this palpable, but they are certainly not infrequent.

As authors in this book have argued, the Christian Right—particularly the evangelical community—has long cultivated a special relationship with the Republican Party and conservative politics in general. Moreover, as this chapter demonstrates, the legal interest groups representing this community have also taken positions that align with those of the GOP. However, as noted previously, some groups—such as the ACLJ and, to a lesser extent, LC—are more comfortable than others in aligning themselves with conservative electoral politics. Despite agreement on many core principles, not every CCLO is comfortable publicly standing with the Republican Party.

What does the future hold for CCLOs and their relationship with the GOP and conservative politics? If the past is any indication, CCLOs will continue to advocate for issues and policies at home in the Republican Party, such as opposition to abortion and support for religious freedom. A Trump administration, however, could reveal some cracks in this foundation: groups like the ACLJ and the TMLC will support Trump's hard-line policies on immigration, while a Pacific Justice Institute attorney told me the Christian legal movement would be wise to reach out to new immigrants and appeal to their shared commitment to conservative social values (Snider 2015).

In the courts, CCLOs will almost surely have greater support for their legal goals from a Trump presidency than they did under the Obama administration. Trump's early picks for the federal judiciary—punctuated by the confirmation of several circuit court judges and the elevation of Neil Gorsuch to the Supreme Court—have drawn rave reviews from those in the Christian legal movement. These actors also have allies elsewhere in the Trump administration—Attorney General Jeff Sessions appeared at an event organized by ADF in June 2017 and praised the group for "the important work that you do every day to uphold and protect the right to religious liberty in this country" (Sessions 2017). After eight years of fighting uphill against the federal government, these are welcome developments for Christian legal groups. And though they will lose the ability to fund-raise off an opposition presidential administration, these potential losses will be offset by gains on the legal front and elsewhere.

The relationship between CCLOs and the Republican Party essentially mirrors the larger relationship between white evangelicals and the Republican Party. And as the 2016 presidential election laid bare, there is little reason to believe that this relationship is in danger of fracturing in the near future. For Christian legal groups, the conservative political arena may not be the domain in which they are *most* comfortable, but it certainly provides more respite and opportunities than they have in any other political context. And even when issues stray from these groups' core mission, CCLOs generally work hard to maintain links to the conservative political movement. If there is an impending crackup between the GOP and the evangelical community, it is clear that CCLOs have not been informed.

NOTES

1. Of the ten CCLOs identified as active today, only seven maintain an archive of their press releases. Thus, this data collection is limited to these seven groups. While collecting these releases, I developed a coding scheme, identifying the primary issue central to each release. This scheme was developed in an ad hoc fashion, which was eventually refined and narrowed to the categories presented in Table 14.2. Issue framing is especially important in this process. For example, in one press release on the Affordable Care Act (ACA), a CCLO may reference its amicus brief emphasizing the ACA's ramifications for religious liberty—this release is coded as *sanctity of life*. But in another release on the ACA, a CCLO may cite its brief emphasizing the act's disregard for the separation of powers and principles of federalism—this release is coded as *other legal issue*. And in another, a CCLO may not mention any of its specific legal activity on the ACA, but it may suggest President Obama is guilty of political overreach—this release is coded as *other nonlegal issue*.

2. An example of a press release coded *other legal issue* is an LC release highlighting the group's defense of a family seeking to regain custody of their daughter (see Liberty Counsel 2014). An example of a press release coded *other nonlegal issue* is a TMLC release informing readers of the death of D. James Kennedy (see Thomas More Law Center 2007).

REFERENCES

Alliance Defending Freedom. n.d. "Who We Are." Available at http://www.adflegal.org/about
-us/who-we-are (accessed March 26, 2018).
——. 2008. "ADF Prepared to Fight Looming Leftist Agenda." November 7. Available at
http://www.adfmedia.org/News/PRDetail/2016.
——. 2016. "ADF: Senate Shouldn't Hold Hearings on Obama Nomination to Supreme
Court." March 16. Available at http://www.adfmedia.org/News/PRDetail/9900.
American Center for Law and Justice. 2010a. "ACLJ: Justice Dept. Suit Challenging AZ Immigration Law 'Flawed' and 'Waste of Taxpayer Funds.'" July 6. Available at http://aclj
.org/immigration/aclj-justice-dept-suit-challenging-az-immigration-law-flawed-and
-waste-of-taxpayer-funds-.
——. 2010b. "ACLJ Represents Members of Congress in Filing Amicus Brief Supporting
VA's Federal Suit Challenging Heath Care Law." June 8. Available at http://aclj.org/
obamacare/aclj-represents-members-of-congress-in-filing-amicus-brief-supporting-va
-s-federal-suit-challenging-heath-care-law.
——. 2011. "ACLJ: Osama Bin Laden's Death: Victory for War on Terror—America's Commitment to Justice Never Ending." May 2. Available at http://aclj.org/war-on-terror/aclj
-osama-bin-laden-s-death-victory-for-war-on-terror---america-s-commitment-to
-justice-never-ending.
——. 2016. "ACLJ: No Action on President Obama's Supreme Court Nominee until after
the Election." March 16. Available at http://aclj.org/supreme-court/aclj--no-action-on
-president-obamas-supreme-court-nominee-until-after-the-election-.
Bennett, Daniel. 2014. "Serving God by Shaping Law: Religious Legal Advocacy in the United
States." In *Mediating Religion and Government: Political Institutions and the Policy
Process*, edited by Kevin R. den Dulk and Elizabeth A. Oldmixon, 83–108. New York:
Palgrave Macmillan.

———. 2017a. *Defending Faith: The Politics of the Christian Conservative Legal Movement.* Lawrence: University Press of Kansas.

———. 2017b. "Why 'Jay Sekulow: Trump Attorney' Makes Perfect Sense." *Religion in Public,* June 20. Available at https://religioninpublic.blog/2017/06/20/why-jay-sekulow-trump -attorney-makes-perfect-sense.

Bowman, Matt. 2016a. "I Watched No Election Coverage." *Twitter,* November 9. Available at https://twitter.com/mattbowman2000/status/796308920881057792.

———. 2016b. "The People Chose." *Twitter,* November 9. Available at https://twitter.com/ mattbowman2000/status/796313650604675072.

Cruz, Ted. 2016. "Justice Scalia Was an American Hero." *Twitter,* February 13. Available at https://twitter.com/tedcruz/status/698634625246195712.

Epp, Charles. 1998. *The Rights Revolution: Lawyers, Activists, and Supreme Courts in Comparative Perspectives.* Chicago: University of Chicago Press.

Everett, Burgess. 2016. "Flake Says It Might Be Garland Time." *Politico,* October 20. Available at https://www.politico.com/story/2016/10/jeff-flake-merrick-garland-vote-supreme -court-230109.

Everett, Burgess, and Glenn Thrush. 2016. "McConnell Throws Down the Gauntlet: No Scalia Replacement under Obama." *Politico,* February 13. http://www.politico.com/ story/2016/02/mitch-mcconnell-antonin-scalia-supreme-court-nomination-219248.

First Liberty. 2012. "An Obama Presidency: What's in Store for Religious Freedom?" November 7. Available at http://blog.libertyinstitute.org/2012/11/an-obama-presidency-whats -in-store-for.html.

———. 2016. "Statement on the Nomination of Merrick Garland to the U.S. Supreme Court." March 16. Available at http://firstliberty.org/newsroom/statement-on-the-nomination -of-merrick-garland-to-the-u-s-supreme-court/.

Green, John, James Guth, Corwin Smidt, and Lyman Kellstedt, eds. 1996. *Religion and the Culture Wars.* Lanham, MD: Rowman and Littlefield.

Kessler, Glenn. 2012. "When Did McConnell Say He Wanted to Make Obama a 'One-Term President'?" *Washington Post,* September 25. Available at https://www.washingtonpost .com/blogs/fact-checker/post/when-did-mcconnell-say-he-wanted-to-make-obama-a -one-term-president/2012/09/24/79fd5cd8-0696-11e2-afff-d6c7f20a83bf_blog.html.

Kruse, Kevin M. 2015. *One Nation under God: How Corporate America Invented Christian America.* New York: Basic Books.

Liberty Counsel. 2008. "Today We Begin to Rebuild the Base and Advance Conservative Values." November 5. Available at http://www.lc.org/newsroom/details/today-we-begin -to-rebuild-the-base-and-advance-conservative-values-1.

———. 2009. "One Step Forward for Racial Equality, Two Steps Backward for Life." January 20. Available at https://lc.org/newsroom/details/one-step-forward-for-racial-equality -two-steps-backward-for-life-1.

———. 2010a. "Arizona Immigration Law Blocked by Federal Court." July 28. Available at https://www.lc.org/newsroom/details/arizona-immigration-law-blocked-by-federal -court-1.

———. 2010b. "Obama and Politicians Willing to Slaughter the Constitution to Ram ObamaCare Agenda." March 18. Available at https://www.lc.org/newsroom/details/031810 -obama-and-politicians-willing-to-slaughter-the-constitution-to-ram-obamacare -agenda.

———. 2011. "Radical Obama Judicial Nominee Withdraws after Failing to Get Enough Votes." May 26. Available at https://www.lc.org/newsroom/details/052611-radical -obama-judicial-nominee-withdraws-after-failing-to-get-enough-votes.

———. 2014. "Motion Filed Today in Court Requests Justina Pelletier Be Returned Home." May 30. Available at https://lc.org/newsroom/details/motion-filed-today-in-court -requests-justina-pelletier-be-returned-home-1.

———. 2016. "No Hearing on Obama Supreme Court Nominee." March 18. Available at http://libertycounsel.com/no-hearing-on-obama-supreme-court-nominee/.

Luo, Michael. 2007. "Romney Lands Big Endorsement." *The Caucus*, November 5. Available at http://thecaucus.blogs.nytimes.com/2007/11/05/romney-lands-big-endorsement/.

Mattox, Casey. 2016a. "Just to Be Perfectly Clear." *Twitter*, February 25. Available at https://twitter.com/CaseyMattox_/status/703070404018114560.

———. 2016b. "Neither History nor the Constitution Compels the Senate to Confirm Obama's Scalia Replacement." Alliance Defending Freedom, March 10. Available at https://www .adflegal.org/detailspages/blog-details/allianceedge/2016/03/10/neither-history-nor-the -constitution-compels-the-senate-to-confirm-obama-s-scalia-replacement.

Nicholas, Peter. 2009. "Tensions between Democrats, Republicans Mount." *Los Angeles Times*, April 24. Available at http://articles.latimes.com/2009/apr/24/nation/na-par tisanship24.

Politi, Daniel. 2016. "Obama: I Plan to Fulfill My Constitutional Responsibilities to Nominate Scalia's Successor." *Slate*, February 13. Available at http://www.slate.com/blogs/the _slatest/2016/02/13/obama_vows_to_fulfill_constitutional_responsibilities_and _nominate_scalia.html.

Schaeffer, Francis A. 1975. *How Should We Then Live? The Rise and Decline of Western Thought and Culture*. Wheaton, IL: Crossway.

Sekulow, Jay. 2016a. "Historical Precedent Favors Letting Our Next President Appoint Justice Scalia's Replacement." American Center for Law and Justice, February 15. Available at http://aclj.org/supreme-court/historical-precedent-favors-letting-our-next-president -appoint-justice-scalias-replacement.

———. 2016b. "Historic Ending to Presidential Primaries." *Jay Sekulow Live!*, June 8. Available at http://www.oneplace.com/ministries/jay-sekulow-live/listen/jay-sekulow-live -536203.html.

———. 2016c. "Pres. #Obama's Admin." *Twitter*, October 24. Available at https://twitter.com/ JaySekulow/status/790590439057416192.

———. 2016d. "Pres. #Obama Will Undoubtedly Bypass." *Twitter*, November 13. Available at https://twitter.com/JaySekulow/status/797831416251908096.

Sekulow, Jordan. 2015. "Excited to Meet All the Good People." *Twitter*, April 25. Available at https://twitter.com/JordanSekulow/status/592055456891207680.

Sessions, Jeff. 2017. "Here's the Speech Jeff Sessions Delivered to Christian First Amendment Lawyers." *The Federalist*, July 13. Available at http://thefederalist.com/2017/07/13/heres -the-speech-jeff-sessions-delivered-to-christian-first-amendment-lawyers.

Shear, Michael D., Julie Hirschfeld Davis, and Gardiner Harris. 2016. "Obama Chooses Merrick Garland for Supreme Court." *New York Times*, March 16. Available at http://www .nytimes.com/2016/03/17/us/politics/obama-supreme-court-nominee.html.

Smith, Wesley. 2016. "Comparing the Democrat and Republican Platforms on Military Issues." American Center for Law and Justice, July 26. Available at http://aclj.org/national -security/comparing-the-democrat-and-republican-platforms-on-military-issues.

Snider, Kevin. 2015. Phone interview by the author. February 19.

Staver, Anita. 2016. "Why the Supreme Court Is the Most Important Issue for Voters." *The Stream*, October 19. Available at https://stream.org/supreme-court-important-issue -voters/.

Staver, Mathew. 2016. "Cruz Wins Wyoming Delegates." *Twitter*, April 17. Available at https:// twitter.com/MatStaver/status/721638160384585733.

Thomas More Law Center. 2007. "Christian Warrior D. James Kennedy Dies." September 5. Available at http://www.thomasmore.org/news/christian-warrior-d-james-kennedy -dies.

———. 2010a. "Thomas More Law Center Asks Court to Stop Enforcement of the Individual Mandate of Health Care." April 8. Available at https://www.thomasmore.org/news/

thomas-more-law-center-asks-court-stop-enforcement-the-individual-mandate-health
-care/.

———. 2010b. "TMLC Files Friend of the Court Brief Supporting Arizona's Immigration
Law." September 7. Available at https://www.thomasmore.org/news/tmlc-files-friend-the
-court-brief-supporting-arizona-s-immigration-law/.

———. 2011. "Justice Done: Osama Bin Laden Killed by American Forces; War on Radical
Islam Is Not Over." May 2. Available at https://www.thomasmore.org/news/justice-done
-osama-bin-laden-killed-american-forces-war-radical-islam-not-over/.

Ward, Jon. 2016. "Transcript: Donald Trump's Closed-Door Meeting with Evangelical Leaders." *Yahoo! News*, June 22. Available at https://www.yahoo.com/news/transcript-donald
-trumps-closed-door-meeting-with-evangelical-leaders-195810824.html.

Weigel, David, Abby Phillip, and Sarah Larimer. 2015. "Kim Davis Released from Jail, Ordered Not to Interfere with Same-Sex Marriage Licenses." *Washington Post*, September
8. Available at https://www.washingtonpost.com/news/post-nation/wp/2015/09/08/
judge-orders-kentucky-clerk-kim-davis-released-from-jail.

15

"God Is a Pretty Fair Guy"

Evangelicalism and Economic Attitudes

Ronald J. McGauvran
Elizabeth A. Oldmixon

I n the November 28, 2015, Republican presidential candidate debate, Dr. Ben Carson, a devout Seventh-Day Adventist, defended his flat-tax proposal by drawing on the biblical practice of tithing: "I think God is a pretty fair guy. And he said, . . . if you give me a tithe, it doesn't matter how much you make. If you've had a bumper crop, you don't owe me triple tithes. And if you've had no crops at all, you don't owe me no tithes. So there must be something inherently fair about that" (Tankersley 2015). Many in the conservative movement support the flat tax, so it is to be expected that it would feature prominently in a Republican presidential debate. It is less common for a high-profile political figure to ground this policy proposal in religious arguments. Carson's joining of the Bible with economic policy is consistent with Christian reconstructionist thought, which is present in some evangelical Protestant circles, in which sacred and secular are considered as one (Iannaccone 1993). This raises questions: How widely diffused is Carson's approach among evangelicals? And to the extent that it is widely diffused, is it salient enough to shape the evangelical partisan alignment? In the 2016 election, for example, Republican nominee Donald Trump appealed to evangelicals using explicitly religious language, such as his "Two Corinthians" remarks on religious liberty at Liberty University, but he also appealed more generally on economic issues, such as bringing jobs back to nonurban areas, where evangelicals are concentrated. If the latter is as important to evangelicals as the former, then white evangelical loyalty to the Republican Party coalition is owed in part to economic position taking.

Economic issues are highly salient among the American people, but religion and politics scholars have been slow to study them (Wilson 2009; also see Deckman et al. 2017; Hart 1996; McCarthy et al. 2016). Among white evangelicals, in particular, religious politics is associated almost exclusively with cultural issues. After all, when white evangelical Protestants were welcomed into the Republican fold in the late 1970s, they were mobilized and recruited on the basis of cultural appeals rather than Reagan's economic agenda. Focusing on evangelicals, then, we address this incongruity by assessing the degree to which religion is associated with economic attitudes. The theoretical puzzle here is that while religion may inform economic attitudes, it does not necessarily speak with one voice. For instance, a Weberian approach underlines the individualist nature of Calvinist theology, whereby believers pursue personal piety and material success as a way to demonstrate their status as elect, as saved (Barker and Carman 2000). But the social-gospel approach emphasizes that the Bible also teaches the importance of social responsibility and charity for the poor. Moreover, religious teachings contain sufficient ambiguity to give believers flexibility when aligning religious and economic values (Iannaccone 1998).

Which approach structures evangelical attitudes? We argue that it depends (of course). Using American National Election Studies (ANES) data, we consider three vectors of religious influence, the so-called three Bs—belonging, believing, and behaving. We demonstrate that economic attitudes vary tremendously based on religious belonging and race. White evangelicals tend to be more economically individualistic than mainline Protestants, while black evangelicals are more communitarian. Behaving (religious commitment) lacks an independent effect on economic attitudes, but it conditions the effect of belonging among evangelicals. Belief in biblical literalism is associated with economic liberalism, but socioeconomic status likely drives this relationship. Echoing Stephen Hart (1996), moreover, we demonstrate that these relationships vary by issue. The influence of religion is strong with respect to welfare spending but weak with respect to support for general free-market principles.

Evangelicalism and Economic Conservatism

Religious belonging structures political attitudes because coreligionists tend to share a social status and are exposed to the same "beliefs connecting theology to public affairs" (Guth et al. 1997, 8). In this sense, affiliation is a shared lens through which people view the political world. German social theorist Max Weber ([1930] 1994) explains one such lens. He makes a clear connection between religion and behavior in the economic marketplace, arguing that for European Calvinists the accrual of wealth is a virtue, a religious duty, and a sign of personal piety. Economic conservatism in the form of free markets and a limited welfare state are natural aftereffects of this line of religious thought.

The Weberian approach to religion and economics builds on patterns of belonging and is rooted in the Enlightenment and the emergence of capitalism. The Enlightenment emphasis on rationality, individualism, and the perfectibility of human beings challenged the existing feudal order, in which earthly destinies were established at birth. The unfettered exchange of goods and capital as the basis of economic advancement was anathema to the deeply rooted class structure. Calvinists embraced a radical form of predestination. According to Weber ([1930] 1994), Calvinists believed themselves to be masters of their earthly destinies, as God had foreordained who was saved. They could not earn salvation through good works, but they could demonstrate their elect status through prudence, hard work, and the accrual of material wealth. From this perspective, the role of the state is to "assure freedom for individual action," unless traditional morality is compromised (Leege 1993, 11). With its emphasis on "hard work, individual initiative, and personal responsibility" (Wilson 1999, 432), the Protestant work ethic prioritizes doctrine and personal holiness over a broader Christian social ethic—the poor must do for themselves. Rodney Stark and Charles Y. Glock argue that this approach is especially prevalent in evangelical Protestantism, "which tends to take a miraculous view of social justice" (1968, 75). Because evangelical theology is more likely rooted in orthodox, Calvinist ideas, evangelical Protestants likely prefer conservative economics policies to the alternative.

Yet care for the poor, economic justice, and social connectedness are central tenets of Christianity and directly inform the ethical roots of the social-gospel tradition. This approach admonishes Christians to reform the social structures associated with poverty, racism, and degradation. It emphasizes care for others as opposed to personal piety (Stark and Glock 1968). Personal piety is well and good, but it is not sufficient and should be accompanied by actions meant to lift up "the least of these." As Clarke E. Cochran and David Carroll Cochran observe, "Say what you will about prayer, about liturgy, about loyalty to the church. These are vital. . . . But—*do you really think that any of us will make it to heaven without feeding the hungry, clothing the naked, ministering to the sick, visiting the imprisoned?*" (2003, 1; emphasis in original). This is the traditional ethic embodied by the Sermon on the Mount (Stark and Glock 1968, 75) that lends itself to liberal economic policy in the form of market interventions and a robust welfare state. This left-leaning theology is somewhat less common among white evangelicals (Kenski and Lockwood 1991; Pyle 1993; Wilson 1999, 2009), but economic conservatism is not uniformly embraced within evangelical communities.

Evidence in support of these approaches is mixed. Angela Farizo McCarthy and colleagues (2016) find almost no connection between affiliation and economic policy preferences. Hart (1996) finds that, contrary to wide-spread stereotypes, evangelicals are not conservative on every issue, including economic issues. Indeed, evangelicals are the third most economically liberal tradition behind black Protestants and Catholics but ahead of Jews, mainline Protestants, and the unaffiliated. David Barker and Christopher Jan Carman (2000, 8), however, find that culturally conservative, white, born-again Christians are more supportive of individualistic (conservative) economic policies than other Christians.[1] In the same way, Melissa Deckman and colleagues (2017) find that white evangelicals are more likely to adopt conservative positions on taxes and infrastructure spending. In regard to support for government spending for the poor, black Protestants are the most supportive, while white evangelical and mainline Protestants are less supportive (Pyle 1993). The upshot here is that when people place more value on individual achievement and responsibility, they are less likely to support government intervention into economic matters and more likely to support economic conservatism.

Religious behavior and belief vary considerably. The Pew Research Center (2015) observes, for example, that while 66 percent of evangelical Americans pray daily, others pray on a weekly or monthly basis or not at all. Some 88 percent of evangelicals believe in God; the remaining 12 percent are divided among those who are "fairly certain" that God exists to those who are confident that God does not exist. This variability is politically significant, because within religious traditions the most observant and believing members tend to be the most conservative (Green 2010; Layman 2001; Smidt, Kellstedt, and Guth 2009). Does this pattern extend to economic issues? McCarthy and colleagues (2016, 4) note that the effect of religious behavior and belief may simply reinforce the core beliefs and teachings endemic to affiliation. Thus, the more one attends a church that emphasizes individualism, the more likely one is to internalize that message.

Bringing behavior and belonging together, J. Matthew Wilson (1999) finds that among observant Protestants, mainline and black Protestants are positively inclined toward people on welfare, while white evangelical Protestants are negatively inclined. In regard to government policy preferences, Ben Gaskins, Matt Golder, and David A. Siegel (2013) find that the relationship between religious participation and economic conservatism is conditioned by income. Among the poor, religious participation and economic conservatism work against each other, but among the rich they complement each other: "The religious poor are more economically conservative than the secular poor but the religious rich are less economically conservative than the secular rich" (Gaskins, Golder, and Siegel 2013, 839; see also Huber and Stanig 2011). Thus, the relationship between religious behavior and economic attitudes calls for a more nuanced assessment. Religious behavior may not necessarily lead to conservatism across the board.

With respect to belief (or what we call orthodoxy), Ralph Pyle (1993) finds that belief in biblical literalism is positively related to support for government efforts to help the poor. Timothy T. Clydesdale (1999) and Hart (1996) confirm these results. While religious commitment pushes believers toward economic conservatism, religious orthodoxy is associated with support for government assistance for the poor. These findings are surprising, as orthodoxy and commitment are thought to produce conservatism across religious traditions (Green 2010; Olson and Warber 2008). However, orthodox and committed believers moved to the right in response to cultural issues (see Chapter 3). The pattern may break down when we move outside that domain. Perhaps orthodox believers are more likely to take biblical admonitions to care for the poor seriously. Another possibility, however, is that belonging overlaps with believing. To the extent that orthodox believers share a diminished, group-based socioeconomic status, their liberal economic attitudes may be more about self-interest than religious orthodoxy.

Hypotheses

Our primary interest is in assessing white evangelical Protestant attitudes on economic issues, and we use Protestants as our primary point of comparison. First, we investigate the influence of religious belonging. The ethnoreligious approach to the study of religion and politics focuses on belonging because it is within religious communities that individuals are exposed to and internalize a common worldview. Moreover, individuals in the same religious community often share a social status that structures their interests vis-à-vis the political system. Since we believe that evangelicalism places tremendous emphasis on the Protestant work ethic and the importance of personal piety, both of which lend themselves to economic conservatism, we hypothesize the following:

> *Hypothesis 1*: White evangelical Protestants will be more supportive of economic conservatism than individuals of other religious affiliations.

Second, we investigate religious commitment (behavior—attendance) and religious orthodoxy (belief—biblical literalism). These expressions crosscut religious traditions, creating what some have called the "New Religion Gap" (Green 2010, 45; see also Smidt, Kellstedt, and Guth 2009). This produces diversity within religious traditions, as the most committed and orthodox align to preserve traditional social and political arrangements. For this reason, we expect religious commitment and orthodoxy to be positively associated with conservatism among evangelicals. Thus, we hypothesize the following:

Hypothesis 2: For white evangelicals, increased religious attendance will increase economically conservative attitudes.

Hypothesis 3: For white evangelicals, belief in biblical literalism will increase economically conservative attitudes.

Data and Methods

To test our hypotheses, we use ANES survey results for all presidential years between 1992 and 2016. The ANES, which is conducted over several months before and after presidential elections, includes questions about individual religious affiliation and economic preferences in addition to a wide variety of demographic data, making it particularly valuable for this research. There are a total of 19,762 respondents, but not every respondent answered all questions. Since the ANES uses similar questions in each round of the survey, this research can include multiple years without problems inherent in differences in question wording. The ANES has been used previously to conduct studies on the effect of religion on politics (e.g., see Barker and Carman 2000; Olson and Warber 2008), producing robust results.

Dependent Variables

The dependent variables in this study are different measures of economic conservatism. By economic conservatism, we refer to support for the free-market, free-enterprise system; support for decreases in the current levels of social welfare spending by the federal government; and the belief that there should be more individual autonomy in economic endeavors. We use several ANES survey questions to measure this conceptualization. To consider attitudes on social spending, we analyze a spending scale derived from measures related to assistance for the poor and education. The scale was generated using Cronbach's alpha ($\alpha = .70$), with high scores reflecting high levels of economic conservatism. Additionally, we feel that it is important to analyze attitudes solely on welfare spending, as this is often the most salient spending issue. The welfare measure is taken from responses to a question asking whether federal spending on welfare should increase, decrease, or stay the same. This variable was coded as one for respondents who stated that federal spending on welfare should be decreased and zero for all other responses. Preferring a decrease in federal spending on welfare spending is consistent with conservative economic preferences; approximately 40 percent of the entire sample desired a decrease in welfare spending.

We also analyze attitudes on the free market, which is derived from a question asking whether strong government or the free market is better positioned to handle economic problems. The variable was coded one if the respondent thought that the government was the appropriate mechanism for handling the economy; coded two if the respondent was ambivalent, did not know, or was indifferent; and coded three if the respondent thought that the free market was most appropriate for handling the economy. We measure support for government-provided job guarantees with a seven-point scale where a value of one represents a respondent who thinks that the government should see to it that each person has a job and a good standard of living, and a score of seven represents respondents who think that government should let each person get ahead on his or her own. A question in the provision of social services assesses opinions on whether government should spend more or less in this area. Respondents were scored a one if they responded that the government should provide many more services and a seven if they responded that the government should provide many fewer services.

To consider economic attitudes holistically, we analyze an economic conservatism scale derived from the previous ANES questions on welfare spending, child care, the poor, and schools; the free market; job guarantees; and government services. The scale scores were generated using Cronbach's alpha ($\alpha = .77$). All questions are coded so that higher positive numbers indicate a conservative direction. Given that the relationship between religion and economic issues may vary by issue (Hart 1996), we also analyze the factor components separately.

Independent Variables

Belonging is a measure of religious affiliation, which is collapsed into larger religious families. Following primarily Corwin E. Smidt, Lyman A. Kellstedt, and James L. Guth (2009), we include indicator variables for white evangelical Protestants and black evangelical Protestants and leave mainline Protestants as the reference category. We distinguish between white and black evangelicals because minority communities within religious traditions tend to be distinctive with respect to styles of worship, shared grievances, and theological emphases (Wald and Calhoun-Brown 2011). Thus, minorities may be more likely to embrace the social-gospel approach.

Behaving is a measure of commitment to one's religious denomination. This typically includes frequency of contact with its organizational structure, monetary giving, and other factors concerning individuals' devotion to their denomination (Green 2010). We use stated frequency of attending a worship service. This variable was coded on a five-point scale: zero means never attends services, and four means attends at least once a week.

Believing measures the strength of a person's belief in the central tenets of his or her denomination. Acceptance of biblical literalism is used to measure religious belief, which is normative among many evangelicals.

Respondents were asked if they think the Bible is the actual word of God and is to be taken literally, word for word; the word of God but not everything in it should be taken literally, word for word; a book written by men and is not the word of God. Respondents indicating that the Bible is to be taken literally, word for word, were coded one with all other responses coded zero.

We include a number of additional covariates in our analysis. Personal income is a consistent predictor of economic policy preferences (Orr 1976; Plotnick and Winters 1985). Furthermore, class has been previously shown to be a mitigating factor between religious affiliation and policy preferences (Green 2010). Income is coded from the respondent's stated household income and grouped by income quintile. An individual's partisan identification should be linked to his or her policy preferences. Previous research has demonstrated that ideological conservatism is linked to other forms of conservatism (Campbell 2002; Johnson and Tamney 2001; Pyle 1993). Republican and Independent indicator variables are included in the analyses. The base category comprises Democrat. Other variables controlled for in this study include the respondent's age, education, and sex. Each of these has been previously shown to affect a respondent's political behavior (Brady, Verba, and Schlozman 1995), and we extend that expectation to preferences.

Analysis and Discussion

While the multivariate analysis focuses on Protestants, Figure 15.1 displays mean economic conservatism scores by religious tradition. Black evangelicals are the most economically liberal, while white evangelicals are the most economically conservative. Only three religious groups have average economic conservatism scores that are net conservative—white evangelicals, white Catholics, and mainline Protestants. Individuals with no religious affiliation, other religious affiliations, and Jews have averages just below zero, indicating a slight liberal preference. These values, however, are not significantly different from the sample mean. Both black evangelicals and nonwhite Catholics have an average economic-index score that indicates economic liberalism.

Given that white and black evangelicals are at opposite poles on economic issues, we thought it important to investigate further. Figure 15.2 breaks down mean evangelical scores by race and religious commitment. The results indicate that white evangelical attitudes are highly sensitive to levels of commitment—higher religious commitment is associated with increased economic conservatism. Among black evangelicals, however, commitment has little to no effect on economic attitudes. Indeed, black evangelical attitudes seem relatively impervious to variation on this basis. Figure 15.3 breaks down mean scores by orthodoxy and race. Here, both black and white evangelical attitudes are sensitive levels of orthodoxy, but

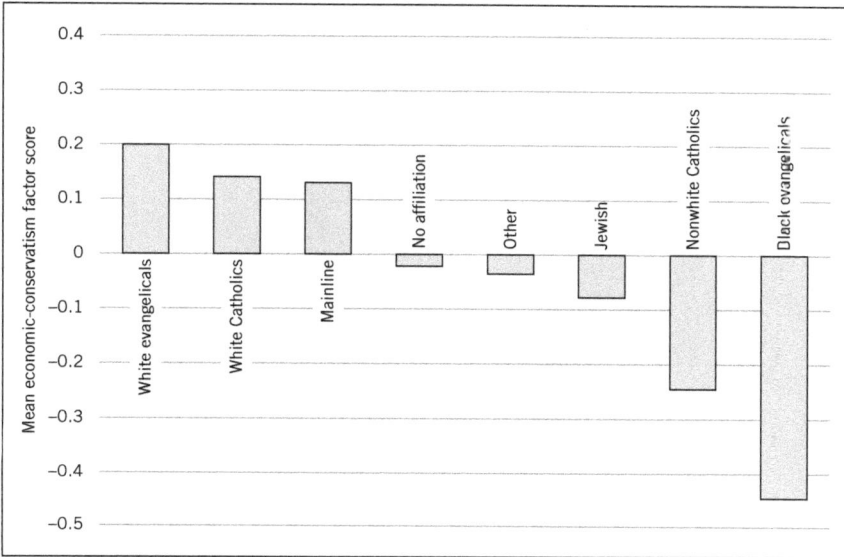

Figure 15.1 Mean economic-conservatism factor scores by religious tradition

Source: American National Election Studies data for all presidential years from 1992 to 2016.
Note: The range of scores is −1.4 to 2.0; the overall mean score is −.005246. Higher positive scores indicate conservatism.

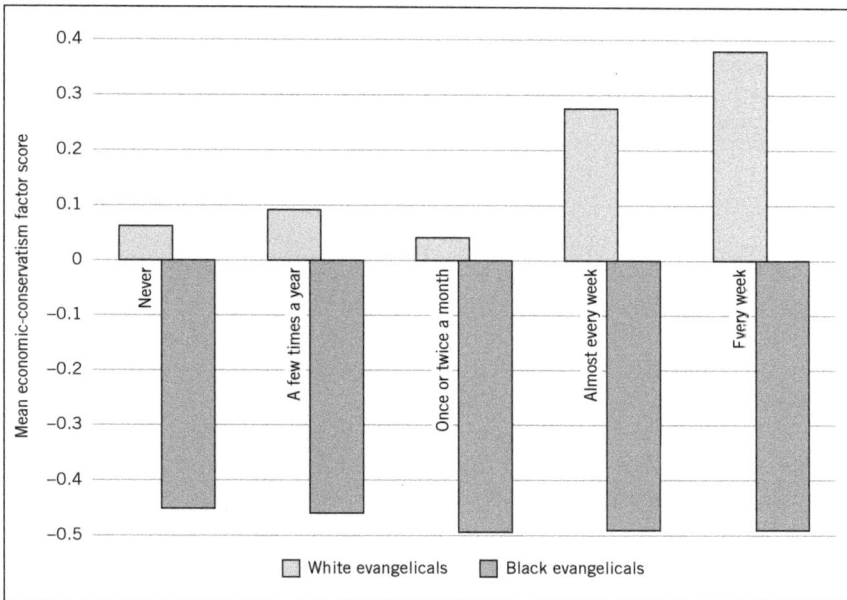

Figure 15.2 Mean economic-conservatism factor scores for religious commitment of white and black evangelicals

Source: American National Election Studies data for all presidential years from 1992 to 2016.
Note: The range of scores is −1.4 to 2.0; the overall mean score is −.005246. Higher positive scores indicate conservatism.

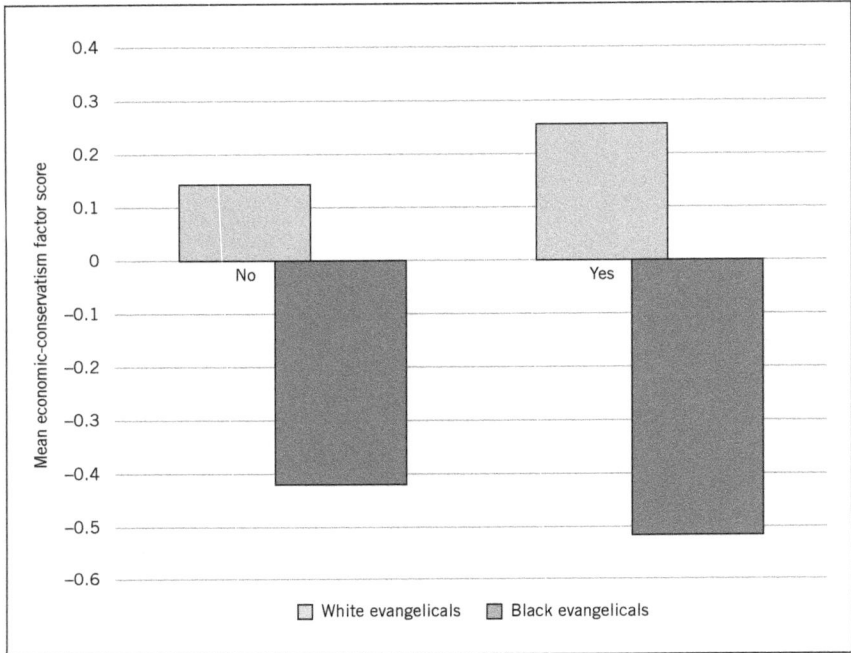

Figure 15.3 Mean economic-conservatism factor scores for belief in biblical literalism by white and black evangelicals

Source: American National Election Studies data for all presidential years from 1992 to 2016.
Note: The range of scores is –1.4 to 2.0; the overall mean score is –.005246. Higher positive scores indicate conservatism.

increased orthodoxy pushes both groups in the opposite direction. White evangelical respondents who agree that the Bible is the word of God and should be taken literally are more conservative on average than unorthodox respondents, while black evangelical respondents who agree that the Bible is the word of God and should be taken literally are more liberal on average than their unorthodox coreligionists. Among both groups, then, orthodoxy strengthens latent economic attitudes.

To investigate the hypotheses with greater rigor, we subject the economic conservatism scores to multivariate analyses. The results for evangelicals are provided in Table 15.1. The first column includes indicators of all three Bs, as well as interactions for behaving and belonging. Across all of the models, the controls perform as expected. Republicans and Independents are more conservative than Democrats, and women are less conservative than men. Age, income, and education are all positively associated with conservatism. Even after considering these key sociodemographic variables, the analyses demonstrate that religion is strongly associated with economic attitudes.

TABLE 15.1 MULTIVARIATE ANALYSIS OF RELIGION AND ECONOMIC-CONSERVATISM MEASURES

	Economic conservatism (OLS)	Welfare spending (logit)	Spending scores (OLS)	Free market (ordered logit)	Job guarantees (OLS)	Social services (OLS)
Religious variables						
White evangelical	.017	.033	.014	.137	.019	.050
	(.033)	(.055)	(.034)	(.093)	(.076)	(.061)
Black evangelical	−.163**	−.126*	−.303**	−.185**	−.403**	−.284**
	(.036)	(.065)	(.043)	(.044)	(.119)	(.090)
Attendance	−.001	−.019*	−.001	.023	−.009	−.006
	(.006)	(.012)	(.008)	(.020)	(.016)	(.013)
Attendance × white evangelical	.039**	.041*	.038**	.017	.075**	.085**
	(.012)	(.020)	(.013)	(.034)	(.028)	(.020)
Attendance × black evangelical	−.016	.009	−.003	−.104**	−.006	−.011
	(.012)	(.029)	(.015)	(.049)	(.042)	(.031)
Biblical literalism	−.047**	.081*	−.067**	−.032	.156**	−.038
	(.021)	(.039)	(.025)	(.065)	(.056)	(.045)
Biblical literalism × white evangelical	.094**	−.021	.134**	−.046	.161*	.106
	(.038)	(.064)	(.040)	(.108)	(.089)	(.073)
Biblical literalism × black evangelical	.026	−.076	.032	.049	−.055	.046
	(.036)	(.086)	(.043)	(.149)	(.123)	(.092)
Control variables						
Republican	.845**	.809**	.713**	1.483**	1.387**	1.301**
	(.020)	(.034)	(.021)	(.059)	(.047)	(.039)
Independent	.376**	.379**	.343**	.760**	.638**	.620**
	(.017)	(.034)	(.020)	(.057)	(.048)	(.037)
Income	.061**	.128**	.065**	-.006	.153**	.090**
	(.006)	(.011)	(.007)	(.018)	(.015)	(.012)
Age	.006**	.000	.007**	.008**	.011**	.007**
	(.000)	(.001)	(.000)	(.001)	(.001)	(.001)
Education	.050**	.043**	.062**	.071**	.066**	.078**
	(.005)	(.010)	(.006)	(.017)	(.014)	(.011)
Woman	−.167**	−.113**	−.139**	−.401**	−.246**	−.238**
	(.015)	(.027)	(.017)	(.045)	(.037)	(.030)
Constant	2.565**	−.851**	.718**		2.594**	2.676**
	(.049)	(.080)	(.046)		(.112)	(.092)
N	10,250	10,241	10,250	9,013	8,247	8,867
Prob > F	.000	.000	.000	.000	.000	.000
R-squared	.805	.114	.533	.078	.213	.233

Source: American National Election Studies data for all presidential years from 1992 to 2016.

Note: Year dummies are omitted from the table. Robust standard errors are in parentheses. The dependent variable is indication of economic conservatism. The sample includes white evangelical Protestants, black evangelical Protestants, and mainline Protestants only. Mainline Protestants are the reference group.

* statistical significance at the 0.10 level (two-tailed tests); ** statistical significance at the 0.05 level (two-tailed tests)

Consistent with our expectations in Hypothesis 1, white evangelical Protestants are more conservative than their mainline counterparts, though this difference falls just short of statistical significance. Black evangelical Protestants are less conservative. The results confirm that within theological traditions, communities of belonging emerge, and these communities are associated with distinct political impulses. In this instance, race crosscuts evangelicalism, producing distinct attitudinal patterns. This is hardly surprising given the strong prophetic tradition among black evangelicals that encourages sociopolitical criticism and given the status of African Americans during much of the country's history: "The very existence of Black churches is in part a testament and a response to social inequality" (Wald and Calhoun-Brown 2011, 277). Thus, the experiences and development of black churches complement the social-gospel tradition in that both call for deep, religiously motivated societal reform. White evangelicals, however, are more conservative. Economic issues tend not to provide their political raison d'être, but as white evangelicals aligned with the Republican Party in the late 1970s, they adopted secular conservative concerns. On economic issues, the theological tradition of individual piety and personal responsibility nicely complements secular economic arguments.

Hypothesis 2 predicts that religious commitment in the form of attendance would be associated with economic conservatism. The results indicate that attendance is positively and significantly related to economic conservatism for white evangelicals, but it does not appear to influence black evangelicals. Hypothesis 3 predicts that religious orthodoxy in the form of support for biblical literalism would strengthen underlying economic attitudes. Here again, our findings indicate that orthodoxy is associated with conservatism among white evangelicals, but the coefficient for orthodox black evangelicals is not statistically significant. The findings support Hypothesis 3.

Here again, we note that the historical status of African Americans makes the black church more amendable to the social-gospel approach. The relationship between black evangelical identification and economically liberal attitudes is so strong that belief and behavior do very little to condition the relationship. In an effort to separate the effects of orthodoxy from those of income, we ran this model again and included an interaction for affiliation, income, and biblical literalism. We do not include the full results, but Figure 15.4 illustrates the interactive effect of income and orthodoxy on economic conservatism for white and black evangelicals. Higher income is linked to economic conservatism in all cases except for nonorthodox black evangelicals. Orthodoxy is associated with liberalism at low-income values; but as income increases, orthodoxy has a positive influence on economic conservatism. However, this effect is much stronger for white evangelicals than it is for black evangelicals. Thus, economic liberalism among orthodox

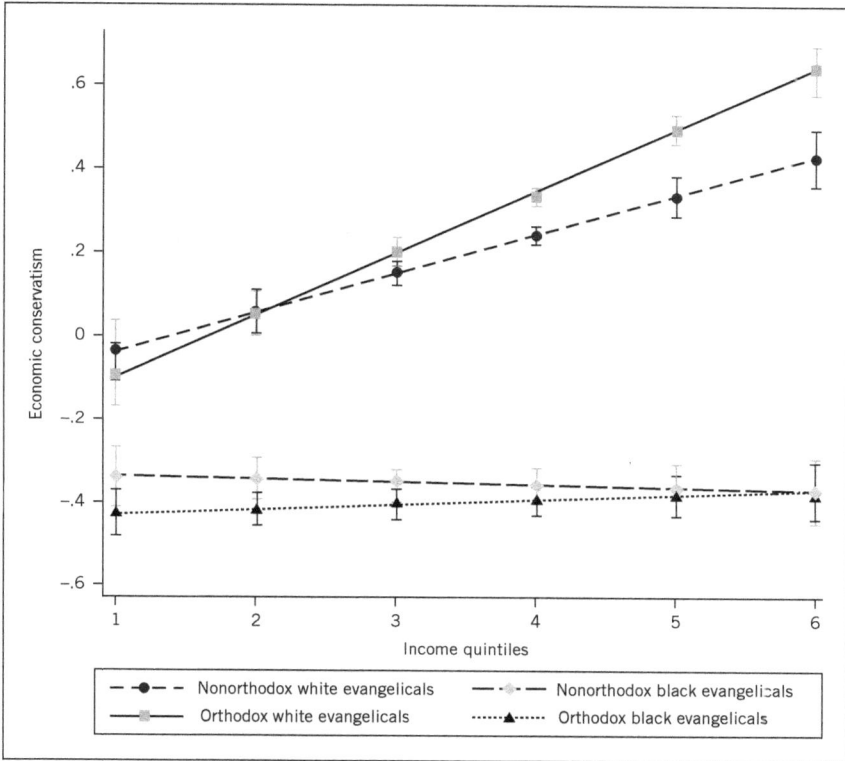

Figure 15.4 Interactive effect of income and orthodoxy on economic conservatism
Source: American National Election Studies data for all presidential years from 1992 to 2016.
Note: Coefficients are significant to at least the .05 level, as is the model overall. Results shown with
   84 percent confidence intervals (see Austin and Hux 2002).

white evangelicals may be more about socioeconomic status than religious
norms. The increase in economic conservatism among white evangelicals
may be an effect not of increased religious stringency but of their increasing
economic status over time.

The association between religion and economic attitudes may vary by
issue (Hart 1996), as all issues are not equally salient and not all salient issues
are salient in the same way. Thus, we analyze the index components individually. These include attitudes on welfare spending, social-service spending more generally, free markets, government job guarantees, and the
provision of social services, shown in columns two through six of Table 15.1.

The results for the other five economic indicators remain relatively consistent with the results from the conservatism index, with a few minor differences. On support for the free market, attendance negatively influences
black evangelical attitudes. The other models demonstrate that at high levels

of religious commitment white evangelicals are more economically conservative than both black evangelicals and mainline Protestants. Additionally, biblical literalism is associated with higher levels of economic conservatism for white evangelicals in two of the models. For all five models, black evangelicals are considerably less economically conservative than both the mainline reference group and white evangelical Protestants.

Conclusion

White evangelicals may have joined the Republican fold because of cultural insecurity, but economic issues reinforce their loyalty. In part, this may be a result of activist efforts to frame their economic agenda using religious language (Deckman et al. 2017), enculturation into Republican politics, and/or a reflection of their improved socioeconomic status. It is difficult to know what this means in the long term. First, there is a clear divide among white evangelicals. The relationship between evangelical identification and economic attitudes is weak among nominal evangelicals, but attitudes among observant, religiously orthodox evangelicals strongly align with Republican economic orthodoxy. Second, Republican economic orthodoxy may change in the Trump era. President Trump makes broadly populist appeals, and as a candidate he expressed support for economic protectionism and single-payer health care.

Thus, to the degree that Republican economic orthodoxy remains traditionally conservative, the party can count on maintaining a strong well of support among observant, orthodox white evangelicals. The relationship of nominal evangelicals to the party is weaker on this dimension, but they might remain in the Republican fold to the degree that cultural issues remain salient. Beyond that, several key findings should be emphasized. First, belonging structures attitudes differently depending on race. Minority communities within evangelical Protestantism were consistently liberal, while whites were consistently conservative. Economically salient religious teachings are a little bit like Ann Swidler's (1986) cultural toolkit—they are plural and contain sufficient ambiguity to give believers flexibility when aligning religious and economic norms (Iannaccone 1998). Thus, people of faith may gravitate toward teachings that support a liberal or conservative approach. Here, we see that minorities gravitate to the left, because, we suspect, it reflects group interests and the social gospel emphasizes interconnectedness and care for the poor. White evangelicals gravitate to the right. We suspect this results from the resonance of the Protestant work ethic. The key point is that religious teachings are heard and internalized through the filter of group-based social status, which often overlies race (Wald and Calhoun-Brown 2011). This speaks to the importance of traditional approaches to the study of religion and politics that prioritize belonging.

Second, religious commitment strongly conditions the effect of religious belonging and mutes the patterns we have seen established. White evangelicals are conservative, but the most conservative are the most religiously committed. Black evangelicals are liberal, but religious commitment does not affect this pattern. We speculate that for black evangelicals, economic preferences align with religious doctrine and group interests, so additional opportunities to internalize religious teachings do not affect preferences. Finally, religious believing—in this case, orthodoxy on the meaning of sacred scripture—appears to reinforce the preexisting preferences of the religious tradition. This pattern does not hold, however, once we consider the effect of economic status. This indicates that economic position is influencing conservatism but not religious orthodoxy, as we find that the wealthiest respondents are the least orthodox in their beliefs while being the most conservative.

Religious belonging, belief, and behavior all inform economic attitudes in interesting and complementary ways. The findings reinforce the importance of religious influences outside a predictable set of culture-war issues. They also serve to underline the complexity of religious politics. Returning to the anecdote from the introduction, how widespread is Dr. Carson's approach to economic issues? Among white evangelicals, the Carson approach likely has a strong presence—especially among the most religiously committed white evangelicals. Thus, the white evangelical commitment to the Republican Party is not just about culture but about culture *and* economics.

President Trump, however, complicates further prognostications. As a candidate, Trump espoused wildly unorthodox economic ideas (at least from a conservative perspective), such as his rejection of free trade and support for universal health care. Trump said the right things on religious liberty and abortion, but his life story belies his standing as a true culture warrior. Yet 81 percent of white evangelicals voted for Trump. It is possible that culture trumped economics, and white evangelicals viewed Trump as an imperfect yet satisfactory vehicle for securing pro-life votes on the Supreme Court. Alternatively, the election may have been about economics but with conservative economic orthodoxy running head-on into white identity politics, which was part and parcel of Trump's campaign rhetoric. From this perspective, "big government" is a problem only insofar as it provides benefits to the undeserving. It goes beyond the scope of this chapter to determine which narrative—if either—explains white evangelical voting in the 2016 election. We can say, however, that observant white evangelicals are strongly conservative on economic issues. As long as the Republican Party champions economic conservatism, and as long as the words "economic conservative" have their traditional meaning, then Republican leaders should count on white evangelical support.

NOTE

1. Born-again identification is commonly used as a proxy for evangelicalism.

REFERENCES

Austin, Peter C., and Janet E. Hux. 2002. "A Brief Note on Overlapping Confidence Intervals." *Journal of Vascular Surgery* 36 (1): 194–195.
Barker, David, and Christopher Jan Carman. 2000. "The Spirit of Capitalism? Religious Doctrine, Values, and Economic Attitude Constructs." *Political Behavior* 22 (1): 1–27.
Brady, Henry, Sidney Verba, and Kay Lehman Schlozman. 1995. "Beyond SES: A Resource Model of Political Participation." *American Political Science Review* 89 (2): 271–294.
Campbell, David E. 2002. "The Young and the Realigning: A Test of the Socialization Theory of Realignment." *Public Opinion Quarterly* 66 (2): 209–234.
Clydesdale, Timothy T. 1999. "Toward Understanding the Role of Bible Beliefs and Higher Education in American Attitudes toward Eradicating Poverty, 1964–1996." *Journal for the Scientific Study of Religion* 38 (1): 103–118.
Cochran, Clarke E., and David Carroll Cochran. 2003. *Catholics, Politics, and Public Policy: Beyond Left and Right.* Maryknoll, NY: Orbis Books.
Deckman, Melissa, Dan Cox, Robert Jones, and Betsy Cooper. 2017. "Faith and the Free Market: Evangelicals, the Tea Party, and Economic Attitudes." *Politics and Religion* 10 (1): 82–110.
Gaskins, Ben, Matt Golder, and David A. Siegel. 2013. "Religious Participation and Economic Conservatism." *American Journal of Political Science* 57 (4): 823–840.
Green, John C. 2010. *The Faith Factor: How Religion Influences American Elections.* Dulles, VA: Potomac Books.
Guth, James L., John C. Green, Corwin E. Smidt, Lyman A. Kellstedt, and Margaret M. Pomona. 1997. *The Bully Pulpit: The Politics of Protestant Clergy.* Lawrence: University Press of Kansas.
Hart, Stephen. 1996. *What Does the Lord Require? How American Christians Think about Economic Justice.* New Brunswick, NJ: Rutgers University Press.
Huber, John D., and Piero Stanig. 2011. "Church-State Separation and Redistribution." *Journal of Public Economics* 95 (7–8): 828–836.
Iannaccone, Laurence R. 1993. "Heirs to the Protestant Ethic? The Economics of American Fundamentalists." In *Fundamentalisms and the State*, edited by Martin Marty and R. Scott Appleby, 342–366. Chicago: University of Chicago Press.
———. 1998. "Introduction to the Economics of Religion." *Journal of Economic Literature* 36 (3): 1465–1495.
Johnson, Stephen, and Joseph B. Tamney. 2001. "Social Traditionalism and Economic Conservatism: Two Conservative Political Ideologies in the United States." *Journal of Social Psychology* 141 (2): 233–243.
Kenski, Henry C., and William Lockwood. 1991. "Catholic Voting Behavior in 1988: A Critical Swing Vote." In *The Bible and the Ballot Box: Religion and Politics in the 1988 Election*, edited by James L. Guth and John C. Green, 173–187. Boulder, CO: Westview Press.
Layman, Geoffrey. 2001. *The Great Divide: Religious and Cultural Conflict in American Party Politics.* New York: Columbia University Press.
Leege, David C. 1993. "Religion and Politics in Theoretical Perspective." In *Rediscovering the Religious Factor in American Politics*, edited by David C. Leege and Lyman A. Kellstedt, 3–25. Armonk, NY: M. E. Sharpe.

McCarthy, Angela Farizo, Nicholas T. Davis, James C. Garand, and Laura R. Olson. 2016. "Religion and Attitudes toward Redistributive Policies among Americans." *Political Research Quarterly* 69 (1): 121–133.

Olson, Laura, and Adam L. Warber. 2008. "Belonging, Behaving, and Believing: Assessing the Role of Religion on Presidential Approval." *Political Research Quarterly* 61 (2): 192–204.

Orr, L. 1976. "Income Transfers as a Public Good: An Application to AFDC." *American Economic Review* 66 (2): 359–371.

Pew Research Center. 2015. "U.S. Public Becoming Less Religious." Available at http://www.pewforum.org/2015/11/03/u-s-public-becoming-less-religious.

Plotnick, Robert, and Richard F. Winters. 1985. "A Politico-Economic Theory of Income Redistribution." *American Political Science Review* 79 (2): 458–473.

Pyle, Ralph. 1993. "Faith and Commitment to the Poor: Theological Orientation and Support for Government Assistance Measures." *Sociology of Religion* 54 (4): 385–401.

Smidt, Corwin E., Lyman A. Kellstedt, and James L. Guth. 2009. "The Role of Religion in American Politics: Explanatory Theories and Associated Analytical and Measurement Issues." In *Oxford Handbook of Religion and American Politics*, edited by Corwin E. Smidt, Lyman A. Kellstedt, and James L. Guth, 3–42. New York: Oxford University Press.

Stark, Rodney, and Charles Y. Glock. 1968. *American Piety: The Nature of Religious Commitment*. Berkeley: University of California Press.

Swidler, Ann. 1986. "Culture in Action: Symbols and Strategies." *American Sociological Review* 51:273–286.

Tankersley, Jim. 2015. "Someone Once Tried Ben Carson's Biblical Tax Plan." *Washington Post*, August 14. Available at https://www.washingtonpost.com/news/wonk/wp/2015/08/14/someone-once-tried-ben-carsons-biblical-tax-plan.

Wald, Kenneth D., and Allison Calhoun-Brown. 2011. *Religion and Politics in the United States*. 6th ed. Lanham, MD: Rowman and Littlefield.

Weber, Max. (1930) 1994. *The Protestant Ethic and the Spirit of Capitalism*. Reprint, New York: Routledge.

Wilson, J. Matthew. 1999. "'Blessed Are the Poor': American Protestantism and Attitudes toward Poverty and Welfare." *Southeastern Political Review* 27 (3): 421–437.

———. 2009. "Religion and American Public Opinion: Economic Issues." In *The Oxford Handbook of Religion and American Politics*, edited by Corwin E. Smidt, Layman A. Kellstedt, and James L. Guth, 191–216. New York: Oxford University Press.

PART IV

The Lasting Political Contributions of Evangelicalism

16

"No One Loves the Bible More Than Me"

The Ironic Continuities of Political Evangelicalism

ROBERT WUTHNOW

Ronald Reagan's much-quoted statement to the assembled evangelical clergy and lay leaders at the 1980 National Affairs Briefing in Dallas, "I know you can't endorse me, but I want you to know that I endorse you," is widely considered to have been a high point in the history of twentieth-century political evangelicalism. Televangelists Jerry Falwell and Pat Robertson, Baptist preacher William Criswell, Presbyterian pastor D. James Kennedy, and the event's organizer revivalist James Robison basked in Reagan's endorsement. For the next quarter century Republican leaders courted evangelicals as allies against abortion and homosexuality and as champions of welfare reform, limited government, and religious freedom.

But now, well into the twenty-first century, the growing conviction among pundits is that the heyday of political evangelicalism may be over. Even though white evangelicals overwhelmingly voted for Donald Trump, the punditry's focus has shifted toward rural resentment, white nationalism, and speculation that evangelicals' hypocrisy surely at last signals their utter demise.

To be sure, much has changed. Evangelicalism has changed. The leaders Reagan endorsed have passed from the scene and been replaced by a new generation with popular ministries of their own. Television ministries are not what they once were. To be young and evangelical is to have more age-mates who are not involved in religion at all. Partisan politics has also changed, driven by new candidacies and issues. Coalitions and voting patterns that seemed unimaginable a few years ago now seem possible. And certainly the role of social media has become increasingly important. The discontinuities are certainly evident.

I suggest, though, that significant continuities must also be taken into consideration. They include the following: first, evangelicals continue to be aligned with the Republican Party, even though these alignments sometimes cross religious traditions; second, the relationship between evangelical leaders and Republican leaders is still, as Reagan's statement suggested, more one of political leaders conferring power on religious leaders than the reverse; and third, political evangelicalism has continued to be fundamentally opposed to "big government" even when evangelicalism becomes involved in the political process.

To understand these continuities, we need to be clear at the outset about what we mean by evangelicalism. I use the term "political evangelicalism" advisedly. Much has been written about evangelicals and politics, which suggests that there is an identifiable segment of the population that can be called evangelicals who then engage in politics in ways that differ from those of other religious traditions' adherents. That view is inaccurate. "Political evangelicalism" is the more appropriate term and is not the same thing.

Evangelicalism is first and foremost a *religious* practice. Any historian of American religion and any practicing evangelical leader would describe it that way. Its theological and denominational roots are diverse, which means that even today its diverse denominational affiliations, beliefs, and practices are important. It includes denominations as different as the Southern Baptist Convention, Assemblies of God, Nazarenes, Pentecostals, and Reformed Presbyterians. Evangelicals do share certain distinctive beliefs, such as an affirmation of the unique divinity of Jesus Christ, the authority of the Bible, and the importance of sharing one's faith with unbelievers. But evangelicals disagree with one another about how literally the Bible should be interpreted, how aggressively evangelicalism should be pursued, and whether speaking in tongues is a legitimate manifestation of the Holy Spirit. Evangelicalism is basically concerned with believers' relationship to God. As it is practiced in the lives of ordinary churchgoers, evangelicalism is a matter of having faith, raising one's children, attempting to be a moral person, dealing with suffering and death, and looking forward to eternal life. Most of these practical day-to-day activities and concerns have very little to do with politics. And this is important to understand because every impetus that may be present for evangelicals to be politically active is countered with an impetus toward focusing instead on faith and family.

Of course, evangelicals do engage in politics and in recent years have often done so in organized ways. But when studies have been conducted to determine how exactly and to what extent evangelicals may be involved in politics, complications arise and simplifications have had to be made. We social scientists have been responsible for many of these simplifications and should be the first to acknowledge them. A few studies have attempted to define evangelicals in terms of specific beliefs about Jesus and the Bible or in terms of self-identity and then compare that group with other groups. But most studies, rather than tap the nuances of belief and practice, have relied on categories that merely happened to be available in survey data or were included because they were simple and cheap.

Statements based on polls and surveys usually reflect these simplifications. They refer to membership in denominations that someone has classified as evangelical, thus leaving out people who hold evangelical beliefs but belong to other denominations. They often fail to distinguish active church-going members from nominal members. And in political polling evangelicals are usually defined by a single question that asks people if they consider themselves an evangelical or born-again Christian. That has been a neat way of suggesting that evangelicals are a huge voting bloc making up some 35 percent of the public. But it is far different from the 7 to 15 percent identified when better questions about belief and practice are asked.

To further complicate things, much of the polling on which conclusions about evangelical politics are drawn is of such poor quality that it is difficult to know whether it means anything at all. The typical poll now has an 8 percent response rate, which means that 92 percent of those who should have been included for the poll to truly be based on a representative sample are missing. The best pollsters tinker with the numbers in terms of what they know about age and gender and who has voted in the past, but they have no such information with which to jigger the numbers about religion. Even the basic electoral horse-race polling is now frequently wrong.

The information pundits report about evangelical politics is, for these reasons, the kind that has to be taken with a large grain of salt. Reports about who evangelicals favor in statewide primaries are often based on as few as a hundred people who were identified by a single question and happened to be among the 8 percent who answered the phone. Rarely do the reports compare evangelicals who attend church regularly with those who merely happened to say they were born-again Christians. And rarely is it possible to know if conclusions about evangelicals would be different if other factors such as age, gender, region, and level of education were taken into account.

What we have from pundits and the polling industry then is *political evangelicalism*—a fabrication that is by no means meaningless but one that has to be understood for what it is rather than for much else about how American evangelicals practice their faith. Political evangelicalism has become a prominent feature of public discussion about American politics, and it is interpretable not only in its own right but also in relation to what we know about organizations, interest groups, and political operatives and from the occasional survey that asks better questions and has a better response rate.

The continuity between political evangelicalism and Republican partisanship has been evident in presidential elections since 1980 and was on its
way toward being established well before then. Although it surprised pundits
that evangelicals supported Reagan as strongly as they did in 1980 against
fellow evangelical Jimmy Carter, prominent evangelical leaders such as William Criswell had endorsed Gerald Ford instead of Carter in 1976, and, to
the extent that data were available, the evidence suggested that conservative
Protestants had favored Eisenhower in 1952 and 1956 and Nixon in 1960,
1968, and 1972. An evangelical living in a red state somewhere in the Midwest or South could thus be a second- or third-generation Republican. Partisan continuities of this kind may be similar to die-hard Cubs or Packers
fans' support of their favorite teams. It seems telling that political evangelicalism in 2012 went for Rick Santorum in the Republican primary, despite
his being a Roman Catholic; for Mitt Romney in the general election, despite
his being a Mormon; and in 2016 for Donald Trump, who seemed to some to
be the devil himself.

The second continuity that needs to be considered is Republican candidates and operatives courting evangelical support. My contention since the
1980s has been that, yes, evangelical votes were sometimes pivotal in close
elections, but in larger terms evangelical leaders gained more from being
courted than political candidates did from courting them. I mean this in
symbolic terms more than in terms of policies. The symbolism of Ronald
Reagan as the presumptive nominee and soon-to-be leader of the free world
endorsing you is far greater than you endorsing him, even if you happen to
have a decent following as a Baptist preacher. Republican presidential candidates have continued to speak at large churches and at conservative political rallies organized by clergy and religiously based pro-life groups with
few exceptions, while Democratic candidates have mostly refrained from
doing so. A few evangelical leaders have refused to be courted in these symbolic ways. But not many.

Of course, the possibility that all this may be changing has been raised
by the 2016 presidential campaign. Did Pat Robertson, Jerry Falwell Jr., and
Franklin Graham gain something by supporting Donald Trump? Would
they have supported him even if Trump did not love the Bible more than
anyone else did? Their support—ironic as it was—at least demonstrated the
continuity of evangelical leaders supporting Republican candidates, no matter who they are.

The third continuity is political evangelicalism's stance toward government, which is persistently against "big government." Whether expressed in
Reagan's assertion about government being the problem rather than the so-
lution or in more recent arguments about Washington being broken, smaller
government has been a featured aspect of Republican discourse. Smaller
government has also been embraced in political evangelicalism's arguments,

lending support to Reagan's view that churches and other local voluntary organizations were the core of American democracy, George W. Bush's compassionate-conservative arguments for faith-based initiatives, Ted Cruz's advocacy for religious freedom in opposition to the Affordable Care Act, and Donald Trump's promise to "drain the swamp."

Evangelicals' opposition to big government is hypocritical, critics say, because they do not seem to mind government telling women what they can do with their bodies or homosexuals whom they cannot marry. But of course, political evangelicalism's leaders do not see it that way. Big government is in their view consistently the problem: the Supreme Court in approving *Roe v. Wade*, the welfare state in perpetuating poverty, and liberal Democratic pro-gay lobbyists in undermining the sanctity of marriage.

The history of evangelical Protestantism's opposition to big government has yet to be written, but I imagine it would demonstrate a tradition deeply rooted in concerns about the infringement of government on religion, whether in repressing upstart Protestant sects in the seventeenth century, imposing imperial power over the American colonies in the eighteenth century, undermining the authority of municipalities and states in the nineteenth century, or ushering in New Deal bureaucracy in the twentieth century.

Opposing big government does not have to win to be successful. Just as it confers power to be endorsed by a political candidate, it enhances a person's reputation to buck something powerful. The biblical David gains stature going up against Goliath. Joshua does so by marching against Jericho. A hometown preacher who proclaims that the president is evil gains a following.

It does, however, take a particular view of politics to argue so consistently that big government is evil. In a two-party system as deeply polarized as that in the United States has been in recent decades, embracing a candidate because that candidate is pro-life or antigovernment often means supporting gerrymandered redistricting and favoring political appointees who undermine public education.

Unless Republican leaders for some unlikely reason experience a change of heart and become outspoken advocates of big government, it seems doubtful that they will lose the support of evangelicals anytime soon—at least not the support of political evangelicalism.

17

The Evangelical Consolidation

JOHN C. GREEN

Popular accounts of the voting behavior of white evangelical Protestants have long had a bipolar character (J. Green 1995). On the one hand, these voters have been regularly portrayed as on the verge of political dominance, with imminent consequences for public policy—a perspective revived by the 2016 presidential election (Montgomery 2016). On the other hand, evangelical voters have been routinely described as in political decline and thus largely irrelevant to government. The essay that inspired this book is a well-written example of the latter (Kirkpatrick 2007). Although these reports often reflect the writers' own fears and hopes, they also capture the waxing and waning of evangelical influence at the ballot box.

The cumulative impact of these episodes has been neither electoral dominance nor decline but instead a consolidation of evangelicals as a major constituency of the Republican Party—similar to black Protestant, Jewish, and religiously unaffiliated voters in the Democratic Party. This partisan consolidation has changed the politics of both evangelicals and Republicans. During the 2016 campaign, these shifts were largely underappreciated by observers both inside and outside the evangelical community.

Over time, evangelical voters have become more cooperative and pragmatic in politics (Newel 2016). On the first count, they have adopted a larger issue agenda, partly from participating in the GOP coalition and partly from exposure to a wide array of policy arenas (J. Green 2013). As a consequence, they have become "multiple-issue" voters, with views on the economy, domestic and foreign policy, and public order. To be sure, evangelicals still have a strong faith-based agenda, including a special concern with sexual issues, but they have many other interests as well (Goren and Chapp 2016). On the second count, evangelicals have become keenly aware of the trade-off between articulating principles and achieving success in politics, and as a consequence, they have become more instrumental in casting ballots (Hinckley 2016). Nowhere is such pragmatism more evident than in their view of politicians: Evangelicals recognize that it is crucial to support the most viable Republican candidate at the ballot box, especially when the options are poor (Jones 2016).

Evangelical political perspectives have also evolved, becoming broader, less distinctive, and more accommodating. At the heart of this change is recognition that their community is a (large) minority in American society (Lipka 2016). J. C. Watts, an African American pastor with the Southern Baptist Convention and former Republican congressman from Oklahoma (and thus a minority on many counts), offered an example of these new perspectives while campaigning in 2015.

"The difference between Republicans and Democrats," Watts said, "is that Republicans believe people are fundamentally bad, while Democrats see people as fundamentally good." He continued, "We are born bad. . . . We become good by being reborn—born again." Turning to the example of a mass shooting, he added that Republicans knew whom to blame: the gunman. But Democrats "look for other causes—that the man was basically good, but that it was the guns, society or some other place where the blame lies and then they will want to control the guns, or something else—not the man" (quoted in Leonard 2017).

Although neither fully comprehensive nor completely novel, this campaign comment is worth a tentative unpacking. First, bad people exist and society needs protection from them. The government is the chief source of such protection, but it is also a flawed instrument, since public officials can be bad people too. Thus, government must be limited in its operation, and its priority must be the protection of individuals (E. Green 2016). This formulation can easily be extended to protecting individuals from violence, crime, poverty, and discrimination but also from foreign terrorists and multinational corporations. However, a comprehensive improvement of the world is largely beyond the scope of government because it is fundamentally the work of faith: a voluntary, spiritual renewal, one individual at a time. Such individuals have a new capacity to be good, including acts of sacrifice, discipline, charity, tolerance, and forgiveness. Protecting the religious activities of the faithful is thus crucial to the well-being of the world.

This emphasis on protection is generally consistent with the goals of the conservative wing of the Republican Party, especially the "nationalist" conservatives (Buchanan 2017). But with modest revisions, it can fit proposals of reform conservatism (Douthat and Salam 2008) and even progressive policies of the "new evangelicals" (Steensland and Goff 2013). Of course, there are numerous ways to frame such arguments, leaving ample room for disagreement, debate, and decision.

The evangelical consolidation has also changed the Republican Party, making it more socially diverse, politically accommodating, and ideologically complex. Aspiring Republican candidates regularly and comfortably tailor their messages to appeal to evangelical voters (see Borkett-Jones 2015). It is worth remembering that the last four Republican presidential nominees—George W. Bush, John McCain, Mitt Romney, and Donald Trump—were not initially the consensus favorites of evangelicals but won the nominations by seeking and obtaining evangelical votes in crucial contests. In 2016, Donald Trump did well among evangelical voters in the face of stiff opposition from a number of candidates with stronger evangelical credentials (Posner 2016a). Once the GOP nomination was settled in each of these elections, a large majority of evangelical voters coalesced behind the Republican nominee in the general election. Trump performed especially well in this regard, doing a bit better than Bush in 2004.[1]

Coming to Terms with Their Candidate

Despite this strong partisan pull, Trump presented a very tough choice for many evangelicals—as it did for many other Republicans. Some evangelical leaders strongly opposed Trump, essentially arguing that he was not a credible protector.[2] Given his three marriages, admitted adultery, and embrace of popular culture, Trump was an unlikely defender of traditional families. Furthermore, his religiosity was nominal at best and his views on sexual issues suspect, offering only modest prospects for protecting faith or morals. These concerns were exacerbated by Trump's many bigoted statements, revealing little inclination to protect women or ethnic and religious minorities. His complete lack of experience in government inspired a lack of confidence, while his tough talk suggested increased insecurity. Behind these principles was a dose of pragmatism: Trump was unlikely to win evangelical votes, let alone the nomination or the general election—and if he somehow got to the White House, he would perform poorly on all counts. In short, "The Donald" was a bad choice for the White House given the alternatives, especially early in the nomination process.

Other evangelical leaders supported Trump, in large part because he was perceived as a potential protector.[3] While he was clearly a flawed individual, it was argued that God regularly uses such people to defend the vulnerable (Gibson 2016). Indeed, some argued that Trump could be forgiven his sinful past. Had not many people—including evangelicals—forgiven Bill Clinton's sexual misbehavior in the White House? In regard to his vague religiosity, devout presidents George W. Bush and Barack Obama had not significantly

increased security at home or abroad. And Trump voiced as much support
for protecting life and religious liberty as any other viable presidential candidate. Although his rhetoric was often nasty, it had a redeeming element of
candor, welcomed by long-suffering victims of political correctness. Trump's
status as a complete outsider was also appealing, given many past disap-
pointments at the hands of establishment Republicans and Democrats. Such
blunt pragmatism had an element of principle as well: Trump could mobilize
evangelicals, win elections, and if elected, increase security on many fronts.
In short, "The Donald" was not a bad choice for the White House under the
circumstances.

All these arguments understated the potential breadth of Trump's appeal to evangelical voters. Trump's support grew throughout the nomination and general election campaigns, despite numerous controversies. These
gains were due in part to Trump's calculated pursuit of evangelicals (Serrie
2016). He explicitly thanked evangelicals for their primary support during
his acceptance speech at the Republican National Convention and, in an
uncharacteristically humble aside, remarked, "Maybe I don't deserve evangelical support." Other appeals included choosing Mike Pence as his vice
presidential running mate, promising a conservative Supreme Court nominee, and repealing of the "Johnson Amendment" on tax-exempt status of
political activity by clergy and congregations (Trump 2016).[4] This pursuit
prompted conservative evangelical leaders—including many who had preferred other Republican primary candidates—to coalesce behind Trump's
general election campaign. These leaders deployed their organizations and
resources to help mobilize the evangelical vote.[5] However, Trump's policy
statements and the GOP platform were even bigger assets to the multiple-
issue evangelical voters, who were more focused on policy results than presidential character.

The contrast between Trump and the Democratic presidential nominee,
Hillary Clinton, also mattered to evangelicals. Many had long disliked Clinton, partly because of her husband and partly because of her perceived lack
of honesty—both issues in the 2016 campaign (Smith 2016). Clinton's comment about the "basket of deplorables," defined as "racist, sexist, homopho-
bic, xenophobic, Islamophobic," angered many evangelicals sensitive to the
characterization of their religious beliefs as bigotry—much as progressives
resent being labeled "immoral" because of religious support for reproductive
rights and marriage equality. On sexual issues, Clinton's strong pro-choice
position, endorsement of same-sex marriage, and especially a promise to
nominate a liberal Supreme Court justice troubled many evangelicals. In this
regard, her strong establishment credentials were a detriment rather than an
asset. Although Clinton was religiously devout, her campaign was perceived
to lack effective appeals to religious voters (Goodstein 2016b). Indeed, a
statement by progressive evangelical leaders highly critical of Trump had

little positive to say about Clinton: "Whether we support Mr. Trump's political opponent is not the question here. Hillary Clinton is both supported and distrusted by a variety of Christian voters. We . . . simply will not tolerate the racial, religious, and gender bigotry that Donald Trump has consistently and deliberately fueled, no matter how else we choose to vote or not to vote" (Jenkins 2016). In short, Clinton was not a good candidate for the White House, despite the poor alternatives.

The Battle in Ohio

Regardless of their views of Trump, most evangelical leaders were as shocked by Trump's Electoral College victory on November 8 as the pundits and pollsters were (Miller 2016). But the role of evangelical voters should not have been such a surprise. Postelection survey data from Ohio is illustrative of the evangelical vote for Trump.[6]

Ohio was once again a battleground, but unlike it had been in recent elections, it was less a bellwether of the national popular vote than a harbinger of the Trump vote. He carried Ohio by eight percentage points—almost as large a margin as in Texas. White evangelicals were a key part of this victory, with more than three-quarters backing Trump and about one-fifth backing Clinton.

As one might imagine, partisanship was a major factor in the Ohio evangelical vote: two-thirds of Trump backers were Republicans, and three-fifths of Clinton backers were Democrats. However, three-fifths reported that the candidate's issue positions were most or more important to their vote than the candidates' personal traits. Trump backers were more likely to be issue voters, and Clinton backers were more likely to be trait voters.

Ohio evangelicals also reported voting on the basis of multiple issues. Almost two-fifths said economic issues were most important to their vote, but one-fifth mentioned foreign policy, one-sixth reported social welfare, one-seventh mentioned the political process (such as poor candidates), and one-eighth picked public order (including sexual issues). Trump backers were more likely to be economic-issue voters, and Clinton backers more likely to be non-economic-issue voters. Although social issues were not a top priority for Ohio evangelicals, three-fifths said social issues were "very important" in deciding their vote. Far more Trump backers gave this response than Clinton backers.

Two-fifths of Ohio evangelicals identified "bringing change to the White House" as the most important candidate personal trait to their vote. Another one-third said honesty, one-seventh chose nonpolitical experience, and less than one-tenth each picked temperament or political experience. Trump backers were more likely to be "change" voters, and Clinton backers were more likely to be "honesty" or "temperament" voters.

Neither Trump nor Clinton was personally popular with Ohio evangelicals, but Clinton was the least liked. Overall, only one-fifth reported a "very favorable" opinion of Trump—and one-fifth a "very unfavorable" view. In contrast, less than one-tenth had a "very favorable" opinion of Clinton; and more than two-thirds, a "very unfavorable" view. When asked why they had a negative view of the candidates, nearly nine in ten mentioned character problems—dishonesty was the top response for Clinton; disrespect was the top response for Trump. Only about one-quarter mentioned a specific issue as a negative for Trump, while almost three-fifths mentioned a specific issue as a negative for Clinton. These issue mentions ranged from the economy to abortion.

Conclusion

Thus, Ohio evangelicals voted as one might expect of a strong party constituency, a pattern that may well fit the national evangelical vote. No doubt this result reflects the strong polarization of American politics, where evangelicals, like other voting blocs, are tied to one major party for special reasons. But it also reflects the dynamics of party politics: it was by no means certain that evangelical voters would strongly back Trump. This support developed because of a particular combination of issues, candidates, and campaigns. Evangelical voters are more open to these many influences than the conventional wisdom suggests.

One need not agree with the majority of evangelical voters to recognize the reasonableness of their choice in the context of the 2016 election. There is, however, a good bit of irony in the outcome. Evangelicals have long been admonished, both from within and outside their communities, to be more cooperative, pragmatic, and accommodating in politics. The 2016 results were surely not what such advocates had in mind. Whether the evangelical consolidation yields promise or disappointment for such voters remains to be seen.

NOTES

1. The 2016 National Election Pool exit polls found that 80 percent of "white, born-again/ evangelical Christians" voted for Trump (and made up 26 percent of the electorate); the comparable figure for Bush in 2004 was 78 percent (and 23 percent of the electorate) (Smith and Martinez 2016). This measure is commonly used by pollsters as a shortcut for members of the evangelical Protestant religious tradition. In some ways, this shortcut captures the politics of this larger religious tradition well—but not in others (Smidt 2013).

2. One of earliest and most vocal Trump critics was Russell Moore, president of the Ethics and Religious Liberty Commission of the Southern Baptist Convention. He was joined by a variety of other evangelical leaders, including prominent evangelical progressives (see Gjelten 2016; Walton 2016; Posner 2016b; Jenkins 2016).

3. One the earliest and most vocal Trump supporters was Jerry Falwell Jr., president of Liberty University and the son of the founder of the Moral Majority. Other conservative

leaders included Ralph Reed of the Faith and Freedom Coalition, Tony Perkins of the Family Research Foundation, and retired leaders James Dobson and Pat Robertson (see Goodstein 2016a; Johnson 2016; Scott, Killough, and Burke 2016; Williams 2016).

4. On his remark about not deserving evangelical support, see *The John Batchelor Show*, July 21, 2016, hour 3, block D, available at http://johnbatchelorshow.com/schedules/thursday -21-july-2016.

5. Among the organizations that worked to mobilize the evangelical vote for Trump were the Faith and Freedom Coalition, the Family Research Council, the Susan B. Anthony List, and a variety of pro-life organizations. Franklin Graham, the son of the legendary evangelist Billy Graham, conducted a nationwide voter-registration drive (see Dias 2016; Leahy 2016).

6. The survey data discussed come from the "Your Vote Ohio Poll." Conducted by the Bliss Institute at the University of Akron in cooperation with the Ohio Media Consortium, the survey was a four-wave panel of adult Ohioans: an initial survey of 1,972 respondents completed in June, and then second surveys of the respondents in August, September, and November. The postelection survey had 800 voters for an overall margin of error of plus-or-minus 3.5 percentage points. Although the number of cases for evangelical voters was small (208), the patterns reported are robust and largely outside the margin of error (plus or minus seven percentage points).

REFERENCES

Borkett-Jones, Lucinda. 2015. "What Do We Know about the Faith of the 2016 Presidential Candidates?" *Christian Today*, July 21. Available at http://www.christiantoday.com/ article/what.do.we.know.about.the.faith.of.the.2016.presidential.cndidates.so.far/51847 .htm.

Buchanan, Patrick J. 2017. "Reagan and Trump: American Nationalists." Available at http:// buchanan.org/blog/reagan-trump-american-nationalists-126426.

Dias, Elizabeth. 2016. "How Evangelicals Helped Donald Trump Win." *Time*, November 9. Available at http://time.com/4565010/donald-trump-evangelicals-win/.

Douthat, Ross, and Reihan Salam. 2008. *Grand New Party: How Republicans Can Win the Working Class and Save the American Dream*. New York: Doubleday.

Gibson, David. 2016. "Is There a 'Trump Effect' on Public Morality?" *Religion News Service*, October 19. Available at http://religionnews.com/2016/10/19/is-there-a-trump-effect-on -public-morality/.

Gjelten, Tom. 2016. "Evangelicals Consider Whether God Really Cares How They Vote." *NPR*, November 1. Available at http://www.npr.org/2016/11/01/500105245/evangelicals -consider-whether-god-really-cares-how-they-vote#.

Goodstein, Laurie. 2016a. "Donald Trump Reveals Evangelical Rifts That Could Shape Politics for Years." *New York Times*, October 17. Available at https://www.nytimes.com/2016/ 10/17/us/donald-trump-evangelicals-republican-vote.html.

———. 2016b. "Religious Right Believes Donald Trump Will Deliver on His Promises." *New York Times*, November 11. Available at https://www.nytimes.com/2016/11/12/us/donald -trump-evangelical-christians-religious-conservatives.html.

Goren, Paul, and Christopher Chapp. 2016. "Evangelical Voters Will Almost Surely Vote for Donald Trump: Here's Why." *Washington Post*, October 3. Available at https://www .washingtonpost.com/news/monkey-cage/wp/2016/10/03/evangelical-voters-will-almost -surely-vote-for-donald-trump-heres-why.

Green, Emma. 2016. "Why Donald Trump Appeals to Evangelicals." *The Atlantic*, August 8. Available at http://www.theatlantic.com/politics/archive/2016/08/donald-trump -christian-libertarianism/494843/.

Green, John C. 1995. "The Christian Right and the 1994 Election: A View from the States." *PS: Political Science and Politics* 38 (1): 5–8.

———. 2013. "New and Old Evangelical Public Engagement: A View from the Polls." In *The New Evangelical Social Engagement*, edited by Brian Steensland and Philip Goff, 129–153. New York: Oxford University Press.

Hinckley, Story. 2016. "Why Presidential Candidates' Faith Matters Less and Less to Voters." *Christian Science Monitor*, July 14. Available at https://www.csmonitor.com/USA/Politics/2016/0714/Why-presidential-candidates-faith-matters-less-and-less-to-voters.

Jenkins, Jack. 2016. "Group of Nearly 80 Evangelical Leaders Publish Letter Condemning Trump." *ThinkProgress*, October 6. Available at https://thinkprogress.org/trump-evangelicals-letter-d86c70f05194#.rkoornpiq.

Johnson, Alex. 2016. "What's behind Evangelical Support for Donald Trump?" *NBC News*, October 16. Available at http://www.nbcnews.com/politics/2016-election/what-s-behind-evangelical-support-donald-trump-less-you-think-n666146.

Jones, Robert P. 2016. "Donald Trump and the Transformation of White Evangelicals," *Time*, November 19. Available at http://time.com/4577752/donald-trump-transformation-white-evangelicals/.

Kirkpatrick, David D. 2007. "The Evangelical Crackup." *New York Times Magazine*, October 28. Available at https://www.nytimes.com/2007/10/28/magazine/28Evangelicals-t.html.

Leahy, Michael Patrick. 2016. "Lift the Vote: Evangelicals Made the Difference in Florida, Other Swing States." *Breitbart*, December 5. Available at http://www.breitbart.com/big-government/2016/12/05/lift-vote-evangelicals-difference-florida-swing-states/.

Leonard, Robert. 2017. "Why Rural America Voted for Trump." *New York Times*, January 5. Available at https://www.nytimes.com/2017/01/05/opinion/why-rural-america-voted-for-trump.html.

Lipka, Michael. 2016. "Evangelicals Increasingly Say It's Becoming Harder for Them in America." Pew Research Center, July 14. Available at http://www.pewresearch.org/fact-tank/2016/07/14/evangelicals-increasingly-say-its-becoming-harder-for-them-in-america/.

Miller, Emily McFarlan. 2016. "Evangelical Christians Celebrate and Urge Unity; Others Wary." *Religion News Service*, November 9. Available at http://religionnews.com/2016/11/09/religious-reactions-to-trump-win-time-to-rebuild-and-to-reconcile/.

Montgomery, Peter. 2016. "The Revenge of the Religious Right?" Right Wing Watch, November 9. Available at http://www.rightwingwatch.org/post/the-revenge-of-the-religious-right.

Newell, Jim. 2016. "Why Evangelicals Are Smart to Support Trump." *Slate*, October 19. Available at http://www.slate.com/blogs/the_slatest/2016/10/19/why_donald_trump_s_deep_evangelical_support_makes_sense.html.

Posner, Sarah. 2016a. "How Donald Trump Divided and Conquered Evangelicals." *Rolling Stone*, July 21. Available at http://www.rollingstone.com/politics/features/how-donald-trump-divided-and-conquered-evangelicals-w430119.

———. 2016b. "The Religious Right's Trump Schism." *New York Times*, October 19. Available at https://www.nytimes.com/2016/10/19/opinion/campaign-stops/the-religious-rights-trump-schism.html.

Scott, Eugene, Ashley Killough, and Daniel Burke. 2016. "Evangelicals 'Disgusted' by Trump's Remarks, but Still Backing Him." *CNN*, October 21. Available at http://www.cnn.com/2016/10/07/politics/donald-trump-evangelical-leaders/index.html.

Serrie, Jonathan. 2016. "Trump's Holy Alliance with Evangelical Voters." *Fox News*, November 16. Available at http://www.foxnews.com/politics/2016/11/16/trumps-holy-alliance-with-evangelical-voters.html.

Smidt, Corwin E. 2013. *American Evangelicals Today.* Lanham, MD: Rowman and Littlefield.

Smith, Gregory A. 2016. "Many Evangelicals Favor Trump Because He Is Not Clinton." Pew Research Center, September 23. Available at http://www.pewresearch.org/fact-tank/2016/09/23/many-evangelicals-favor-trump-because-he-is-not-clinton/.

Smith, Gregory A., and Jessica Martinez. 2016. "How the Faithful Voted: A Preliminary 2016 Analysis." Pew Research Center, November 9. Available at http://www.pewresearch.org/fact-tank/2016/11/09/how-the-faithful-voted-a-preliminary-2016-analysis.

Steensland, Brian, and Philip Goff, eds. 2013. *The New Evangelical Social Engagement.* New York: Oxford University Press.

Trump, Donald. 2016. "Full Text: Donald Trump 2016 RNC Draft Speech Transcript." *Politico,* July 21. Available at https://www.politico.com/story/2016/07/full-transcript-donald-trump-nomination-acceptance-speech-at-rnc-225974.

Walton, Andy. 2016. "Has the 2016 Election Sounded the Death Knell of the Religious Right?" *Christian Today,* November 8. Available at https://www.christiantoday.com/article/has.the.2016.election.sounded.the.death.knell.of.the.religious.right/100122.htm.

Williams, Daniel K. 2016. "Why Values Voters Value Donald Trump." *New York Times,* August 20. Available at https://www.nytimes.com/2016/08/21/opinion/sunday/why-values-voters-value-donald-trump.html.

18

What If . . . ?

Evangelicals and the Future of American Politics

RYAN L. CLAASSEN
PAUL A. DJUPE

Counterfactuals offer unique insights into the way things work. Accordingly, we conclude as we began, by noting that the 2016 election offered religion and politics scholars opportunities to see how evangelicals would respond to an unusual set of circumstances. What if the Democrats nominated an overtly religious candidate and the Republicans nominated a very secular candidate? Would the leaders in the Christian Right take a left turn? Would evangelicals in the mass public return to the party of William Jennings Bryan, three-time Democratic presidential nominee and fiery evangelical best remembered for his role prosecuting John Thomas Scopes for the crime of teaching evolution in a public school in Tennessee? While some prominent evangelical leaders advocated against Trump, a message that was not widely known, most legacy Christian Right leaders and organizations provided the same sort of support enjoyed by George W. Bush—a candidate evangelicals were able to embrace as a devout leader. And if the crackup of support among elites was only minor, it was nonexistent in regard to the voting behavior of evangelicals in the mass public. Apparently a devout candidate is not much of a requirement for evangelical support of a Republican.

We hasten to add, however, that support for an irreligious candidate need not imply that evangelicals' motivations are not religious. After all, Trump made several efforts—albeit very awkwardly—to invoke religion as a guiding force in his life. He embraced the positions of the Christian Right on a range of political issues—giving Tony Perkins, president of the Family Research Council, a major role writing the Republican platform. He selected a running mate evangelicals embraced as devout. He even went as far as to circulate likely judicial nominees in advance of the election to allay worries that his nominees might look more like 1970s, 1980s, or 1990s Trump than the "baby Christian" presidential candidate endorsed by James Dobson. This is all to say that the biography of Trump might not be very enlightening as a counterfactual after all if virtually any candidate can erase a long record of irreligious behavior during a comparably short campaign.

Yet the idea of exploring the motivations of evangelicals through the lens of counterfactuals is intriguing. For example, what if the Access Hollywood video, in which Trump bragged about being able to sexually assault women with impunity, had surfaced during the primary? This is an interesting counterfactual for several reasons. First, several people knew of the existence of the video during the primary (obviously). In fact, it would not be at all surprising to us if the video was known to Democratic operatives during the primary, so the fact that it did not surface until the general election suggests the possibility of a strategic calculation that Democrats thought Trump would be beatable. In fact, given that many thought a Trump nomination would hasten a crackup in the relationship between evangelicals and the Republican Party (ahem), it would not surprise us if Democratic operatives saw Trump as especially vulnerable because of his irreligious background and salacious past. Second, the decision faced by evangelical leaders and members of the mass public would have been very different during the primary when there were several contenders with solid Christian Right backing. The fact that the video was only a temporary setback for the Trump campaign—including only fleeting criticism by evangelical leaders followed by renewed support—suggests evangelicals discounted Trump's vulgar words as "locker-room talk." On the one hand, this is an indictment of a group that professes a great deal of concern about moral social behavior. On the other hand, by largely ignoring the video and subsequent accusations, evangelicals appear to do what social psychologists say nearly everyone does—avoid cognitive dissonance. However, if Ted Cruz had been an alternative to Donald Trump when the tape story broke, Trump's misdeeds would not have been a source of cognitive dissonance because congenial alternative candidates were available. Again, the counterfactual is interesting and reveals that evangelicals exercise the same sort of moral elasticity everyone else does to avoid cognitive dissonance as they make political decisions.

What if the Democratic nominee had been hostile to immigrants and the Black Lives Matter movement? What if Trump had failed to embrace a pro-life position? The opening paragraphs imply that pro-life positioning blunted problematic parts of Trump's biography. Yet abortion was not the only issue on which Trump and Clinton differed. Unfortunately, the 2016 campaign did not provide much new leverage for disentangling the effects of different issues on evangelical voting behavior. In a campaign that will surely go down in history as setting a record for setting new records, not much changed in regard to Democratic and Republican positions on major political issues. In fact, virtually any alternative set of political positions would have been more enlightening for those interested in understanding the issue motivations of voters, be they evangelicals or others, than the ones the candidates staked out in 2016. When Democratic candidates take similar positions in election after election and Republican candidates do the same thing, it becomes difficult to say which issues matter.

Considering counterfactual issue positions—even if only theoretically— helps highlight important theoretical questions that lie at the heart of understanding the role religion plays in American politics. Are social and moral issues the key to winning large numbers of evangelical voters? If so, then institutional religion shapes the political coalitions because the traditional values evangelical worship instills demand pro-life and traditional family-policy positions. If, however, social and moral issues appear to be important only because they are currently aligned with partisan positions on the economy and on the proper role of the federal government addressing racial inequality, then the current political alignment may be more about whiteness than worship.

Digging into these questions, authors in this book investigate the issue priorities of evangelicals in a variety of ways. Ronald McGauvran and Elizabeth Oldmixon conclude that Republican evangelicals come for the culture and stay for the economic policy. Other authors focus on the positioning of parties, candidates, and religious leaders on issues of religious freedom. Looking for an electoral connection between the stated political priorities of evangelicals and the positions the parties stake out in their platforms, Kevin den Dulk finds that Republicans are "doubling down on one side of the culture wars, with an emphasis on Judeo-Christian heritage and repeated clarion calls about threats to the traditionalist vision of family and community."

But demographic trends in the United States are surely undermining the electoral strength of evangelicals. Accordingly, Andrew Lewis explores whether evangelicals will pivot as the majority status of white Christians comes to an end in the United States. Such a pivot would lead to more tolerant orientations toward other minority groups as evangelicals attempt to preserve their political priorities despite diminishing political power. Or, as Kimberly Conger finds, evangelicals may resist embracing the rights of other minorities in favor of controlling state governments in places where their numbers remain strong. Or, as Tobin Grant and Joshua Mitchell discuss, evangelicals may turn to more symbolic efforts at more local levels. In addition, evangelicals continue to avail themselves of institutions where electoral strength matters less. Daniel Bennett investigates the work of Christian conservative legal organizations and again finds that opposition to abortion, gay marriage, and defense of religious freedom is central to their work.

In contrast, Ryan Claassen highlights the importance of attitudes about race explaining *changes* in the voting behavior of evangelicals. Claassen confirms that the voting choices of evangelicals and their positions on abortion and gay marriage are strongly correlated, but explaining the vote in a single election is very different from explaining changes in voting behavior over the course of several elections. Although recent elections have not provided much variation in the positions of Democrats and Republicans on important issues, Barry Goldwater's opposition to the Civil and Voting Rights Acts in 1964 marked a dramatic shift on the issue of race. Indeed, one way of viewing religious-freedom laws is as a new way of justifying discrimination for religious reasons. Today such laws are being used to enable bakers to refuse service to homosexuals, but the logic is very similar to the defenses racially segregated parochial schools mounted a few short decades ago. In regard to understanding the political motivations of evangelicals, the counterfactuals highlight something that is terribly important. Partisans were not divided on the issue of abortion until nearly a decade after the *Roe v. Wade* decision (Highton 2004) and the sides have remained the same ever since. In contrast, partisans have been divided in different ways on the issue of race, with partisanship shifting as the parties "evolved" on the issue (Carmines and Stimson 1989). Thus, it is difficult to say whether abortion is the "third rail" of evangelical politics, as evangelicals' stated policy priorities would suggest, or whether the moral elasticity extended to Trump reveals other issue priorities that have less to do with the values instilled by evangelical worship.

Pushing counterfactuals to extremes, is there some scenario in which institutional religion is the catalyst for the crackup imagined in the title of this book? In the first place, although the 2016 election was unusual in many respects, it also delivered a great deal of continuity, as Robert Wuthnow and John Green note in their concluding thoughts about evangelicalism and the most recent presidential election. Setting aside the unusual candidates, evangelical politics was "business as usual" in 2016. Geoffrey Layman and Mark Brockway reveal evangelical presence among convention delegates continued apace. Kimberly Conger demonstrates that Christian Right political organizations in states were able to deliver Republican votes in 2016 just as they had in other recent elections.

Even in places where one might expect to see a crackup in the making—see Jeremy Castle on evangelical young people and Benjamin Taylor, Sarah Gershon, and Adrian Pantoja on evangelical Hispanics—authors find distinctively conservative orientations. Some speculate that reduced social isolation in the modern age will end evangelical political distinctiveness, but Juhem Navarro-Rivera, Daniel Cox, Robert Jones, and Paul Djupe, as well as Djupe, Jacob Neiheisel, and Anand Sokhey, find that evangelicals with more diverse social networks are more likely, not less, to embrace the embattled mentality of the Christian Right. The emergent church movement discussed by Ryan Burge is positioned within evangelicalism and promotes beliefs at odds with the moral absolutism of the Christian Right, but it could also be a case of "preaching to the choir" if the evangelicals most affected by the movement tend to be political progressives in any case. Moreover, when exposed to dissonant messages from a credible evangelical elite, evangelicals react negatively (increasing their Trump support) or not at all, as Paul Djupe and Brian Calfano find. Perhaps the lesson of 2016 is that there is no "what-if" scenario that would have altered the political proclivities of evangelicals in the short term. And if that is the case, what inference does one draw about the role of religion structuring the political behavior of evangelicals?

The belief that everyone is obsessed with politics has long been an occupational hazard within the discipline of political science, and we wonder whether the 2016 election is evidence that institutional religion has never been as political as political scientists imagined. What if the correlation between what evangelicals say about their churches in surveys and what they do in the voting booth is more about projection than pulpit power, prayer, or piousness?

We grant that the Christian Right organizations so well documented in the religion and politics literature are very engaged in politicking. But the handful of organizations created and supported by institutional religion that are *explicitly political* are a tiny fraction of the whole and interact very little with very few in the mass public. The real potential of institutional religion exists in the monetary, time, and doctrinal commitments of hundreds of millions who meet weekly in places of worship. And if clergy and parishioners alike tend to avoid politics during worship, then the similar political behavior of white evangelicals, or black evangelicals, or Catholics, and so on, may actually be an artifact of other forces that bring these groups together, especially their shared communities. For example, for white evangelicals, race and concentration in former Confederate states may be more potent forces for understanding their political behavior than sermons and voting guides. Perhaps political science should not be surprised that evangelicals embraced Trump if the fact that many whites in the South are evangelicals actually does not matter as much as the fact that they are whites in the South.

In some ways this conclusion is disheartening for those who long for religion to be salient in American politics. But for those who worry about sectarian divisions undermining democratic institutions, our take is much more optimistic. In any case we hope it stimulates renewed interest in examining the mechanisms that connect the political behavior of different religious groups.

REFERENCES

Carmines, Edward G., and James A. Stimson. 1989. *Issue Evolution: Race and the Transformation of American Politics*. Princeton, NJ: Princeton University Press.
Highton, Benjamin. 2004. "Policy Voting in Senate Elections: The Case of Abortion." *Political Behavior* 26:181–200.

Contributors

Daniel Bennett teaches political science at John Brown University. His research focuses on the intersection of politics, law, and religion in the United States. He is the author of *Defending Faith: The Politics of the Christian Conservative Legal Movement* (2017).

Mark Brockway is a Ph.D. candidate in the Department of Political Science at the University of Notre Dame. His research interests include political parties, religion and politics, and political behavior. His work has appeared in *American Politics Research* and *Politics and Religion*.

Ryan P. Burge is an instructor of political science at Eastern Illinois University with research interests focused on the intersection of religiosity and political behavior (especially in the American context). He has published articles in a number of academic journals, including the *Journal for the Scientific Study of Religion*, *Politics and Religion*, and *Representation*. In addition, his work has been highlighted in the *Washington Post* and *Christianity Today*.

Brian R. Calfano is assistant professor of political science and journalism at the University of Cincinnati. His research interests include religion and politics, minority groups, and media. Calfano has published more than fifty academic journal articles and book chapters and is coauthor of *God Talk: Experimenting with the Religious Causes of Public Opinion* (2013) and *A Matter of Discretion: The Politics of Roman Catholic Priests in the United States and Ireland* (2017).

Jeremiah J. Castle teaches political science at Central Michigan University, including courses on Congress, campaigns and elections, and research methods. His research on public opinion has been published in journals including *Social Science Quarterly*, *Journal for the Scientific Study of Religion*, and *Politics and Religion*.

Ryan L. Claassen is professor of political science at Kent State University. His research interests include political participation, citizen competence, public opinion, election administration, religion and politics, interest groups, and racial and ethnic politics. He is author of *Godless Democrats and Pious Republicans* (2015) and author and coauthor of numerous articles in top political science journals.

Kimberly H. Conger teaches political science and public administration at the University of Cincinnati. Her current projects examine the influence of the Christian Right and Religious Left in lobbying and political advocacy and investigate the role of religious activism in reducing political inequalities in the United States.

Daniel A. Cox is the research director at the Public Religion Research Institute (PRRI), specializing in survey research, youth politics, and religion. He has coauthored several academic book chapters and journal articles on topics relating to religious polarization, anti-Muslim attitudes in the United States, religious tolerance of atheists, and the origins of free-market ideology among evangelical Protestants. He regularly writes for major news outlets such as *FiveThirtyEight*, *Yahoo! News*, and *U.S. News and World Report*.

Kevin R. den Dulk is the Paul B. Henry Professor of Political Science and the executive director of the Henry Institute for the Study of Christianity and Politics at Calvin College in Grand Rapids, Michigan. He has coauthored or coedited several books, including *Religion and Politics in America* (2010), *The Disappearing God Gap? Religion in the 2008 Presidential Election* (2010), and *The Challenge of Pluralism: Church and State in Six Democracies* (2017).

Paul A. Djupe teaches political science at Denison University and is an affiliated scholar with PRRI, with research interests in religion and politics, social networks, and gender dynamics. He is the series editor of the Religious Engagement in Democratic Politics series at Temple University Press and a coauthor of *God Talk: Experimenting with the Religious Causes of Public Opinion* (2013). He blogs at https://religioninpublic.blog.

Sarah Allen Gershon is an associate professor at Georgia State University. Her research focuses on the incorporation of traditionally underrepresented groups (including women and racial and ethnic minorities) into the American political system. Her research has been published in *Political Research Quarterly, Journal of Politics, Du Bois Review, Journal of Women, Politics and Policy, Politics and Religion*, and several other journals. She co-edited (with Nadia Brown) *Distinct Identities: Minority Women in U.S Politics* (2016).

J. Tobin Grant teaches political science at Southern Illinois University Carbondale, where he also serves as chair of the Department of Political Science. He is editor in chief of the *Journal for the Scientific Study of Religion*.

John C. Green is dean of the College of Arts and Sciences, director of the Ray C. Bliss Institute of Applied Politics, and Distinguished Professor of Political Science at the University of Akron. He has published widely on political parties, campaign finance, religion, and politics in the United States.

Robert P. Jones is the founding CEO at PRRI, a nonpartisan independent research organization in Washington, D.C. He is the author of *The End of White Christian America* (2016) and two other books, writes a regular online column on politics and culture at the *Atlantic*, and appears frequently as a commentator on religion and politics in the media. He serves as the national cochair of the Religion and Politics steering group for the American Academy of Religion and sits on the editorial board for the *Journal of the American Academy of Religion*.

Geoffrey Layman is professor of political science at the University of Notre Dame. His research interests are religion and politics, political parties, and public opinion. He has published articles in most of the top journals in political science and is the author of *The Great Divide: Religious and Cultural Conflict in American Party Politics* (2001).

Andrew R. Lewis teaches political science at the University of Cincinnati and researches the intersection of religion, politics, and law in the United States. He is the author of *The Rights Turn in Conservative Christian Politics: How Abortion Transformed the Culture Wars* (2017), and he serves as the book review editor for *Politics and Religion*.

Ronald J. McGauvran is an assistant professor in the Department of Sociology and Political Science at Tennessee Tech University. His research examines the political repercussions of economic inequality and has appeared in journals including *Political Research Quarterly, Politics and Policy*, and *Congress and the Presidency*.

Joshua L. Mitchell teaches public administration courses at the University of Arkansas. His research interests are policy diffusion, political geography, spatial statistics, and campaign finance.

Juhem Navarro-Rivera is a Gratis Research Scholar at El Instituto: Institute of Latino/a, Latin American, and Caribbean Studies at the University of Connecticut. He is cohost of *The Benito Juárez Experience*, a podcast about Latino/Latina secularism and is managing partner and research director at SocioAnalítica Research LLC, a research consulting firm. He is a graduate of the University of Puerto Rico at Río Piedras (B.A.) and the University of Connecticut (M.A.; Ph.D.).

Jacob R. Neiheisel is associate professor of political science at the University at Buffalo, SUNY, with research interests that include religion and politics, political parties, election administration, and political communication. His work has been published in the *American Journal of Political Science*, *Legislative Studies Quarterly*, *Political Research Quarterly*, and *American Politics Research*.

Elizabeth A. Oldmixon is professor of political science at the University of North Texas and editor in chief of *Politics and Religion*. She is formerly a Fulbright Scholar (2010) and an American Political Science Association Congressional Fellow (2001–2002). Her research investigates religion and legislative behavior and political activism among clergy. She is coauthor of *Matter of Discretion: Priests, Politics, and Institutional Context* (2017).

Adrian D. Pantoja is professor of political studies and Chicano studies at Pitzer College. He has published extensively in the fields of Latino politics, immigration politics, and racial and ethnic politics. He is also a senior analyst with Latino Decisions, a public-opinion polling firm that works with a number of political and advocacy groups seeking to understand the Latino electorate.

David Searcy is a doctoral candidate in political science at Southern Illinois University Carbondale. His research focuses on the relationship between religious behavior and political behavior. His dissertation examines patterns of political behavior within American Christianity. He is a recipient of the Morris Doctoral Fellowship at SIUC.

Anand E. Sokhey is associate professor of political science at the University of Colorado Boulder. His research examines voting behavior, public opinion, and political participation in the United States, focusing on problems of social and contextual influence. He is the director of the Keller Center for the Study of the First Amendment.

J. Benjamin Taylor is assistant professor of political science at Kennesaw State University. His research and teaching interests are in American political behavior, with a particular focus on political communication and public opinion.

Robert Wuthnow is Gerhard R. Andlinger '52 Professor of Social Science and director of the Center for the Study of Religion at Princeton University. His publications include *Red State Religion: Faith and Politics in America's Heartland* (2011) and *The Left Behind: Decline and Rage in Rural America* (2018).

Index

Abortion, 5, 23; candidate stances on, 2, 61, 103, 231, 253, 274; Christian conservative legal organizations and, 234; Christian Right and, 5, 34, 51, 54, 65, 68, 78, 195, 224; early evangelical attitudes toward, 52; Latino views on, 148–149; picketing of clinics that provide, 96; Republican party and, 49, 51, 54, 63–64, 70–71, 259; state policies on, 99–102; as study measure, 23, 44–45n4, 57–58; views of evangelicals on, by denomination, 116–118; voting and, 59–60, 205, 269; young evangelicals and, 36, 125–139

Activists, 4, 32–34, 65–66, 98; cultural views of, 34–35, 38; economic views of, 35, 38–39; ideological purism of, 34–35, 40, 43; impact of, on the Republican Party, 32–35, 69–72, 102, 276; religious composition of, 37–38, 43; and support for compromise, 36, 38, 40, 43, 45n5; and support for Trump, 41–43; tolerance for out-group activists, 87; views of, on minorities, 40, 43, 44–45n4

Affordable Care Act (ACA), 99, 229, 263

African Americans: and abortion, 131; economic attitudes of, 240, 242, 245–246, 248–253; and evangelicalism, 109, 153; and gay marriage, 131; and homogeneity, 151, 179, 188; and political tolerance, 85; as tied to Democratic Party, 64, 145, 264; and vote in 2012, 138, 195; and welfare, 242

Alexander v. Holmes County Board of Education, 52–53

Alliance Defending Freedom, 80, 223, 225, 229, 231–232, 234

American Center for Law and Justice (ACLJ), 80, 222, 225–234

American Family Association, 98, 185, 190n5

Atheists, 84, 87, 160, 201–202, 205

Attendance, church: and economic attitudes, 244–245, 250–251; and ideology of young evangelicals, 130–131; among Latinos, 149; by Republican National Convention delegates, 37; in strict churches, 176; and support of Trump, 41–43; and view of Supreme Court, 89; and views on environment, 133; and views on welfare, 133; and vote choice, 180, 183. *See also* Religious commitment

Authority, 8, 164; religious dimension of, 17, 109, 163–165, 167–169

Balmer, Randall, 52–54, 60

Barton, David, 69, 74

Bauer, Gary 66

Becket Fund for Religious Liberty 79, 225

Beliefs, religious: among Christian denominations, 115; and economic attitudes, 239–246, 248, 250; emergent versus evangelical, 165–167; and political issues, 34; as unifying evangelicals, 65, 109, 125, 127, 147, 163, 260

Bell, Rob, 161, 163

Benedict Option, 6, 67, 101

Bob Jones University, 53

Brown v. Board of Education, 52

Bryan, William Jennings, 50–51

Bush, George H. W., 2

Bush, George W.: AIDS/HIV initiative of, 70; Christian Right's dissatisfaction with, 100; Christian Right's support of, 2, 9–10, 150, 152, 194, 230, 263, 266, 273; compared to Mitt Romney, 138; and immigration reform, 145